Marketing Luxury Goods Online

Schriften zu Marketing und Handel

Herausgegeben von Martin Fassnacht

Band 19

PL ACADEMIC RESEARCH

Philipp Nikolaus Kluge

Marketing Luxury Goods Online

PL ACADEMIC RESEARCH

Bibliographic Information published by the Deutsche Nationalbibliothek
The Deutsche Nationalbibliothek lists this publication in the Deutsche Nationalbibliografie; detailed bibliographic data is available in the internet at http://dnb.d-nb.de.

Zugl.: Vallendar, Wiss. Hochsch. für Unternehmensführung, Diss., 2016

Library of Congress Cataloging-in-Publication Data
Names: Kluge, Philipp Nikolaus, 1985- author.
Title: Marketing luxury goods online / Philipp Nikolaus Kluge.
Description: Frankfurt am Main ; New York : Peter Lang, [2016] | Series: Schriften zu Marketing und Handel, ISSN 1862-605X ; Band 19 | Includes bibliographical references.
Identifiers: LCCN 2016025321 | ISBN 9783631678657
Subjects: LCSH: Luxury goods industry. | Luxuries--Internet marketing. | Internet marketing. | Electronic commerce.
Classification: LCC HD9999.L852 K5185 2016 | DDC 658.8/72--dc23 LC record available at https://lccn.loc.gov/2016025321

D 992
ISSN 1862-605X
ISBN 978-3-631-67865-7 (Print)
E-ISBN 978-3-653-07000-2 (E-PDF)
E-ISBN 978-3-631-69407-7 (EPUB)
E-ISBN 978-3-631-69408-4 (MOBI)
DOI 10.3726/978-3-653-07000-2

PL Academic Research is an Imprint of Peter Lang GmbH.

Peter Lang – Frankfurt am Main · Bern · Bruxelles · New York · Oxford · Warszawa · Wien

This publication has been peer reviewed.

www.peterlang.com

To my father

Preface by Martin Fassnacht

The domain of luxury goods is a relatively new phenomenon for both the scientific community as well as for the corporate world. Given the increased sales volume of the personal luxury goods the topic of luxury goods has increased in its importance in both fields. If we are looking at the existing scientific literature, there is no comprehensive contribution that captures the topic of the marketing of luxury goods online as well as offline from both a scientific and managerial perspective.

Against this background, the dissertation of Dr. Philipp Nikolaus Kluge can be regarded as the state of the art of luxury goods. In his dissertation, Dr. Kluge addresses very relevant topics of luxury goods. The second chapter makes the reader familiar with the concept of luxury goods. He is talking about constituent characteristics of luxury goods as well as about the motives for buying luxury goods. In this chapter, he provides us with a very profound understanding of luxury goods. We got to take into account that there is no established definition of luxury goods either in the scientific or managerial world.

Dr. Kluge enriches and provides us with many insights about the marketing mix of luxury goods for the so called "4P's": product, price, communication and distribution management. In two very comprehensive chapters, he provides us with the state of the art of the marketing-mix for luxury goods for the offline as well as for the online world. Such an inspiring and detailed description of all "4P's" for both worlds for luxury goods is almost impossible to find in the current literature. He makes us aware about the specificities of luxury goods and all "4P's" for the traditional (offline) and the new (online) field.

Dr. Kluge is not only providing us with the above mentioned marketing specificities in both worlds, but he is also empirically investigating based on a theoretical approach the effects of online accessibility of luxury goods on perceived scarcity, desirability, convenience, and willingness-to-buy. It is worthwhile mentioning, that Dr. Kluge is not asking students in his empirical study, but luxury consumers which is very positive in terms of the external validity. His empirical results do show that, surprisingly, the online accessibility does not influence the consumer perceptions of scarcity.

All in all, Dr. Kluge's dissertation will be without any doubt very inspiring for both the scientific as well as for the corporate world.

Prof. Dr. Martin Fassnacht
The Otto Beisheim Endowed Chair of Marketing & Commerce
WHU – Otto Beisheim School of Management

Acknowledgements

The following dissertation was submitted in partial fulfilment of the requirements of the degree doctor rerum politicarum to the WHU – Otto Beisheim School of Management. I would like to express my appreciation and gratitude to all the persons who supported me in completing this dissertation.

Firstly, I would like thank my supervisor, Professor Martin Fassnacht, for the continuous guidance and encouragement I received throughout the years as research assistant and doctoral student at his chair. He is genuinely committed to the research, teaching, and business projects on marketing luxury goods. I also wish to thank my second supervisor, Professor Walter Herzog, for providing valuable feedback and helping me broaden the perspectives on my research project.

I would like to express my appreciation to the Stipendienstiftung Rheinland-Pfalz and my home institution WHU – Otto Beisheim School of Management for funding parts of my research project with a research scholarship.

Special thanks go to my friend and colleague Dr. Jerome Alexander Königsfeld. Throughout the years we shared an office at WHU, Jerome's sense of humour and intellect was my daily dose of motivation. More than a companion on the road to completing this doctoral dissertation, Jerome has become a true friend.

Throughout my time as doctoral student, I am immensely grateful for having met and intellectually exchanged with my doctoral peers and friends Alexander Stich, Dr. Julia Gäckler, Dr. Kristina Schmidt, Markus Szajna, and Dr. Toni Schmidt. I also would like to dedicate special thanks to our team at the Chair of Marketing and Commerce, Stephanie Krause (‚die gute Seele des Lehrstuhls'), Barbara Luig, Jan Josten, and Katrin Dötsch, for the exceptional support and fun time throughout these years.

Above all, I feel deepest gratitude for my mum Ulrike, my dad Wolfgang, my sister Julia and her family, my grandparents Annette and Hans, my girlfriend Juliana, as well as my oldest friends André, Michael, and Sascha. Without your genuine caring and unconditional love this work would not have been possible – thank you so much for being part of my life!

Dr. Philipp Nikolaus Kluge

Overview of Content

Contents

Figures

Tables

Abbreviations

ad	advertisement
AMT	Amazon Mechanical Turk
ANOVA	analysis of variance
ATL	above-the-line communication
B2C	business-to-consumer
BMW	Bayerische Motoren Werke Aktiengesellschaft
bn	billion
BTL	below-the-line communication
c.p.	ceteris paribus (other things being equal)
CAGR	compound annual growth rate
CC BY	creative commons attribution license
CC BY-SA	creative commons attribution-share-alike license
CEO	chief executive officer
CFA	confirmatory factor analysis
CFI	comparative fit index
CGC	company-generated content
COD	country-of-design
COGS	costs of goods sold
COM	country-of-manufacturing
COO	country-of-origin
CPC	cost-per-click
CPM	cost-per-mille
CRM	customer relationship management
CTR	click-through-rate
df	degrees of freedom
DIY	do-it-yourself
DFS	Duty-Free Shoppers Group (travel retail group)
DOS	directly operated store
e-	electronic
e.g.	exempli gratia (for example)
etc.	et cetera (and other things)
EBIT	earnings before interest and taxes
ECCIA	European Cultural and Creative Industries Alliance
EUR	Euro (currency)
H	hypothesis
HIT	human intelligence task
HNWI	high-net-worth individual
i.e.	id est (that is)
k	thousand
KaDeWe	Kaufhaus des Westens

LVMH	Moët Hennessy Louis Vuitton Société Anonyme
m	million
ml	millilitres
ns	non-significant
p.	page
pp.	pages
p.a.	pro anno (per year)
POS	point of sale
PPR	Pinault-Printemps-Redoute Société Anonyme (now Kering)
PR	public relations
PV	page view
R&D	research and development
RMSEA	root mean square error of approximation
RQ	research question
Q	quote
QR	quick response
S-E-D	Scarcity-Expensiveness-Desirability model
SD	standard deviation
SE	standard error
SEA	search engine advertising
SEM	structural equation modeling
SEO	search engine optimization
SERVCON	service convenience scale
SKU	stock keeping unit
SOV	share of voice
SRMR	standardized root mean square residual
TV	television
UGC	user-generated content
UK	United Kingdom
URL	uniform resource locator
US	United States (of America)
USD	US dollar
VW	Volkswagen Aktiengesellschaft
WOM	word-of-mouth
WWW	World Wide Web

Symbols

&	and
%	per cent
$	US dollar (currency)
D_a	market demand curve
D_S	individual demand curve of snobbish consumers
D_V	individual demand curve of Veblenian consumers
E	point of market equilibrium
k	number of factor levels
M	mean
m	number of pairwise comparisons
N	sample size
p	statistical significance level
p_t	price at time t
q_t	quantity at time t
S	supply curve
t	t-value, i.e. factor loading divided by standard error
α	level of significance
β	standardized path coefficient
ρ_{AVE}	average variance extracted
ρ_{CR}	composite reliability
ρ_{IR}	indicator reliability
λ^*	standardized factor loading
χ^2	chi-square test statistic

Marketing Luxury Goods Online[1]

1. Introduction

1.1 Motivation

The phenomenon of luxury fascinates consumers, marketers, and researchers alike. Goods and services designed beyond any necessity are desired by the mass but reserved for the happy few. Brands like Hermès, Rolls-Royce, Cartier, and Patek Philippe create an aura of good taste, finest quality, and exclusiveness. They convey a deeper meaning beyond their functional quality; something individuals desire not only to signal status but also to reward oneself and significant others for meaningful moments in life.

The marketing of luxury goods is built on a paradox: "The more desirable the brand becomes, the more it sells but the more it sells, the less desirable it becomes", says Patrick Thomas, former CEO of Hermès (Interbrand, 2011). **Balancing sales growth against exclusiveness** represents the major strategic challenge for luxury goods manufacturers (Kastanakis & Balabanis, 2012, p. 1399; Keller, 2009, p. 293; Wetlaufer, 2001, p. 121). The worldwide market for personal luxury goods has shown strong post-recession growth of 9.2 per cent p.a. from EUR 153 billion in 2009 up to EUR 223 billion in 2014 (Bain & Company & Fondazione Altagamma, 2014, p. 10). Across all categories the luxury goods market realized EUR 865 billion sales worldwide in 2014 (Bain & Company & Fondazione Altagamma, 2014, p. 10). European luxury goods manufacturers, many of them small and medium-sized enterprises, account for about 70 per cent of the worldwide luxury goods market, contribute as much as 3 per cent to the European gross domestic product and employ approximately one million workers (Frontier Economics & ECCIA, 2012, p. 1).

Despite the continuing growth luxury marketers must preserve the brand's fragile image of exclusiveness. Exclusiveness is top-of-mind among luxury brand managers as the following quotes show:

1 Parts of this manuscript are based on: Kluge & Fassnacht (2015): Selling Luxury Goods Online: Effects of Online Accessibility and Price Display, in: International Journal of Retail & Distribution Management, Vol. 43, No. 10/11, pp. 1065–1082; Kluge & Fassnacht (2014): Selling Luxury Goods Online? Effects of Making the Inaccessible Accessible, presented at the 2014 Monaco Symposium on Luxury, April 10th–11th 2014, Monaco; Kluge, Königsfeld, Fassnacht, & Mitschke (2013): Luxury Web Atmospherics: An Examination of Homepage Design, in: International Journal of Retail & Distribution Management, Vol. 41, No. 11/12, pp. 901–916; Fassnacht, Kluge, & Mohr (2013): Pricing Luxury Brands: Specificities, Conceptualization, and Performance Impact, in: Marketing ZFP – Journal of Research and Management, Vol. 35, No. 2, pp. 104–117; Kluge, Fassnacht, Stich, Königsfeld, & Mitschke (2013): Preserving Brand Luxury Online? An Examination of Luxury Homepage Design, in: Proceedings of the 42th European Marketing Academy Conference, June 4th–7th 2013, Istanbul, Turkey.

"In luxury, **ubiquity** will kill you."
– *Angela Ahrendts, former CEO of Burberry (Ahrendts, 2013, p. 40)*

"Defending the **exclusivity** of its products in the eyes of its customers is crucial."
– *Marco Bizzarri, former CEO of Bottega Veneta (Sanderson, 2013)*

"Wir dürfen unsere **Exklusivität** nicht gefährden."[2]
– *Luca di Montezemolo, CEO of Ferrari (Freitag & Katzensteiner, 2013)*

"Wir als Hüter der Marke wollen sie hochgradig begehrlich und **exklusiv** halten."[3]
– *Torsten Müller-Ötvös, CEO of Rolls-Royce (Schaal, 2014)*

The trade-off between sales growth and exclusiveness is reflected in the on-going discussion about the suitability of the Internet for luxury goods (Kapferer & Bastien, 2012, p. 233; Quintavalle, 2012, p. 75). A luxury brand's fragile concept of exclusiveness is seemingly incompatible with the ubiquitous accessibility provided by the mass medium Internet. This apparent mismatch is often referred to as "**Internet dilemma**" (Kapferer & Bastien, 2012, p. 247) or "**love/hate relationship**" (Chevalier & Gutsatz, 2012, p. 63). However, considering that the number of Internet users worldwide has grown dramatically by annually 29 per cent over the past two decades reaching 3 billion in 2014 (Internet Live Stats, 2014a), online marketing has become an imperative to luxury marketers.

To the affluent clientele the opportunity to shop online has become the second most important feature of a luxury brand website (Roland Berger & Meisterkreis, 2013, p. 8) whereas it was considered least important ten years ago (Riley & Lacroix, 2003, p. 100). The growing demand is reflected in a strong growth in sales through monobrand online stores like Hermes.com and Cartier.com or through multibrand online retailers like Net-a-porter.com, Yoox.com, and Mytheresa.com of annually 28 per cent over the past five years thereby outpacing total market growth (see Figure 1(a)).

2 Translation by the author: "We must not jeopardize our exclusiveness."
3 Translation by the author: "As the guardian of the brand we want to keep it desirable and exclusive."

Figure 1 – Online sales of personal luxury goods.

(a) Online sales of personal luxury goods[a] worldwide from 2009 to 2014 (in EUR bn)

(b) Share of online sales in worldwide personal luxury goods sales 2014

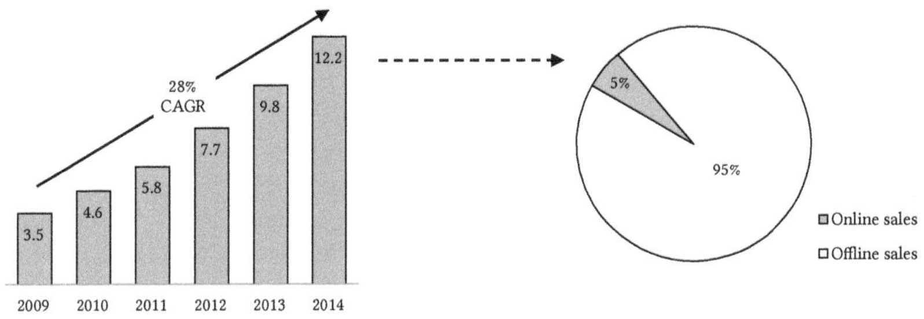

[a]include ready-to-wear, leather goods & accessories, jewellery & watches, perfume & cosmetics, other
Source: Bain & Company & Fondazione Altagamma (2014, pp. 10, 19; 2011, p. 10)

Yet, online sales account for less than 5 per cent of total personal luxury goods sales (see Figure 1(b)). Many luxury goods manufacturers have long been or still are hesitant to exploit the Internet as a channel of distribution (Gastaldi, 2012, p. 112; Okonkwo, 2009, p. 302; Quintavalle, 2012, p. 92). To date specialist watchmakers like A. Lange & Söhne, Patek Philippe, and Rolex are reluctant to install monobrand online stores. Other luxury brands like Bulgari, Chanel, and Fendi limit their online offering to US customers only. According to recent studies by Bain & Company & Fondazione Altagamma (2013, p. 10), L2 (reported in Chevalier & Gutsatz, 2012, p. 68), and Roland Berger & Meisterkreis (2013, p. 16) as many as **40 to 50 per cent** of luxury goods manufacturers still **do not sell their products online**.

The controversy whether or not to sell luxury goods online is reflected by the opposing statements of François-Henri Pinault, CEO of the multinational luxury goods conglomerate Kering (formerly PPR) and Miuccia Prada Bianchi, CEO of Prada Group, on the one hand, and Bernard Arnault, Chairman and CEO of the multinational luxury goods conglomerate LVMH, on the other hand.

> "There was a time when accessing luxury was difficult – you had to go to Paris, London, Milan or New York to get it. That aspect has disappeared [...] with the Internet. How do you compensate for that **loss of exclusivity**?"
> *– François-Henri Pinault, CEO of Kering (Daneshkhu, 2012)*

> "We don't like it [e-commerce]. I don't care. [...] We think that, for luxury, **it's not right**. [...] Personally, I'm not interested."
> *– Miuccia Prada Bianchi, CEO of Prada Group (Soller, 2014)*

> "The Internet will not transform business the way many people initially thought it would. **It will enhance it**. Success on the Internet, like any other business, will take time. You need patience."
> *– Bernard Arnault, Chairman and CEO of LVMH (Wetlaufer, 2001, p. 121)*

Despite the growing importance of online marketing to luxury goods manufacturers **literature in this field remains scarce**. Figure 2 shows: when systematically searching for luxury-related publications from 1948 to 2013 we find that the number luxury-related publications (grey shaded area in Figure 2) has increased tremendously over the past five years (mainly driven by special issues as in Journal of Business Research (2012), Journal of Brand Management (2009, 2012), International Journal of Retail & Distribution Management (2013), Marketing ZFP (2013)). At the same time, however, disproportionally less attention has been paid to the research on marketing luxury goods online as illustrated by the relatively smaller, black shaded area in Figure 2.

To conclude: despite the growing importance of the Internet for marketing luxury goods, scientific literature on marketing luxury goods online remains scarce. In particular, the question whether or not to sell luxury goods online has been controversially discussed among both marketing scholars and executives. Yet, we lack empirical evidence on the effects of the online accessibility of luxury goods on consumer perceptions of exclusiveness.

1.2 Objectives of manuscript

The objective of the following manuscript is threefold: first, the manuscript conceptually examines the specific marketing-mix of luxury goods. Second, the manuscript discusses the benefits, concerns, and practices of marketing luxury goods in the Internet. Third, the manuscript empirically tests the effects of the online accessibility and price display of luxury goods on consumer evaluations of scarcity, brand desirability, convenience, and willingness-to-buy. As identified in Chapter 1.1 we lack research on how to market luxury goods online in general and whether or not to sell luxury goods through the Internet in particular. The present manuscript is an attempt towards closing these research gaps.

Figure 2 – Luxury-related publications from 1948 to 2013.

[a]based on a search analysis in scientific journals (see Appendix 1 for a list), book chapters, and books for the keywords "luxury", "prestige", "status", "conspicuous", "symbolic", and "scarcity" as of January 2014
Source: author

Conceptually, the general purpose of the manuscript is to discuss the benefits, concerns, and specificities of marketing luxury goods online. Yet, examining how the Internet affects the marketing of luxury goods necessitates a thorough understanding of the essential principles of marketing luxury goods in general. Online marketing initiatives should not be considered as an isolated decision. Rather they represent an integral part of a luxury brand's overall marketing strategy. Offline and online channels should complement rather than substitute each other. Hence, before conceptually examining the online marketing-mix of luxury goods, we are first interested in identifying the essential principles of marketing luxury goods in terms of product management, pricing, communication, and distribution management (Chapter 3).

Conventional marketing principles do not equally apply to luxury brands. To create and preserve consumer perceptions of finest quality, rarity, and aesthetic appeal marketing luxury brands requires specific procedures that may be counterintuitive to traditional marketing approaches (Kapferer & Bastien, 2009b, pp. 315–320): products are not designed to merely meet functional needs. Prices are not regularly reduced to drive sales. Communication is not designed to sell but to create dreams. And, luxury goods marketers do not aim at ubiquitous availability but rather rely on an exclusive distribution network. The present manuscript attempts to systematically contrast conventional versus luxury-specific marketing practices. Hence, the first objective of the present manuscript is to address the following research question:

RQ1: What are the specificities of marketing luxury goods in terms of product management, pricing, communication, and distribution management?

In a second step, we are interested in how these luxury-specific marketing principles apply online. Particularly, we aim at conceptually examining the benefits and concerns about marketing luxury goods online and how the Internet affects the marketing of luxury goods in terms of product management, pricing, communication, and distribution management (Chapter 4). At first sight, the Internet is commonly associated with mass availability, bargain prices, and transparency of information. Luxury, in contrast, is characterized by exclusiveness, stable, high-end prices and discretion (Chevalier & Gutsatz, 2012, p. 67; Kapferer & Bastien, 2012, pp. 247 & 249; Okonkwo, 2009, p. 304; Seringhaus, 2005, p. 15; Wiedmann, Hennigs, & Klarmann, 2011, p. 34). At second sight, the Internet has become an omnipresent companion in consumers' everyday lives, which allows for increasing reach and intensity of brand communication and selling to clients who live in geographically distant places. More than discussing the general suitability of the Internet for marketing luxury goods, we aim at examining how the marketing-mix of luxury goods can be adapted to the online world. Hence, the second objective of this manuscript is to address the following research question:

RQ2: What are the specificities of marketing luxury goods online in terms of product management, pricing, communication, and distribution management?

Empirically, the manuscript examines consumer responses to the online accessibility and price display of luxury goods. On the one hand, as an additional distribution channel the Internet serves as a potential source of profit by reaching new customers at lower cost and a higher share of margin (Chevalier & Gutsatz, 2012, p. 66; Quintavalle, 2012, p. 77). To the affluent clientele, the possibility to shop online has become a must-have as it represents a convenient alternative to in-store shopping (Liu, Burns, & Hou, 2013, p. 888). Hence, luxury goods should not only be communicated online but also offered for sale (Okonkwo, 2010, p. 173).

On the other hand, selling luxury goods online is commonly believed to dilute a brand's fragile appeal of exclusiveness (Seringhaus, 2005, p. 15). The mass medium Internet apparently contradicts with the exclusive distribution of luxury goods (Curtis, 2000). Consequently, leading scholars in the field of luxury goods marketing like Jean-Noël Kapferer & Vincent Bastien (2012, p. 248) argue that luxury goods "should *not* be sold" via the Internet. And indeed (as shown above) about every second luxury goods manufacturer does not sell online. The suitability of the Internet as an additional channel of distribution for luxury goods manufacturers will be discussed from a conceptual (Chapter 4.5), managerial (Chapter 5), and theoretical perspective (Chapter 6).

In essence, luxury goods marketers face the dilemma of making additional profit at the expense of perceived exclusiveness. It is this dilemma of making the inaccessible accessible which makes the online distribution challenge a luxury-specific one. In light of this controversially discussed online distribution challenge for luxury goods marketers, the third objective of the present manuscript is to address the following research question:

RQ3: How does the online accessibility and price display of luxury goods affect consumer perceived scarcity, desirability, convenience, and willingness-to-buy?

In particular, we first approach the online distribution challenge for luxury goods from three perspectives: conceptual, managerial, and theoretical. Second, based on these considerations we develop hypotheses about the effects of selling luxury goods online on consumer brand evaluations. Finally, we test these hypotheses in two experiments: first, we conduct experiment 1 using 183 high-income individuals from Germany to test for the effects of online accessibility on consumer perceived scarcity, desirability, convenience, and willingness-to-buy. Second, we conduct experiment 2 using 142 qualified luxury insiders from the US to test consumer responses to the online accessibility and price display of luxury goods. Results indicate that the online accessibility of luxury goods does *not* affect consumer perceived scarcity and, thus, does not dilute a luxury brand's desirability. This "no-dilution" finding applies to both high- and low-involvement goods, for both German and US luxury consumers and persists independently of whether or not retail prices are explicitly displayed.

1.3 Outline of manuscript

Figure 3 illustrates the outline of the present manuscript. Subsequent to the introduction we discuss the concept of luxury to gain a common understanding of what a luxury brand is and why consumers desire luxury brands (Chapter 2). Next, we address RQ1 by conceptually examining the specificities of marketing luxury goods in terms of product management, pricing, communication, and distribution management (Chapter 3). Next, we are interested in how these luxury-specific marketing principles apply online. To address RQ2, we conceptually examine the luxury-specific marketing-mix elements in an online context with a particular focus on the online communication and distribution of luxury goods (Chapter 4). In addition to these conceptual considerations we present the results of a qualitative study among luxury industry experts in order to deepen our understanding of the online distribution challenge for luxury goods (Chapter 5). Since both conceptual and managerial insights provide mixed results on whether or not luxury goods should be sold online, we rely on socio-economic and social-psychological theory in order to derive hypotheses how the online accessibility of luxury goods affects consumer perceived scarcity and brand desirability (Chapter 6). We then empirically test these hypotheses. Two experiments are presented: First, we conduct an experiment using high-income individuals from Germany to test the effects of online accessibility of luxury goods on consumer brand evaluations (Chapter 7). Second, we conduct a second experiment using luxury insiders from the US to replicate and extend the findings of the first experiment by testing for potential effects of another factor, i.e. price display (Chapter 8). Finally, we conclude with a discussion of major findings, limitations, future research directions, and implications for managerial practice (Chapter 9).

Figure 3 – Outline of manuscript

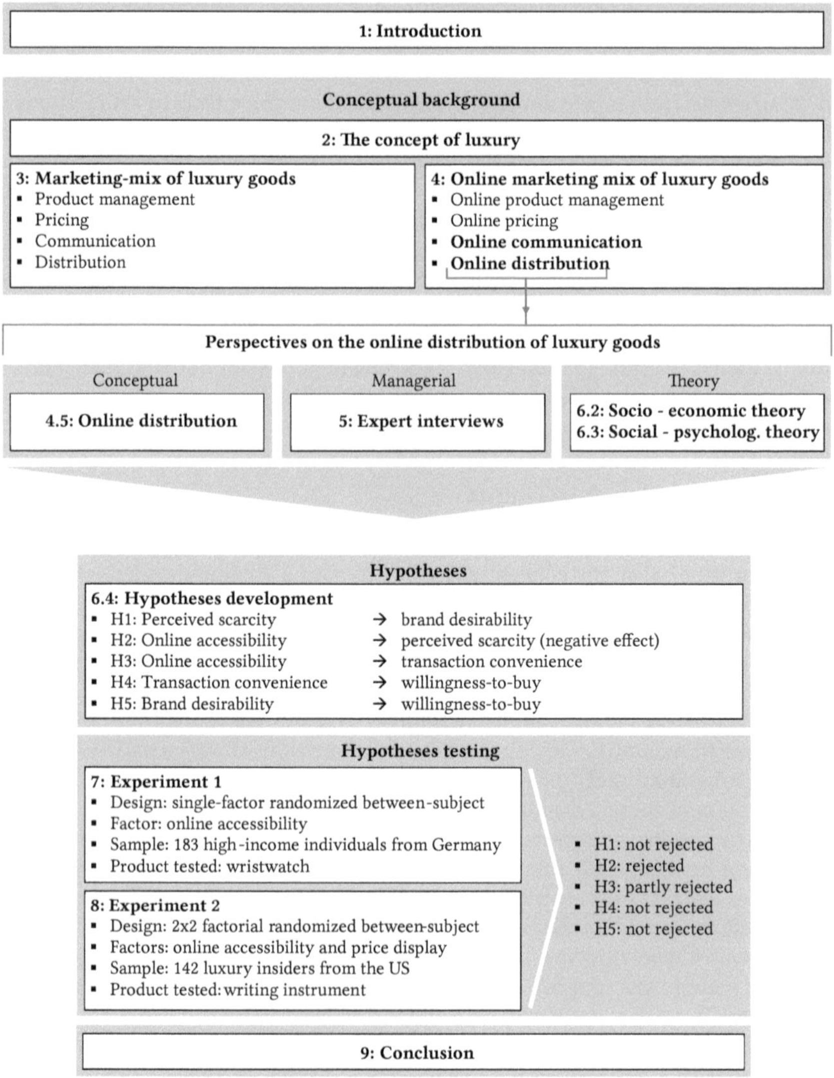

Source: author

2. The Concept of Luxury

The phenomenon of luxury is "particularly slippery to define" (Cornell, 2002, p. 47). Its individual meaning changes from one person to another. Something perceived as extraordinary by one individual might be regarded as ordinary by another (Kapferer & Bastien, 2009b, p. 314). Water, food, and shelter are necessities in developed countries, but luxuries in the wilderness. Owning a car and drinking champagne is ordinary to the high-net-worth individual (HNWI), but luxury for a student. Above all, luxury and necessity both depend on subjective judgement and context.

After numerous attempts to approach the concept of luxury within different disciplines such as history (e.g., Berry, 1994), sociology (e.g., Bourdieu, 1984; Sombart, 1913), economics (e.g., Leibenstein, 1950; Mason, 1998; Veblen, 1960[1899]), and marketing in particular (see Miller & Mills, 2012 for a review) academics have come to agree that the subjectivity and intangibility inherent to luxury **defies an objective, universally valid definition of luxury** (Christodoulides, Michaelidou, & Ching Hsing Li, 2009, p. 397; Heine, 2012, p. 9; Kapferer, 2014, p. 3; Miller & Mills, 2012, p. 41; Phau & Prendergast, 2000, p. 123; Valtin, 2005, p. 20).

In the absence of a commonly accepted definition, luxury goods can be defined by their **constituent characteristics** (e.g., Dubois et al., 2001, pp. 8–17; Kisabaka, 2001, p. 75) and the consumer **motives** for buying them (e.g., Berthon, Pitt, Parent, & Berthon, 2009, p. 49; Vickers & Renand, 2003, pp. 469–471; Vigneron & Johnson, 1999, p. II, 2004, p. 488; Wiedmann, Hennigs, & Siebels, 2009, p. 629). Characteristics like excellent quality, high-end prices or rarity represent "means to an end" to satisfy consumer needs ("ends") like status, differentiation or self-reward that motivate individuals to buy luxury goods (Heine, 2012, p. 27). For example, an individual high in need for pleasure and self-reward (motive) indulges in the consumption of a grand cru because of its fine taste and rare vintage (characteristics). Another individual high in need for social status (motive) ostentatiously consumes an expensive and superfluous leather bag or sportscar (characteristics) to demonstrate wealth. This difference between characteristics of luxury goods and what needs and motives they satisfy is often confused in existing definitions (Heine & Phan, 2011, p. 110). Throughout the following chapters both the constituent characteristics of luxury goods and the motives for buying luxury goods are described separately and in more detail.

2.1 Constituent characteristics of luxury goods

For the purpose of the present manuscript we define luxury goods by the following six constituent characteristics as identified by Dubois et al. (2001, pp. 8–17): **excellent quality, high-end prices, rarity, aesthetics, heritage,** and **superfluousness.**

These characteristics overlap with those presented by other sources as shown in Table 1.

2.1.1 Excellent quality

Excellent quality is an indispensable ingredient of luxury goods, "a sine qua non" (Quelch, 1987, p. 39). The words luxury and quality are almost used synonymously (Dubois et al., 2001, p. 8). In a study among 31 millionaires every individual associated luxury goods with excellent quality (Heine & Phan, 2011, p. 111). The quest for excellence includes both the product attributes and the manufacturing process (Dubois et al., 2001, p. 8; Kisabaka, 2001, pp. 85–96; Lasslop, 2005, p. 473).

Luxury goods are typically best-in-class in terms of product attributes. Depending on the category, luxury goods excel in major product attributes like **material, function, and durability**. For example, the Italian brand Loro Piana specializes in weaving finest cashmere and wool products. The firm operates a nature reserve in the high alpine area of the Andes to preserve the natural habitat of the Vicuñas, a type of camelid, whose wool is considered as one of the finest and rarest animal fabrics and functionally superior over other fabrics in terms of heat insulation (Loropiana.com, 2014). Similarly in categories other than fashion, luxury goods outperform non-luxury goods in terms of material (e.g., jewellery and watches made of precious metals) and function (e.g., horse power of a sportscar, comfort of a limousine, or skin tolerance, scent, and effects of luxury skin care products).

As a result of processing finest material durable luxury goods excel in terms of **longevity** (Kapferer & Bastien, 2009a, p. 164; Kisabaka, 2001, p. 95). Luxury brands like Patek Philippe emphasize the longevity of its precious timepieces by communicating: "You never actually own a Patek Philippe. You merely look after it for the next generation" (Patek.com, 2014d). Patek's quest for excellent quality is backed by the in-house production of all parts, lifetime maintenance, and an own quality seal, which exceeds the official Swiss watchmaking standards (Patek.com, 2014c, 2014e). The extraordinary longevity is a fundamental pre-requisite for a luxury good to become a collectible.

Table 1 – Characteristics of luxury goods

	Characteristics of luxury goods by Dubois et al. (2001, pp. 8–17)						
Sources (by date)	**Excellent quality**	**High-end price**	**Rarity**	**Aesthetics**	**Heritage**	**Superfluousness**	**Other**
Nueno & Quelch (1998, pp. 63–64)	Premium quality	Premium pricing	Limited production, distribution		Heritage, COO, values of creator		Recognizable style, global reputation,
Kisabaka (2001, p. 75)	High quality		Scarcity				Luxury image (incl. aesthetics, heritage, superfluousness)
Valtin (2005, p. 121)	Quality	Premium pricing	(In-) accessibility	Aesthetics	Brand history		Innovation, reputation
Keller (2009, pp. 291–293)	Premium image, quality products	Premium pricing	Selective channel strategy	Pleasurable experience	Heritage, COO		Consistent brand architecture, style elements
Frontier Economics/ ECCIA (2012, pp. 9–13)	Aura: craftsmanship, material		Selective distribution				Industrial property, development of new markets
Heine (2012, p. 72)	High level of quality	High level of price	Rarity	Aesthetics		Extra-ordinariness	Symbolism
Brun & Castelli (2013, pp. 830–831)	Premium quality	Premium pricing	Exclusivity	Emotional appeal	Heritage, COO		Recognizable style, innovation

COO = country-of-origin
Source: author

The excellent material and functional quality is the result of the **expertise, craftsmanship,** and **complexity** in manufacturing luxury goods (Dubois et al., 2001, p. 8). Luxury goods are produced with care and attention to detail (Kisabaka, 2001, p. 89). Manufacturing luxury goods is less automated than the mass production of their non-luxury counterparts and involves human expertise and craftsmanship (Frontier Economics & ECCIA, 2012, p. 9; Lasslop, 2005, p. 473). Thus, processing precious material requires time. For example, the delicate manufacturing of haute horlogerie timepieces like A. Lange & Söhne wristwatches "often takes one and a half years" (Heine & Phan, 2011, p. 111). At Van Cleef & Arpels creating a brooch using the Mystery Set technique requires 300 hours or 37.5 working days (Vancleefarpels.com, 2015d). Similarly, at the Porzellan Manufaktur Nymphenburg painting one single Cumberland porcelain plate, the world's most complicated flower motive, takes three weeks (Nymphenburg.com, 2015a). Not surprisingly, finest craftsmanship also requires a substantial investment in time for the education of workmen. At Munich-based porcelain specialist Porzellan Manufaktur Nymphenburg, for example, it takes up to 15 years in order to learn how to paint the most complicated decorations (Nymphenburg.com, 2014).

Ironically, the quest for excellence in quality does not imply perfection in all aspects. Rather luxury goods are characterized by minor imperfections or flaws (Nueno & Quelch, 1998, p. 63). For example, a Patek Philippe watch is inferior to a Seiko quartz watch in terms of accuracy and legibility (Kapferer & Bastien, 2009b, p. 317). A Ferrari sportscar is inferior to a Volkswagen in terms of comfort, space, and fuel consumption. And, a Waterford vase might have minor imperfections as a result of its hand-blown manufacturing (Nueno & Quelch, 1998, p. 63). After all, these minor flaws add to the quality appeal of a luxury good rather than reducing it (Heine, 2012, p. 75).

2.1.2 High-end price

Luxury goods are expensive. The price of a luxury good, i.e. the monetary value a luxury brand requires in exchange for a product or service it delivers, by far and continuously exceeds prices of comparable non-luxury products and services (Mohr, 2013, p. 15; Simon & Fassnacht, 2009, p. 62). A high-end price first comes to consumers' minds when thinking about luxury goods (Heine & Phan, 2011, p. 111). In addition, prices are fairly objective and easy to measure (Heine, 2012, p. 73). Consequently, a study by McKinsey & Co. (1990) defines luxury goods as "those that, over a 5 year minimum period, could justify a high price – i.e., a price substantially higher than that of products with comparable tangible functional features" (p. 16; cited in Mohr, 2013, p. 13). Yet, a high-end price per se does not constitute a luxury good. It must come along with excellent quality and other value dimensions as shown in Figure 4.

To be considered as a luxury good, the price premium should be at least **30 per cent** vis-à-vis a comparable non-luxury good (Kapferer & Bastien, 2009a, p. 183). However, identifying a minimum price level for luxury goods by category is complicated. Some indication is provided by Dubois & Duquesne (1993, p. 39) and Heine (2010, p. 137) who differentiate between accessible and exceptional luxury goods: accessible luxury goods include a bottle of champagne worth more than EUR 30, a pen or lighter

Figure 4 – High-end price positioning of luxury goods

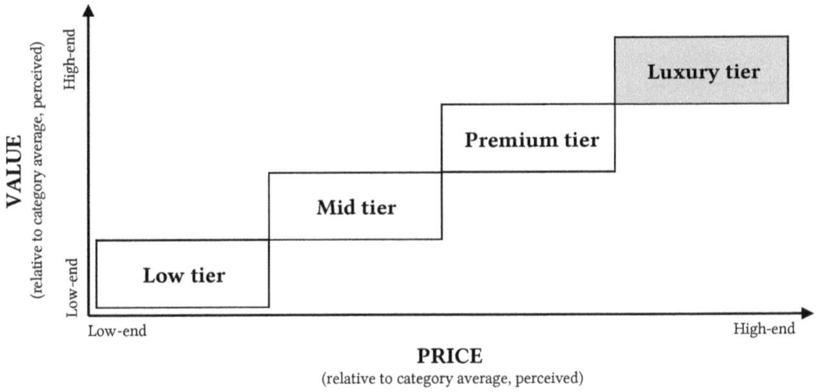

Source: Mohr (2013, p. 15)

worth more than EUR 100, a leather good worth more than EUR 200, jewellery worth EUR 150 to 500, or a watch worth EUR 400 to 5,000. Exceptional luxury goods include clothing, jewellery, and silverware worth more than EUR 500, a watch or piece of furniture worth more than EUR 5,000, or a car worth more than EUR 60,000.

From a consumer perspective, reported levels of minimum prices for luxury goods by category are highly heterogeneous (Kapferer & Laurent, 2014, p. 13). For example, the consumer stated minimum price for a luxury wristwatch ranges from about EUR 50 to more than EUR 3,000 (Kapferer & Laurent, 2014, p. 22). Across all categories, the 5th and 95th percentile of stated minimum prices differ by the factor of 37.5 (Kapferer & Laurent, 2014, p. 13). This enormous heterogeneity reflects the subjectivity of perceptions of luxury.

2.1.3 Rarity

Rarity refers to the state of being "infrequently found" (Oxforddictionaries.com, 2014). Limited availability and perceptions of being hard-to-get is an essential element of luxury goods. "By definition, necessities are possessed by virtually everyone, while luxuries have a degree of exclusivity" (Bearden & Etzel, 1982, p. 184). Although being slightly different, the terms rarity, scarcity, exclusiveness are often used interchangeably. In luxury marketing literature the term scarcity refers to physical or natural paucity while rarity refers to perceived or virtual paucity (e.g., Catry, 2003, p. 10; Kapferer, 2012, p. 457). Rarity is a more generic term while scarcity is understood as a form of rarity. Exclusiveness on the other hand is the result of rarity in the sense that limited availability excludes other individuals from possessing the same thing.

Luxury goods are rare by nature or design. Originally, their rarity originates from the **natural scarcity** of material and human resources and from limitations in production

(Catry, 2003, p. 11; Kapferer, 2012, p. 457; Nueno & Quelch, 1998, p. 62). Hence, the physical availability of a luxury good is limited in number (Kisabaka, 2001, p. 97). A vineyard is naturally limited in size. Gems of a certain size are limited in occurrence. Well-educated individuals capable of designing and crafting fine products are limited in number (recall that it takes about 15 years of education to paint a complicated porcelain decoration; see Chapter 2.1.1). And, luxury goods manufacturers like Ferrari or Patek Philippe deliberately restrict production capacity to a certain number of units (Kapferer, 2012, p. 457). All these restrictions, whether in fact natural or somewhat imposed by management, result in a limited number of physically available products.

The concept of rarity inherent to luxury goods has evolved from natural scarcity to perceived or **virtual rarity** (Catry, 2003, p. 11). Natural scarcity implies a limited number of physically available products and thus impedes fast growth to the discontent of shareholders (Kapferer, 2012, p. 457). In an attempt to somewhat circumvent this rarity-growth-trade-off luxury goods manufacturers artificially induce rarity through limited editions, custom-made products, a highly selective distribution, and communication (Catry, 2003, p. 17; Kapferer, 2012, p. 458; Kisabaka, 2001, pp. 102–104).

For example, as a statement of creativity and revitalization of rarity the Parisian malletier Louis Vuitton has launched some **limited editions** of its iconic Speedy 30 bag like the "Multicolour", "Cherry Blossom", or "Graffiti" line (Rebelle.de, 2014). Similarly, in 2012 the British limousine manufacturer Rolls-Royce has launched a special "Year of the Dragon" edition of its Phantom extended wheelbase model dedicated to the Chinese market (Cho, 2012). And, the LVMH-owned perfume house Guerlain even allows for fully **customizing** perfumes (Guerlain.com, 2015).

To nurture perceptions of rarity luxury goods manufacturers increasingly rely on directly operated monobrand stores (DOS; Bain & Company & Fondazione Altagamma, 2014, p. 15). The European umbrella association ECCIA considers a highly **selective distribution** as a key characteristic of luxury goods (Frontier Economics & ECCIA, 2012, p. 3). The most prominent example refers to Louis Vuitton, which fully controls the distribution of its products (Manninger, 2012, p. 245).

Finally, perceived rarity may be induced by **brand communication**. For example, the iconic fashion brand Chanel primarily advertises its haute joaillerie line rather than its relatively more accessible jewellery line (Kapferer, 2012, p. 458). Another good example of communicating rarity refers to the stepwise launch of the One 77 model by the British sportscar manufacturer Aston Martin, which was limited to 77 units and priced at nearly two million Euros. Before its actual launch at the Geneva Motor Show in 2009, the sports car was first presented to the world at the Paris Motor Show in 2008 – however, one quarter of the car only. The remainder was covered by a grey pin-stripe fabric (Astonmartin.com, 2014b).

2.1.4 Aesthetics

Luxury goods appeal to all senses. They are manufactured with attention to detail and do "not only look beautiful but also are (and should be) pleasant to hear, smell, taste or touch" (Dubois et al., 2001, p. 13). Aesthetic appeal is considered a key differentiating characteristic of luxury goods (Heine & Phan, 2011, p. 112). Kapferer (1997) emphasizes: "Luxury defines beauty; it is art applied to functional items. [...] They offer more than mere objects: they provide reference of good taste. [...] Luxury items provide extra pleasure and flatter all senses at once" (p. 253; cited in Vigneron & Johnson, 2004, p. 486). As a result, luxury goods were empirically found to excel non-luxury goods in terms of hedonic potential (Hagtvedt & Patrick, 2009, p. 612).

Aesthetic appeal refers to the pleasure of sensually experiencing a luxury good: smelling the leather of a handmade pair of shoes, feeling the weight of a piece of jewellery, tasting and feeling a fine sparkling champagne, unpacking a carefully wrapped luxury gift, hearing the sound when starting the engine of a sports car or simply enjoying the silence when sitting in a luxury limousine. However, aesthetic appeal goes beyond indulging in using or consuming a luxury good. It already starts when shopping for a luxury good: when passing by and being caught by an artistically arranged shopping window, when entering the store on a red carpet passing the security, when sitting down in a heavy leather chair and being presented a precious item by a sales person using white gloves.

2.1.5 Heritage

Luxury brands are typically built on a rich heritage. They are deeply rooted in history and place from which they have been carefully created over time. Heritage is a sign of authenticity, consistency, and longevity (Beverland, 2006, pp. 251–253; Hudson, 2011, p. 1538). Luxury brands have created legends to tell; something that competition cannot easily copy and whose appreciation requires some competence of the consumer (Dubois et al., 2001, p. 14). As empirically shown by Wiedmann, Hennigs, Schmidt, & Wuestefeld (2011, p. 209) brand heritage is mainly driven by credibility and consistency and positively affects consumer brand evaluations.

Examining the brand portfolio of the two largest luxury conglomerates LVMH and Richemont reveals that the average luxury brand was founded **100 years** ago (see Table 2). In addition to their roots in history, luxury brands are also rooted in place. About **75 per cent** of luxury brands have a **European heritage** (see Table 2). European luxury brands represent the "old luxury" with an average tradition of 123 years. Non-European luxury brands are relatively younger with an average tradition of 27 years.

2.1.6 Superfluousness

Finally, luxury goods are characterized by some extent of superfluousness. In essence, "luxury is anything that exceeds the necessary" notes Sombart (1913, p. 17; cited in Thomas, 2007, p. 7). Individuals do not necessarily need a yacht, diamond necklace, a car whose maximum speed by far exceeds the general speed limit, or a handmade, complicated mechanical wristwatch while the watch of a mobile phone works equally well or even better. Individuals desire luxury goods for reasons other than rationality. In contrast to mass-market goods, luxury goods defy any reason.

Table 2 – Heritage of brands: LVMH- and Richemont-owned brands

(a) **LVMH** brands

Brand	Year of foundation	Country of origin
Château d'Yquem	1593	France
Dom Pérignon	1668	France
Ruinart	1729	France
Moët & Chandon	1743	France
Hennessy	1765	France
Veuve Clicquot	1772	France
Chaumet	1780	France
Ardbeg	1815	UK
Guerlain	1828	France
Chateau Cheval Blanc	1832	France
Krug	1843	France
Glenmorangie	1843	UK
Loewe	1846	Spain
Louis Vuitton	1854	France
Mercier	1858	France
TAG Heuer	1860	Switzerland
Zenith	1865	Switzerland
Bulgari	1884	Italy
Berluti	1895	France
Acqua di Parma	1916	Italy
Loro Piana	1924	Italy
Fendi	1925	Italy
Fred	1936	France
Céline	1945	France
Emilio Pucci	1947	Italy
Parfums Christian Dior	1947	France
Wenjun	1951	China
Givenchy	1952	France
Parfums Givenchy	1957	France
Bodega Chandon	1959	Argentina
Cape Mentelle	1970	Australia
Kenzo	1970	France
Perfumes Loewe	1972	Spain
D. Chandon California	1973	USA
beneFit	1976	USA
Newton Vineyard	1977	USA
Hublot	1980	Switzerland
Marc Jacobs	1984	USA
Thomas Pink	1984	UK
Donna Karan	1984	USA
Make Up For Ever	1984	France
Cloudy Bay	1985	New Zealand
Fendi Perfumes	1985	France
D. Chandon Australia	1986	Australia
Kenzo Parfums	1988	France
Fresh	1991	USA
Belvedere	1993	USA
Numanthia	1998	Spain
Terrazas de los Andes	1999	Argentina
Cheval de Andes	1999	Argentina
De Beers	2001	UK
Nicholas Kirkwood	2004	UK
Edun	2005	USA
Nude	2007	UK
NOWNESS	2009	France
Dom. Chandon India	2013	India
Dom. Chandon China	2013	China

(b) **Richemont** brands

Vacheron Constantin	1755	Switzerland
Purdey	1814	UK
Baume & Mercier	1830	Switzerland
Jaeger-LeCoultre	1833	Switzerland
A. Lange & Söhne	1845	Germany
Cartier	1847	France
Officine Panerai	1860	Italy
IWC	1868	Switzerland
Piaget	1874	Switzerland
Lancel	1876	France
Alfred Dunhill	1893	UK
Van Cleef & Arpels	1906	France
MONTBLANC	1906	Germany
Chloé	1952	France
Azzedine Alaia	1983	France
Shanghai Tang	1994	Hong Kong
Roger Dubuis	1995	Switzerland
Net-a-Porter.com	2000	UK
Peter Millar	2001	USA
Giampiero Bodino	2013	Italy

Source: LVMH.com (2014a, 2014b, 2014c, 2014d, 2014e, 2014f, 2014g, 2014h, 2014i, 2014j, 2014k, 2014l, 2014m, 2014n, 2014o, 2014p, 2014q, 2014r, 2014s, 2014t, 2014u, 2014v, 2014w, 2014x, 2014y, 2014z, 2014aa, 2014ab, 2014ac, 2014ad, 2014ae, 2014af, 2014ag, 2014ah, 2014ai, 2014aj, 2014ak, 2014al, 2014am, 2014an, 2014ao, 2014ap, 2014aq, 2014ar, 2014as, 2014at, 2014au, 2014av, 2014aw, 2014ax, 2014ay, 2014az, 2014ba, 2014bb, 2014bc, 2014bd, 2014be) and Richemont.com (2014)

Superfluousness means having something valuable in excess like the freedom to choose, space to live, time, or quietness (Dubois et al., 2001, p. 16). A first class flight saves time for checking in, provides a menu of dishes to choose from as well as a separated and quiet space to calm down and relieve stress. Considering that both first and economy class passengers arrive at the same time at the same destination, these additional services are not necessary at all. Still, if money was no option most passengers would certainly prefer a first over an economy class flight.

2.2 Motives for buying luxury goods

2.2.1 Introduction

Luxury brands are desired by many but reserved for the happy few. But why do individuals desire, buy, and indulge in goods that are beyond necessity? Previous literature has identified multiple values of luxury goods, both functional, emotional, and symbolic in nature, that motivate consumers to prefer luxury goods over their non-luxury counterparts (Berthon et al., 2009, p. 49; Hudders, 2012, p. 614; Leibenstein, 1950, p. 188; Vickers & Renand, 2003, pp. 469–471; Vigneron & Johnson, 1999, p. II, 2004, p. 488; Wiedmann et al., 2009, p. 629). For example, the high-end quality standard of luxury goods in terms of finest material, craftsmanship, and longevity meet consumer needs for perfection (functional value).

The aesthetic appeal of luxury goods provides pleasure and a sense of self-reward (emotional value). And the rarity, high-end prices, and superfluousness of luxury goods may satisfy consumer needs for status, uniqueness, and a sense of belonging to the upper class (symbolic values). Figure 5 illustrates the six most prominent motives for buying luxury goods: perfectionism, hedonism, status, uniqueness, affiliation, and gift-giving.

On a first level, motives for buying luxury goods can be differentiated by whether an individual buys a luxury item for oneself (i.e. buyer equals consumer) or for a significant other (i.e. buyer and consumer differ). When buying for oneself, an individual's motives can be further differentiated into personal and interpersonal motives (Vigneron & Johnson, 2004, pp. 7–8). Personal motives, also titled "**luxury for oneself**" (Kapferer & Bastien, 2009b, p. 314), refer to motives like perfectionism and hedonism that are independent from other individuals.

Interpersonal motives for buying luxury goods, also titled "**luxury for others**" (Kapferer & Bastien, 2009b, p. 314), include signalling wealth and social status to others (Veblenian: status-seeking), assimilate with others (bandwagon: affiliation), or dissimilate with others (snob: uniqueness).

An individual's luxury buying behaviour is typically influenced by a combination of different motives. For example, an individual might value an excellent, scarce vintage of champagne (perfectionist), indulge in the act of opening, pouring, and drinking it (hedonist), and eventually enhance one's self-esteem by consuming it in public (Veblenian). The six central motives for buying luxury goods are described below in more detail.

Figure 5 – Motives for buying luxury goods.

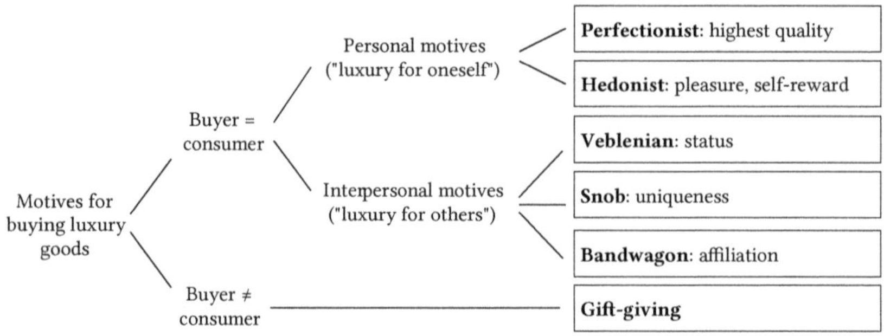

Source: adapted from Hudders (2012, p. 614), Kapferer & Bastien (2009b, p. 314), Lasslop (2005, p. 480), Valtin (2005, p. 121), Vigneron & Johnson (1999, pp. 7–8; 2004, p. 488), Wiedmann et al. (2009, p. 629)

2.2.2 Perfectionist: highest quality

In psychology, perfectionism refers to an individual's personal trait of aiming at flawlessness and setting high personal standards (Flett & Hewitt, 2002, p. 5; Frost, Marten, Lahart, & Rosenblate, 1990, p. 450). Similarly, the perfectionist consumer is characterized by highest expectations concerning the functional quality of a product or service (Vigneron & Johnson, 1999, p. 9). These expectations typically go beyond necessity and require attention to detail.

Luxury goods are generally associated with highest levels of quality and durability (Dubois et al., 2001, p. 9; Nueno & Quelch, 1998, p. 62), even though the core function of luxury goods is often comparable to that of non-luxury goods (e.g., watches telling the time, clothes keeping warm, or cars transporting the driver and his belongings from A to B) or in some aspects even inferior (e.g., higher accuracy of quartz watches as compared to watches with mechanical movements; Kapferer & Bastien, 2009, p. 317). Perfectionist consumers value luxury brands for their "endless quest of art for art's sake" (Kapferer & Bastien, 2009b, p. 317). Due to their lasting quality consumers consider luxury goods as an investment, i.e. as collectibles that are passed on to the next generations (Kisabaka, 2001, p. 33). Here, "higher prices may even make certain products or services more desirable" (Groth & Mcdaniel, 1993, p. 10) since consumers refer to the price as a indicator of quality.

2.2.3 Hedonist: pleasure and self-reward

The hedonic individual consumes a luxury good for reasons of pleasure, indulgence, and the meaning it confers to her- or himself like a sense of self-reward. More specifically, hedonic consumption "designates those facets of consumer behavior that relate to multisensory, fantasy, and emotive aspects of one's experience with products" (Hirschman & Holbrook, 1982, p. 92). Hedonic consumption motives are becoming increasingly important as compared to perfectionist and interpersonal consumption motives (Dubois & Laurent, 1996, p. 476; Nueno & Quelch, 1998, p. 62).

Hedonic value is inherent to luxury goods. The purchase and consumption of a luxury good arouses feelings of **pleasure** and **indulgence** (Dubois & Laurent, 1994, p. 275; Vigneron & Johnson, 1999, p. 8). Luxury goods are associated with an aesthetic and multisensory appeal (Dubois et al., 2001, p. 12). The hedonic individual enjoys the feel and smell of a handmade leather bag, the taste and sparkling feeling of a good vintage of champagne, or the acceleration of a sportscar. This emotional pleasure enhances the private self independently of whether or not is visible to and recognized by significant others (public self; Lasslop, 2005, p. 480; Reich, 2005, p. 41).

In addition to pleasure and indulgence, the purchase and consumption of a luxury good arouses feelings of **self-reward** and enhances the individual's **self-esteem** (Kisabaka, 2001, pp. 26–27; Lasslop, 2005, pp. 479–481). The hedonic individual does not only enjoy the multisensory pleasure of drinking champagne or steering a yacht but also derives a sense of accomplishment and enhanced self-esteem. Individuals purchase extraordinary goods as manifestations of meaningful moments in life (e.g., love, anniversaries, and accomplishments like graduation or job promotion). Luxury goods serve as a source of self-reward and enhanced self-esteem as high-end prices, exclusive distribution, and limited human and material resources make them desirable but unavailable to most individuals.

2.2.4 Veblenian: status

Veblenian or conspicuous consumption motives refer to the purchase and consumption of luxury goods in order to signal wealth to significant others and enhance one's **social status** within society (Bagwell & Bernheim, 1996, p. 349; Corneo & Jeanne, 1997a, p. 55; R. Mason, 1984, p. 26). The seminal work by John Rae (1905[1834]) and Thorstein Veblen (1960 [1899]) suggests that an individual's consumption behaviour may be influenced by the anticipated reactions of others, i.e. a reference group (Bearden & Etzel, 1982, p. 184). Individuals buy and consume goods that they anticipate to evoke desired reactions by significant others.

According to Bourne (1957, p. 218), to create the desired reactions by others a good should meet two requirements: first, the item consumed must be "**exclusive**" by any means. Any characteristic of being scarce or hard-to-obtain excludes others from possessing the same item and thus bears the potential to elevate the owner's social status within society. Exclusion of others may be created by an item being unavailable to others in terms of natural scarcity like limited human or material resources as well as in terms of high levels of effort needed to obtain the item like high-end prices and an exclusive distribution.

Second, the item must be visible in order to be "**seen or identified by others**" (Bearden & Etzel, 1982, p. 184; Bourne, 1957, p. 218). Any symbol has the potential to evoke desired reactions by others only if it is recognized and decoded by other individuals. Affluent individuals high in need for status, also known as "parvenus", engage in signalling their wealth through the conspicuous consumption of symbols that may be easily decoded by the general public (Han, Nunes, & Drèze, 2010, p. 17). The status-seeking parvenu thus prefers expensive goods that are consumed in public like clothing, accessories, or cars and brands that are commonly known and easily recognizable like a conspicuously branded Louis Vuitton bag carrying the LV monogram rather than a less known and subtly branded Bottega Veneta bag.

2.2.5 Snob: uniqueness

The snobbish consumer uses a luxury good as a mean of uniqueness and self-differentiation from others (Corneo & Jeanne, 1997b, p. 335; Leibenstein, 1950, p. 189). Snobs buy and consume goods that are not consumed by the masses. They seek to dissociate from the common and ordinary. Hence, snobbish consumption behaviour is characterized by the early adoption of goods that are not yet heavily diffused and the decreasing interest in goods that are becoming too common over time (Vigneron & Johnson, 1999, p. 5). The purchase and consumption of luxury goods provides a potential source of self-differentiation as scarcity of human and material resources, selective distribution, and high prices limit their diffusion among population.

Like the Veblenian individual, the snobbish consumer prefers goods that are exclusive, i.e. unavailable to others. However, Veblenian and snobbish individuals differ in the following two aspects: first, while the Veblenian mostly relies on price as an indicator of unavailability, the snob judges the exclusiveness of an item based on its diffusion among the population (Leibenstein, 1950, p. 189). Second, while the Veblenian engages in the conspicuous consumption of visible symbols in order to enhance perceptions about his or her social status within society (public self-consciousness), the snob is rather concerned about how similar or dissimilar he or she perceives him- or herself as compared to others (private self-consciousness; Vigneron & Johnson, 1999, p. 6).

Both the phenomenon of snobbism and the Veblenian will be further explained from a socio-economic and socio-psychological perspective in Chapter 6.

2.2.6 Bandwagon: affiliation

In contrast to snobs, the bandwagon consumer buys and consumes luxury goods as a symbol of group affiliation rather than dissociation (Corneo & Jeanne, 1997b, p. 334; Kastanakis & Balabanis, 2012, p. 1400). The bandwagon individual seeks to conform with an exclusive social group he or she desires to be associated with like gourmets, classical music lovers, sailing clubs etc. (Gierl & Huettl, 2010, p. 226). This individual aims at being perceived as "one of the boys" (Leibenstein, 1950, p. 189). In order to signal his or her **membership with the exclusive social group** the bandwagon individual consumes goods that other members of that group appreciate. Hence, a bandwagon consumer's demand for a certain good increases as it becomes popular within the social group of interest.

Luxury goods can serve as signals of group membership as they are often unavailable to others (i.e. non-members) in terms of limited supply or high-end prices (Gierl & Huettl, 2010, p. 227). For example, a bandwagon individual might aim at belonging to the group of Ferrari old-timer car owners. Ferrari old-timers are unavailable to the masses as they are limited in number (i.e. not being produced anymore) and hard-to-obtain (i.e. knowing how to get a model, affording it etc.). The bandwagon individual might possess a Ferrari old-timer as a signal of being one of the "Ferraristi". Hence, in order to signal group membership the owned or consumed object must be (a) appreciated by members of the group and (b) unavailable to others as a symbol of differentiation of the group and its members from non-members.

Importantly, the purchase, ownership and consumption of luxury goods is hardly driven by a single motive but rather a combination of multiple motives. The same individual might be to some extent both perfectionist, hedonist, Veblenian, snob, and bandwagon or any combination of these motives. Again referring to the example of buying a Ferrari old-timer: the purchase might be motivated by the desire to belong to the exclusive group of Ferraristi (bandwagon), to differentiate from the mass (snob), to purely signal status to others (Veblenian), or simply because one enjoys the aesthetics, heritage and the pleasure of driving a Ferrari old-timer (hedonist).

2.2.7 Gift-giving

The gift-giving individual buys luxury goods as a symbol of appreciation, friendship, or love to a significant other in order to provide and obtain pleasure (Banks, 1979, p. 322; Belk, 1977, p. 3). The phenomenon of gift-giving is deeply rooted in our social system and characterized by reciprocity (Mauss, 1967 [1923] cited in Belk, 1976, p. 155). Reciprocity implies that gift-giving hardly represents a purely altruistic act where the giver is nothing given in return (Banks, 1979, p. 319). Rather, the social system of gift-giving somewhat obliges the receiver to repay in form of a material equivalent at a later period of time (Mauss, 1967 [1923] in Belk, 1976, p. 155). Apart from the material, Levi-Strauss (1965) emphasizes the emotional reward like gratitude and appreciation the giver immediately receives in return to his gift-giving behaviour (Belk, 1976, p. 156). Hence, by giving a gift the individual not only provides but also obtains pleasure.

In meaningful occasions in life, individuals often give luxury gifts as an extraordinary symbol of appreciation, friendship, and love. Luxury goods are given to celebrate important accomplishments (e.g., graduation, retirement) or special moments in life (e.g., birth, wedding). In fact, gifts account for about 50 per cent of luxury goods purchases (Dubois, Czellar, & Laurent, 2005, p. 120). Sarett (1960, pp. 53–54) reports that about one in two pieces of jewellery and two out of three watches are given as a gift. The significance of gift-giving for the luxury goods industry is further illustrated by looking at historical sales patterns over time. As shown in Figure 6, sales for luxury fashion and jewellery & watches repeatedly peak within the fourth quarter of each year, i.e. the Christmas season.

Figure 6 – Seasonality of fashion, jewellery & watches sales.

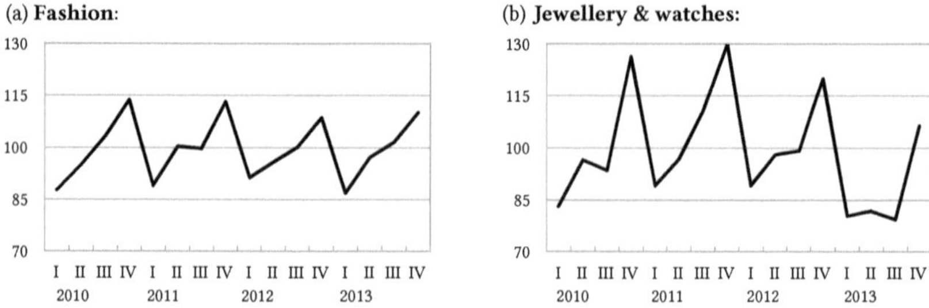

Note: sales index Germany by quarters 2010–2013 with 2010 = 100
Source: Statistisches Bundesamt (2015)

3. Marketing-Mix of Luxury Goods

Researchers show an increasing interest into the phenomenon of luxury goods (see Figure 2). Part of the fascination arises from the observation that luxury goods manufacturers apply specific marketing principles that may be counterintuitive to conventional marketing theory. Understanding the essential principles of marketing luxury goods is subject to this manuscript and a necessary prerequisite for discovering how the Internet affects the way luxury goods are marketed. Online marketing initiatives should be considered as integral part of a luxury brand's overall marketing strategy rather than as an isolated decision.

Hence, we are first interested in identifying the essential specificities of the marketing-mix for luxury goods. Introduced in 1960 by the American marketing scholar Edmund Jerome McCarthy the marketing-mix framework refers to a set of parameters that companies manage to satisfy customer needs. In particular, McCarthy (1964, p. 38) suggests four groups of parameters, which he calls "The 4 P's", i.e. product, price, promotion (or communication), place (or distribution). How these marketing-mix elements can be applied to luxury goods will be conceptually examined throughout this chapter. Specifically, Chapter 3 addresses the first research question (compare Chapter 1.2):

RQ1: What are the specificities of marketing luxury goods in terms of product management, pricing, communication, and distribution management?

3.1 Product management of luxury goods

3.1.1 Introduction

A product is anything of value (tangible or intangible; goods or services) that a company offers to the market with the potential to satisfy customer wants or needs (Homburg, 2015, p. 551; Kotler & Armstrong, 2012, p. 224). It is the essence of any business activity. Products are created and offered by suppliers and bought and used by customers. The term **product management** (also product policy) refers to all decisions and actions a company makes to create and manage its products (Bruhn & Homburg, 2004, p. 685; Herrmann, 1998, pp. 4–5). These decisions include strategic considerations (objectives, strategic direction, product-mix) and product design decisions (function, aesthetics, packaging, add-on services, branding; Albers & Herrmann, 2007, pp. 5–6; Bruhn, 2014, p. 127; Herrmann & Huber, 2013, p. 2; Kotler & Armstrong, 2012, p. 229).

In luxury, the affluent clientele seeks to satisfy needs that are **beyond mere function**. They do not drink a flute of champagne to simply satisfy their thirst. The connoisseur enjoys the routine of unpacking and opening a bottle of a rare vintage, carefully pouring it, taking a smell, and finally indulging in feeling and tasting the fine sparkling wine. For reasons other than hedonistic reasons the parvenu might simply consume

Figure 7 – Overview: specificities of product management in luxury.

Product strategy

Objectives by range
- High-end range: awareness and desire
- Core range: sales and profit
- Entry range: trial

Strategic direction
- Designer driven
- Long-term consistency

Product-mix
- Consistency of product categories
- Moderate accessibility

Product design

Product excellence in terms of
- Function
- Aesthetics
- Durability
- Craftsmanship
- Packaging

Add-on services
- Customization
- Gift-wrapping
- Lifetime product maintenance and spare parts supply

Brand signature
- Monograms, emblems, design
- Consistency across products and over time

Source: author

it as a signal of wealth and status. Similarly, the educated luxury consumer values a pair of hand-sewn calfskin leather shoes, a woven horsehair handbag, or a handmade tourbillon watch beyond their basic function of keeping one's feet warm, storing personal belongings, or telling the time. The affluent clientele is looking for perfection, pleasure and self-reward as well as for signals to significant others (see Chapter 2.2).

Product management is directed towards satisfying these sophisticated needs by **consistently managing highest levels of quality, rarity, and aesthetic appeal**. Consistency of product management is essential for the long-term success of the company. A luxury good is the physical embodiment of what the company stands for. It is the tangible result of a company's expertise, aim for perfection, and attention to detail it has developed over decades or centuries. Hence, luxury goods are carefully managed in terms of strategic considerations (objectives, strategic direction, product-mix) and product design decisions (function, aesthetics, packaging, add-on services, branding). Figure 7 provides an overview of the specificities in the product management of luxury goods, which will be described in more detail throughout this chapter.

Please note that throughout this manuscript we mainly refer to luxury goods rather than to luxury services. On the one hand, the marketing of services differs from that of goods in many instances (Wilson, Zeithaml, Bitner, & Gremler, 2012, p. 11–20). On the other hand, physical goods like cars, fashion & accessories, jewellery & watches, perfume & cosmetics, food & beverages, furniture, yachts, and jets account for more than 80 per cent of the worldwide luxury market in 2014 (Bain & Company & Fondazione Altagamma, 2014, pp. 3–6).

3.1.2 Product strategy

In general, product management starts with defining a product strategy in terms of objectives, strategic direction, and product-mix decisions (Herrmann & Huber, 2013, p. 85). Based on these strategic considerations product elements like function, aesthetics, packaging, add-on services, and branding are designed. Hence, the product strategy determines what a company aims at, how it plans to achieve it within a given time period and how new products fit into the current product-mix.

3.1.2.1 Objectives

In general, marketing objectives include economic and psychological objectives (Becker, 1990, pp. 48–52; Homburg, 2015, p. 434; Meffert, Burmann, & Kirchgeorg, 2008, p. 242): economic objectives refer to absolute or growth targets in terms of unit sales (amount of units sold), value sales (amount of units sold weighted by price), market share (company's sales relative to total market sales), contribution margin (values sales minus unit costs), or profit (value sales minus unit and fixed costs). Psychological objectives refer to absolute or growth targets in cognitive (e.g., brand awareness), affective (e.g., attitudes, preferences), and conative (e.g., trial, repeat purchases) consumer responses to the market offering. In general, market share has become a major objective in conventional marketing practice as it indicates a company's market performance relative to its competitors (Bruhn, 2014, p. 26).

In luxury, multiple marketing objectives apply. Considering that clients often spend years of dreaming of a luxury good before actually being able to afford it, objectives are both **psychological** (e.g., awareness and desire) and **economic** (e.g., sales and profit) in nature. Market share, however, is less important. "Nothing is more foreign" to luxury brands than "any comparison with a competitor" (Kapferer & Bastien, 2009b, p. 316). To identify the diverse marketing objectives it is helpful to consider the different levels of a luxury brand's product-mix. These levels are illustrated in the luxury pyramid as suggested by Kapferer & Bastien (2009a, pp. 141 & 251; see Figure 8).

First, as an ultimate statement of creativity luxury goods manufacturers typically develop a "**griffe**", which is at the very top of the luxury pyramid (Kapferer & Bastien, 2009a, p. 250). Like art a griffe is a signature product, which is designed beyond any necessity, usually not for sale, and the pure expression of a luxury brand's accumulated expertise and creativity. Griffes are haute couture dresses, complicated watches, or concept cars like the Lamborghini Egoista or the Aston Martin CC100 Speedster. The objective of creating a griffe is usually purely psychological in nature. It triggers both brand **awareness** through its diffusion in media (cognitive consumer response) and **desirability** through its unique, aesthetic, and superfluous character (affective consumer response).

Figure 8 – The luxury pyramid.

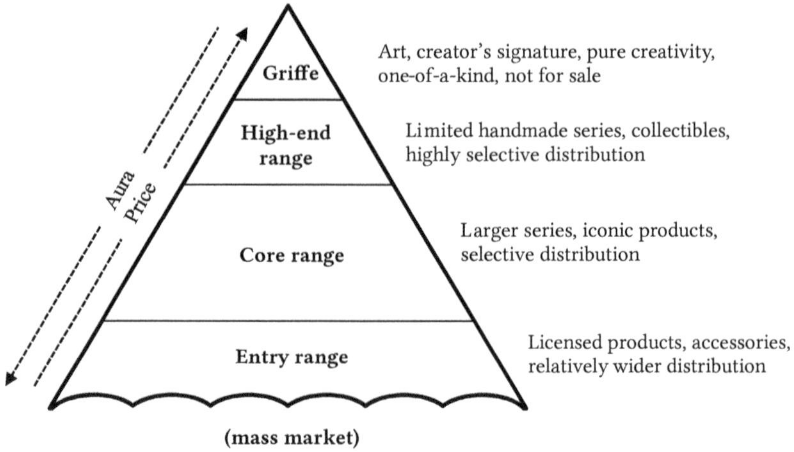

Source: Kapferer & Bastien (2009a, pp. 141 & 251)

The second highest level of the luxury pyramid refers to the **high-end range**, i.e. a small, handmade series whose distribution is highly selective (Kapferer & Bastien, 2009a, p. 251). The high-end range often includes precious limited editions, which are extremely hard-to-get and often sold out prior to release; something an elite group of connoisseurs desires to collect. Examples of high-end range products include Aston Martin's sports car One-77, Montblanc's Patron of Art Edition fountain pens, or a rare vintage wine. The objective of a high-end range product is rather psychological than economic in nature. Like for the griffe, the high-end range primarily aims at creating and reinforcing brand **awareness and desirability** through its unique and highly exclusive character. In contrast to the griffe, these limited series are intended to be sold and generate some value sales. However, the sales are not only limited considering the small amount of units produced and clients capable of paying the extreme prices. Also, the expenses involved in producing high-end range products make them "**very rarely profitable**" (Kapferer & Bastien, 2009a, p. 245).

Third, **core range** products primarily aim at generating **sales and profit**. The core range refers to larger serieses, whose production is fully controlled by the manufacturer and organized in a more standardized manner (Kapferer & Bastien, 2009a, p. 244). It is typically created around a luxury brand's most iconic products like a Montblanc Meisterstück fountain pen, a Rolex Oyster wristwatch, the Louis Vuitton Speedy bag series, or the Boucheron Collection Quatre. The objective of generating sales does not imply that core range products are widely distributed. Their distribution is still highly selective through own monobrand stores or authorized multibrand retailers only. However, within this highly selective distribution network the core range is typically available at any of these stores while the distribution of high-end range products are far more restricted to few representative points of sale like flagship stores, for example. To survive in the long run, luxury goods manufacturers must realize a **minimum gross margin of 80 per cent** (Kapferer & Bastien, 2009a, p. 227), i.e. unit price (e.g., USD 1,000) should be at least **5 times the unit cost** (e.g., USD 200). While this number might seem high at first sight, high margins are necessary to cover the enormous expenses for initial creation, brand communication and distribution (Kapferer & Bastien, 2009a, p. 227).

Finally, the primary objective of **entry range** products is **trial**, i.e. giving prospects access to the brand by offering less sophisticated, more affordable products. Kapferer & Bastien (2009a, pp. 132 & 169) further differentiate between entry-level products for the "future faithful", i.e. prospects with the potential to become loyal customers, and entry-level products for "day trippers", i.e. consumers who occasionally buy luxury goods independent of specific brand preferences. The latter include products **outside the core expertise** of the brand like Gucci branded sunglasses or fragrances that are often licensed to contract manufacturers, made available through a relatively wider distribution (e.g., Sephora, Douglas, or DFS duty free shops) and sold at **high margins** (Kapferer & Bastien, 2009a, p. 169). Those entry-level products for ‚day trippers' we consider as an access to the brand rather than to the brand's core range.

In contrast, entry-level products for the "future faithful", how Kapferer & Bastien (2009a, pp. 132 & 169) call it, actually represent the lower end of the core range. These are relatively less sophisticated products **within the core expertise** of the brand rather than accessories or fragrances (e.g., a less sophisticated Hermès bag rather than a perfume). Despite their lower level of sophistication and price, this kind of entry-level products must still meet highest quality standards to make the "future faithful" clientele dream of going up the range. Providing quality at relatively affordable prices results in **relatively lower margins** (Kapferer & Bastien, 2009a, pp. 169 & 244). Hence, the objective of this kind of entry range is generating **trial and potential repeat purchase** rather than making profit. Please note that in the following the terms entry range and entry-level products refer to the "day-tripper" type of entry-level products like accessories or fragrances, for example.

Conclusion. Luxury product strategy follows multiple objectives both economic and psychological in nature. The ultimate creativity and inaccessibility of griffes continuously nurtures desires. The entry range lures new clients to enter the brand universe and subsequently move up the range. The core range with its iconic and high-margin products aims at generating excess profits to cover expenses for product creation, communication, and distribution. Finally, the high-end range reinforces desire among the loyal clientele by regularly launching limited, handmade editions that become precious collectibles.

3.1.2.2 Strategic direction

Once objectives have been identified and prioritized a strategic direction or roadmap defines how the company plans to achieve these objectives within a given time frame. Conventionally, non-luxury consumer goods manufacturers aim at gaining sales and market share (see above). In the pursuit to serve more consumers better than competition, developing a strategic direction typically involves going through a process of (1) segmenting consumers based on geographic, demographic, psychographic, or behavioural variables (**segmentation**), (2) identifying a target segment (**targeting**), its needs and how they are met by competitive products, and (3) positioning the product in the market with a specified value proposition (**positioning**; Herrmann & Huber, 2013, pp. 89–108; Kotler & Armstrong, 2012, p. 191). This value proposition should be both of lasting relevance for the consumer and difficult for competitors to copy (Bruhn, 2014, p. 124). In essence, product strategy defines how to profitably satisfy relevant customer needs that are currently not met by competitive offerings.

Designer-driven. In luxury, product strategy is designer-driven rather than consumer- and competitor-driven. A luxury good emanates from the "mind of its creator", his or her "intrinsic passion" rather than being the response to customer wishes or the result of a deliberate positioning vis-à-vis competition (Kapferer & Bastien, 2009a, pp. 62–65). Unlike conventional marketing practice of deriving new product ideas from regular market research and prototype testing, it is the owner of the brand, its creative director, designer, horologist or any other experienced artisan who drives luxury product development. A creator's personality is a key determinant of luxury brands (Nueno & Quelch, 1998, p. 63). **Karl Lagerfeld**, for example, the German fashion designer and creative director at the Parisian fashion house Chanel, is leaving his mark on the brand and its collections for more than 30 years now.

Yet after all, luxury goods manufacturers must satisfy the needs of their demanding clientele in order to generate sales and profit. Finding the **balance between creative independence and customer orientation** has been referred to as the paradox of luxury product management (Dubois, 1992, p. 31; Heine, 2012, p. 81).

To exemplify different positions between the two extremes we may again consider the different levels of the luxury pyramid (see Figure 8). First, the **griffe** is the ultimate statement of a luxury brand's **creative independence**. When developing a griffe its creator does not ever ask a single consumer for his or her opinion. Griffes are often superfluous and ahead of time instead of satisfying current customer needs. Refusing to design what market research recommends, **Tom Ford**, designer and former creative director at Gucci and Yves Saint Laurent, once argued (Bastien & Kapferer, 2013, p. 26): "I look at research then throw it away and forget it for this is about yesterday. I must create dreams for tomorrow".

The same thinking applies to the **high-end range**, i.e. a limited, handmade series of finest quality, whose distribution is highly selective (Kapferer & Bastien, 2009a, p. 251). Like the griffe, a high-end range product is the result of its creator's immanent drive for perfection and irrepressible creativity rather than deliberate market research. Often dedicated to art, sports or unique moments (e.g., anniversaries), the high-end range product is the physical embodiment of a story its creator wants to share.

Third, a luxury brand's **core range** exemplifies both creative independence and customer orientation. The luxury goods manufacturer defines the essential features and design of its products. Often, however, the customer is given the possibility to decide on specific design elements like materials or colours to personalize the product – either within a pre-defined set of options or fully tailored. For example, while the design of the iconic Vitra Eames Plastic Armchair has remained unchanged since its first creation in 1950, the customer today may choose from more than 3.000 possible combinations of colours and material (Vitra.com, 2015). Hence, parts of a luxury good are manufactured based on consumer preferences.

Fourth, not only design elements of the product but the product idea itself might follow consumer trends. This may hold true for **branded accessories within the entry range** only rather than to a luxury brand's griffe, high-end, or core range. For example, today we find a considerable variety of luxury-branded iPad and iPhone cases. While these items are still uniquely designed and made of fine materials that go beyond mere function, they represent a response to customer needs rather than the genuine vision of the brand. Another example refers to branded fragrances, which are often licensed to consumer goods manufacturers like Coty (e.g., Chloé, Chopard), Estée Lauder (e.g., Tom Ford, Michael Kors), L'Oréal Luxe (e.g., Gorgio Armani, Yves Saint Laurent), or Procter & Gamble Prestige Products (e.g., Gucci, Dolce & Gabbana). These manufacturers and their product development are essentially driven by **customer orientation** (Kapferer & Bastien, 2009a, p. 65). Overall, with the exception of some of these entry range products the genuine signature of the creator mainly drives the strategic direction for a luxury product rather than deliberate market research.

Time frame. In addition to defining a roadmap how to achieve product management objectives, a strategic direction also involves deciding on within which **time frame** they should be achieved. Conventionally, product management is rather short-term oriented. To achieve growth in sales and market share (see objectives above), non-luxury consumer goods manufacturers aim at responding to current consumer needs better and more quickly than competition. The need for quickly responding to market changes may be observed in fast fashion or consumer electronics where manufacturers always seek for the latest fashion or technology trends, respectively.

In luxury, product strategy is about **long-term consistency** rather than speed. Norbert Platt, former CEO at Richemont Group, notes: "There is no place for a short-term mindset within Richemont; we invest in individuals, in businesses and in infrastructure for the long term, not for tomorrow" (Richemont.com, 2006, p. 10). In a similar, however, less rigid manner Bernard Arnault, Chairman and CEO at LVMH, states his strategy for the group of about 60 luxury brands: "While sticking firmly to our long-term strategy, we are adapting our decisions and actions to the ever faster changes in our market environment" (LVMH.com, 2014, p. 1). Consistency across the entire product range is needed to preserve the identity of the brand (Nueno & Quelch, 1998, p. 62). In the pursuit of consistency the long-term commitment of a luxury brand's creative and management team is crucial (Kapferer & Bastien, 2009a, p. 234).

3.1.2.3 Product-mix

Launching a new product is not an isolated decision. Each product should fit into the general product-mix strategy of a manufacturer. A product-mix (also assortment or product program) refers to the entirety of products and services a manufacturer offers to the market (Homburg, 2015, p. 603; Kotler & Armstrong, 2012, p. 235; Meffert et al., 2008, p. 400). A product-mix strategy defines the **width** (i.e. number of product lines), **length** (i.e. number of products within a product line), and **depth** (i.e. number of variants of each product) of a manufacturer's product range based on which products are added or eliminated (Bruhn, 2014, p. 157; Herrmann & Huber, 2013, p. 2; Kotler & Armstrong, 2012, pp. 235–236).

Width and length. In luxury, a **moderate width and length** of product-mix is preferred (Nueno & Quelch, 1998, pp. 64–65; Reddy, Terblanche, Pitt, & Parent, 2009, p. 190). While some width and length is needed to provide variety and realize a critical level of sales, the luxury product-mix should remain adequately narrow for reasons of higher margins, lower operation and complexity costs, and preserving a coherent brand image (Kapferer & Bastien, 2009a, pp. 132 & 227; Nueno & Quelch, 1998, pp. 64–65). An empirical study of 150 luxury brands shows that profitability is higher among manufacturers with a logically consistent, rather narrow product-mix (Reddy et al., 2009, p. 190). However, both extremes, i.e. a luxury product-mix being too narrow or too broad, may endanger the long-term success of a brand.

On the one side, **broadening the product-mix** either vertically or horizontally is tempting as it generates additional sales and profit while leveraging existing capabilities and a strong brand name. Yet, there is a fine line between extending the client base and diluting the brand's luxury cachet. In essence, the decision whether or not to extend a luxury brand's product-mix reflects the major trade-off between sales growth and exclusiveness (compare Chapter 1.1). In particular, luxury goods manufacturers face two major product-mix challenges: (1) adding lower-priced items within existing product categories (**vertical downwards extension**), and (2) adding product lines that are loosely related to the brand's core product category (inconsistent **horizontal extension**; Kapferer & Bastien, 2009, p. 140).

The French fashion designer Pierre Cardin, for example, used to be one of 21 members of the elite "Chambre Syndicale de la Couture Parisienne", a French association of haute couture designers, before excessively licensing its brand name (more than 800 licenses by 1988) and extending its product-mix from fashion into more affordable, loosely related product categories like cigarettes, wine, baseball caps (Reddy et al., 2009, p. 191). While being economically successful, the once-elite brand Pierre Cardin has become a rather mass-market phenomenon (Kapferer & Bastien, 2009a, pp. 145–146).

On the other side, having a **too narrow product-mix** of few, high-end range products often implies high total cost per unit in terms of R&D, production, and marketing & sales while having a very limited client base. The VW-owned super sports car manufacturer Bugatti, for example, is assumed to make a loss for any EUR

1.5 million Veyron model it sells resulting from the imbalance of enormous R&D costs on the one hand and extremely low volume sales (about 40 per year) on the other (Davies, 2013). Similarly, haute joaillerie manufacturers are rarely profitable given the limited client base able to afford their fine pieces of jewellery (Kapferer & Bastien, 2009a, p. 227).

A **moderate vertical downwards extension** of the product-mix can help those highest-end luxury goods manufacturers to increase the client base to a critical size and realize a reasonable level of economies of scale. Before 2009, the British car manufacturer Rolls-Royce, for example, faced profitability problems (Kapferer & Bastien, 2009a, p. 227) with relatively low annual unit sales of around 1,000 cars delivered and offering a too narrow product-mix with the high-end Phantom series only priced at around EUR 350,000 for the base model (Stankeviciute, 2012, p. 147). By introducing the Ghost series in 2009, a relatively less voluminous sedan with retail prices starting at around EUR 215,000, Rolls-Royce succeeded in extending its client base while not diluting its parent brand (see Figure 9(a); Stankeviciute, 2012, pp. 147–148). Economic figures prove the success of this vertical downward extension – a **moderate** democratization of the elite brand Rolls-Royce. As shown in Figure 9(b), total unit sales went up by about 170 per cent from 1,002 in 2009 up to 2711 in 2010 and have further increased up to 3,630 in 2013. For comparison, Bentley, Ferrari, and Maserati recorded unit sales of 10,876, 7,000, and 15,400 in 2013, respectively (FCAGroup.com, 2013, p. 49; VolkswagenAG.com, 2013, p. 33).

Depth. Finally a luxury product-mix should have an adequate depth, i.e. a reasonable number of variants of each product. Particularly a brand's most iconic product should be **constantly reinvented** (Kapferer & Bastien, 2009a, p. 131). It is about adding a touch of modernity to otherwise timeless icons (Wetlaufer, 2001, p. 121). Louis Vuitton, for example, has constantly reinvented the design of its iconic Speedy bag series through editions like the Cherry Blossom, Graffiti, or Multicolour edition (Chevalier & Mazzalovo, 2008, p. 233). Its recognizable form, however, remained unchanged.

3.1.3 Product design

A product is a bundle of components both tangible and intangible, which combined create value for the consumer (Bruhn, 2014, p. 123; Herrmann & Huber, 2013, p. 7). Designing a product or market offering involves deciding on how to design **function, aesthetics, packaging, add-on services, and branding** (Herrmann & Huber, 2013, p. 320; Homburg, 2015, p. 552; Nieschlag, Dichtl, & Hörschgen, 2002, p. 666; Zanger, 2007, p. 100). Decisions in product design aim at best satisfying consumer needs and evoke desired perceptions of excellent quality, rarity, aesthetic appeal, heritage, and superfluousness – constituent characteristics of a luxury good (compare Chapter 2.1). In general, the honourable task of designing the product and its elements rests with the creative team, not the product or marketing manager (Herrmann, 1998, p. 461; Koppelmann, 2006, p. 107). However, as the product is the materialization of what the brand stands for, any luxury brand marketer and salesperson should know its components. In luxury, function, aesthetics,

Figure 9 – Vertical downward extension: Rolls-Royce Ghost.

(a) Rolls -Royce product-mix: downwards extension through launching the Ghost series 2009

(b) Rolls -Royce Motor Cars unit sales by model series worldwide, from 2006 to 2013

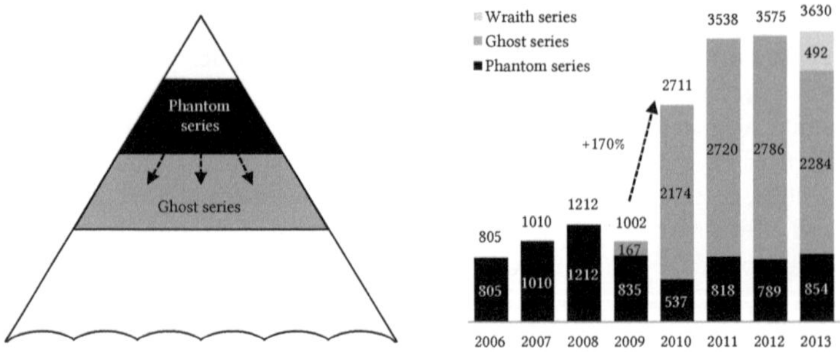

Source: BMWGroup.com (2009, 2011, 2013)

packaging, add-on services, and a brand's aura must meet highest standards. In the following we address these components beginning with functional core features and subsequently adding aesthetic features, packaging, add-on services, and branding. Please note, however, that these components are deeply interlinked and thus difficult to address in a fully separate manner.

3.1.3.1 Function

Function refers to the core of a product developed to satisfy a customer's basic need (see Figure 10). In its core a product is a physical, chemical, and technical combination of materials that constitutes its generic function needed by the customer (Zanger, 2007, p. 102). A bag stores belongings, a watch tells the time, clothes protect the body, and a car transports persons and objects from one place to another. Even in luxury, it is the core function of a product that "justifies its purchase" (Kapferer & Bastien, 2009a, p. 160). Contrary to the common perception of luxury merely being the result of good branding, luxury starts with excelling in the core functions of a product (Kapferer & Bastien, 2009a, p. 162; Keller, 2009, p. 291).

In general, the materialisation of a product involves decisions on *what* the product is composed of and *how* these elements are combined to perform the desired function. The "what" refers to product design characteristics like **material**, **form**, **colour**, and **texture** (Koppelmann, 1997, p. 323). These characteristics contribute to both function and aesthetic appeal of a product. Depending on the product category these characteristics merely add to the aesthetic appeal of the product or constitute its basic function. The scent of material, for example, adds to the aesthetic appeal of leather goods while constituting the core function of perfumes. The "how" refers to the physical, chemical, or technical combination of these characteristics in a way that the resulting product performs the desired function (Koppelmann, 1997, p. 397; Zanger, 2007, p. 102).

Figure 10 – Components of a product.

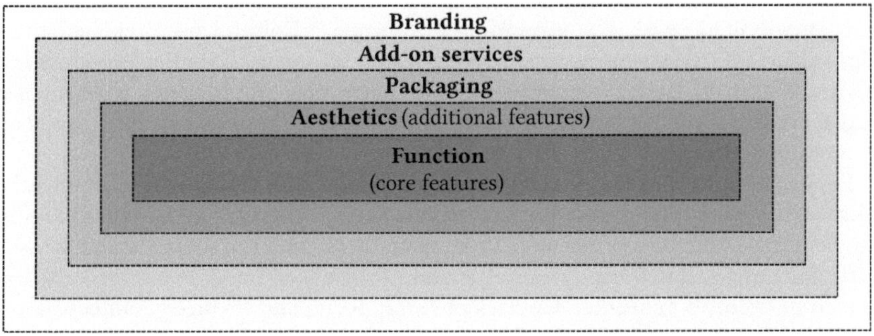

Source: Herrmann & Huber (2013, p. 320), Homburg (2015, p. 552), Nieschlag et al. (2002, p. 666), Zanger (2007, p. 100)

In luxury, decisions on product design characteristics like material, form, colour and texture (the "what") and their construction (the "how") are guided by multiple objectives including the aim for excellent quality, rarity, aesthetic appeal, heritage, and some degree of superfluousness to justify high-end prices (compare Chapter 2.1). Considering merely the core function of a luxury good, product characteristics like material, form, and texture should be selected based on their potency to deliver **highest possible quality** in terms of **function and durability** (Heine & Phan, 2011, p. 112).

Functional quality. Recall the example of Vicuña wool, a high-quality garment: besides its highly aesthetic appeal the wool of a Vicuña, a rare type of camelid living in high-alpine areas of the Andes, is a superior wool type in terms of both fineness and heat insulation. Hence, a USD 4,000 Vicuña wool scarf by the Italian wool specialist Loro Piana or a EUR 860 pair of Vicuña wool socks by the German sock specialist Falke does not only look and feel extremely pleasant but does in fact protect the owner's body from loosing heat better than other wool products (Falke.com, 2015; Loropiana.com, 2014).

Durability. In addition to their functional quality materials of luxury goods are selected based on their durability. The longevity of a luxury good does not only help justifying high-end prices. It is also essential for the product to become a collectible, which is passed on from generation to generation. The aim for longevity is well expressed by the well-known slogan of the Geneva-based watchmaker **Patek Philippe**, which states: "You never actually own a Patek Philippe. You merely look after it for the next generation" (Patek.com, 2014d).

Form. The form of a product also contributes to its function. The ergonomic form of a Vitra Eames armchair is not only visually appealing but also increases comfort of sitting. The flat form of a Lamborghini Aventador contributes to its driving efficiency. And in its most basic sense, the form of a Baccarat Champagne Flute is designed to do what it is supposed to do, i.e. contain a certain amount of champagne.

Craftsmanship. The manufacturing of luxury goods, i.e. "how" single parts are combined to deliver the desired function and form, is characterised by fine craftsmanship (Dubois et al., 2001, p. 8). According the European Cultural and Creative Industries Alliance (ECCIA), craftsmanship is the "DNA" of luxury (Frontier Economics & ECCIA, 2012, p. 9). Both the expertise, aim for perfection, and attention to detail of a skilled artisan as well as some degree of manufacturing complexity qualify a good as a luxury good (Heine & Phan, 2011, p. 111).

For example, the German luxury handbag manufacturer **Comtesse** consequently follows its slogan "Handmade Perfection since 1929" to satisfy its famous clientele like Princess Madeleine of Sweden. Processing finest material (in particular woven horsehair) necessitates the careful eye and experienced hand of a highly skilled artisan in order to guarantee flawless material, form, and texture (Comtesse.com, 2015a). At Comtesse, a certificate personally signed by its artisan accompanies each precious handbag (Comtesse.com, 2015a).

Another example of unique craftsmanship refers to the Richemont-owned, haute joaillerie house **Van Cleef & Arpels**. The jeweller has patented a sophisticated gem-setting procedure called *Mystery Set* which allows setting a stone on a precious metal without using visible prongs (Vancleefarpels.com, 2015d). As a result, stones may stand freely and close to each other in a way that the jeweller is able to design a surface with seemingly no interruption. Due to its complexity, however, completing a single brooch using the Mystery Set procedure takes more than 300 hours or around 37.5 working days of a highly skilled master jeweller (Vancleefarpels.com, 2015d).

However, while aiming at perfection in crafting a luxury good (Heine & Phan, 2011, p. 112), the resulting function is not necessarily superior as compared to its mass-market or premium counterparts. Rather, luxury goods are characterized by some "imperfections" (Nueno & Quelch, 1998, p. 63) or "flaws" (Kapferer & Bastien, 2009b, p. 316). Examples are minor imperfections of a hand-blown crystal vase (Nueno & Quelch, 1998, p. 63), the inferior accuracy of a mechanical watch as compared to a quartz watch (Kapferer & Bastien, 2009b, p. 317), or the weight of a hand-sewn leather bag as compared to lighter synthetic-fibre-made bags. This is the result of luxury goods being designer-driven rather than being fully customer-oriented. Manufacturing luxury goods aims at highest perfection – however, within the boundaries of a heritage of craftsmanship and aesthetic standards.

3.1.3.2 Aesthetics

In luxury more than in any other segment goods are expected to be aesthetically appealing beyond mere function (Dubois et al., 2001, p. 12; Heine & Phan, 2011, p. 112; compare Chapter 2.1). Aesthetics refer to "visual forms of objects and sensory experiences associated with, texture, harmony, order and beauty" (Venkatesh, Joy, Sherry, & Deschenes, 2010, p. 460). Aesthetics add to the mere function of a luxury good (compare Figure 10) as the beauty of an object satisfies hedonistic consumer needs for pleasurable experiences (compare Chapter 2.2). According to Kapferer (1997) "luxury defines beauty; it is art applied to functional items. [...] Luxury items provide extra pleasure and flatter all senses at once" (p. 253; cited in Vigneron & Johnson, 2004, p. 486). Luxury is commercialized art.

Luxury product design aims at creating goods that **appeal to multiple senses** (Okonkwo, 2007, p. 192; Wiedmann, Hennigs, Klarmann, & Behrens, 2013, p. 66). To stimulate consumers' visual, haptic, auditory, gustatory, and olfactory perceptions luxury goods manufacturers decide on specific product design characteristics in terms of **material, form, colour and texture** (Schmitt & Simonson, 2005, p. 318). How these product design characteristics are selected and designed differs by product category.

Material. First, in addition to its functional quality a material (i.e. organic materials, metals, or non-metals like glass or porcelain) is selected based on its look, consistency, and shape (visual perception), its feel, weight, and temperature (haptic perception), its acoustic tone and volume (auditory perception), and its sensation and intensity of taste and scent (gustatory and olfactory perception; Kisabaka, 2001, p. 165). The **rarity** of material adds to the aesthetic appeal of luxury goods (Kisabaka, 2001, p. 167). Of course, types of aesthetically appealing material vary across product categories.

The German handbag manufacturer Comtesse, for example, processes only finest, rare **animal hides and skins** like horsehair, python, lizard, ostrich, and crocodile leather (Comtesse.com; 2015b). In haute joaillerie, fine pieces of jewellery are made of precious metals like platinum, gold, silver, copper, or rhodium and specific alloys of these metals like white or pink gold (Boucheron.com, 2015b). In addition to precious metals, gemstones represent a classic example of a rare and aesthetically appealing material. The Richemont-owned jeweller Van Cleef & Arpels, for example, decorates its pieces of jewellery with a broad array of rare gemstones like diamonds, sapphire, ruby, emerald, or turquoise (Vancleefarpels.com, 2015b).

Form. Second, the form or design of a product is often considered the most important product characteristic (Bloch, 1995, p. 16). Even more in luxury, an aesthetically appealing form is essential to product design (Brun & Castelli, 2013, p. 830; Kisabaka, 2001, p. 168; Nueno & Quelch, 1998, p. 62). A study among 1,102 consumers from seven different countries by Godey et al. (2012, p. 1465) shows that the visual appearance (design, style, form) of a luxury good is the most important product attribute and significantly more important as compared to non-luxury goods purchases (see Figure 11).

The form, style, design of a luxury good stimulates mainly visual and haptic perceptions. In some product categories an aesthetically pleasing form is the primary or single "function". For example, the iconic sculpture Rhinoceros Clara by the German Porzellan Manufaktur Nymphenburg is purely designed to appeal to the eyes of its beholder (see Nymphenburg.com, 2015c). Another example of a unique form refers to the form of the iconic Bvlgari Serpenti collection that replicates a snake wrapped around its owner's neck, arm, or finger (see Bulgari.com, 2015). Its exceptional, open-ended form makes it look and feel different to conventionally closed watches and pieces of jewellery. Also, beyond the power and dynamics of driving, individuals desire luxury cars because of their unique forms. Sports cars by the German manufacturer Wiesmann, for example, have become iconic for their puristic form; an "amalgamation of vintage and modern lines" which represents the "perfect combination of dynamics and design" (Wiesmann.com, 2015).

Figure 11 – Importance of design: luxury versus non-luxury goods.

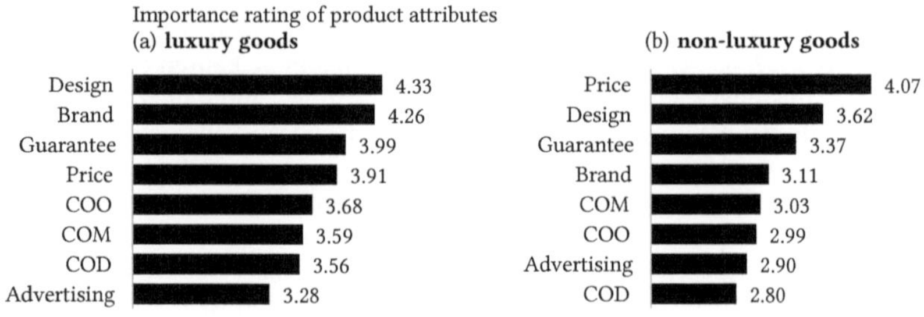

COO = country-of-origin; COM = country-of-manufacturing; COD = country-of-design; Sample: 1,102 students from China, France, India, Italy, Japan, Russia, and the USA; importance was rated on a five-point scale
Source: Godey et al. (2012, p. 1465)

Colours. Third, colours refer to an elementary product design characteristic, which stimulates visual perceptions. Colour tones are categorized into spectral (e.g., red, blue, green), achromatic (i.e. white, grey, black), earth (e.g., brown), metal and metallic (e.g., golden, silver), and special tones like mother-of-pearl (Koppelmann, 1997, p. 367). In general, the colour tones, white, black, golden, and silver evoke associations with luxury (Schmitt & Simonson, 1998, p. 131). However, the selection of an aesthetically appealing colour differs by product category and brand and does not follow something like a universally valid colour tone catalogue for luxury goods. The Parisian fashion house Chanel, for example, is known for its classic chic black and white branding. Coco Chanel once said: "I have said that black has it all. White too. Their beauty is absolute. It is the perfect harmony" (Wikiquote.org, 2015). Similarly, pumps by designer Christian Louboutin have become iconic for their red soles.

Texture. Fourth, texture of material adds to the visual and haptic appeal of luxury goods (Kisabaka, 2001, p. 172). While some materials are selected for their natural texture (e.g., animal skins), other materials are treated to modify their texture. Precious metals or car lacquers, for example, may be given a glossy or matt finish. Leather may be used in plain or perforated form. The surface of a precious wood may be natural rough or smooth after oiling or painting.

3.1.3.3 Packaging

Once function and aesthetics of the core product have been designed, the physical good is usually packaged (compare Figure 10). Packaging refers to any kind of wrapping, coating, or encasement of a product (Bruhn, 2014, p. 148; Meffert et al., 2008, p. 443) and is designed for both functional and aesthetic reasons.

Functional aspects. Functional aspects of packaging include protection, portioning, product usage, information and branding (Kotler & Armstrong, 2012, p. 232;

Meffert et al., 2008, pp. 443–444). For example, a bottle of **Veuve Clicquot** Brut Yellow Label champagne serves all these functions (see Figure 12). First, the primary function of the bottle is to contain and protect its content. As opposed to clear, colourless bottles, green glass protects the sparkling wine from ultraviolet rays of sunlight. Also, as opposed to non-sparkling wines, champagne bottles typically have thicker walls and a deep punt necessary to cope with the excess pressure inside the bottle. Second, particularly in product categories like perfume & cosmetics or wine & spirits the packaging is essential to hold and portion the core product, e.g., a certain amount of liquid or powder. In the example of Veuve Clicquot, the standard bottle contains 750 ml of champagne. Like other champagne labels, Veuve Clicquot offers a wide array of portions starting from a demi or fillette (0.375 litres) up to a nebuchadnezzar (15 litres). Third, packaging often facilitates the usage of the product. The tapered top-end of the Veuve Clicquot bottle helps pouring the champagne in a controlled manner. Other examples of usage facilitation refer to the vaporizer of perfumes or the brush and mirror of a make-up packaging. Fourth, the bottle provides information to prospect clients. While the form of the bottle signals to the educated shopper that it contains about 0.7 litres of sparkling wine, the label explicitly states that the bottle contains "750 ml" of "champagne" with "12 % Vol." alcohol which is a "product of France". Finally, the packaging serves branding purposes. The form, labels, and signs of the packaging communicate the brand. In our example of Veuve Clicquot both the front label, the banderol, and the cork contain the logo that helps the shopper identifying the brand and differentiating it from other sparkling wines. More than the brand name and logo, the characteristic form of a bottle of Ruinart champagne, for example, makes it stand out from competitive products.

Aesthetic aspects. In luxury, packaging is designed beyond mere function. Luxury goods packaging meets highest standards in terms of **aesthetic appeal**, quality and exclusiveness (Kisabaka, 2001, p. 183). As for the core product, the same design characteristics apply to packaging design: **material, form, colour, and texture** (Koppelmann, 1997, p. 323). Again, the specific packaging design largely differs by product category and brand.

To illustrate the aesthetic appeal of packaging, we again refer to the example of the LVMH-owned champagne brand Veuve Clicquot, which is well known for its creativity in designing gift boxes (see Figure 13). By providing aesthetically appealing gift boxes on top of the primary packaging, i.e. the bottle, Veuve Clicquot differentiates from mass-market sparkling wines. The design of these gift boxes reflects the brand's high standards in terms of quality and aesthetic appeal. The classic Veuve Clicquot Design Box (see Figure 13 (a)), for example, is exclusively made with eco-friendly, fully recyclable paper (Veuve-clicquot.com, 2015b), presented in the iconic orange colour tone and with a discreet diamond-pattern texture. The form allows smoothly sliding the bottle out of the box. More creatively, the form of the limited Veuve Clicquot Clutch case edition (see Figure 13(h)) replicates a classic chic envelope carrier made of leather and isothermal textile to keep a previously chilled bottle of champagne cool for about one hour (Veuve-clicquot.com, 2015b).

Figure 12 – Functional aspects of packaging: Veuve Clicquot.

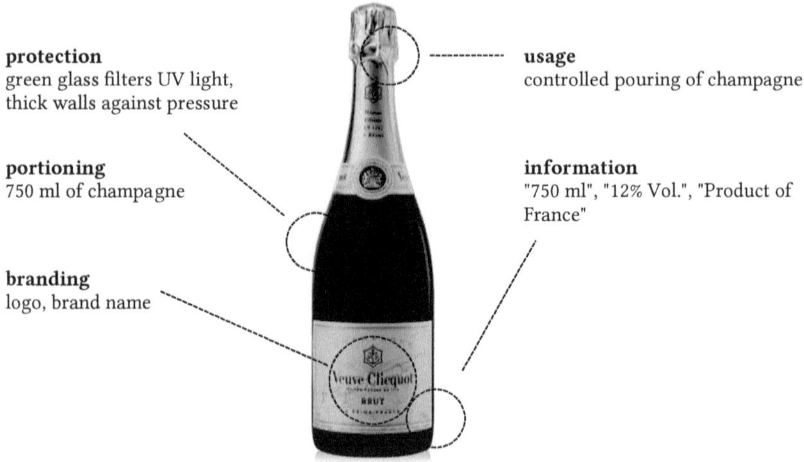

Source: © image by courtesy of Veuve Clicquot (Veuve-clicquot.com, 2015a)

Figure 13 – Aesthetic aspects of packaging: Veuve Clicquot.

Source: © images by courtesy of Veuve Clicquot (Veuve-clicquot.com, 2015b)

3.1.3.4 Add-on services

Add-on services (also secondary or value-added services) refer to those services that accompany and **add value to the core product** as opposed to primary services that satisfy basic consumer needs like being treated in a spa or transported by an airline (Bruhn, 2014, p. 150; Homburg, 2015, p. 553; Kotler & Armstrong, 2012, p. 233). Manufacturers add services to their core offering in order to differentiate from competitive offerings (pre-purchase) and to create and retain a close customer relationship in the long run (post-purchase). Specifically in luxury, physical goods are complemented with excellent add-on services to provide a holistic brand experience and augment the brand's quality appeal (Heine & Phan, 2011, p. 112; Kapferer & Bastien, 2009a, p. 158; Kisabaka, 2001, p. 236).

Managing add-on services is at the intersection between product and distribution management. On the one hand, theses services become an integral part of the overall market offering and may thus influence consumers' purchase decision-making (product management). On the other hand, these services are mostly delivered to the customer by the sales person at the point of sale (distribution management). We may generally differentiate between add-on services that are directly related to the core product and those that are not directly related to the core product. The management of **directly related add-on services** generally entails decisions on **delivery policy, client service, and guarantee policy** (Bruhn, 2014, pp. 151–155; Kisabaka, 2001, pp. 237–242; Koppelmann, 2006, p. 115).

Delivery policy. In general, delivery policy management starts with deciding on whether the product is delivered to or picked up by the customer (Koppelmann, 2006, p. 113). In case of product delivery, service levels need to be defined in terms of reliability, quality, and availability (Bruhn, 2014, p. 151; Koppelmann, 2006, p. 113). In luxury, a high-end, zero-defect service level in terms of reliability (in-time delivery) and quality (delivered good is complete and undamaged) is an absolute must (Kisabaka, 2001, p. 237). In terms of availability, service levels differ by product category. More accessible luxury goods, i.e. accessible non-durable goods like wine & spirits or perfume & cosmetics or iconic items of the core range of durable luxury goods, are typically expected to be readily available. In contrast, the educated clientele that appreciates the time and craftsmanship involved in producing precious goods tolerates to wait for goods that are high-end range products, limited editions, or made to order (Kisabaka, 2001, p. 237). If clearly justified, **waiting lists** serve as a symbol of rarity and thus create desire. For example, due to limited production, clients wait for about two years for a Ferrari sports car or a Mikimoto pearl necklace (Kapferer & Bastien, 2009a, p. 67). Clients' tolerance to wait for something they have long been dreaming of is in contrast to the delivery policy of non-luxury goods that are expected to be readily available to satisfy consumer needs on short call.

Client service. Client services refer to all add-on services supporting the consumer in buying and using a good. In general, client services include installation/ adaptation, maintenance/ repairs, spare parts supply, and disposal, which are particularly relevant in business-to-business marketing settings (Bruhn, 2014, p. 153;

Koppelmann, 2006, p. 115). In luxury, specific client services include **customization**, **gift-wrapping**, **product maintenance**, and **spare parts supply** (Kisabaka, 2001, pp. 238–240; Nueno & Quelch, 1998, p. 65; Valtin, 2005, p. 109).

First, **customization** is inherent to luxury. Traditionally, fine shoes and suits were made to measure (Nueno & Quelch, 1998, p. 65). At the LVMH-owned perfume house Guerlain, for example, privileged consumers may fully customize their own eau de perfume in close collaboration with the Director of Fragrance Development, Sylvaine Delacourte (Guerlain.com, 2015). Rather than full customization, luxury goods manufacturers often allow personalizing materials, colours, or features of the product. The "Ad Personam" individualization program by the Italian sports car manufacturer Lamborghini, for example, allows the client to choose from a variety of interior and exterior materials, colours, and features (Motorauthority.com, 2015). Even finished goods are often personalized through a **serial number or an engraving**. One of the most recognizable examples refers to the "Return to Tiffany" collection by the US jeweller Tiffany & Co. First introduced in 1969, any item of the collection is given a unique serial number, which allows the identification of the owner once the item has been lost and returned to Tiffany New York (Tiffany.com, 2015). In addition, Tiffany offers a personal engraving for most of its pieces of jewellery.

Second, a **gift-wrapping** service (whether in-store or online) should complement a luxury market offering considering that gift-giving account for about 50 per cent of luxury goods sales (Dubois et al., 2005, p. 120). A gift-wrapping service adds value to both the gift-giver (saving time and effort while showing appreciation to a significant other) and the gift-receiver (pleasure of carefully unpacking the wrapping and packaging to get to the actual product). Other than standardized, aesthetically appealing gift boxes as some kind of secondary packaging as shown for Veuve Clicquot (Figure 13), gift-wrapping is done on a individual level either upon customer request (e.g., the iconic Blue Box wrapping at Tiffany) or as a surprise effect for the customer (e.g., a car cover wrapping of a Rolls-Royce limousine).

Third, considering that durable luxury goods are made for a lifetime, **product maintenance** and **spare parts supply** are essential to client service in luxury (Kisabaka, 2001, p. 239). Product maintenance includes both providing advise to the consumer on how to ideally care for the product (e.g., how treat leather, metal, or wood surfaces) and periodic maintenance by a professional (e.g., periodic car inspection, jewellery polishing; Kisabaka, 2001, p. 239). Additionally, manufacturers of durable luxury goods should provide a long-term supply of spare and complement parts (Koppelmann, 2006, p. 114). For example, once you have bought or inherited a Nymphenburg porcelain tableware set you are given a lifetime guarantee of replacing broken pieces or complementing your set with additional pieces all made by hand (Nymphenburg.com, 2015b).

Guarantee policy. The guarantee policy defines both the **scope of services** (e.g., repairs, replacement of parts or the total product) that is covered by the manufacturer and the **time frame** of the guarantee being valid (Koppelmann, 2006, pp. 114–115). In luxury, to signal confidence in the excellent quality of goods guarantees should cover a wide range of services valid for a decent period of time

(Kisabaka, 2001, p. 242). The British, BMW-owned limousine manufacturer Rolls Royce, for example, offers a "4-year unlimited mileage warranty" for all new models to his private clients (Rolls-roycemotorcars.com, 2015c). As opposed to conventional car warranties, both the time frame (from conventionally two to four years) and the scope of services (e.g., roadside assistance and replacement car) are extended (Rolls-roycemotorcars.com, 2015c). Another example of an extended service level refers to the leather goods manufacturer Hermès as a consumer notes: "You get a lifelong guarantee with a Hermès belt. If you need a new hole, you just send it to them and they do that for free" (Heine & Phan, 2011, p. 112).

The abovementioned add-on services are directly related to the core product: the product may be delivered, customized, wrapped, maintained, and repaired. In addition, luxury goods manufacturers may offer add-on services that are not directly linked to the delivery or usage of a product. Typically, clients are invited to become part of a **brand community** whose members enjoy specific privileges like participating in cultural or sports events or being offered concierge services (Cailleux, Mignot, & Kapferer, 2009, p. 410). The management of this kind of add-on services is at the intersection of product management (privileges add value to the market offering), communication management (events serve a mean of brand communication; see below Chapter 3.3.5.3), and distribution management (managing customers relationships).

3.1.3.5 Branding

Finally, a brand or mark adds value to the market offering (see outside layer in Figure 10) in two important ways: first, a brand **identifies** the product of a manufacturer and **differentiates** it from competitive market offerings (Bruhn, 2014, p. 144; Kotler & Armstrong, 2012, p. 231). Second, once recognized a brand **evokes consumer perceptions** of the functional, emotional, and symbolic value of product (Homburg, 2015, p. 617; Kotler & Armstrong, 2012, p. 243). In increasingly saturated markets consumers are looking for brands they can trust in. Even more in luxury, the brand is of significant importance when making a purchase decision (Godey et al., 2012, p. 1465; compare Figure 11 above). The importance of brands when buying luxury goods may be explained by (a) consumers' inexperience with luxury (as a result of the relatively lower purchase frequency) while facing high prices and (b) by the signals a brand confers to the owner and his or her significant others (e.g., good taste, wealth, status).

Definition of brand. The term *brand* has been defined in mainly two ways: first, a **brand is any kind of mark added to a product** as a mean of identification and differentiation (Homburg, 2015, p. 617; Kotler & Armstrong, 2012, p. 231; Nieschlag et al., 2002, p. 674). More specifically, the American Marketing Association (2015a) defines a brand as a "name, term, design, symbol, or any other feature that identifies one seller's good or service as distinct from those of other sellers".

Second, a brand is often referred to as the **overall consumer associations with a market offering** and its manufacturer (Homburg, 2015, p. 617; Kotler & Armstrong, 2012, p. 243). More specifically, Achenbaum (1993) argues that a brand should be considered as the "sum total of consumers' perceptions and feelings about the product's attributes and how they perform, about the brand name and what it stands for, and about the company associated with the brand" (cited in Keller, 1998, p. 5). Following this definition of a brand becoming synonymous with the overall value of a product, branding is often considered to be the "heart" of product management (Bruhn, 2014, p. 144). Rather than simply deciding on brand names or logos brand management is understood as a holistic discipline that manages activities across all points of contact with the consumer (e.g., through products, advertising, point of sale) to create a consistent brand image. In luxury, holistic brand management entails designing a specific marketing-mix that reflects the brand's identity in terms of finest quality, high-end prices, rarity, aesthetics, heritage, and superfluousness (compare Chapter 2.1).

Elements of brand signature. In the concrete context of product design, we focus on branding as any kind of marking the product. Product branding entails designing and applying a set of marks, i.e. a **brand signature** that is **identifiable, differentiated, and consistent**. Elements of a brand signature include any kind of marks like names, monograms, emblems, colour tones, slogans, marks of heritage, or design elements (Kapferer & Bastien, 2009a, pp. 220–221; Kisabaka, 2001, pp. 174–177; Nieschlag et al., 2002, p. 674).

In luxury, **brand names** often relate to the founder (e.g., Alfred van Cleef & Salomon Arpels, Coco Chanel, Ferruccio Lamborghini, Guccio Gucci, Louis Vuitton, Thierry Hermès) or its geographic origin (e.g., Bottega Veneta referring to the Italian city Venice, Glashütte Original referring to the Saxonian city Glashütte, or Porzellan Manufaktur Nymphenburg referring to the Munich-based Nymphenburg Palace). Artificial creations like Montblanc, Philipp Plein, or Rolex are less common.

In luxury, the initials of the founders name are often combined as a **monogram**. Examples include the "AP" monogram engraved in the crown of an Audemars Piguet Royal Oak wristwatch (see Audemarspiguet.com, 2015), the "CC"-formed signature buckle of a Chanel Flap bag (see Chanel.com, 2015a), the "FF"-formed signature buckle of a Fendi Baguette bag (see Fendi.com, 2015), or the "RR" monogram on the wheel hub of an Rolls-Royce Ghost limousine (see Rolls-roycemotorcars.com, 2015b).

In addition to textual marks like brand names and monograms, a luxury brand's signature might also include **emblems or symbols**. Products marked with a recognizable emblem include, for example, the Montblanc Meisterstück pen with the six-pointed "White Star" on the top cap (see Montblanc.com, 2015b), cuff links in the form of the Patek Philippe "Calatrava Cross" (see Patek.com, 2015b), the Rolls-Royce Ghost with the iconic "Spirit of Ecstasy" bonnet ornament (Rolls-roycemotorcars.com, 2015d) or a Versace ring engraved with the "Medusa" emblem (see Versace.com, 2015).

Other than textual marks or emblems unique **colour tones** also serve to identify and differentiate a luxury good from competitive products. Examples of recognizable colour tones include the Ferrari red, the Tiffany blue, or the Veuve Clicquot orange.

Slogans, i.e. a recognizable phrase complementing a brand name and other marks, are rather rarely applied to luxury brands. Examples include Asprey's "The Art of Giving", Bottega Veneta's "When Your Own Initials Are Enough", De Beers iconic "A Diamond is Forever", or Patek Philippe's "Begin Your Own Tradition".

Rather than by slogans, luxury brand names are often complemented by **marks of heritage** like the city or country-of-origin or the year of foundation. Examples of marking the geographic origin include "Boucheron Paris", "A. Lange & Söhne Glashütte I/SA", "Patek Philippe Genève", "William & Son London", or the Italian flag in Ferrari's logotype. Examples of marking the year of foundation include "Beguet, Depuis 1775", "Breitling, 1884", "Burberry, Established 1856". Examples for a combination of both marks of geographic origin and year of foundation include "IWC Schaffhausen since 1868", "Prada Milano dal 1913", "1729, Ruinart, Plus Ancienne Maison de Champagne", or "Vacheron Constantin, Manufacture Horlogère, Genève, depuis 1755".

Finally, recognizable **design elements** should complement a luxury brand's visual signature (Kapferer & Bastien, 2009a, p. 64; Nueno & Quelch, 1998, p. 62). Rolls-Royce, for example, is not only known for its brand name, "RR" monogram, or "Spirit of Ecstasy" bonnet ornament, but also for its handmade, Parthenon-style radiator grille. Similarly, instead of a visible brand name, logo, or any other sign, Bottega Veneta products identify and differentiate through the iconic *Intrecciato* pattern resulting from a specific leather-weaving technique (Bottegaveneta.com, 2015e).

All these single **marks combined** constitute a luxury brand's signature. As shown in Figure 14, the Rolex Datejust II wristwatch is an excellent example of adding multiple marks, which combined clearly identify and differentiate the Rolex watch from competitive products: the dial contains the Rolex brand and product name in capital letters and a serif font (name) as well as the iconic golden five-point crown emblem on the twelve-o'clock-position (emblem).

The dial is surrounded by a fluted bezel (design element), "a genuine Rolex signature feature" (Rolex.com, 2015a). Also, the winding crown, the dial knob, is embellished with the Rolex five-point crown (emblem). Finally, the watch crystal is equipped with a Cyclops lens magnifying the date, which has become iconic for Rolex watches (design element).

Consistency of brand signature. Finally, given the importance of identifiable and differentiated marks added to luxury goods, a luxury brand's signature should be **consistent across the brand's product range and over time** (Beverland, 2006, p. 253; Kapferer & Bastien, 2009a, p. 64; Keller, 2009, p. 291). In case of Bottega Veneta, for example, the iconic *Intrecciato* pattern is consistently applied to large parts of the brand's product range whether the pattern is truly woven like for leather bags or a pair of sandals or replicated like on a pair of earrings or the cap of the Coty-licensed Knot fragrance (see Bottegaveneta.com, 2015a, 2015b, 2015c, 2015d). In addition to consistency across the product range, a brand's signature should be consistent over time. While it is obvious that names or logos of powerful luxury brands should remain constant, the need for long-term consistency also refers to less obvious marks like stylistic features. For example, in addition to the brand name, the "RR" monogram, and the "Spirit of Ecstasy" ornament, any Rolls-Royce limousine is marked with the Parthenon-style radiator grille. As shown Figure 15, any Rolls-Royce model starting from the very first model, the 10 HP from 1904, up to the current Phantom, Ghost, and Wraith series is equipped with this colossal radiator grille.

Figure 14 – Elements of brand signature: Rolex Datejust II.

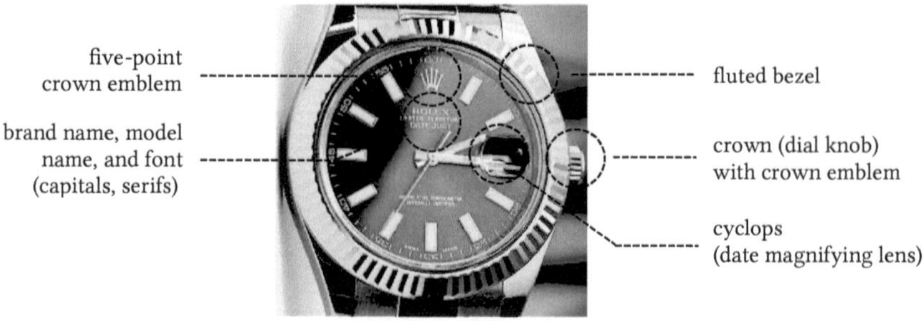

Source: © image by hypo.physe (2010, CC BY-SA 2.0 license)

Figure 15 – Consistency of brand signature: Rolls-Royce radiator grille.

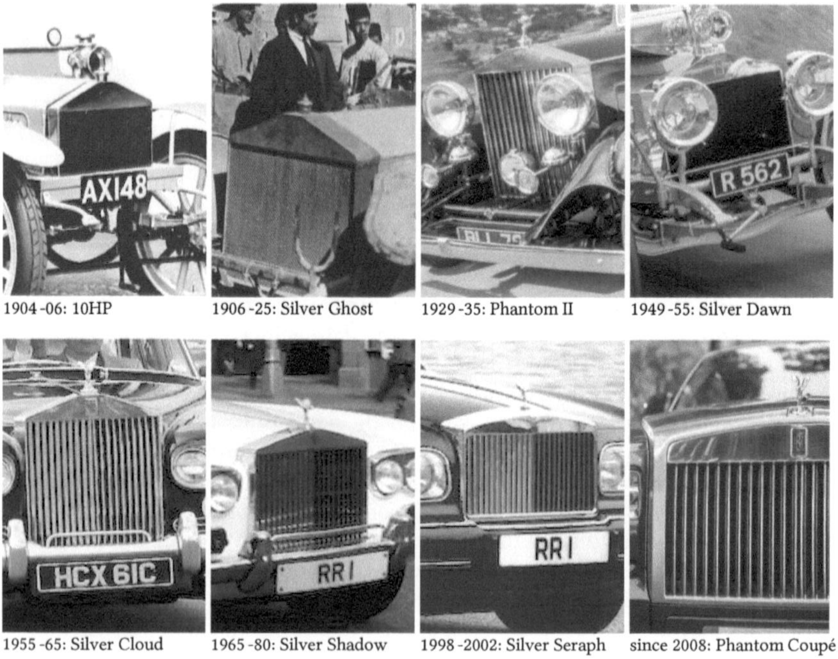

Source: © images by courtesy of Rolls-Royce Motor Cars Limited
(Rolls-roycemotorcars.com, 2012, 2013a, 2013b, 2013c, 2014a, 2014b, 2014c, 2014d)

3.2 Pricing of luxury goods

3.2.1 Introduction

"Pricing refers to a firm's procedure of determining the monetary value it receives in exchange of products or services it delivers to customers" (Fassnacht, Kluge, & Mohr, 2013, p. 105). Pricing can be referred to as the **strongest marketing instrument** (Rao, 1984, p. 39) given the following considerations: first, other than product, communication, or distribution management pricing decisions directly impact a firm's profit. Considering the profit equation price represents one of three direct profit drivers, i.e. volume, price, costs (Simon & Fassnacht, 2009, p. 2).

Second, price is the strongest among theses profit drivers. Based on an analysis of 2,463 companies Marn & Rosiello (1992, p. 85) show that a 1 per cent improvement in price induces an operating profit increase of 11.1 per cent whereas a 1 per cent improvement in volume, variable costs, and fixed costs increases operating profit by only 3.3 per cent, 7.8 per cent, and 2.3 per cent, respectively.

Third, prices impact demand more than other marketing instruments. A relative change in price causes a disproportionately greater change in volume demanded by customers. More specifically, a large-scale analysis with 1,851 observations by Bijmolt, van Heerde, & Pieters (2005, p. 145) reveals a mean price elasticity of demand of -2.62, i.e. a 10 per cent decrease in price comes along with a 26.2 per cent increase in demand. In absolute terms the value of price elasticity of demand well exceeds that of advertising elasticity of demand. A meta-analysis by Sethuraman, Tellis, & Briesch (2011, p. 457) reveals a mean short-term advertising elasticity of demand of .12 (751 observations) and a mean long-term advertising elasticity of demand of .24 (402 observations) only, i.e. in the long run a 10 per cent increase in advertising comes along with a 2.4 per cent increase in demand.

The importance of price particularly applies to luxury goods for three reasons: first, other profit levers are limited. Luxury goods manufacturers may not unlimitedly increase volume sales without diluting parts of the brand's fragile perception of exclusiveness (Dubois & Paternault, 1995, p. 73). At the same time, the potential for cost reductions is somewhat limited (Mohr, 2013, p. 2). Cost-intensive aspects of manufacturing (e.g., precious material, highly skilled craftsmen), communication (e.g., high-end magazines like Vogue), and distribution (e.g., boutiques in prime locations of world's city centres, highly skilled sales personnel) represent essential elements of the luxury experience.

Second, more than for non-luxury goods a consumer uses the price of a luxury good as a surrogate for the overall value it is likely to deliver (Fassnacht et al., 2013, p. 104; Völckner, 2006, p. 474). On the one hand, since luxury goods are usually purchased less frequently than non-luxury (fast moving) consumer goods, consumers often lack a reference point for assessing the value of a given luxury good (Fassnacht et al., 2013, p. 105). Consequently, consumers rely on the price as informational cue. On the other hand, in luxury the price does not only reflect a monetary sacrifice but adds to the value a luxury good delivers to the consumer (Simon & Fassnacht, 2009, p. 78). The high price of a luxury good signals both a feeling of personal achievement to oneself and wealth and social status to significant others.

Third, given the increased information-function of price the price elasticity of demand for a luxury good may actually be zero or even positive (Fassnacht et al., 2013, p. 106). Thus, an increase in price does not necessarily come along with a decrease in demand, but may even cause a increase in demand. This paradoxical effect, also known as Veblen effect (Bagwell & Bernheim, 1996, p. 349; Kapferer & Bastien, 2009a, p. 95; Leibenstein, 1950, p. 189; Veblen, 1960), will be described below in more detail.

The price of a luxury good should be managed towards two fundamental objectives: prices should be (1) high-end in the relevant market and (2) remain stable (Fassnacht et al., 2013, p. 104; Kapferer & Bastien, 2009a, pp. 183 & 189; Kisabaka, 2001, pp. 224–225). In luxury more than in any other segment, consumers refer to the price as an indicator of the quality level, hedonic appeal, and prestige a luxury good is likely to deliver. Hence, the price should continuously reflect a luxury brand's highest quality standard, aesthetic appeal, and symbolic meaning by being both high-end and stable.

To establish high-end and stable prices luxury goods manufacturers apply specific pricing procedures that differ from conventional pricing procedures. Fassnacht et al. (2013, p. 105) and Mohr (2013, p. 55) conceptualize a luxury-specific pricing process along four phases: strategic direction, analysis, decision, and implementation (see Figure 16). Hence, pricing is not only a decision. It is a process, a "system of rules and procedures to determine and implement prices" (Fassnacht et al., 2013, p. 105).

Along these four phases Fassnacht et al. (2013, p. 106) contrast traditional versus luxury-specific characteristics of the pricing process derived from previous literature and expert interviews. Based on a large-scale survey among managers of 114 European luxury goods manufacturers Fassnacht et al. (2013, p. 114) empirically show that manufacturers that apply a luxury-specific pricing process outperform their competitors not only in terms of a relatively higher EBIT margin (price as profit driver) but also in terms of relatively higher perceptions of quality, scarcity, and hedonic value (price as informational cue) by realizing high-end, stable prices. The specificities of luxury price management as illustrated in Figure 16 will be described in more detail throughout this chapter.

Figure 16 – Overview: specificities of pricing in luxury.

Strategy	Analysis	Decision	Implementation
Objectives ▪ Long-term profitability ▪ Exclusiveness	**Economic analysis** ▪ Costs ▪ Competitors ▪ Customers	**Long - term decisions** ▪ Continuous increase of the average price of product-mix	**Internal** ▪ Centralized pricing authority
Price positioning by range ▪ High-end: inaccessible ▪ Core: intermediate ▪ Entry: accessible	**Behavioural analysis** ▪ Price-response function (eventually positive) ▪ Price as a signal of quality, rarity, and prestige	**Short - term decisions** ▪ Rare-to-no discount policy ▪ Rare-to-no use of price discrimination ▪ Price-volume stability	**External** ▪ Selective to exclusive distribution ▪ Discreet price communication ▪ Monitoring of realized prices

Source: adapted from Fassnacht et al. (2013, p. 106), Mohr (2013, p. 83)

3.2.2 Strategy

Before actually determining and implementing prices, luxury goods manufactures should outline a strategic direction to be followed. This first step entails defining precise pricing objectives and an adequate price positioning. Strategic pricing objectives include both profit-oriented objectives like profit growth, EBIT margin, or return on investment and sales-oriented objectives like unit sales, value sales, sales growth, or market share (Monroe, 2003, pp. 30–34; Nagle, Hogan, & Zale, 2011, pp. 17–21; Simon & Fassnacht, 2009, p. 25). Firms often face a certain level of trade-off between profit- and sales-oriented objectives (Doyle & Hooley, 1992, p. 60). As shown above, the positive (negative) profit impact of a relatively higher (lower) price (price as profit driver) typically comes along with a negative (positive) sales impact (given a negative price-response function). In luxury, an additional strategic objective further complicates balancing this trade-off: **preserving the brand's fragile image of exclusiveness** (Fassnacht et al. 2013, p. 105; Kastanakis & Balabanis, 2012, p. 1399; Keller, 2009, p. 293; Wetlaufer, 2001, p. 121). Excessive sales growth may jeopardize perceptions of exclusiveness (Dubois & Paternault, 1995, p. 73).

Considering the strategic pricing objectives defined luxury goods manufacturers should position each branded product on the price-value continuum accordingly. As shown in Figure 17(a) the consumer should perceive a luxury brand's product range as delivering high-end value (functional, emotional, and symbolic) at a high-end price (Simon & Fassnacht, 2009, pp. 32 & 64; Vigneron & Johnson, 2004, pp. 488–491; Wiedmann, Hennigs, & Siebels, 2009, pp. 629–633). As for non-luxury goods, the consumer perceived price should adequately reflect the consumer perceived value. Given the information-function of price, an adequate price-value balance becomes particularly relevant for luxury goods since "any inconsistency in price jeopardizes the luxury perception of a brand" (Fassnacht et al. 2013, p. 106).

Figure 17 – Luxury-price positioning.

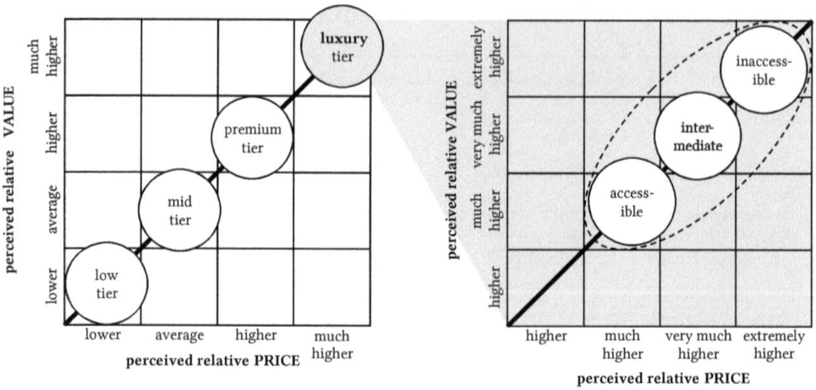

Source: adapted from De Barnier et al. (2012, p. 634), Mohr (2013, pp. 15–16), Monroe (2003, p. 209), Sebastian & Maessen (2003, p. 58), Simon & Fassnacht (2009, p. 34)

Notably the relative distance between the premium and the luxury tier shown in Figure 17(a) is deliberately illustrated to be greater than the distances between the low, mid, and premium tier, respectively, to account for the fact that a luxury good is not just an extension, not just a "better" version of premium goods, but different in terms of the value dimensions it delivers (Kapferer & Bastien, 2009b, pp. 312–313). Nueno & Quelch (1998, p. 62) state that "luxury brands are those whose ratio of functional utility to price is low while the ratio of intangible and situational utility to price is high". In functional terms, a mechanical luxury watch, for example, is not necessarily superior over a more affordable electronic watch (i.e. it still tells the time) or sometimes even less precise (Kapferer & Bastien, 2009b, p. 317). However, it conveys high levels of emotional value (i.e. "luxury for oneself") and symbolic value (i.e. "luxury as a badge") to its owner (Kapferer & Bastien, 2009b, p. 314).

Within the luxury tier as shown in Figure 17(a), De Barnier et al. (2012, p. 634) further differentiate three, more granular levels of luxury as shown in Figure 17(b): accessible luxury, intermediate luxury, and inaccessible luxury. Based on a sample of 501 French individuals the authors find that consumers perceive brands like Chanel and Montblanc as accessible, Rolex as intermediate, and Ferrari and Van Cleef & Arpels as inaccessible luxury brands (De Barnier et al., 2012, p. 632). While the authors apply a between-brand perspective in their study, these different levels of luxury can be similarly applied to a **within-brand perspective**, i.e. across different products of the same brand. Referring to the pyramidal product-mix as shown above in Figure 8 we may differentiate between the high-end, core, and entry range depending on the level of product sophistication. We may consider the price positioning of a brand's different ranges accordingly: the **high-end range** is priced at an **inaccessible**, the **core range** at an **intermediate,** and the **entry range** at an **accessible** price positioning. For example, the product range of a fashion brand like Dior typically includes unique, haute couture pieces designed for the world's fashion shows (inaccessible luxury), a small series of prêt-a-porter pieces for sale at directly operated monobrand stores (intermediate luxury), and a variety of licensed products like perfumes, eyewear or other accessories available at monobrand stores as well as multibrand retailers (accessible luxury).

Depending on the strategic pricing objectives luxury goods manufacturer extend the core of the product range vertically, i.e. down- or upwards (Rumpf, 2010, p. 37). Downwards extensions from intermediate to accessible luxury (e.g., from Porsche 911 to Porsche Boxster) are directed towards sales growth while upwards extensions from intermediate to inaccessible luxury (e.g., from Porsche 911 to the limited supercar series Porsche 918 Spyder) are typically directed towards reinforcing the luxury perceptions of the brand (Kapferer & Bastien, 2009a, p. 144).

3.2.3 Analysis

Another requirement for determining adequate prices refers to a sound analysis of price-relevant information, i.e. information about **internal cost structures**, **competitors**, and **customers** (Monroe, 2003, p. 12; Nagle et al., 2011, pp. 18–21; Simon & Fassnacht, 2009, p. 82). As for non-luxury goods, costs represent the lower limit (price floor), customers' willingness-to-pay the upper limit (price ceiling) of the price range (Monroe, 2003, p. 12; Simon & Fassnacht, 2009, p. 82). As luxury goods manufacturers tend to have a high degree of vertical integration (e.g., from mining to retailing in the case of the South African diamond group De Beers; Cadieux, 2005) luxury managers need to account for multiple cost information like cost of material, manufacturing, marketing and sales. Similar to the findings for non-luxury goods, a survey among managers of 114 luxury goods manufacturers reveals that managers mostly rely on cost and competitor information and less on information about customer perceptions and intentions (Mohr, 2013, pp. 165–166).

However, collecting information about customer perceptions and intentions is necessary for understanding how demand changes in response to variations in price (i.e. price-response function; Monroe, 2003, p. 43; Simon & Fassnacht, 2009, p. 91). While the price-response function for non-luxury goods is typically characterized by a negative slope (i.e. demand decreases as price goes up), the **price-response function for luxury goods may actually have three different slopes**: negative, zero, or positive (Kapferer & Bastien, 2009a, pp. 179–180; Mohr, 2013, p. 64).

In the first case (Figure 18(a)), an increase in price comes along with a decrease in the quantity demanded, i.e. both the slope of the price-response function and the price elasticity are less than zero. Negative price elasticity scores are common for non-luxury goods. As noted above, the mean price elasticity of demand is -2.62 (Bijmolt et al., 2005, p. 145). For luxury goods price elasticity of demand may happen to be negative as well but it rarely really is (Kapferer & Bastien, 2009a, p. 179). Importantly, Kapferer & Bastien (2009a, p. 179) recommend not dropping the price if a luxury good is not selling well but rather rethinking the entire market offering.

Figure 18 – Price-response functions for luxury goods.

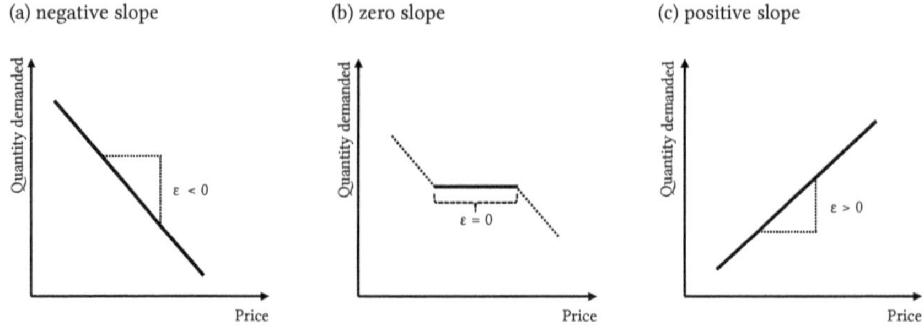

ε = price elasticity of demand; note: straight lines are illustrated for simplicity reasons. For different, more complex line forms please see Simon & Fassnacht (2009, pp. 92–109)
Source: Bagwell & Bernheim (1996, p. 349), Kapferer & Bastien (2009a, p. 95), Leibenstein (1950, p. 189), Mohr (2013, p. 64), Simon & Fassnacht (2009, p. 96), Veblen (1960)

In the second case (Figure 18(b)), any variation in price does not come along with a variation in quantity demanded, i.e. both the slope of the price-response function and the price elasticity are zero. Within a certain price range (continuous line) the number of customers remains constant independently on whether the price rises or falls, i.e. customers are price insensitive (Kapferer & Bastien, 2009a, pp. 179–180). Only after an excessive price variation (dotted lines) demand rises or falls.

In the third case (see Figure 18 (c)), an increase in price comes along with an increase in quantity demanded, i.e. both the slope of the price-response function and the price elasticity are greater than zero. This paradoxical effect is also known as **Veblen effect**, named after the Norwegian theoretician Thorstein Veblen (Bagwell & Bernheim, 1996, p. 349; Kapferer & Bastien, 2009a, p. 95; Leibenstein, 1950, p. 189; Veblen, 1960). Amaldoss & Jain (2005, p. 38) empirically show for snobbish consumers (i.e. consumers seeking for uniqueness as opposed to conformism) that the demand for a good increases as its price goes up. Also, we know from an anonymous source the case of a high-end watchmaker whose annual sales figures in the Japanese market went up 60 per cent after having increased retail prices by 20 per cent. This reflects a positive price elasticity of demand of 3.0.

To better understand this counterintuitive effect we again refer to the dual role of price (Völckner, 2006, p. 474): monetary sacrifice on the one hand and informational cue on the other. The latter becomes more relevant when shopping for luxury than for non-luxury goods. Luxury goods are typically infrequently purchased (Fassnacht et al., 2013, p. 105). For many consumers, a Porsche represents an once-in-a-lifetime purchase, a childhood dream coming true. Additionally, the overall value of a luxury good is more complex. It entails multiple value dimensions beyond its functional value. A non-luxury pen, for example, is mainly bought for its writing quality (i.e. functional value). In contrast, a luxury pen is bought not only for its high-end functional quality (e.g., writing quality, handcrafted, precious material), but particularly for the meaning it conveys to oneself (i.e. experiential value; e.g., self-reward for a personal achievement like job promotion) or to significant others (i.e. symbolic value; e.g., as signal of status or, when given as a gift, as manifestation for a special moment in life; Amaldoss & Jain, 2005, p. 30; Grubb & Grathwohl, 1967, p. 24; Kapferer & Bastien, 2009b, p. 314; Vigneron & Johnson, 2004, p. 488). "Luxury items are bought for what they mean, beyond what they are" (Dubois & Paternault, 1995, p. 71). When consumers cannot easily judge the quality of a luxury good they "tend to heavily rely on price as a cue for a luxury brand's quality, prestige, rarity, and hedonic value" (Fassnacht et al., 2013, p. 105). Hence, the demand for luxury goods might increase as prices go up as a result of elevated consumer perceptions of the functional, emotional, and symbolic value a luxury good is likely to deliver.

3.2.4 Decisions

Once the strategic direction is defined and price-relevant information have been analysed prices are actually determined. We differentiate between long-term and short-term pricing decisions (Fassnacht et al., 2013, p. 107; Simon & Fassnacht, 2009, p. 309). Figure 19 illustrates common practices how to manage prices in the long run. For non-luxury goods we mainly differentiate between (a) a skimming strategy, i.e. the introductory price is relatively high (to yield high contribution margins) and subsequently lowered over time, and (b) a penetration strategy, i.e. the introductory price is relatively low to quickly gain market share (Monroe, 2003, pp. 381–383; Simon & Fassnacht, 2009, pp. 328–329).

Continuity. Luxury goods manufacturers follow a different strategy. As shown in Figure 19(c) the average price of a luxury brand's product-mix should start at the high-end level (in contrast to penetration strategy) and continuously increase over time (in contrast to skimming strategy; Fassnacht et al., 2013, p. 104; Kapferer & Bastien, 2009a, p. 72; Kisabaka, 2001, p. 259). In fact, the Cost of Living Extremely Well Index issued by Forbes (2012) shows that luxury prices have increased considerably faster than general consumer goods prices. Kapferer & Bastien (2009a, pp. 72–73) argue that continuously increasing the average price of a luxury brand's product range is needed as a mean of re-stratification, i.e. reinforcing the gap between the mass and the class. Also, as mentioned above, the quantity demanded often remains constant or even increases as prices go up. Thus, by continuously increasing prices luxury goods manufacturers may remain or even extend contribution margins without necessarily lowering volume sales.

Figure 19 – Long-term pricing strategy for luxury goods.

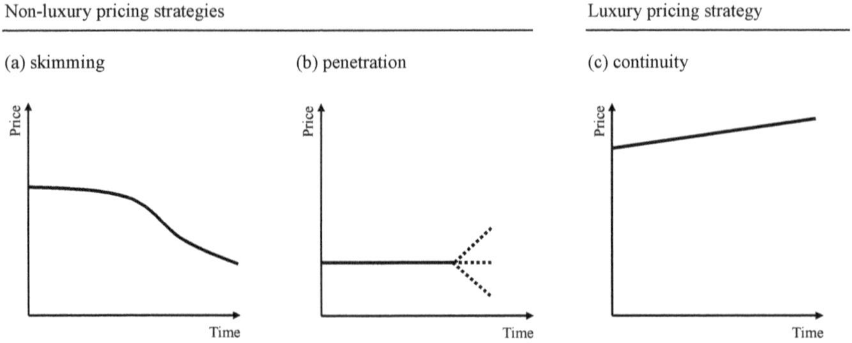

Source: Kapferer & Bastien (2009a, p. 72), Kisabaka (2001, p. 259), Monroe (2003, pp. 381–383), Simon & Fassnacht (2009, p. 328), Voigt (2003, p. 711)

Rare-to-no discount policy. In the short run, luxury goods manufacturers should pursue a strict rare-to-no discount policy as "excessive price movement or volatility could send the wrong signal as to the worth of the brand" (Keller, 2009, p. 292). Avoiding bargain sales represents one of the key principles to the French malletier Louis Vuitton (Nagasawa, 2008, p. 44). Louis Vuitton even destroys unsold seasonal items rather than selling them at a discount (Kapferer & Bastien, 2009a, p. 189). And the Swiss watchmaker Rolex even bought back some of its timepieces from retailers as to avoid sales at reduced prices during the financial crises 2009 (Adams, 2009). With respect to a no-discount policy Kapferer & Bastien (2009a, p. 189) point at a fundamental difference between luxury and fashion brands: luxury brands should be timeless, something that is collected and passed on to the next generation like Hermès bags, Van Cleef & Arpels jewellery and Patek Philippe watches. In contrast, fashion quickly becomes outdated as a result of seasonal collections and short innovation cycles. As soon as a new collection arrives end-of-season items are sold at reduced prices and often through special channels, e.g., outlet stores outside the prestigious city centres.

Rare-to-no price discrimination. A continuity-driven pricing policy also implies a rare-to-no use of price discrimination, i.e. selling identical or slightly modified products at different prices in order to increase profits (Fassnacht, 1996, p. 25; Tellis, 1986, p. 147). In luxury, firms typically apply the following four forms of price discrimination (Fassnacht, Kluge, & Mohr, 2012, p. 125) based on:

(a) **special editions**: in 2012 the British car manufacturer Rolls-Royce launched the "Year of the Dragon" special edition of its flagship car Phantom Extended Wheelbase at a heavy price tag of around EUR 900,000 – about double the price of the basic version (Cho, 2012; Fassnacht et al., 2012, p. 125).
(b) **quantity**: like other Champagne brands the LVMH-owned brand Moët & Chandon charges different litre prices for different quantities. The litre price for a 0.75 litre bottle of Moët & Chandon Brut Impérial of EUR 42.90 goes up to for

smaller bottles (e.g., price premium of more than 60 per cent for the 0.2 litre bottle) as well as for larger bottles (e.g., price premium of more than 200 per cent for 15 litre Nebukadnedzar; Fassnacht et al., 2012, p. 125).

(c) **customer status**: on an individual level sales personnel may grant a discount to a loyal customer. However, giving discounts should be done on a highly personalized level, e.g., at the end of a face-to-face sales talk (Kapferer & Bastien, 2009a, pp. 189–190). For example, for Saint Valentine's Day in 2012 the Austrian jeweller Swarovski sent a digital 10% off voucher to all of its E-Mail subscribers to incentivize purchases above EUR 120 (R. Lamb, 2012). While this approach relies on the right intention of rewarding loyal customers, experts have criticised its implementation by arguing "don't discount love" (R. Lamb, 2012). Swarovski highlighted the price, not the rich value of the product which a salesperson should communicate first (Kapferer & Bastien, 2009a, p. 192).

(d) **country**: in general, firms often charge different prices in different countries, among other reasons, as to account for country-specific differences in consumers' price elasticity of demand (Simon & Fassnacht, 2009, p. 281). This reasoning is based on the assumption that goods and services within a given country are mostly consumed by local inhabitants. The luxury goods market, however, increasingly depends on tourist spendings. In Europe, for example, about 50 per cent of luxury goods sales are accounted for by tourists (Bain & Company & Fondazione Altagamma, 2014, p. 21). To communicate a consistent price image across countries, the fashion and leather goods brands Louis Vuitton, Gucci, and Prada charge highly similar prices for identical handbags in different countries when accounted for differences in consumption taxes (Fassnacht et al., 2012, p. 127).

Price-volume stability. Additionally to keeping prices constant in the short run by pursuing a rare-to-no-discount policy, luxury goods manufacturers should also limit the number of units produced and sold per period (Mohr, 2013, pp. 70–71; Simon & Fassnacht, 2009, pp. 64–65). The balanced specification of both price and volume (i.e. price-volume stability) should be defined ex ante and communicated to the market as to signal the firm's commitment (Fassnacht et al., 2013, p. 107; Simon & Fassnacht, 2009, p. 64). Luxury goods manufacturers keep both prices and volumes stable irrespectively of whether short-term changes in demand occur.

3.2.5 Implementation

Once the price for a given product is defined, it needs to be implemented both within the organization and the market (Homburg & Totzek, 2011). Internally, a solid implementation firstly requires a precise allocation of the pricing decision-making authority, i.e. deciding whether to centralize or delegate the pricing authority (Fassnacht et al., 2013, p. 107; Mohr, 2013, p. 76). Although the delegation of pricing authority can be beneficial to an organization (Hansen et al., 2008, p. 103), luxury goods manufacturers should **centralize the pricing authority** in order to create and preserve a consistent price image over time (the average price of the product range should continuously increase over time), across countries and channels (careful use of price discrimination; Fassnacht et al., 2013, p. 107; Kapferer & Bastien, 2009a, p. 72). Simon & Fassnacht (2009, pp. 360–361) argue that the allocation of pricing authority should be more centralized in cases where the product is of high importance to the organization and if the organization needs to send consistent signals to competitors and customers.

Externally, to implement prices in the market luxury goods manufacturers should operate and supply an **exclusive distribution** network and **discreetly communicate** prices (Mohr, 2013, pp. 77–79). Luxury goods manufacturers increasingly forward-integrate into directly operated monobrand stores (Nueno & Quelch, 1998, p. 66). In 2013, directly operated store formats account for about one third of personal luxury goods sales worldwide (Bain & Company & Fondazione Altagamma, 2014, p. 15). Directly operated store formats allow luxury goods manufacturers to fully control not only in-store brand communication but also retail prices and how they are communicated. In contrast, selling wholesale to retail partners (e.g., department stores, specialty stores etc.) provides no control over prices or their communication and thus requires an extremely careful selection of distribution partners.

In general, prices should not be publicly communicated through brand advertisements or press releases (Kapferer & Bastien, 2009a, p. 191; Simon & Fassnacht, 2009, p. 68). However, recent experimental studies by Parguel, Delécolle, & Valette-Florence (2014, pp. 15–18) reveal that the display of price in a shopping window may actually have a positive influence on consumers' perceptions of conspicuousness and quality while it does neither increase nor decrease consumer perceived uniqueness of the brand. In any case, prices should be communicated in a discreet manner, ideally through sales personnel in-store (Kapferer & Bastien, 2009a, p. 199).

3.3 Communication of luxury goods

3.3.1 Introduction

In marketing, communication refers to the creation and transmission of relevant information through selected communication instruments in order to influence cognitive, affective, and behavioural responses among a targeted audience (Bruhn, 2013, p. 3; De Pelsmacker, Geuens, & Van den Bergh, 2013, p. 3; Homburg, 2012, p. 747; Kotler & Keller, 2012, p. 498). In light of ever more competitive markets consumers are confronted with a wide array of products and services meeting the same set of basic needs (e.g., watches telling the time, handbags storing belongings). Communication then has the essential function of making consumers aware of the differentiating benefits of a brand (e.g., design, material, heritage; Bruhn, 2013, p. 3).

Figure 20 illustrates a generic communication model: a sender encodes a relevant message that may be decoded by the targeted receiver. The sender transmits the message through a selected communication instrument that reaches the targeted receiver. The decoded message then influences the receiver's cognitive (e.g., awareness), affective (e.g., liking or preferences), and behavioural (e.g., trial or repeat purchase) responses.

Figure 20 – Generic communication model.

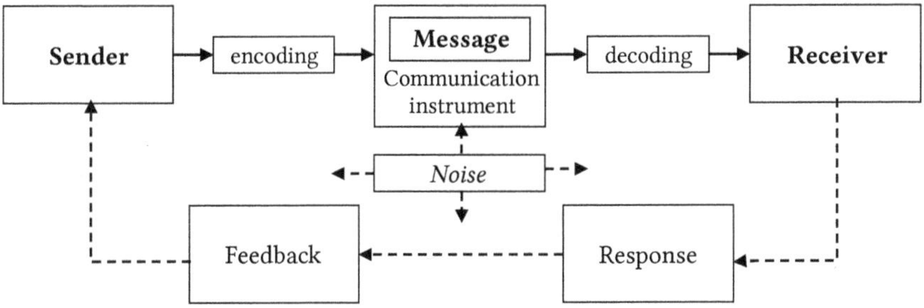

Source: Belch & Belch (2012, p. 17), Bruhn (2013, p. 42), Kotler & Keller (2012, p. 502), Schweiger & Schrattenecker (2013, p. 12)

For example, the Geneva-based luxury watchmaker Patek Philippe (sender) emphasizes the tradition and longevity of its branded timepieces (message) through print advertisements (communication instrument) in order to create awareness and desire (communication objective/ response) among the readers of the Financial Times *How to Spend It* (receiver). Here, the encoding of the message refers to the textual ("You never actually own a Patek Philippe. You merely look after it for the next generation.") and graphical cues (father and son sharing the same passion for sailing) used in the print advertisement to signal the rich tradition and longevity of the Patek Philipp's timepieces.

In luxury, communication represents an important marketing instrument to cater consumers' dreams. The importance of communication to luxury goods is highlighted by the **dream formula** (see Figure 21) which Dubois & Paternault (1995, p. 73) have empirically derived from a survey among 3,000 US consumers. According to the regression formula the dream value of brand (brand choice if money is not an issue) is function of brand awareness and purchase, i.e. brand diffusion. Notably, higher levels of brand awareness fuel the dream value (indicated by the positive regression coefficient) whereas higher levels of brand diffusion decrease the dream value of a brand (indicated by the negative regression coefficient). Luxury goods manufacturers do not follow conventional communication procedures. Luxury brand communication is not about "making the sale", but about creating and recharging dreams (Kapferer & Bastien, 2009a, p. 210). Figure 22 illustrates a generic communication process (Bruhn, 2013a, p. 54; Homburg, 2012, p. 749; Kisabaka, 2001, pp. 261–272; Kotler & Keller, 2012, p. 504) and systematically contrasts conventional versus luxury-specific procedures. Each phase of the communication process will be explained in more detail in following chapters.

Figure 21 – Dream formula.

DREAM = – 8.6 + 0.58 * AWARENESS – 0.59 * PURCHASE	
DREAM	Imagine that you are given the possibility of choosing a beautiful present because you won a contest. Which are the five brands you like the best?
AWARENESS	Here is a list of luxury brands. Please indicate which ones you know at least by name.
PURCHASE	Please indicate from which you have bought an item during the past two years.

Source: Dubois & Paternault (1995, p. 70 & 73)

Figure 22 – Overview: specificities of brand communication in luxury.

Objectives	**Audience**	**Message**	**Instruments**	**Budget & control**
▪ Focus on cognitive and affective consumer responses ▪ Create and feed the dream ▪ Do not "sell"	▪ Target audience is beyond target clientele ▪ Prospect clients, existing clients, *and* significant others	▪ Focus on aesthetic and symbolic rather than functional attributes ▪ Use subtle images and abstract descriptions ▪ Do not communicate prices ▪ Communicate globally consistent	▪ Focus on print, public relations, events, sponsoring, and direct marketing ▪ Embrace online communication channels	▪ Relatively higher percentage of sales invested in brand communication

Source: author

3.3.2 Objectives

Brand communication is about influencing consumer responses by sending relevant information through relevant communication instruments. At the very beginning of a communication planning process it is essential for marketers to precisely define communication objectives, i.e. the level of consumer response they intend to achieve. Figure 23 shows the generic hierarchy of consumer responses to brand communication stimuli (Bruhn, 2013, pp. 49 & 189; Homburg, 2012, p. 751; Kotler & Keller, 2012, p. 503) and which consumer responses luxury brand communication is aimed at.

Figure 23 – Hierarchy of consumer responses to communication stimuli.

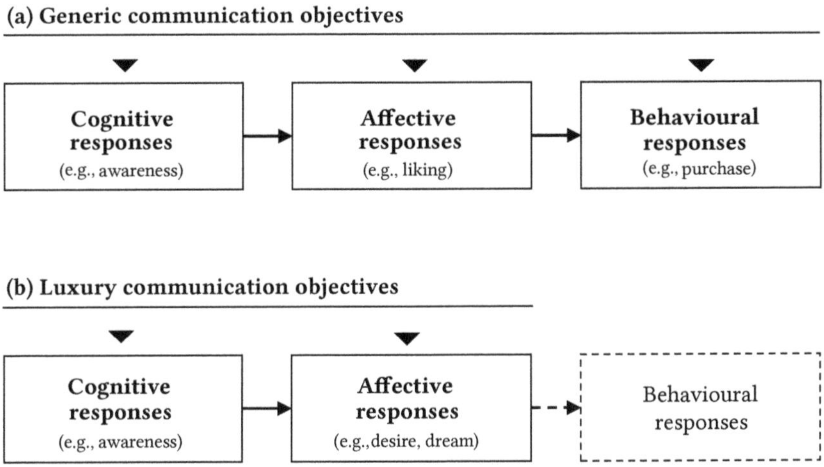

Source: author

In general, brand communication aims at three different levels of consumer responses: cognitive, affective, and behavioural responses (Bruhn, 2013, p. 49 & 189; Homburg, 2012, p. 751; Kotler & Keller, 2012, p. 503). First, a consumer is aware of and knowledgeable about a brand and its market offering (cognitive stage). Then, the consumer consciously or subconsciously builds a personal attitude towards the brand, i.e. she or he likes the brand, prefers its products over other brands' products and ideally desires the brand (affective stage). Lastly, if a consumer desires a brand she or he tries the product, purchases it for the first time or repeatedly (behavioural or conative stage).

In luxury, brand communication does not "sell" (Kapferer & Bastien, 2009a, p. 68). It aims at cognitive and affective rather than short-term behavioural consumer responses. It is about creating and recharging awareness and dreams in the long run among the targeted client base and their significant others. On the one hand, the dream formula shows (see Figure 21) that a certain level of awareness is needed to generate brand desirability (cognitive and affective stage). However, pushing sales to hard in luxury brand communication (behavioural stage) may come at the expense of a luxury brand's dream value.

On the other hand, the luxury purchasing process is characterized by a considerable time lag between the initiation of the dream (brand desirability) and – in happy few cases – the actual purchase. Other than for frequently purchased consumer goods, individuals typically do not shop for luxury goods on a regular basis. The thirsty individual goes for a Coca-Cola softdrink while the freshly married couple goes for a Moët & Chandon champagne. And while the student goes for a BIC ballpoint pen, the graduated doctorate goes for a Montblanc Meisterstück fountain pen. Shopping luxury goods represents a "lengthy act" (Kapferer & Bastien, 2009a, p. 200), a dream that is built over time and comes true in special moments of life. Luxury brand communication should add to an individual's projection of those special moments of life (affective stage) rather than triggering the unlikely event of immediate purchase (behavioural stage).

Please note, however, that creating awareness does not apply in all cases. Often, smaller luxury brands build on their image of being reserved for those in the know, something that is not openly communicated but becomes known mainly through word-of-mouth (Kisabaka, 2001, p. 261). For those "connoisseur brands" excessively increasing awareness may actually decrease demand (Heine, 2012, p. 86). By becoming known among too many unqualified individuals the brand attracts bandwagon consumers who intend to signal their belonging to the elites by owning the same brands and products while at the same time distracting snobbish consumers who intend to differentiate themselves from the masses by consuming carefully selected goods (Leibenstein, 1950, p. 189).

3.3.3 Audience

A communication message should be designed for and sent to the relevant audience. Knowing the targeted audience is therefore a pre-requisite for deciding on when to send which message through which communication instrument (Kotler & Keller, 2012, p. 504). For non-luxury goods, brand communication aims at generating awareness, interest, and trial among prospects as well as reconfirmation and repeat purchase among existing clients. In luxury, brand communication not only targets prospects and existing clients, but also their **significant others**. After all, a luxury brand is not only bought for its functionally and experientially superior quality but also for the meaning it conveys to significant others, i.e. symbolic value (Grubb & Grathwol 1967, p. 24; Kapferer & Bastien, 2009a, p. 69). The conspicuous consumption of a luxury good increases the status of its owner among the relevant references group (e.g., friends, colleagues) only if the members of the reference group are aware of the brand and what it stands for (Kapferer & Bastien, 2009a, p. 70).

For example, the iconic Italian supercar manufacturer Ferrari counts about 16 million fans on its branded Facebook page (Facebook.com/Ferrari, 2015). Its fan base is by far larger than its actual client base. Considering that Ferrari sells about 7,000 supercars each year less than 0.05 per cent of Ferrari's Facebook fans actually buys one of its supercars. Still, Ferrari benefits from its large fan base that goes beyond actual clients in three ways: first, all fans and admirers are prospects that may turn into actual clients once they are one of the happy few to have the money at hand. Second, a large fan base increases the symbolic value of the brand as significant others are more likely to recognize and estimate the ownership of a Ferrari supercar. Third, the 99.95 per cent of Ferrari's Facebook fans that are teased by but cannot afford one of Ferrari's supercars are offered a broad portfolio of fan articles ranging from fashion and accessories to toys and electronic devices. In 2012, Ferrari recorded EUR 200 mn sales in Ferrari fan articles only (Freitag, 2013).

But building awareness and desire among significant others is not only some pre-requisite of the symbolic value for oneself. When given as gift, luxury goods also convey a symbolic value to significant others. Hence, significant others also need a certain level of connoisseurship to appreciate a precious gift. A Tiffany's diamond engagement ring is appreciated only to the extent to which a woman recognizes Tiffany's iconic blue box and estimates the rich heritage of the brand.

3.3.4 Message

Message refers to the content a brand intends to communicate to the targeted audience. In general, designing a message involves deciding on a message strategy, a creative strategy, and a message source (Kotler & Keller, 2012, p. 506). In a message strategy the marketer first defines *what message* the brand communication campaign conveys to the audience. The content of a message should be consistent with the brand identity and the functional, emotional, and symbolic value it delivers. Then, the creative strategy defines *how* the message is conveyed to the audience, i.e. how it is encoded using informative/rational or emotional appeals (Bruhn, 2013a, p. 491; Schweiger & Schrattenecker, 2013, p. 261). Finally a marketer decides on *who* is conveying the message, i.e. the product itself, a celebrity, an avatar, a brand ambassador etc.

For example, since 1991 the well-known German entertainer Thomas Gottschalk (message source) conveys the message of the German candy brand HARIBO "Kids and grown-ups love it so, the happy world of HARIBO" (message strategy) in TV advertisements which show him sharing happy moments in life with kids and adults (creative strategy: emotional appeals). In the TV advertisement for its Mach3 series, the Procter & Gamble owned razor brand Gillette demonstrated its new three-razor-blade technology (creative strategy: informative appeal) advocated by some of the world's best sportsmen Roger Federer, Thierry Henry, and Tiger Woods (message source) in order to convey what the brand uses to stand "The best a man can get" (message strategy).

In luxury, message strategies focus less on functional, but rather on the emotional and symbolic attributes of a brand and the aesthetic beauty of its products. Recall that luxury brands are those "whose ratio of functional utility to price is low while the ratio of intangible and situational utility to price is high" (Nueno & Quelch, 1998, p. 62). The content of luxury brand messages typically refers the heritage and country-of-origin of the brand, aesthetics and product details, limited editions, special moments in life like marriage or personal achievements, but never to price (Kisabaka, 2001, p. 263; Kapferer & Bastien, 2009a, p. 191; Simon & Fassnacht, 2009, p. 68). The message strategy applied should be consistent across countries in order to avoid irritation among mobile, frequently travelling clients (Kisabaka, 2001, p. 265). Also, luxury brands usually convey their message using purely emotional appeals rather than explicitly demonstrating and explaining the functional superiority of its products. An empirical investigation by Hansen & Wänke (2011, p. 794) shows that luxury goods manufacturers tend to describe their brands and products using a more abstract manner than non-luxury goods manufacturers do and that a more abstract description of branded product evokes higher perceptions of luxury. These message and creative strategies are consistent with the objectives of luxury brand communication: creating and feeding dreams rather than making the sale.

For example, in its 360 degree campaign "L'Odyssée de Cartier" from 2012 the Richemont owned French haute joaillerie brand Cartier emphasizes its rich tradition, elegance, sophistication and exclusiveness (message strategy) by showing the journey of a powerful, yet elegant and rare panther (message source) through different epochs and countries paving its way to the prestigious, Parisian Place Vendôme (known for its heritage of fine jewellery) where the panther walks up the stairs to an adorable woman (creative strategy: emotional appeal; see movie on Odyssee. Cartier.us, 2014). Throughout the panther's journey Cartier's products are shown subtly only, e.g., a tree made of precious gems, bracelets rolling down the mountain, or the woman wearing a Cartier ring. Production cost for this sophisticated movie total as much as USD 5.3 million (Jardine, 2012).

A recent empirical investigation of 750 print advertisements of 30 luxury and 30 non-luxury brands in different magazines from 2011 to 2013 by Dahm (2013) reveals some specific differences in the creative design of a luxury versus a non-luxury brand advertisement: Text and logos are less explicitly emphasized, i.e. smaller in size and positioned in the corners. Models shown are mostly female and photographed with a withdrawing gaze. In only 27 per cent of cases benefits are explicitly claimed (as opposed to 47 per cent in non-luxury brand advertisements). Luxury brands hardly ever communicate prices (1 per cent as opposed to 14 per cent for non-luxury brands). And, around 80 per cent of luxury brands do not use celebrities.

This finding matches the postulation by Kapferer & Bastien (2009a, p. 73): "Keep stars out of your advertising", i.e. celebrities should not be used as message source since the message a brand intends to convey does heavily depend on the (potentially volatile) image of the celebrity. Also, the authors argue that the use of a celebrity weakens the brands as it shifts the brand and the product itself to the background. Thus, Bastien & Kapferer (2013, pp. 32–33) recommend that celebrities should be used locally only and as "testimonial [...] for existing customers" as they may re-confirm the owners' feelings of status and personal achievement.

3.3.5 Instruments

Communication instruments refer to the channels or media used to convey a message to the targeted audience. We generally classify into "above-the-line" (ATL, i.e. advertising and public relations) and "below-the-line" communication instruments (BTL, i.e. events, sponsoring, direct marketing, sales promotion; Schweiger & Schrattenecker, 2013, p. 125). Figure 24 provides a generic overview of the variety

Figure 24 – Communication instruments.

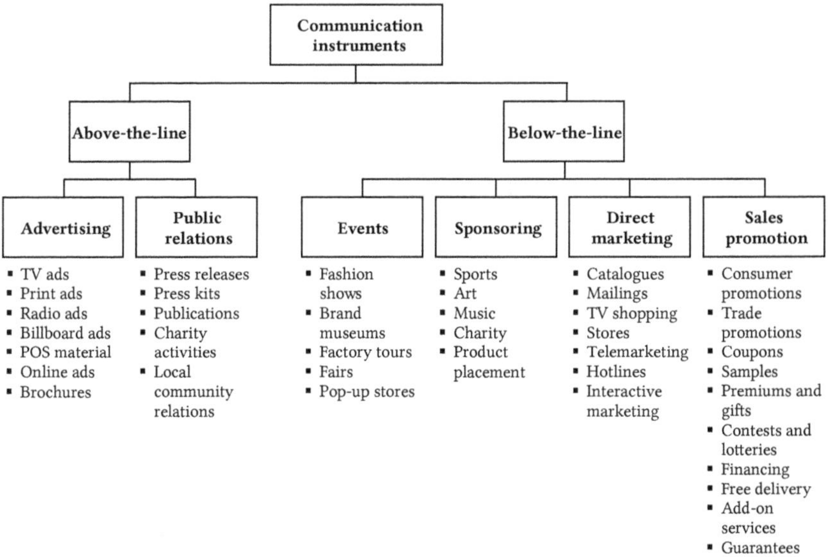

Source: adapted from Bruhn (2013, p. 322), Homburg (2012, pp. 778–835), Kotler & Keller (2012, pp. 512–514), Schweiger & Schrattenecker (2013, p. 126)

of communication instruments. Often, online communication is considered as a separate BTL communication instrument (e.g., Bruhn, 2013, p. 322; Schweiger & Schrattenecker, 2013, p. 126). While the increasing digitalization has enabled new, powerful ways of communication, online and offline communication instruments should not be considered as separate but rather integrated elements of brand communication. In fact, most of ATL and BTL communication instruments can be applied both in the offline and online world: an advertisement can be placed both in a print and online magazine, fashion shows can be live-broadcasted on the branded YouTube channel, and the interactive communication with clients can take place in-store or online on the branded website or with the help social media. Hence, the array of communication instruments has not changed as such but the ways they are applied to online media. The specificities of online communication are explained in more detail in Chapter 4.4.

Selecting a mix of communication instruments should not be considered an isolated decision. The choice of communication instruments depends on the objectives (cognitive, affective, or behavioural consumer responses), target audience (e.g., broad audience versus connoisseurs only), and messages (e.g., visual only versus multi-sensory stimuli) of a brand communication campaign.

3.3.5.1 Advertising

Advertising refers to an above-the-line communication instrument (see Figure 24) that aims at creating awareness (cognitive response) and desire (affective response) among a selected group of prospects, existing clients and their significant others by distributing brand communication messages through selected media like Print, TV, or own brochures. For being desired, a luxury brand must be recognized first. Brand awareness is a prerequisite of a luxury brand's dream value (Dubois & Paternault, 1995, p. 70). Yet, it is important to note that not all luxury brands might aim at high awareness among the general public but rather prefer remaining a secret to the mass and being known by few connoisseurs only.

Not surprisingly, awareness requires capital investement. According the market research data, the covetousness of a luxury brand is positively related to the absolute advertising expenditure (Bernstein Research, 2009, p. 26). On average, luxury goods manufacturers spend around **5 to 15 per cent of sales** for advertising only, i.e. excluding other communication instruments (Okonkwo, 2007, p. 145). For example, in 2014 the LVMH Group spend 11.3 per cent of sales for "advertising and promotion", i.e. media coverage and POS advertising (LVMH.com, 2015, p. 52).

Aiming at high levels awareness among and beyond the targeted clientele does not imply communicating to the masses. Hence, a luxury-specific mix of above-the-line communication instruments does typically not include expensive mass media like **television** (TV). As a common exception, luxury perfumes (often licensed to cosmetics manufacturers like L'Oréal or Coty) are heavily advertised on TV. One of the rare (non-perfume) examples of a luxury branded TV commercial refers to the Swiss wristwatch brand Rolex, which supports the broadcasting of the Ryder Cup on the pay TV channel Sky Germany.

Rather than on TV, luxury goods manufacturers commonly advertise in **print media**. In order to reach a more selective target audience luxury marketers typically focus on high-end special interest and lifestyle formats like Vogue (29,700 EUR per 1/1-page), How to Spend it (17,100 EUR per 1/1-page), or The Private Journey (17,770 EUR per 1/1-page; Dahm, 2013, p. 17).

With the advance of the Internet luxury goods manufacturers increasingly rely on **online advertising** (e.g., banners) placed at the websites of pure online magazines (e.g., worlds-luxury-guide.com) and traditional print magazines and newspapers (e.g., vogue.com; howtospendit.ft.com). More details and examples will be provided in Chapter 4.4.

In addition to advertising brands in third-party print media, luxury goods manufacturers and retailers typically provide own branded brochures, catalogues, books or so called "magalogues", a mixture between editorial content like in a magazine and product promotion like in a catalogue (Kapferer & Bastien, 2009a, p. 200). The French fashion house Hermès, for example, issues its seasonal magalogue "Le Monde d'Hermès" both as hard and digital copy through the app stores of iTunes and Google Play (Hermes.com, 2015d).

3.3.5.2 Public relations

Public relations (PR) refer to another above-the-line communication instrument (like advertising, see Figure 24). While in advertising, the luxury goods manufacturer or retailer itself designs the message to be communicated to the relevant audience, PR refers to the communication through (independent) mediators who transmit a message to the targeted audience, for example, in the form of press releases or editorial content in magazines. Essentially, PR activities aim at being mentioned by independent, yet relevant third parties (e.g., press, magazines, TV) within a positive context.

In luxury, PR represents an essential element of luxury brand communication (Kapferer & Bastien, 2009a, p. 213; Kisabaka, 2001, p. 270) and often is even more important than traditional advertising (Simon & Fassnacht, 2009, p. 67). The extraordinariness and inaccessibility of luxury goods makes them become part of movies, articles, songs or events. One may easily find numerous articles and TV documentaries presenting the world's fastest car, the making of champagne, or the processing of rare gems. Since the independent third party acts as an advocate of the brand, this "free" PR creates high levels of credibility among its audience (Kotler & Keller, 2012, p. 513). Successful PR requires building and cultivating a trustful relationship with the independent third parties to make them mention the luxury brand name in a positive context.

3.3.5.3 Events

As opposed to traditional above-the-line communication, below-the-line communication (BTL) instruments like events, sponsoring, direct marketing, and sales promotion (see Figure 24) are becoming increasingly important (Schweiger & Schrattenecker, 2013, pp. 125–126). Most BTL communication instruments well support a luxury brand's communication objectives, i.e. targeting a selected audience and creating awareness and desire through emotional and symbolic appeals. By organizing **events** like fashion shows or pop-up stores the luxury goods manufacturer can stage its brand and immerse a selected audience into the brand's world in absence of other, non-brand-related stimuli. When advertised or reported in a public magazine, the reader is confronted with numerous impressions distracting attention from each single brand.

An excellent example of creating brand credibility through events refers to the "Festival des Métiers" hosted by the French saddler brand **Hermès** in the world's fashion cities like in September 2012 in New York, USA, or in May 2014 in Hamburg, Germany. The events emphasized the complexity and precision of workmen needed to craft Hermès' fine products. Hermès artisans demonstrated how they create the iconic Kelly Bag, silk scarves, saddles, wristwatches, and porcelain (see Figure 25; Hoffmann, 2014).

Figure 25 – Brand communication event: Hermès "Festival des Métiers".

(a) Poster (b) Saddlery (c) Jewellery (d) Silk

Sources: © images by 準建築人手札網站 Forgemind ArchiMedia (2011a, 2011b, 2011c, 2011d, CC BY 2.0 license)

3.3.5.4 Sponsoring

Sponsoring, i.e. the patronage and financial support of a person, institution, or event in exchange for communicating a brand or product, refers to another BTL communication instrument (see Figure 24) which is commonly applied by luxury goods manufacturers (Kapferer & Bastien, 2009a, p. 214; Simon & Fassnacht, 2009, p. 67). Kapferer & Bastien (2009a, p. 67) argue that, in luxury, manufacturers should sponsor the event itself, not its actors in order to control all parameters of the event. Also, marketers should ensure a strong coherence between the brand and the sponsored event. An empirical study by Bruhn & Batt (2012, p. 40) shows that a strong coherence or fit between the luxury brand and the sponsored object significantly enhances consumer attitudes towards the brand and thus the overall success of the sponsoring activity.

There are several good examples of coherent sponsoring activities by luxury goods manufacturers. The Geneva-based watchmaker **Rolex** sponsors the prestigious Ryder Cup, the most renowned golf tournament between the best European and the best US players (Rydercup.com, 2008). Both Rolex timepieces and the world's elite in golf are known for status and highest precision. The Parisian leather and fashion manufacturer **Hermès** sponsored the Grand Prix de Diana, an elite horse race tournament in Chantilly, France, established in 1843 (France-galop.com, 2014). This esteemed equestrian event embodies the roots of Hermès back in 1837, i.e. crafting leather saddles. And, the French crystal and joaillerie brand **Lalique** used to sponsor the Lalique Trophy, an international senior-level figure skating tournament in Paris (International Skating Union, 2002). Both Lalique and figure skating evoke associations of fine crystal and elegant arts.

A rather poor example refers to **Aston Martin**. The British sportscar manufacturer sponsors the down-to-earth football team of 1860 München which is playing in the second national football league of Germany (Gierke, 2011). On the one hand, by sponsoring a specific actor instead of an event the reputation of the Aston Martin brand strongly depends on the reputation and performance of one single team. In contrast, by sponsoring an event Rolex, Hermès, and Lalique may celebrate their brand and the sportsmen quite independently of the outcome of the tournament. On the other hand, the fit between 1860 München and Aston Martin is weak. Apart from both having some rich tradition, they have hardly anything in common. The brand 1860 München is associated with second-class football supported by the working-class whereas Aston Martin is associated with first-class sportscars driven by the happy few.

A special type of sponsoring refers to **product placements**, i.e. the practice that manufacturers pay a monetary amount in order to place a branded product in an event, movie or video (Homer, 2009, p. 21). Brand communication through product placements is subtler than other sponsoring types since the brand is not explicitly communicated. Rather, a branded product is used instead of a generic product that is needed as an element of the event, movie, or video (Schweiger & Schrattenecker, 2013, p. 136). Product placements in movies have been found to positively affect firm performance (Wiles & Danielova, 2009, p. 56). More specifically, research by Homer (2009, p. 28) shows that while product placements are generally well recognized by consumers (cognitive responses) they diminish consumer attitudes (affective responses) if the brand is exposed too prominently and repeatedly. Subtle product placements, however, do in fact enhance consumer attitudes (Homer, 2009, p. 28). Despite multiple examples of luxury product placements, literature in this field is scarce.

A classic best practice is **James Bond** driving an **Aston Martin** sportscar (Astonmartin.com, 2014a). The secret agent James Bond, the fictitious main character of the homonymous action film series, well embodies the values of Aston Martin: British, discreet, nearly invincible, and made for highest demands.

A more recent example refers to **Louis Vuitton**. The French malletier provides the flight case for the prestigious, golden trophy for the winner of the football tournament FIFA World Cup 2014 in Rio de Janeiro, Brazil. Before the final match between Germany and Argentina, the trophy is presented to the public in a customized flight case with the renowned LV monogram. This product placement communicates what Louis Vuitton stands for: precious cases safeguarding the most precious items (the origins of the trunk-maker Louis Vuitton), and Louis Vuitton branded products being dedicated to the special moments in life.

3.3.5.5 Direct marketing

The abovementioned ATL and BTL brand communication instruments are targeted at a selected *group* of receivers, not a specific individual. In contrast, **direct marketing**, another BTL communication instrument, comprises all activities directed towards communicating with consumers on an individual level, for example, through mailings or interactive communication by phone or social media (see Figure 24; Bruhn, 2013, p. 405). Direct marketing activities include one-way communication (e.g., mailings, catalogues) and interactive communication intended to create a dialogue with the individual consumer, e.g., in-store or through hotlines, social media or instant chats on the website (Bruhn, 2013b, pp. 405–407; Holland, 2009, p. 28; Schweiger & Schrattenecker, 2013, pp. 131–135).

In luxury, direct marketing represents a fundamental communication instrument as it allows, per definition, the highest possible level of selectivity in reaching the targeted audience. Luxury goods manufacturers rely on advertising, public relations, events, and sponsoring in order to create awareness (cognitive response) and desire (affective response) among a selected, yet broader group of prospects, clients and their significant others. In contrast, through direct marketing luxury goods manufacturers can target a refined group of prospects and existing clients not only to inform and make them dream about the brand but also to trigger trial and repeat purchases (behavioural responses).

Personalizing is essential to luxury direct marketing. In today's digitalized world, communication has become extremely efficient and anonymous. It takes firms only few clicks to send out tons of mass-customized E-Mails. Even more appreciated are the **personalized, handwritten notes** sent, for example, by the Italian fashion house Fendi or by the European luxury accessories brand Montblanc (Robeson, 2012). An effective, highly personalized direct marketing requires luxury goods manufacturers to install and maintain a detailed customer relationship management (CRM) system on a worldwide level (Cailleux et al., 2009, p. 411).

In light of the increasing digitization the issue of interactive marketing is becoming ever more important. In particular, **social media** platforms allow luxury goods manufacturers to increase both the reach of brand communication to virtually anyone in the world as well as the intensity of communication. Individuals are not only confronted with brand communication material but can immediately respond to it thereby initiating an publicly visible dialogue with the brand. Social media marketing as a form of interactive marketing will be explained as part of online brand communication in more detail in Chapter 4.4.2.4.

3.3.5.6 Sales promotion

Sales promotion refers to another below-the-line communication instrument intended to stimulate consumer or retailer behaviour through time-limited changes in the market offering like temporary price reductions, samples, free delivery or guarantees (see Figure 24; Chandon, 1995, p. 420; Gedenk, 2002, p. 11). While other communication instruments like advertising, public relations, events, or sponsoring are directed towards evoking cognitive and affective consumer responses (e.g., awareness and desire) sales promotions actually stimulate behavioural consumer responses at the point of sale (POS) like product trial, purchase, or repeat purchase. Sales promotion activities can be either directed towards consumers (consumer promotions, e.g., temporary price reductions, promotion packs, samples) or retailers (trade promotions, e.g., rebates, supportive POS material) and classified into either price promotions (e.g., promotion packs, coupons) or non-price promotions (e.g., sampling, POS material; Gedenk, Neslin, & Ailawadi, 2010, p. 393). Sales promotions are frequently considered as an element of the brand communication mix while in fact it often involves making temporary changes to multiple marketing mix elements (Fassnacht & Königsfeld 2015, pp. 71–74; Gedenk, 2002, p. 13): pricing (e.g., price discounts, rebates), product management (e.g., promotion packs, samples), distribution (e.g., second shelf space), and communication (e.g., POS communication material, flyers).

In mass markets, sales promotions account for 12 to 25 per cent of retailers' sales (A.C. Nielsen 2004; reported in Gedenk et al., 2010, p. 394) with the average price discount being a 20 per cent temporary price reduction (Fassnacht & Königsfeld, 2015, p. 73). An extreme example refers to the German beer market where about two out of three beers are sold with a price discount (Handelsblatt, 2011). However, while most sales promotion instruments can be extremely effective in stimulating short-term behavioural responses in terms of sales, it may eventually harm the brand in the long run (Blattberg & Neslin, 1989, pp. 90–91).

In luxury, marketers maintain and nurture the brand's fragile concept of exclusiveness in the long run rather than realizing short-term gains in sales. As shown by examples of Rolex and Louis Vuitton in Chapter 3.2.4, luxury goods manufacturers pursue a **rare-to-no discount policy** even if it implies buying back or destroying unsold items. Similarly, other sales promotion tools like promotional or value packs, buy-one-get-one-free offers, financing, or coupons hardly apply to luxury goods.

The choice of sales promotion tools often depends on the specific category: a glass of champagne is frequently offered during a sales talk for durable luxury goods like cars, yachts, or real estate. Samples are frequently provided along with a purchased perfume or cosmetics product. Luxury online retailers may wrap purchased items as Christmas gifts and deliver them for free. Jewellers may offer free name engraving as an additional service for Saint Valentine's Day. And luxury fashion retailers may give price discounts for few, selected end-of-season items.

3.3.5.7 Integrated communication mix

Finally, efficient brand communication requires an integrated communication approach, i.e. communicating and interlinking a message consistently between multiple ATL and BTL communication instruments. Again, Cartier's campaign "L'Odyssée de Cartier" serves as a best practice example for applying a 360 degree integrated communication campaign. Cartier conveys the same message (heritage, elegance, sophistication and exclusiveness embodied by the panther's journey through different epochs and countries) simultaneously through multiple media channels: full-page image on the landing page of cartier.com, a noticeable posting on the official Cartier branded Facebook page, the movie in full length shown on the official Cartier Youtube.com channel, the title story of Cartier's dedicated online magazine "Rouge Cartier", banner advertisements on selected websites like FT.com, editorial articles in fashion magazines like Vogue.com, cinema advertisements, and even television advertisement on March 4th 2012 in the US during commercial breaks of prime time formats like Desperate Housewives (Carr, 2012; Jardine, 2012; Odyssee. Cartier.us, 2014).

3.3.6 Budget and monitoring

Budgeting, i.e. the allocation of financial resources to brand communication initiatives, represents a complicated task since the cause-effect relationship between communication instruments and communication objectives is typically hard to measure (Bruhn, 2013, p. 267; Kotler & Keller, 2012, p. 510). An efficient budgeting requires accurate monitoring of each communication instrument and consumer responses to it. Here, collecting "hard" data of behavioural consumer responses (e.g., sales) is often easier than measuring "soft" data of cognitive and affective consumer responses (e.g., awareness and desire). A retailer can track the uplift in sales as a consequence of a temporary price reduction for a particular product. An online retailer can easily track the click-through-rate of a banner ad displayed. In contrast, it is far more difficult to measure how effectively a product placement of an Aston Martin sportscar in a James Bond movie creates awareness and desire among the targeted audience.

Firms generally use heuristic rather than analytic approaches for allocating budget to brand communication initiatives. Heuristic approaches include allocating budgets based on a reference value like a firm's sales figures ("percentage-of-sales" method), a firm's maximum disposable communication budget ("all-you-can-afford" method), budgets applied by competitors ("competitive-parity" method) or a firm's communication objectives ("objective-and-task" method; Bruhn, 2013, pp. 272–276; Kotler & Keller, 2012, p. 511). For more detail both on heuristic and analytic approaches please refer to Bruhn (2013b, pp. 272–279).

In luxury, these budgeting approaches apply equally. However, it may be assumed that luxury goods manufacturers allocate relatively higher budgets to brand communication initiatives. In terms of percentage of sales, communication budgets differ a lot between categories and firms ranging from 5 to 10 per cent in industrial equipment to an extreme of more than 40 per cent in cosmetics (Kotler & Keller, 2012, pp. 510–511). In luxury, total communication budget, i.e. including both ATL and BTL communication, equals around **25 per cent of sales** (Okonkwo, 2007, p. 145; Simon & Fassnacht, 2009, p. 67).

3.4 Distribution of luxury goods

3.4.1 Introduction

Distribution is about making goods available to relevant customers. Once a product is created, priced, and communicated to relevant customers, it is being made available at a point of sale (POS) and sold to the customer, i.e. physically transferred (either immediately or upon delivery) in exchange for a monetary amount to be paid. In marketing, distribution management covers all decisions related to profitably serving consumers with goods and services for use or consumption at the right place, at the right time, and at the right cost (Kotler & Armstrong, 2012, p. 341; Som & Blanckaert, 2015, p. 309). These decisions include strategic considerations like objectives, channel length, and channel width as well as store-level decisions like location, store format, store atmosphere, merchandising, and service level. Based on these aspects a manufacturer designs a directly operated store or carefully selects its retail partners. Figure 26 provides an overview of the specificities of distribution management in luxury, which will be described in more detail throughout this chapter.

Figure 26 – Overview: specificities of distribution management in luxury.

Distribution strategy

- Objectives:
  - Supply of affluent locals and tourists
  - Profitability
  - Brand communication
  - High levels of control
- Low channel length (preferably own retail)
- Low channel width (selective and exclusive distribution)

Store-level decisions

- Prestige locations in major cities, tourist destinations and airports
- Monobrand and carefully selected multibrand store formats
- Freeform store layout and aesthetically appealing store design
- Low product density
- Discreet price ticketing
- Exceptional service (knowledge, courtesy, no pressure)

Source: author

3.4.2 Distribution strategy

The formulation of a distribution strategy involves defining objectives of distribution, i.e. the desired future state of the firm, and a strategic roadmap on how to achieve these objectives within a given time frame (Ahlert & Kenning, 2007, p. 73). Throughout this chapter, the objectives of distribution in luxury and major strategic aspects (i.e. channel length and channel width) will be addressed.

3.4.2.1 Objectives

The objectives of a distribution strategy should be defined in accordance with overall corporate objectives like growth targets and return on investment (Schögel, 2012, p. 245; Specht & Fritz, 2005, p. 245). With respect to a manufacturer's distribution strategy we may generally differentiate between supply-oriented, economic, and managerial objectives of distribution (Bruhn, 2014, pp. 247–248; Manninger, 2012, p. 242).

Supply-oriented objectives. Making goods available to relevant customers at the right time, space, and quantity of items can be considered as the fundamental objective of a distribution strategy (Hollensen & Opresnik, 2010, p. 240; Som & Blanckaert, 2015, p. 309). Supply-oriented objectives are first of all about defining which target clientele to aim at, in which geographical area, how best to reach them, and at which intensity of distribution (Bruhn, 2014, p. 247; Kotler & Armstrong, 2012, p. 352). Mass-market consumer goods manufacturers typically aim at serving more consumers, more frequently, through more points of sale.

The Coca-Cola Company, for example, serves about 1.9 billion beverages per day in more than 200 countries (Coca-colacompany.com, 2015). In luxury, the target clientele is far more limited given the high price tags. Luxury distribution is about serving places where the world's upper class meets, i.e. places with **affluent locals and tourists**. Consequently, large luxury goods manufacturers have points of sale in nearly all top 20 tourist destinations in terms of annual tourist arrivals, e.g., Hong Kong, Singapore, London (Euromonitor.com, 2015). However, luxury retail expansion must not come at the expense of the brand's perceived exclusiveness. Hence, luxury goods manufacturers aim at **low distribution intensity** (Frontier Economics & ECCIA, 2012, p. 12; Keller, 2009, p. 292). For example, to preserve its luxury appeal, Louis Vuitton has announced to deliberately slow down expanding its retail network of about 460 stores in 50 countries worldwide (Reuters.com, 2013).

Economic objectives. Ultimately, any mode of serving the target clientele in geographically relevant places must be economically viable for the manufacturer and its distribution partners. **Profitability** is of primary importance to luxury distribution strategy (Manninger, 2012, p. 241). In simple terms, profit is a function of **reach**, **share of margin**, and **costs** (Bruhn, 2014, p. 247; Manninger, 2012, p. 242; Som & Blanckaert, 2015, pp. 309–310). Reach and share of margin should be sufficiently high to generate revenue in excess of incurred set-up and fixed cost of running the store (e.g., cost of logistics, rent, and staff). For example, given their ample size and exorbitant rent per square metre in the world's prime locations, flagship stores are considered to be hardly profitable and to primarily serve brand communication purposes (Manninger, 2012, p. 241). However, directly operating stores may be a profitable strategy given that demand and share of margin are sufficiently high to overcompensate the enormous capital expenditures of setting up and running the store (Chevalier & Gutsatz, 2012, p. 16; Manninger, 2012, p. 242). In contrast, wholesale distribution reduces the manufacturer's share of margin but comes at lower costs and risks of selling as orders are typically secured upfront.

Managerial objectives. Finally, more than profitably making goods available to the affluent clientele at few, selected points of sale, luxury distribution is about **brand communication** (Kapferer & Bastien, 2009a, p. 198). To shoppers the store often represents the very first physical point of contact – a place where the brand comes to life. Considering the elevated importance of the retail outlet for communicating the luxury brand, the manufacturer typically aims at **high levels of control** over location, assortment, store atmosphere, prices, and service levels of any point of sale carrying its products. "If you control your distribution, you control your image", Bernard Arnault, Chairman and CEO at LVMH, emphasizes (Chevalier & Gutsatz, 2012, p. 15). Similarly, Kapferer & Bastien (2009a) point that "strict control over distribution, in all the key aspects of the brand (product policy, price, merchandizing, communication) is vital in luxury" (p. 201). In the pursuit of a maximum of control and **exclusiveness**, we observe an ongoing "retailization" of the luxury goods market, i.e. a positive trend towards directly operated monobrand stores (Bain & Company, 2014, p. 4; Manninger, 2012, p. 244; Som & Blanckaert, 2015, p. 310).

Overall, luxury distribution strategy aims at making goods available to affluent locals and tourists at relevant places in a profitable, highly selective, and controlled manner. However, when deciding on a specific store format, manufacturers face a major **trade-off** between high levels of margin, control, and exclusiveness on the one hand and capital investment, running costs, risks involved, and a market coverage to generate a critical level of sales on the other.

In the following, we further address fundamental distribution-strategic options, i.e. channel length (retail or wholesale distribution; see Chapter 3.4.2.2) and channel width (intensive, selective, and exclusive distribution; see Chapter 3.4.2.3), and how they help meeting the distribution objectives described.

3.4.2.2 Channel length: retail and wholesale distribution

A manufacturer can sell its goods either directly to end consumers (retail distribution) or wholesale to intermediaries (wholesale distribution). Channel length refers to the **number of tiers of intermediaries** (Homburg, Kuester, & Krohmer, 2013, p. 204; Kotler & Armstrong, 2012, p. 343). In luxury, we mainly differentiate between retail and wholesale distribution (Bain & Company, 2014, p. 18; Chevalier & Gutsatz, 2012, p. 20; Manninger, 2012, p. 244; Moore & Birtwistle, 2004, p. 420): in a **retail distribution model**, i.e. direct distribution (see Figure 27(a)), the luxury goods manufacturer directly sells its branded merchandise to the consumer without any intermediary. The manufacturer itself operates the point of sale (commonly referred to as directly operated store or DOS) and completes the purchase with the shopper. In the **wholesale distribution model**, i.e. indirect distribution, the luxury goods manufacturer does not directly sell to the consumer but sells its merchandise *wholesale* to an intermediary. The intermediary is either a retail partner that operates a point of sale and sells to the end consumer (single-tier distribution, see Figure 27(b)), or a wholesale partner that resells the merchandise to one or more retailers (two-tier distribution). A common example of a wholesale distribution model is branded merchandise sold through department stores like Selfridge's or KaDeWe, specialty stores like Bucherer or Wempe, or duty-free stores like DFS Group or Dufry.

Figure 27 – Distribution models in luxury: retail and wholesale.

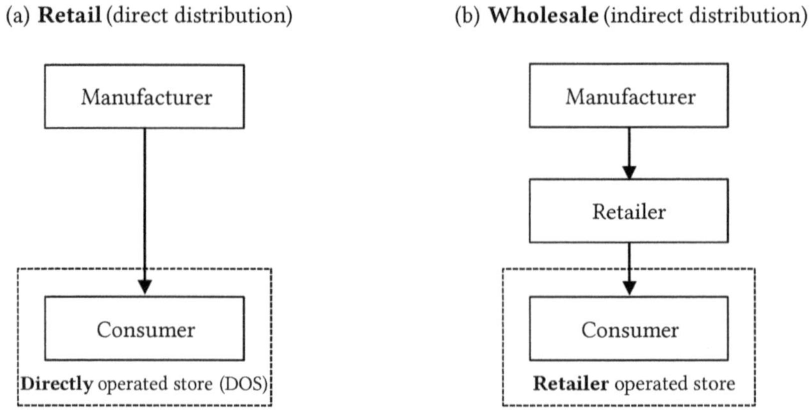

→ flow of merchandise
Source: author

Retailization. In luxury, manufacturers increasingly aim at a **low channel length**, i.e. as few tiers of intermediaries as possible, ideally none (Cervellon & Coudriet, 2013, p. 870; Quintavalle, 2012, p. 88). More specifically, over the past decade we can observe an ongoing "**retailization**" of the luxury goods market, i.e. an ongoing distribution-strategic shift of manufacturers towards directly operated store formats (Bain & Company, 2014, p. 17). As shown Figure 28(a), the share of retail-generated (as opposed to wholesale-generated) sales in the worldwide personal luxury goods market has continuously increased over the past years by annually 11 per cent from 20 per cent in 2006 up to 32 per cent in 2014 (Bain & Company & Fondazione Altagamma, 2008, p. 9, 2014, p. 16).

The growth of retail-generated sales is accounted for by both organic sales growth and an increasing number of new store openings of around 500 stores in 2014 only (Bain & Company, 2014, p. 18). Between 2000 and 2009/10 luxury goods manufacturers like Bulgari (from 126 to 273 stores), Gucci (from 143 to 283 stores) or Tiffany & Co. (from 119 to 220 stores) have considerably expanded their distribution networks (Chevalier & Gutsatz, 2012, p. 25). In addition to freestanding monobrand stores, we may also observe an increasing retailization of traditional wholesale formats like department stores (see Figure 28(b); Bain & Company, 2014, p. 17). For example, luxury goods manufacturers rent a selling area inside a department store and directly operate monobrand concession stores (store formats will be described in more detail in Chapter 3.4.3.1 below).

Figure 28 – Share of retail versus wholesale.

Share of retail- versus wholesale-generated personal luxury goods sales worldwide

(a) trend, in EUR bn from 2006 to 2014 (b) by store format, in EUR bn in 2014

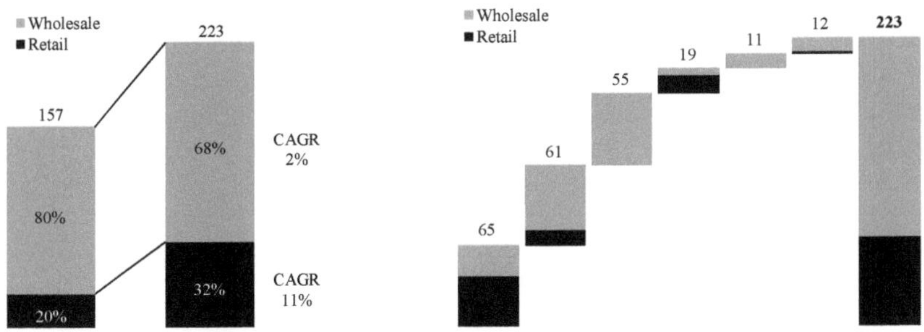

Note: numbers on top of bars indicate worldwide personal luxury goods sales in EUR billion
Source: Bain & Company & Fondazione Altagamma, 2008, p. 9, 2014, p. 16

Benefits of retail. Reasons for the ongoing retailization are manifold. To the manufacturer, the retail model provides several advantages over wholesale distribution including: margin, control, and client contact (Chevalier & Mazzalovo, 2008, p. 349; Manninger, 2012, pp. 244–246; Som & Blanckaert, 2015, p. 310). First of all, direct distribution leaves the manufacturer with a **higher margin** since the margin is not shared with an intermediary. As illustrated in Figure 29, the Keylens Research Center reports a positive correlation between the percentage share of sales generated through directly operated stores and the firm's EBIT margin. This is also reflected in a higher return on investment reported for manufacturers with a higher share of retail sales (Fondazione Altagamma & SDA Bocconi, 2014, p. 17).

Second, for manufacturers a vertical forward integration implies being in **full control** over brand communication, prices, assortment and service levels. Here, we recall the statement by Bernard Arnault, Chairman and CEO at LVMH: "If you control your distribution, you control your image" (Chevalier & Gutsatz, 2012, p. 15). Similarly, Sebastian Suhl, former Chief Operating Officer at Prada, argues: "We can't control what department stores do to wholesale merchandise" (Dodes & Passariello, 2011). By integrating downstream functions like distribution and store operations, luxury goods manufacturers gain control and flexibility.

Figure 29 – Retail sales and EBIT margin.

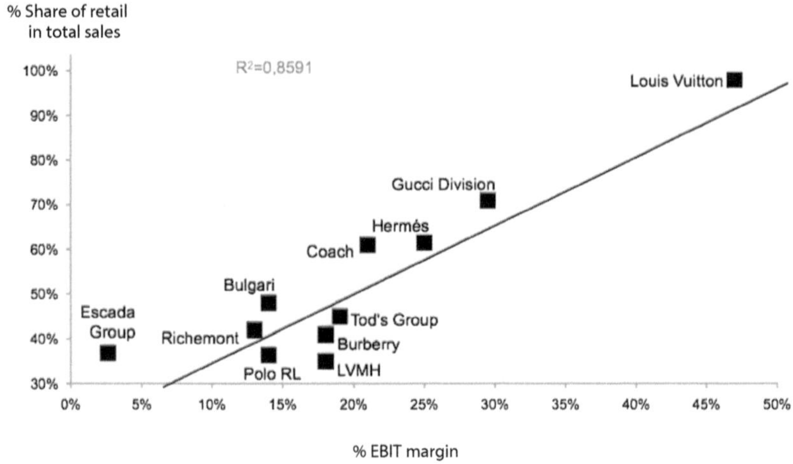

Source: Keylens Research Center 2008 (cited in Manninger, 2012, p. 245)

Finally, through own stores luxury goods manufacturers meet clients face-to-face. They deliver to and interact with end consumers, not wholesalers or retail partners. **Direct client contact** may provide the manufacturer with valuable insights into clients' needs, preferences, and shopping behaviour. Yet, in order to fully leverage the potential of direct client contact luxury goods manufacturers need to systematically collect, process, and analyse up-to-date client data in a customer relationship management database, which is integrated across all different store formats.

Benefits of wholesale. Given its advantages the retail model (direct distribution) is often considered as the *ideal* model (Chevalier & Mazzalovo, 2012, p. 282). Yet, there are common exceptions from this *ideal* and capital-intensive distribution model. After all, sales must generate a contribution margin in excess of the enormous fixed costs incurred by a directly operated store in terms of rent and qualified personnel. Luxury goods manufacturers benefit from a wholesale distribution model (indirect distribution) in multiple ways: first of all, wholesale distribution is **less capital-intensive** since the retail partner bears the cost of rent, personnel, and merchandise (Som & Blanckaert, 2015, p. 310). Second, if the client base is relatively large and diffuse, e.g., in categories like wine & spirits and perfume & cosmetics, selling through intermediaries **increases efficiency** and reduces complexity (Hollensen & Opresnik, 2010, p. 234; Homburg et al., 2013, p. 202). Third, particularly to small- and medium-sized luxury goods manufacturers wholesale distribution helps to geographically **expand the business**

and generate a critical level of sales volume needed to cover fixed costs. For a manufacturer to successfully sell through direct retail stores, its brand awareness must be sufficiently high among target clients and its product assortment must be sufficiently broad to generate a critical level of sales.

Conclusion. Retail and wholesale models differently address supply-oriented, economic, and managerial objectives of luxury distribution. On the one hand, directly operated store formats like flagships, monobrand stores, or concession stores yield higher shares of margin and a maximum of control to the manufacturer while being costly and risky. On the other hand, at the expense of margin, control, and exclusiveness selling wholesale to multibrand specialty stores, department stores, or duty-free stores comes at no capital investments, lower costs, secured upfront orders, and typically allows a relatively faster and broader market coverage to generate a sufficient level of sales.

Most luxury goods manufacturers pursue a **pyramidal distribution strategy** consisting of **both retail and wholesale** distribution (see Figure 30; Manninger, 2012, p. 249; Nueno & Quelch, 1998, p. 67; Quintavalle, 2012, p. 88): depending on firm size, product category, and the targeted geographic market, a luxury goods manufacturer may have one or few flagship stores, operate or franchise some monobrand stores and concession stores, and additionally sell wholesale to several retail partners. Ultimately, for each location the mode of distribution should be considered as a separate business case that needs to be economically viable.

The decision ‚retail versus wholesale' also varies depending on the product category. For example, wholesale dominates in product categories like perfume & cosmetics, wine & spirits, and large parts of the watch industry. With few exceptions like Guerlain's flagship boutique in 68 Champs-Elysées boutique in Paris, **perfumes & cosmetics** are primarily sold through multibrand specialty retailers (e.g., Sephora, Douglas), department stores (e.g., KaDeWe, Harrod's, Les Printemps, or Nordstrom), duty-free formats (e.g., DFS, Dufry, Lagardère Services, Heinemann) and online retailers (e.g., flaconi.de).

Similarly, **wine & spirits** are commonly distributed via agents and wholesale partners that resell the cases to off-trade (e.g., supermarkets, duty-free shops) or on-trade retail partners (e.g., restaurants, hotels, clubs). Considering the relatively large and diffused network of point of sales directly serving each retail store would be a complex and inefficient task (Homburg et al., 2013, p. 202).

Finally, large parts of the luxury **watch business** are made wholesale (Chevalier & Mazzalovo, 2012, p. 84). Luxury watches are commonly sold through multibrand specialty stores like Bucherer, Tourbillon Boutiques, PISA or Wempe. One of the rare exceptions refers to the Swatch-owned watchmaker Breguet that operates 32 monobrand boutiques in prestigious locations like London's New Bond Street, Milan's Via Monte Napoleone, Paris' Place Vendôme and New York's Fifth Avenue in addition to its network of retail partners like Bucherer and Wempe (Breguet.com, 2015).

Figure 30 – Pyramidal distribution strategy.

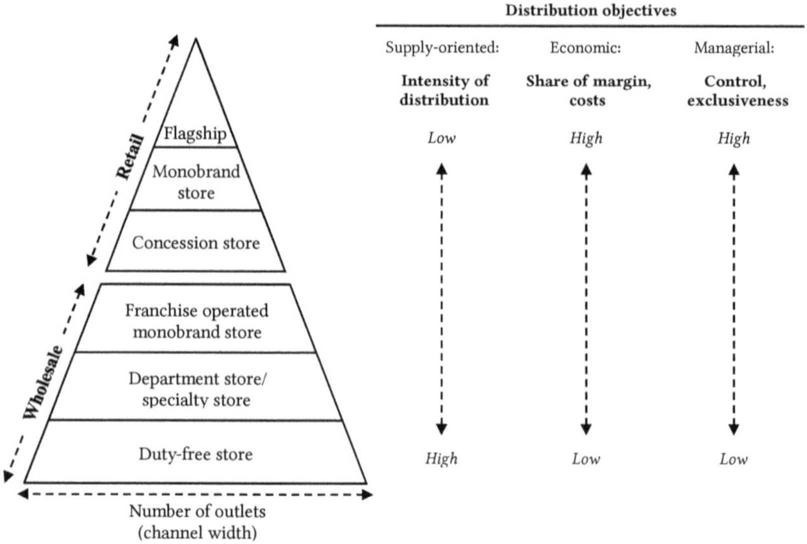

Source: adapted from Manninger (2012, p. 249), Nueno & Quelch (1998, p. 67), Som & Blanckaert (2015, p. 310)

3.4.2.3 Channel width: selective and exclusive distribution

In addition to the number of tiers of intermediaries (channel length) manufacturers need to decide on the **number of intermediaries per tier** (channel width) within a given wholesale distribution channel (Homburg et al., 2013, p. 205; Kotler & Armstrong, 2012, p. 352). Specifically, we are interested in the number of intermediaries at the most downstream level of the distribution channel, i.e. the retail stores or point of sales where a manufacturer's merchandise is sold to end consumers. This number is referred to as **distribution intensity** (Frazier & Lassar, 1996, p. 39). As illustrated in Figure 31, we generally differentiate between three different levels of the distribution intensity continuum: intensive, selective, and exclusive distribution (Frazier & Lassar, 1996, p. 39; Hollensen & Opresnik, 2010, pp. 241–242; Kotler & Armstrong, 2012, pp. 352–353).

Non-luxury manufacturers of convenience goods typically pursue an **intensive distribution** strategy to serve more consumers more frequently. Intensive distribution is about placing a manufacturer's products in as many points of sale as possible (see Figure 31(a); Kotler & Armstrong, 2012, p. 351). It aims at providing a maximum of product availability, brand exposure, and shopping convenience in order to skim as much sales potential as possible (Hollensen & Opresnik, 2010, p. 242). In its extreme, intensive distribution results in the nearly ubiquitous availability of a manufacturer's product. Coca- Cola's carbonated soft drinks, for example, are available wherever

Figure 31 – Channel width: intensive, selective, and exclusive distribution.

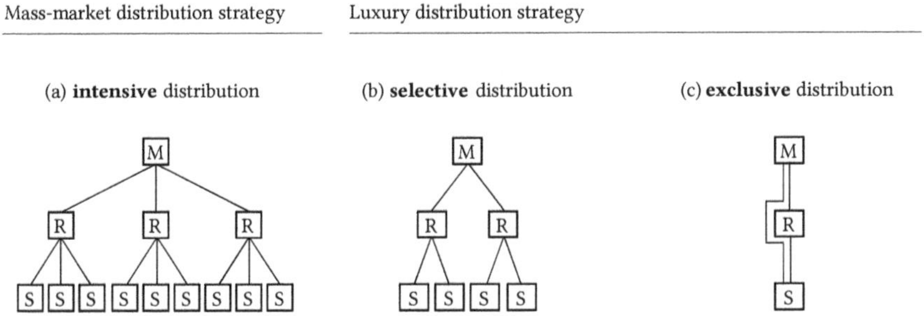

M = manufacturer; R = retailer; S = store/point of sale; exemplary illustration
Source: author

consumers might become thirsty, i.e. both on-trade like in restaurants, hotels, clubs, or in airplanes and off-trade like in supermarkets, gas stations, or vendor machines.

In contrast, as ubiquity is the opposite of exclusiveness luxury goods manufacturers pursue a selective or exclusive distribution strategy intended to **limit the accessibility** of their goods to few, carefully selected points of sale (Frontier Economics & ECCIA, 2012, p. 12; Keller, 2009, p. 292). **Selective distribution** refers to selling through "more than one, but fewer than all" stores within a given geographical area (see Figure 31; Kotler & Armstrong, 2012, p. 353). For example, while mass-market cosmetics and skincare products are available in nearly any supermarket or drugstore across the urban area of a larger city, its luxury counterparts are only available in few selected department stores (e.g., Breuninger) and specialty stores (e.g., Sephora, Douglas), which are typically located in the city centre. The limited set of retail partners is carefully selected based on qualitative criteria like location, quality of merchandise, service level etc. (Bruhn, 2014, p. 260; Meffert et al., 2008, p. 573). Advantages of a selective distribution include a moderate market coverage (products are sufficiently available to generate sales, but not over-diffused), higher levels of control over brand communication, service, and price levels, and less complexity than intensive distribution.

Exclusive distribution refers to an extreme form of selective distribution following which a product is sold at only one store within a given geographic area only, which may be either directly operated by the manufacturer or retailer-operated (see Figure 31(c); Hollensen & Opresnik, 2010, p. 242). The selection of retailers is not only qualitative (e.g., location, assortment, service level) but also quantitative (Bruhn, 2014, p. 260; Meffert et al., 2008, p. 573). In the extreme form, the quantitative limitation leaves the retailer in a monopoly position in a given city or area. In Zurich, for example, products of Hermès, Loro Piana, and Louis Vuitton are available only at the respective monobrand store all of which are located in the prestigious Bahnhofstrasse (Hermes.com, 2015b; Loropiana.com, 2015; Louisvuitton.com, 2015a). Similarly in Berlin, Aston Martin, Ferrari and Rolls-Royce cars are available at only one authorized dealer each all of which are located on Hindenburgdamm while Audi and BMW cars can be bought at eight and six dealers, respectively (Astonmartin.com, 2015; Audi.de, 2015; BMW.de, 2015; Ferrari.com, 2015; Rolls-roycemotorcars.com, 2015a).

In luxury, we may conclude that manufacturers typically pursue **a mix of both** levels of distribution intensity depending on the geographic area targeted. For example, while the fine jewellery by Van Cleef & Arpels is available in Geneva at one monobrand store only (exclusive distribution), it can be found in Paris at five point of sales including a flagship store, two monobrand stores, and at the department stores Le Printemps and Les Galeries Lafayette (selective distribution; Vancleefarpels.com, 2015c). The tendency towards either a selective or more exclusive distribution also varies depending on the product category concerned. We observe that **non-durable** luxury goods manufactures like perfume & cosmetics and wine & spirits mainly follow a selective distribution strategy while **durable** luxury goods manufacturers like in cars, fashion, furniture, jewellery or yachts rather follow an exclusive distribution strategy.

3.4.3 Store-level decisions

Having discussed different channel designs in terms of number of tiers of intermediaries (channel length) and number of intermediaries per tier (channel width), we now address decisions on the store-level. Store-level decisions include location, store format, store atmosphe, merchandising, and service level. Depending on the channel length, these decisions are implemented by either the manufacturer itself (in case of direct distribution) or the independent retailer according to bilateral agreements with the manufacturer (in case of wholesale distribution). In following, we discuss the major store-level decisions in more detail.

3.4.3.1 Location

According to a common proverb there are three critical success factors in stationary retailing: "location, location, and location" (Kotler & Armstrong, 2012, p. 387). Once decided on the geographic market to be served (i.e. country, region, and city) manufacturers must decide on a concrete location (i.e. district, street) that is accessible to the target clientele, in line with luxury brand's image and financial resources (Kotler & Armstrong, 2012, p. 387; Zentes et al., 2011, p. 203). Depending on the channel length, the manufacturer selects a site for a directly operated store (retail) or a retail partner based on its concrete location (wholesale).

In general, locations for non-luxury store formats like supermarkets, drugstores, DIY stores, or bakeries are typically selected based on multiple criteria including customers (e.g., population, income, housing density), competitors (e.g., location, assortment, price-level), site accessibility (e.g., visibility, pedestrian or traffic flows), and costs (e.g., purchase price, rent, operating cost; Zentes et al., 2011, p. 211). In essence, conventional retailing is about profitably serving places with customer needs not yet or insufficiently met by competitors.

In luxury, differently branded stores next to each other do not compete, but rather complement each other (Quintavalle, 2012, p. 79). Luxury site selection is primarily based on the **prestige factor** of a location (Okonkwo, 2007, p. 78; Quintavalle, 2012, p. 79). This implies that, in luxury, sites are selected because, not despite of competitors being located nearby (Berthon et al., 2009, p. 54; Chevalier & Mazzalovo, 2012, p. 277). An excellent example of this specificity in luxury retailing refers to the Place Vendôme. This prestigious location at the heart of Paris is a hotspot for haute joaillerie and haute horlogerie brands like Boucheron, Cartier, Chaumet, Van Cleef & Arpels, Bulgari, Chopard, Piaget, Patek Philippe, and Breguet.

Prestigious sites are typically located in the **city centre** of major cities like London, New York, or Paris (see Figure 32), in smaller, yet prestigious **tourist destinations** like Saint Tropez or Sylt, or at high-traffic **airports**. All these locations account for high tourist traffic, which is important considering that the personal luxury goods market increasingly depends on tourist spending, e.g., up to 50 per cent of sales in Europe (Bain & Company & Fondazione Altagamma, 2014, p. 21).

The importance of being present in the city's prime location has been emphasized by a managing director of a luxury fashion brand (Moore et al., 2010, p. 149):

> *"In London, we could not secure a shop on Old Bond Street so we leased a site nearby. But we may as well have been on the moon. I cannot emphasise enough the* ***importance of the address*** *in this business. We learned to our cost the impact of getting that address wrong."*

Given the importance of the prestige factor, luxury goods manufacturers would **rather have a small boutique in prestige location** than having a large store in second-choice location (Chevalier & Mazzalovo, 2012, p. 277; Kapferer & Bastien, 2009a, p. 271; Quintavalle, 2012, p. 79). In Europe, the average annual rent per square metre for those prestige locations ranges from under EUR 3,000 like Amsterdam's P.C. Hooftstraat, Berlin's Kurfürstendamm, Brussels' Avenue Louise, or Madrid's Calle Serano up to more than EUR 6,000 like London's New Bond Street, Milan's Via Monte Napoleone, Moscow's Stoleshinkov Lane, Paris' Avenue Montaigne, or Zurich's Bahnhofstrasse (Jones Lang LaSalle, 2011, p. 4). Certainly, smaller luxury goods manufacturers may not financially afford being present in all these prestige locations. Instead of prestige locations in major city centres, smaller luxury goods manufacturers may select smaller, yet **prestigious tourist destinations**. The German knitwear specialist Iris von Arnim, for example, operates its flagship store at the Strönwai Street in Kampen, a prestigious tourist destination on the Frisian Island of Sylt, Germany. The flagship store is not only highly visible for affluent tourists looking for cozy knitwear on the windy island, but also in finest company of other luxury stores like Bottega Veneta, Brunello Cucinelli, Burberry, Chopard, Louis Vuitton, Tod's, and Wempe. Given that the site selection represents a long-term capital commitment to both large and small luxury goods manufacturers the final site selection should be a **top-management decision** (Kapferer & Bastien, 2009a, p. 202).

Figure 32 – Prestige locations worldwide.

Source: author

3.4.3.2 Store format

Selecting a store format is a core decision in distribution management. A store format is defined as "a specific configuration of the retail marketing mix" (Zentes, Morschett, & Schramm-Klein, 2011, p. 3). Hence, store formats differ in multiple economic (share of margin, costs) and managerial aspects (store size, location, merchandise, store atmosphere, and service levels; Müller-Hagedorn, 2002, p. 70; Sullivan & Adock, 2002, p. 40; Zentes et al., 2011, p. 3). As shown in Figure 33, we may differentiate between retail and wholesale formats (compare Chapter 3.4.2.2) as well as between offline (also stationary or brick-and-mortar stores) and online stores (also e-commerce). Throughout this chapter we focus on offline store formats, which will be described in the following. Online store formats will be addressed separately in Chapter 4.5.

Monobrand store. When thinking about luxury retailing what typically first comes to mind are monobrand stores of well-known luxury brands located in the world's major city centres, tourist destinations or airports. The term *monobrand* indicates that the store carries products of one single brand only. Typically, a monobrand store is a **medium-sized**, freestanding outlet on a rented or owned property with direct access to and **high visibility** from the street, which stocks the full entry and **core range** of a brand (Chevalier & Gutsatz, 2012, pp. 35 & 38; Chevalier & Mazzalovo, 2012, p. 261). The monobrand store format provides several managerial advantages including preserving the brand's **exclusiveness**, highest levels of **control** over brand communication, stockings, prices, and services levels, as well as the **direct interaction** with the end consumer (Kapferer & Bastien, 2009a, p. 204; Quintavalle, 2012, p. 89; Som & Blanckaert, 2015, p. 310). Financially, both

Figure 33 – Luxury store formats.

	Offline 95 %	**Online** 5 %
Retail (direct distribution) **32 %**	▪ Monobrand store (directly operated) ▪ Flagship store ▪ Concession store ▪ Outlet store	▪ Monobrand online stores (integrated in or separate from brand website)
Wholesale (indirect distribution) **68 %**	▪ Monobrand store (franchise operated) ▪ Department stores ▪ Specialty stores ▪ Duty-free stores	▪ Online department stores ▪ Online specialty stores ▪ Multibrand online outlets

higher share of margin, higher levels of control, exclusiveness, direct client contact

↕

market coverage, lower cost and risks

Note: percentages indicate relative share of worldwide personal luxury goods market sales 2014
Source: adapted from Chevalier & Gutsatz (2012, p. 35), Chevalier & Mazzalovo (2012, p. 261), Kapferer & Bastien (2009a, pp. 204–206), Manninger (2012, p. 244), Quintavalle (2012, p. 88), Som & Blanckaert (2015, p. 310); data from Bain & Company & Fondazione Altagamma (2014, p. 16)

share of margin and capital requirements for cost of rent and qualified personnel are highest given that the manufacturer directly operates the monobrand store (compare Chapter 3.4.2.2; Som & Blanckaert, 2015, p. 310).

In contrast, instead of the manufacturer itself a **franchise partner** may be given the privilege to operate a monobrand store according to mutually specified regulations and in exchange for sales royalties of around 3 to 5 per cent of net sales (Chevalier & Gutsatz, 2012, p. 40; Quintavalle, 2012, p. 91). In this case, the monobrand store still provides full brand exclusiveness (as the brand's product range is offered only) as well as relatively high levels of control and access to client information depending on the mutual agreements. For the consumer, there should be no recognizable difference between a directly operated and a franchise operated monobrand store (Chevalier & Gutsatz, 2012, p. 41). While realizing a relatively lower share of margin, the manufacturer benefits from a franchise operated store in terms of a fast geographic market expansion without any investment or fixed cost (Chevalier & Gutsatz, 2012, p. 41; Quintavalle, 2012, p. 91).

Flagship store. The flagship store represents the **largest** and most impressive monobrand store format (Chevalier & Mazzalovo, 2012, p. 261; Som & Blanckaert, 2015, p. 312). The colossal flagship stores are typically located in a luxury brand's country- and place-of-origin or the world's most **prestigious locations** (Chevalier & Mazzalovo, 2012, p. 261; Quintavalle, 2012, p. 88). The haute joaillerie brand Van Cleef & Arpels, for example, operates flagship stores both at its place-of-origin, i.e. the Place Vendôme at the heart of Paris, and in prestigious locations like at New York's Fifth Avenue or Tokyo's Ginza (Vancleefarpels.com, 2015c). The assortment of a flagship store covers a luxury brand's **full product range**, including high-end and limited collections (Manlow & Nobbs, 2013, p. 59; Quintavalle, 2012, pp. 88–89; Som & Blanckaert, 2015, p. 312). **Enormous store sizes** provide highest possible site visibility. Louis Vuitton's Parisian flagship store, for example, counts a total of 1,800 square metres across seven storeys (Okonkwo, 2007, p. 87).

Given their exorbitant size in expensive locations, flagship store are **rarely profitable**, i.e. profitability per square metre is inferior as compared to monobrand stores or even negative (Chevalier & Gutsatz, 2012, p. 35; Paton, 2012; Quintavalle, 2012, p. 89). The objective of operating a flagship store is primarily strategic rather than economic. It aims at "something other than profit generation" (Moore, Doherty, & Doyle, 2010, p. 150). A flagship store is intended to communicate the brand's heritage, expertise, and creativity rather than solely making profits (Kozinets et al., 2002, p. 17; Manlow & Nobbs, 2013, p. 51). It is designed to create the "**ultimate luxury experience**" (Som & Blanckaert, 2015, p. 312). And indeed, empirical research shows that a flagship store increases the brand experience as compared to a similar monobrand store (Dolbec & Chebat, 2013, p. 464). Given its strategic importance and poor economic efficiency a flagship store is typically owned and directly operated by the luxury goods manufacturer (Kozinets et al., 2002, p. 17; Moore et al., 2010, p. 150).

Concession store. In a concession-based model the concessionaire, i.e. the brand-owning manufacturer, rents a selling area, which is **located inside a department store**, clearly separated from other merchandise, and **directly operated** by the manufacturer (Ausschuss für Definitionen aus Handel und Distribution, 2009, pp. 60–61, cited in Zentes et al., 2011, p. 101). The concession-based model is sometimes also referred to as a "store-within-a-store" model (Dodes & Passariello, 2011; Jerath & Zang, 2010, p. 748; Williams, 2015, p. 403), which is not to be confused with the traditional shop-in-shop model. Other than in a shop-in-shop agreement, in a concession-based model the brand-owning manufacturer (e.g., Louis Vuitton) – not the retailer (e.g., KaDeWe) – owns the merchandise, bears the risk of selling it, educates and employs the service personnel, and – in the purest form – controls the cash register (Chiu, 2014; Dodes & Passariello, 2011; Grüger, 2007, pp. 47–55; Probe, 2007, p. 62; Williams, 2015, p. 403). The manufacturer benefits from the location and the high pedestrian traffic generated by the department store's established name and high-quality offering, while being in full control over the exclusive selling area.

In exchange for providing the selling area and infrastructure (e.g., electricity, storage) and according to the individual contractual agreements, the lessor (i.e. the department store) typically receives both a fixed flat rate as well as a sales-related **concession fee** (Chiu, 2014; Jerath & Zang, 2010, p. 750; Zentes et al., 2011, p. 62). This concession fee is assumed to be at around **20 to 30 per cent of sales** (Dodes & Passariello, 2011; Williams, 2015, p. 403). In essence, the concession store format is highly similar to conventional directly operated monobrand stores (Manninger, 2012, p. 247) with the two key differences being (1) location, i.e. a concession store is located inside a department store while a directly operated store is free-standing, and (2) share of margin, i.e. margin is shared with department store operator in a concession-based model (sales-related concession fee) while for directly operated stores the manufacturer retains the full margin.

Like for stand-alone monobrand and falgship stores, the concession-based model serves as a mean of **vertical forward integration** enabling the brand-owning manufacturer to control downstream functions, i.e. distribution and the point of sale (Grüger, 2007, pp. 53–54). While to the general shopper a manufacturer-operated concession store can look very similar to a retailer-operated shop-in-shop, the concession-based model (like monobrand and flagship stores) provides several advantages to the manufacturer: (1) keeping **control** over store atmosphere, brand communication, merchandise, and, particularly, prices (recall the need for a rare-to-no-discount policy when pricing luxury goods; see Chapter 3.2.4), (2) increasing in-store **service** level as the sales staff is employed and educated by the manufacturer, (3) increasing **profitability** as the manufacturer does not sell the merchandise wholesale to the department store and thus retains a large share of margin, and (4) the manufacturer enjoys direct **client contact** (Chiu, 2014; Grüger, 2007, p. 188; Williams, 2015, p. 403).

Louis Vuitton is often considered as the most promiment, leading example of operating concession stores (Chiu, 2014). For example, since 2013 Louis Vuitton operates one of the biggest ever concession stores, the Louis Vuitton Townhouse, which is located inside the prestigious Selfridge's department store, Oxford Street, London, which spans around 10,000 square foot over three storeys and features a separated elevator and entrance from Oxford Street (Dacre, 2013). Other brands like the Italian fashion labels Gucci and Prada operate concessions stores, for example, on the ground floor Luxury Boulevard of Berlin's prestigious department store KaDeWe in Germany (Kadewe.de, 2015) or in some of Sak's stores in the US (Dodes & Passariello, 2011).

Factory outlet. The factory outlet is referred to as an **off-price** monobrand store format. A brand's factory outlet store is typically located **outside expensive city centres** either isolated at the premises of production or integrated in a factory outlet centre (Chevalier & Gutsatz, 2012, p. 56; Zentes et al., 2011, p. 97). Its assortment primarily covers **overstock**, out-of-season, and second-choice items sold at discount prices ranging from 30 to 70 per cent of original retail prices (Ahlert & Kenning, 2007, p. 340; Chevalier & Gutsatz, 2012, pp. 56–57; Quintavalle, 2012, p. 89). While the concept of a factory outlet as an off-price store format actually contradicts the need for price stability of luxury goods (compare Chapter 3.2), it has become increasingly popular particularly among luxury **fashion** manufacturers given the high seasonality of their collections. For example, luxury fashion brands like Bottega Veneta, Chloé, Dior, Fendi, Gucci, Loro Piana, Prada and others operate stores at Bicester Village, a factory outlet centre located between London and Oxford, which is part of the collection of *Chic Outlet Shopping* villages operated by Value Retail Group (Bicestervillage.com, 2015).

The major advantage of operating a factory outlet is clearing stock at controlled discount prices and **low rental cost**. In addition, the outlet may also serve as a **controlled environment** used to experiment with new product or store concepts at low risk (Chevalier & Gutsatz, 2012, p. 56; Quintavalle, 2012, p. 90). The major drawback of factory outlet stores refers to their **lack of luxury appeal**: discount prices, locations distant to glamorous city centres, and the co-existence with mass-market brands like Nike, Mexx, or Adidas strongly contradicts with a brand's luxury appeal (Okonkwo, 2007, p. 98). Hence, some luxury goods manufacturers, particularly those in the high-end segment, tend not to sell via factory outlet stores and if they do, they avoid publicly communicating the existence and location of such a factory outlet (Chevalier & Gutsatz, 2012, p. 57; Okonkwo, 2007, p. 98).

Factory outlet, monobrand, flagship, and shop-in-shop stores are all monobrand store formats (i.e. carry products of one single brand only) controlled by the manufacturer through either direct management or franchise systems. In the following, we discuss store formats whose assortment covers multiple brands and that are not controlled by the manufacturer but a trusted retail partner. In particular, the department store, multibrand specialty store, and duty-free store formats are described (see Figure 33).

Department store. The department store is a **large** store format characterized by its wide and deep assortment, i.e. it carries **multiple product categories** and multiple brands within each product category "under one roof" (Kotler & Armstrong, 2012, p. 375; Zentes et al., 2011, p. 52). The term department store refers to the different departments within the store built around different product categories like women's and men's ready-to-wear, accessories, perfume & cosmetics, jewellery & watches, home design, wine & spirits, and gourmet food. Hence, the department store is referred to as a "one-stop" shop carrying nearly anything a shopper needs (Zentes et al., 2011, p. 53). Well-known examples of high-end department stores include Harrods and Selfridge's in London, Le Bon Marché and Les Galeries Lafayette in Paris, the KaDeWe in Berlin, Nordstrom, Neiman Marcus and Saks Fifth Avenue in the US.

The department store typically owns the merchandise and controls prices, assortment, service levels, and how the brand is communicated. To the manufacturer selling wholesale to a department store implies the following downsides: a relatively lower share of **margin,** low levels of **control** over prices, assortment, service and promotional activities, a lack of **exclusiveness** given the multibrand environment, as well as the lack of direct **client contact** (Chevalier & Gutsatz, 2012, pp. 20 & 35; Som & Blanckaert, 2015, p. 310). Recall the statement by Sebastian Suhl, former Chief Operating Officer at Prada: "We can't control what department stores do to wholesale merchandise," (Dodes & Passariello, 2011).

Yet at the same time, by selling wholesale to a department store the manufacturer benefits from **low costs** involved (no cost of rent, personnel, or inventory), guaranteed **upfront orders** (the department store owns the merchandise), and the established **location, name,** and **visitor traffic** provided by the department store (Chevalier & Gutsatz, 2012, pp. 24 & 35; Som & Blanckaert, 2015, p. 310).

While the ultimate control over prices, assortment, and service rests with the retailer, the manufacturer may typically influence the way its branded merchandise is presented and communicated in-store according to mutual agreements with the retailer. In particular, the manufacturer may be given a specified selling area (i.e. shop-in-shop or a corner), which is separated from the merchandise of competing brands. To the manufacturer both the shop-in-shop and the corner allow for a differentiated, identifiable design and product display. Both concepts mainly differ by size and format: the shop-in-shop is a relatively larger selling area clearly separated by three or more walls while the corner is somewhat smaller and more open selling area that still allows for differentiating the brand from other merchandise.

Overall, to the manufacturer selling wholesale through a department store (as opposed to direct retail) involves relatively lower cost and risks while benefiting from the established location, name, and visitor traffic provided by the retail partner (Chevalier & Gutsatz, 2012, pp. 24 & 35; Som & Blanckaert, 2015, p. 310). Still, given the non-exclusive, multibrand environment, the lack of control and direct client contact, department stores should be carefully selected based on qualitative criteria including an location and brand name, quality of assortment, luxury-price levels, store atmosphere, and service levels (Quintavalle, 2012, p. 90; Zentes et al., 2011, p. 53).

Specialty store. The specialty store format is relatively smaller than a department store and characterized by a narrow, but deep assortment (i.e. **few product categories** with a broad **variety** within each category) as well as a **high price** and **service** level (Chevalier & Gutsatz, 2012, p. 46; Quintavalle, 2012, p. 90; Zentes et al., 2011, p. 50). Category specializations range from perfume & cosmetics (e.g., Sephora, Douglas), jewellery & watches (e.g., Bucherer, Wempe), to furniture (e.g., Cairo, designfunktion) and tableware & home design (e.g., individual specialty stores like Franzen at the prestigious Königsallee, Düsseldorf, carrying products of Baccarat, Christophle, Robbe Berking, or Prozellan Manufaktur Nymphenburg).

Like for department stores, the specialty store operator orders a specified, rather limited product range from the manufacturer upfront (e.g., at a trade fair), covers the cost of rent, inventory, and staff, and ultimately controls price, merchandise, service level, and promotional activities (Chevalier & Gutsatz, 2012, p. 35; Som & Blanckaert, 2015, p. 316). Hence, advantages and downsides of selling multibrand specialty store are very similar to that of selling through high-end department stores: the benefits of **no operating costs, secured upfront orders**, and the retailer's **established location** and name come at the cost of lower levels of **margin and exclusiveness** as well as a **lack of control and client contact** vis-à-vis directly operated monobrand store formats (Kapferer & Bastien, 2009a, p. 206; Som & Blanckaert, 2015, p. 310). Again, the lack of control requires a meticulous selection of multibrand specialty retailers based on qualitative criteria including location, quality of assortment, price levels, store atmosphere, and service levels (Quintavalle, 2012, p. 90; Zentes et al., 2011, p. 53).

Duty-free store. Duty-free stores refer to a special type of multibrand retail stores in that they are typically located inside the transit area of airports, on board of cruise ships or in few exceptional cases on land like in Waikiki, Seoul, or Okinawa Island (Quintavalle, 2012, p. 91; Som & Blanckaert, 2015, pp. 307 & 324). International, often affluent travellers spend their time waiting for arrival or departure with browsing product categories like perfume & cosmetics, wine & spirits, leather goods & accessories, or eyewear. For product categories like wine & spirits or perfumes duty-free sales account for about 20 to 30 per cent of total worldwide sales (Chevalier & Gutsatz, 2012, p. 58; Chevalier & Mazzalovo, 2012, p. 70). Major duty-free operators include LVMH-owned DFS Group (Duty-Free Shoppers), Dufry, Lagardère Services, and Heinemann.

Manufacturers benefit from strong volume sales and brand visibility at relatively low financial risks (Chevalier & Mazzalovo, 2012, p. 88; Som & Blanckaert, 2015, p. 326). Like for other multibrand store formats, the downsides of selling via multibrand duty-free shops include lower levels of margin and exclusiveness as well as a lack of client contact and control over prices, merchandise, service level, and promotional activities (Kapferer & Bastien, 2009a, p. 206; Som & Blanckaert, 2015, p. 310).

3.4.3.3 Store atmosphere

In luxury more than in other segments the retail outlet serves as a powerful mean of brand communication (Kapferer & Bastien, 2009a, p. 198; Quintavalle, 2012, p. 78). More than merely making goods available for sale, the store becomes an ultimate expression of a luxury brand's sophistication, creativity, and good taste. A store's physical appearance becomes even more important considering that the retail store often represents the very first, physical contact a shopper has with the brand (Okonkwo, 2007, p. 81). Despite its sophistication, the retail outlet must not "show off" in a way that is intimidating and discourages shoppers from entering (Kapferer & Bastien, 2009a, p. 199; Okonkwo, 2007, p. 82; Quintavalle, 2012, p. 79). The store atmosphere refers to the overall, multi-sensory impression a store evokes among shoppers (Okonkwo, 2007, p. 85). It is the result of the effective combination of store layout and aesthetic features like architecture, materials, colours, or lighting directed towards making shoppers aware of and enter the store, enjoy their stay, and finally making them buy (Okonkwo, 2007, p. 82).

Layout. In general, store layout design refers to arranging product shelves, counters, and corners in a way that guides shopper traffic flows and optimizes sales-space efficiency in terms of sales and profit per square metre (Okonkwo, 2007, p. 82; Zentes et al., 2011, p. 275). As illustrated in Figure 34, we generally differentiate between the grid layout and the free-form layout. The grid store layout is typically applied to supermarkets, drug stores, or DIY stores, not luxury retail outlets. It is characterized by having aisles and counters arranged in a highly structured, typically parallel manner that provides orientation to the shoppers and makes efficient use of sales space (Zentes et al., 2011, p. 275). In contrast, in a **freeform** store layout shelves and counters are arranged in an open, less structured manner that allows shoppers to **freely discover goods** and **experience the brand** (Zentes et al., 2011, p. 275). The freeform layout is typically applied to luxury store formats like monobrand boutiques, shop-in-shops, and multibrand specialty stores, as well as to single departments within larger high-end department stores (Okonkwo, 2007, p. 82; Quintavalle, 2012, p. 79).

Aesthetics. Like the luxury good as such (see Chapter 3.1.3.2), the retail outlet should create an atmosphere that appeals to all senses, i.e. visual, auditory, haptic, olfactory, and gustatory (Dion & Arnould, 2011, p. 503; Okonkwo, 2007, p. 85).

Figure 34 – Store layouts.

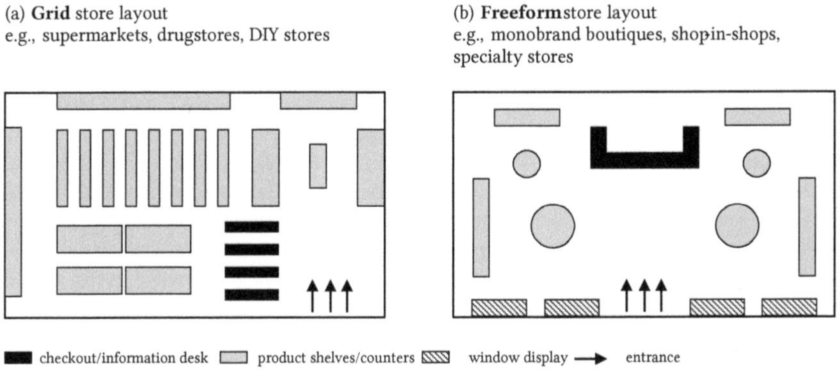

Note: store layouts are illustrative only.
Source: adapted from Levy & Weitz (2009, pp. 512–514), Okonkwo (2007, p. 82), and Zentes et al. (2011, p. 276)

The design of a luxury retail outlet should reflect the "**aesthetic ideology**" of the charismatic creator or creative director of the brand (Dion & Arnould, 2011, p. 502). A Chanel store, for example, is typically characterized by its elegant, yet puristic design and its black and white colour codes (Okonkwo, 2007, p. 83). In general, aesthetic features of a store include the site's architecture, the materials used, colours, sounds, and light exposure. While the **architecture** of conventional retail stores primarily serves functional purposes, luxury retail outlets typically have a delicate, visually appealing architecture with high windows and ceilings (Quintavalle, 2012, p. 80). Not rarely, these buildings have their own rich heritage like the historic, but sophisticatedly refurbished Broadway Guggenheim Building, which is now the home of Prada's New York flagship store (Moore et al., 2010, p. 149). The touch and feel of both the high-quality **materials** used and the products is essential for in-store shopping (Quintavalle, 2012, p. 80). The **colour tones** used in-store may vary from monochrome chic like for Chanel or Montblanc stores to warm, earth-coloured like for Hermès, Louis Vuitton or Patek Philippe stores (Okonkwo, 2007, p. 83). Furthermore, the in-store brand communication should be supported by adequate **sounds**. For example, while the typical sound in conventional fashion stores is a combination of pop music and noise of numerous co-shoppers, retail outlets of established luxury brands are rather characterized by pleasant silence or lower-volume and slow music (Okonkwo, 2007, p. 83). Finally, in-store **lighting** influences the visual perceptions of the store and product display in terms of size, colour tones, and product details (Okonkwo, 2007, p. 83; Quintavalle, 2012, p. 80).

3.4.3.4 Merchandising

The product assortment is the core of any store format (Zentes et al., 2011, p. 227). Making the right product available at the right time and place is the essence of retailing. The term merchandising refers to all decisions related to (1) defining the breadth and depth of **product assortment** (also merchandise-mix), and (2) how the merchandise is **displayed** and promoted **in-store** (American Marketing Association, 2015b; Zentes et al., 2011, p. 227). Depending on the distribution strategy, the manufacturer controls itself all merchandising activities for directly operated outlets (retail) or selects a retail partner based on the retailer's merchandising activities (wholesale).

Assortment. Deciding on the number of product categories (breadth of assortment) and stock keeping units (SKUs) within each product category (depth of assortment) the retail outlet should carry for a specific brand is closely related to the manufacturer's product-mix (see Figure 8 and Chapter 3.1.2.3) and the specific store format (see Figure 33 and Chapter 3.4.3.1). Naturally, in **monobrand** retail outlets the assortment is **broad and deep**, i.e. the store carries most of the brand's categories and SKUs. A brand's flagship store carries the full product range, including limited, high-end range items (Manlow & Nobbs, 2013, p. 59; Som & Blanckaert, 2015, p. 312). Monobrand stores and shop-in-shops (whether directly or franchise operated) typically offer the full core and entry range (Chevalier & Gutsatz, 2012, pp. 35; Quintavalle, 2012, p. 89). Depending on the width of the manufacturer's product-mix, however, monobrand stores can be further differentiated. For example, the fashion houses of Chanel and Dior each operate a monobrand store at Place Vendôme specifically dedicated to their jewellery lines "Chanel Fine Jewelry" and "Dior Joaillerie", respectively (Chanel.com, 2015b; Dior.com, 2015).

In **multibrand** outlets the breadth and depth of merchandise the manufacturer sells to the retailer very much depends on the format of the retail partner and its average **assortment quality within each category**. For example, the high-end department store KaDeWe in Berlin lists nearly all of Chanel's product lines from ready-to-wear, watches and jewellery to eyewear and fragrances (broad assortment) while there is only one corner of Chanel perfumes & cosmetics at mid-level department stores like Galeria Kaufhof or Karstadt (Chanel.com, 2015b). Ideally, each retail outlet is evaluated individually and separately for each product category in order to ensure that quality and price levels fit the brand's luxury appeal.

Product display. In addition to deciding on the breadth and depth of the product assortment, merchandising involves decisions on how to best present the merchandise in-store in order to generate sales (American Marketing Association, 2015b; Okonkwo, 2007, p. 91). In luxury, retailers face a trade-off between maximizing sales-space efficiency in terms of sales and profits per square metre and the generous use of space in order to present each single item as unique (Quintavalle, 2012, p. 81; Zentes et al., 2011, p. 384). Luxury retail outlets should avoid unnecessarily duplicating window and product displays or using idle space for in-store stocking (Quintavalle, 2012, p. 81). Rather, idle space serves as a signal of exclusiveness as a marketing director at a British fashion brand points (Moore et al., 2010, p. 148):

"Space, and what we call "the ***extravagant use of the empty space****", defines a luxury experience. By having commercially inactive space we signal exclusivity, luxury and an extravagance that is at the heart of luxury."*

To make each item stand out, the sales space of luxury retail outlets should be characterized by a **low product density** (Quintavalle, 2012, p. 81). Like in museums, the items sold are so precious that they need to be protected in voluminous glass cases with spotlights from different angels to make them glitter (Quintavalle, 2012, p. 81). Finally, **price ticketing** should be done as discreetly as possible (Kapferer & Bastien, 2009a, p. 195).

3.4.3.5 Service level

Exceptional service is inherent to luxury. In the context of product management we have discussed the scope of services added to the actual luxury good including delivery policy, guarantee policy, and client services like customization, gift-wrapping, product maintenance and spare parts supply (see Chapter 3.1.3.4). The service level defines the scope and quality of performing these services at the retail level. Scope refers to deciding on *who* performs the service, i.e. the store personnel (e.g., gift-wrapping) or the manufacturer (e.g., spare parts supply and product replacement in guarantee cases). More importantly from a consumer point of view, the service level defines the quality of interaction with the consumer.

Brand knowledge. First of all, as the frontline salesperson represents the primary, face-to-face communicator of the brand, she or he should be highly knowledgeable about the brand (Wieseke, Mauer, & Alavi, 2013, p. 362). Acoording to the WealthSurvey by the Luxury Institute (2012) among individuals with an average annual income of USD 310,000 and a reported wealth of USD 3.6 million, luxury shoppers consider brand and product knowledge as the **prime attribute of a "good" salesperson** across all luxury product categories. Another empirical study of 277 sales conversations reveals that providing brand information when personally selling luxury goods positively affects both perceived product value, purchase intention, and loyalty (Wieseke, Alavi, Habel, & Dörfer, 2013, p. 133). A salesperson's knowledge should cover the brand universe (e.g., heritage, anecdotes, iconic products), product details (e.g., material, finishing), aesthetics (e.g., design principles), and manufacturing details (e.g., techniques, processes, complications; Quintavalle, 2012, p. 105). The importance of a salesperson's brand knowledge is even elevated considering the increased availability of information provided by the Internet (Chevalier & Gutsatz, 2012, p. 75; Quintavalle, 2012, p. 105). Hence, the manufacturer should invest in regular and intensive trainings of its sales personnel (Wieseke, Mauer, et al., 2013, p. 362).

Courtesy. Second, a luxury salesperson should meet clients with respect and courtesy, not arrogance. Courtesy ranks among the **top three attributes** of a good salesperson in luxury according to the WealthSurvey by the Luxury Institute (2012). While the luxury brand as such respectfully dominates and educates its clients in terms of dictating good taste and serving as "sociological guide" (Kapferer & Bastien,

2009a, p. 67), the classy salesperson is charming and elegant, rather than arrogant or persistent (Kapferer & Bastien, 2009a, p. 197).

Yet, recent research identifies circumstances in which snobbish salesperson behaviour might actually turn out to have positive effects on shoppers. A series of laboratory experiments by Ward & Dahl (2014, pp. 595–604) shows that a "condescending" (versus a neutral) behaviour of a luxury salesperson may actually enhance brand attitude and willingness to pay among consumers if the individual aspires to the brand and the salesperson authentically represents the brand. This effect does not hold true for "regular luxury shoppers" or "if the salesperson doesn't match the brand", Dahl argues (Manriquez, 2014). More interestingly, the positive effect of snobbish salesperson behaviour is short-term only: two weeks after having been confronted with condescending salesperson behaviour the individual's attitude towards the brand turns negative (Ward & Dahl, 2014, p. 604).

Hence, from a **long-term perspective** luxury brand marketers should aim at courteous and respectful, rather than condescending or rude salesperson behaviour (Manriquez, 2014). Milton Pedraza, CEO of the Luxury Institute, confirms: "The biggest reason why a consumer won't come back isn't the product – it's a rude and inattentative salesperson" (Sabharwal, 2015). In the end, anyone who is interested in but cannot yet afford the brand's products might one day return as a loyal and affluent client (Kapferer & Bastien, 2009a, p. 194).

No pressure. Third, salespersons should support the client in his or her purchase decision, but never exert pressure towards closing the deal (Wieseke, Mauer, et al., 2013, p. 362). The salesperson assists the client in understanding why a luxury good is worth paying a premium price and reassures the client's decision rather than pushing him or her towards it. Often, clients take some time and have multiple points of contact (e.g., stores, Internet, friends and peers) before actually making a purchase decision. The length of the customer decision journey in luxury makes it difficult to identify which point of contact may be regarded as most influential. Hence, unlike conventional personal selling practices, luxury sales personnel should be motivated by his or her intrinsic passion rather than by a direct sales commission (Kapferer & Bastien, 2009a, p. 196; Quintavalle, 2012, p. 100). To the affluent clientele persistency is the least valued attribute of a luxury salesperson (Luxury Insitute, 2007).

Customer relationships. Finally, luxury salespersons should build long-term personal relationships or "commercial friendships" with clients (Cailleux et al., 2009, p. 408; Kapferer & Bastien, 2009, p. 194; Rosenbaum, 2014, p. 3). Wieseke, Alavi, et al. (2013, p. 139) empirically show that building a personal relationship significantly affects purchase intention and customer loyalty. In a commercial friendship the customer feels recognized (ideally welcomed by name), well understood and as a respected member of the brand universe (Cailleux et al., 2009, p. 408; Wieseke, Alavi, et al., 2013, p. 134). A valuable, long-term customer relationship requires a globally centralized, frequently updated database containing socio-demographic client data (e.g., name, address, gender, age etc.), a client's purchase history (e.g., products, price levels, serial numbers, maintenance), and qualitative data (e.g., purchase motives like special moments in life; Cailleux et al., 2009, p. 411; Nueno & Quelch, 1998, p. 66).

4. Online Marketing-Mix of Luxury Goods

Having conceptually examined the specificities of marketing luxury goods in Chapter 3, we are now interested in the benefits, concerns, and approaches to marketing luxury goods online in terms of product management, pricing, communication, and distribution management. Particularly, Chapter 4 addresses the second research question (compare Chapter 1.2):

RQ2: What are the specificities of marketing luxury goods online in terms of product management, pricing, communication, and distribution management?

Prior to conceptually discussing the marketing-mix elements and how they may be adapted to the online world in Chapters 4.2 to 4.5, the general suitability of the Internet for marketing luxury goods will be described first in Chapter 4.1.

4.1 The Internet and luxury

The digital revolution has changed society and economy. With the advance of the Internet speed and reach of communication has increased. Individuals and firms exchange data and information through Internet applications like the World Wide Web (WWW) and electronic mail (e-mail). The Internet (**inter**connected **net**) refers to a worldwide system of computer networks sharing a common standard that can be accessed through a desktop computer, mobile phone, digital TV etc. via wired or mobile networks in order to exchange information (Fritz, 2001, p. 21; Internet Live Stats, 2014a; Kollmann, 2013b, p. 27).

The number of Internet users has grown dramatically over the past two decades at 29 per cent p.a. reaching nearly 3 billion users worldwide (see Figure 35(a); Internet Live Stats, 2014a). As of July 2014, about 40 per cent of worldwide population has access to the Internet (see Figure 35(b); Internet Live Stats, 2014a). For the next decade, this number can be expected to further increase considering that the fast penetration of smartphones facilitates access to the Internet.

Figure 35 – Worldwide Internet usage 2014.

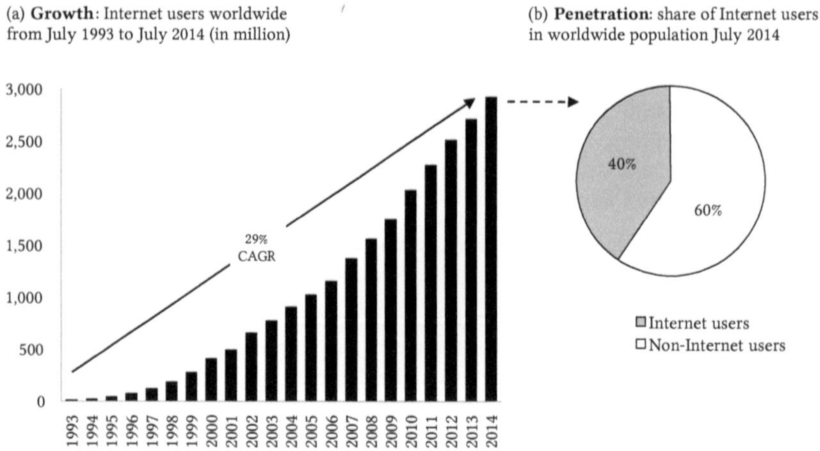

Source: Internet Live Stats (2014a)

Not only the penetration of the Internet continues to increase but also its usage intensity. The **time spent online** via desktop computers, tablets, and smartphones **has increased by about 15 per cent annually** from 2011 to 2015 (eMarketer, 2015a, 2015b, 2015c). Hence, in absolute terms, the Internet has become one of the most heavily used media (see Table 3). In Germany, for example, consumers at the ages of 14+ spend about 2 hours and 24 minutes per day online as compared to an average of 4 hours and 19 Minutes per day watching TV (SevenOne Media, 2014, p. 16). In other countries, daily Internet usage has even surpassed daily TV consumption. In China, for example, adults spend 3 hours and 5 minutes online versus 2 hours and 40 minutes for watching TV (eMarketer, 2015a). In the United Kingdom, adults spend around 4 hours and 39 Minutes per day online versus 3 hours and 12 Minutes for watching TV (eMarketer, 2015b). In the US, adults even spend as much as 5 hours and 38 minutes online as opposed to 4 hours and 15 minutes of watching TV (eMarketer, 2015c).

Given its strong presence in consumers' everday lives, the Internet has become the most influential medium when making a purchase decision. Two out of three consumers search in the Internet before making a purchase, while personal recommendations, TV, and magazines are considered influential by 61 per cent, 42 per cent, and 28 per cent of consumers respectively (Fleishmann Hillard & Harris Interactive, 2012, p. 3).

Table 3 – Daily media consumption by country in 2015

Time spent per day by medium and country in hours:minutes

Country	Internet*	TV	Radio	Print**
China	**3:05**	2:40	0:11	0:11
Germany***	2:24	**4:19**	2:09	0:29
United Kingdom	**4:39**	3:12	1:23	0:19
United States	**5:38**	4:15	1:27	0:21

*includes desktop/laptop, tablets, smartphones; **includes newspapers and magazines; ***data from 2014; figures in bold = most heavily consumed medium in respective country
Source: eMarketer 2015a, 2015b, 2015c; SevenOne Media, 2014, p. 16

Likewise the Internet has affected marketing practices (Fritz, 2001, p. 15). Competitive pressure increases as product and price information becomes easily comparable. Products like music, books, or tickets are digitized and directly sold online. Other, physical products can be ordered online and delivered home. And brand communication becomes increasingly interactive. Now, the term **online marketing refers to all marketing activities related to the medium Internet** (Kollmann, 2013b, p. 17; Lammenett, 2014, p. 22). In the context of the present manuscript the term online marketing is used interchangeably with other terms like "Internet marketing", "web marketing", or "e-marketing". The simplicity of this definition implies that the Internet does *not* change the fundamental understanding of marketing but rather represents an new medium for achieving traditional marketing objectives (Kreutzer, 2014, p. 5; Tiedtke, 1998, p. 79). Also, the term online is not restricted to Internet usage via a desktop computer but similarly includes mobile Internet usage through smartphones and tablets.

The online marketing of luxury goods can be thought of as **love at second sight**. At first sight, the suitability of the Internet for marketing luxury goods has been referred to as a "**dilemma**" (Kapferer & Bastien, 2012, p. 248) or a "**love/hate relationship**" (Chevalier & Gutsatz, 2012, p. 63). Despite the growing penetration and influence of the Internet on consumer behaviour, the contradictions between the concept of luxury and the Internet appear to be immense (see Figure 36).

Figure 36 – Internet dilemma for luxury brands.

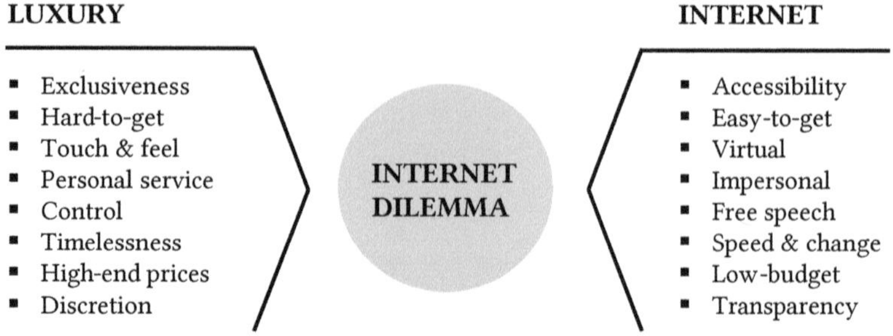

Source: author based on Chevalier & Gutsatz (2012, p. 67), Kapferer & Bastien (2012, pp. 247 & 249), Okonkwo (2009, p. 304), Seringhaus (2005, p. 15), and Wiedmann, Hennigs, & Klarmann (2011, p. 34)

Luxury goods are exclusively made for the happy few while the Internet is accessible to nearly everyone (Seringhaus, 2005, p. 15). Obtaining a luxury good requires effort while the Internet provides convenience and easiness (Kapferer & Bastien, 2012, p. 247). Luxury is about sensorial experience, the touch and feel of finest material while the Internet is virtual and intangible (Chevalier & Gutsatz, 2012, p. 67). Human interaction is an essential ingredient of luxury shopping while the online shopping is impersonal (Kapferer & Bastien, 2012, p. 249; Okonkwo, 2009, p. 304). Marketing luxury goods is about control and consistency while the Internet allows all users to generate content that is beyond the control of luxury goods marketers (Chevalier & Gutsatz, 2012, p. 67; Keller, 2009, p. 291). Luxury brands are built on rich heritage and embody classy and timeless design while the digital world is inconsistent and changes quickly (Chevalier & Gutsatz, 2012, p. 67). Prices for luxury goods are high-end and stable while the Internet is commonly considered as a low-budget sales channel attracting mostly bargain hunters (Kapferer & Bastien, 2009a, p. 208). Finally, true luxury is about discretion and subtleness while the Internet makes information transparent to virtually everyone.

At second sight, the Internet represents as powerful medium to **increase reach and intensity** of brand communication and sell to affluent clients who live in geographically distant places. As shown in Figure 35, the number of Internet users worldwide is constantly increasing. By July 2014, two out of five individuals worldwide have access to the Internet.

In luxury-savvy markets Internet penetration is twice as high. Nearly **four out of five individuals have access to the Internet**. As shown in Figure 37, the top ten countries in terms of luxury goods sales 2014 USA, Japan, Italy, China, France, United Kingdom, Germany, South Korea, Hong Kong, and Russia altogether account for about 78 per cent of the worldwide personal luxury goods market (Bain & Company & Fondazione Altagamma, 2014, p. 31). Within these ten countries Internet penetration is about 77 per cent of population and thus nearly twice as high as the worldwide Internet penetration of about 40 per cent of population (Internet Live Stats, 2014a, 2014b).

Figure 37 – Luxury sales and Internet penetration by country.

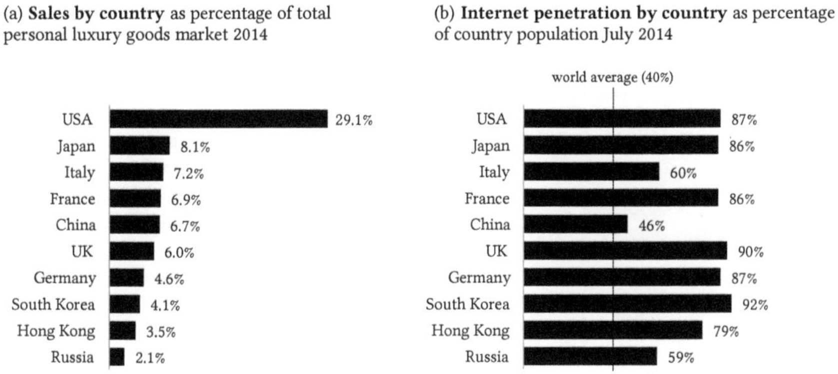

Source: Bain & Company & Fondazione Altagamma (2014, p. 31), Internet Live Stats (2014a, 2014b)

For 60 per cent of consumers the Internet has become the prime source of information when shopping for luxury goods (WHITE Communications, 2012, p. 9). In particular, when searching for relevant product and brand information luxury shoppers across all ages increasingly rely on digital media. As recent market research among luxury shoppers reveals, to find relevant information 69 per cent of luxury shoppers browse the official brand website, 54 per cent browse websites of luxury retailers, 35 per cent rely on online magazines and newsletters, and 31 per cent on social media (see Figure 38(a); Roland Berger & Meisterkreis, 2013, p. 4). When browsing the official brand website luxury shoppers do not only retrieve product information but consider the possibility to order products online as the second most important feature while it ranks eighth among luxury marketers (see Figure 41(b); Roland Berger & Meisterkreis, 2013, p. 8). And indeed, online sales of personal luxury goods have grown at 28 per cent p.a. over the past years (see Figure 1; Bain & Company & Fondazione Altagamma, 2014, p. 10). Not surprisingly, fashion, accessories, perfumes & cosmetics are the most frequently shopped luxury goods categories online (Roland Berger & Meisterkreis, 2013, p. 11). In light of the increasingly growing influence of the Internet **online marketing has become an imperative** for luxury goods marketers. Marketing scholars and executives must not shy away from a medium, which has become omnipresent in consumers' everyday lives. How the marketing-mix for luxury goods can be applied to the online world will be described in more detail throughout the following chapters.

Figure 38 – The importance of the Internet for luxury shopping.

(a) **Sources of information** by popularity among luxury shoppers in Germany 2013

(b) **Features of a luxury brand website** by importance rate, Germany 2013

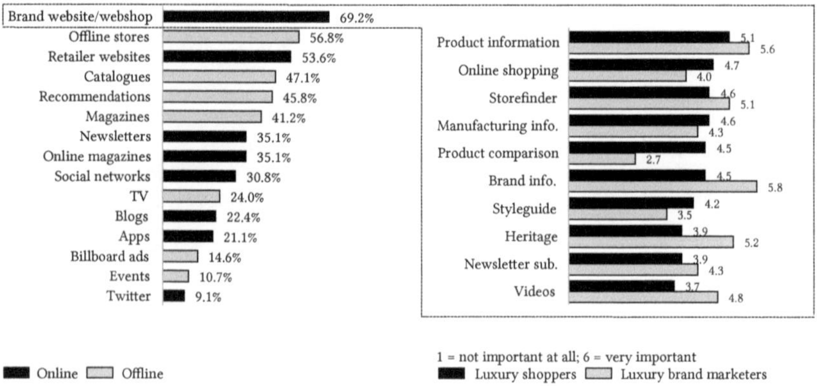

Source: Roland Berger & Meisterkreis (2013, pp. 4 & 8)

4.2 Online product management

The advance of the Internet has affected consumer goods markets in three major ways: first, it has given room for new product categories, i.e. hardware like smartphones and tablets, software like apps and games, and web-based consumer services like search engines, social media, and online retailers. Second, it has substantially transformed existing product categories, i.e. products like books, music, travel bookings or banking services can be fully digitized. Third, it supplements existing product categories by additional service components, e.g., physical goods may be ordered and home delivered. Depending on which product category is concerned, the meaning of online product management varies accordingly. As luxury goods fall into the third category, we define the term online product management as all decisions related to managing a firm's goods and services that are sold through the Internet (Albers, Bachem, Clement, & Peters, 1998, p. 268). Hence, to traditional luxury goods manufacturers online product management is primarily about adapting their existing product management considerations to the online world rather than creating new, fully digitized products. It does not substitute but complements the current product management. Online product management involves analysing the online suitability of a given product and deciding on the online product-mix, online product display, and online add-on services that complement the core product (Chaffey & Ellis-Chadwick, 2012, p. 264; Fritz, 2001, pp. 126–132; Kollmann, 2013b, pp. 69–81; Mülder & Weis, 1996, p. 356; Wolf, 2007, p. 91). These decisions will be addressed in the following.

4.2.1 Online suitability of luxury goods

Online product management typically starts with analysing to which extent a given product is actually suitable for being sold online from both a managerial and a consumer perspective (Albers et al., 1998, pp. 268–274; Fritz, 2001, pp. 126–127; Kollmann, 2013b, p. 68). From a managerial perspective, a product's online suitability is referred to as its "e-potential", i.e. the extent to which a product can be **digitized** (Bliemel & Fassott, 2000, p. 193). A product's "digitizability" mainly depends on the extent to which it consists of information like text, sound, or images (Albers et al., 1998, p. 269). Products high in information may be fully digitized (e.g., music, banking services, travel bookings). Physical goods low in information cannot be digitized but supplemented by online services. Luxury goods are characterized by a **low e-potential**. Traditional luxury product categories like cars, jewellery & watches, fashion & accessories, wine & spirits, perfume & cosmetics, or home designs are physical in nature and cannot be fully digitized. However, they can be well supplemented by online add-on services. For instance, luxury goods manufacturers can enhance the overall market offering by providing additional product information online and allowing shoppers to configure and order selected products online as will be described below.

From a consumer perspective, the online suitability of a given good mainly depends on its "**online assessability**", i.e. the extent to which the digital information provided about product attributes and quality may be considered sufficiently accurate and conclusive for consumers to justify an order (Albers et al., 1998, pp. 271–274; Kollmann, 2013a, pp. 279–280). From an information economics perspective, the attributes and quality of physical goods are typically easy to assess prior to purchase (search goods) whereas the actual performance of services may be assessed only during or after consumption (experience goods; Nelson, 1970, p. 312; Zeithaml, 1981, p. 186). Accordingly, the online suitability is considered to be higher for search than for experience goods (Peterson, Balasubramanian, & Bronnenberg, 1997, p. 334).

Luxury goods categories like ready-to-wear, jewellery, leather goods, cars or furniture are generally classified as search goods (Nelson, 1974, p. 312; Zeithaml, 1981, p. 186). Given the high-end prices of luxury goods and the typically low purchase frequency, individuals tend to intensively study the brand and product of interest prior to purchase. However, particularly when shopping a luxury brand for the very first time, the physical **touch and feel** of a luxury good as well as the **human interaction** with a sales expert is of major importance for an individual's purchase decision-making. Both Riley & Lacroix (2003, p. 100) and Liu et al. (2013, p. 890) find that the lack of touch and feel ranks as top reason why luxury consumers prefer traditional brick-and-mortar shopping over online shopping. Particularly to first-time luxury shoppers, the product information provided online might not appear sufficiently conclusive to justify a first-time purchase of a high-end priced item.

To conclude, the **online suitability** of luxury goods may be considered as **limited** for two reasons: first, unlike music, banking, travel bookings or other products high in information luxury goods are physical in nature and cannot be digitized (low e-potential). Second, consumers may not fully assess and appreciate the sophistication of luxury goods solely based on the product information provided online (moderate online assessability). Yet, apart from this isolated point of view, prospect clients today do not simply rely on one single point of contact with the brand. They experience a particular brand or good either through prior consumption, in-store inspection or peers along their decision-making journey (Manninger, 2012, pp. 239–240) and may actually order online. Then, issues like online product-mix, online product display, and online add-on services like shopping advisory, customization, and home delivery become increasingly important. These issues will be addressed in the following. The reader interested in a detailed discussion on the suitability of the Internet as a channel of distribution for luxury goods is kindly referred to Chapter 4.5.1.

4.2.2 Online product-mix

One of the fundamental decisions luxury goods manufacturers need to address in their online strategy refers to the question whether to sell the full product range or just a limited selection (Kapferer, 2015, p. 120; Okonkwo, 2010, p. 225). More specifically, luxury goods manufacturers need to decide on the online product-mix, i.e. the width (which product lines), length (which products within a each line), and depth (which variants or versions of each product) of the product range offered online (Kotler & Armstrong, 2012, pp. 235–236; Mülder & Weis, 1996, p. 356). Recalling the different ranges along the luxury pyramid (see Figure 8), Kapferer & Bastien (2012) explicitly argue that, in luxury, the online product-mix should include a limited number of entry-range products only, but "no core products" (p. 253). Accordingly, Louis Vuitton's website integrated online store should feature small accessories only, "but no bags" (Kapferer & Bastien, 2012, p. 253). The intention behind their postulated online product-mix strategy is primarily about seducing prospect clients, i.e. generating trial and potential repeat purchase, rather than making profit (Kapferer & Bastien, 2012, p. 253).

What we observe in practice, however, very often deviates from Kapferer & Bastien's (2012) recommended strategy. If at all committed to any form of online distribution, luxury goods manufacturers frequently offer both their **entry *and* core range products**, but usually not their limited high-end range products. Certainly, a manufacturer's most iconic bestsellers (typically within its core range) should be offered online (Okonkwo, 2010, p. 225). For example, in addition to accessories the online stores of fashion and leather goods manufacturers like Fendi, Gucci, and Louis Vuitton often feature their most iconic core-range bags like the Fendi Baguette, the Gucci New Bamboo, or the Louis Vuitton Speedy, respectively (Fendi.com, 2015; Gucci.com, 2015; Louisvuitton.com, 2015d). The core range versions of the most iconic timepiece series by Jaeger-LeCoultre and Piaget can be instantly ordered online (e.g., the Jaeger-LeCoultre Reverso Taille or the Piaget Altiplano ultra-thin mechanical watch), whereas consumers need to request purchase information first or visit brick-and-mortar store to access the high-end versions like the Jaeger-LeCoultre

Reverso Gyrotourbillon Two watch or the Piaget Altiplano Skeleton watch, respectively (Jaeger-lecoultre.com, 2015a, 2015c; Piaget.com, 2015a, 2015b). Jeweller Van Cleef & Arpels offers its iconic Alhambra collection online while its high-end, haute joaillerie pieces need to be requested by phone call (Vancleefarpels.com, 2015a). Montblanc offers its iconic Meisterstück writing instruments series online, but not its high-end limited edition fountain pens (Montblanc.com, 2014b).

4.2.3 Online product display

Offline retail outlets allow for a rich, multisensory brand and product experience (compare Chapter 3.4.3.3). While this experience cannot be fully replicated online (Chevalier & Mazzalovo, 2012, p. 281; Kapferer, 2015, p. 32; Okonkwo, 2009, p. 304), the enhanced possibilities to create visual and auditory stimuli online help compensate for the lack of touch and feel (Som & Blanckaert, 2015, p. 332). In general, the online product display results from a combination of text, images, graphics, sound, video, or interactive elements (Kollmann, 2013b, pp. 74–75). To help shoppers discover and appreciate the sophistication and detail of each carefully crafted item, the online display of luxury goods is typically enhanced by high-resolution images, multiple-angle product views, close-ups of product details (e.g., stitching and structure of textiles), zooming options, product colour selections, videos on the heritage and manufacturing of products, or even augmented reality like virtual fitting rooms (Okonkwo, 2010, p. 145; Quintavalle, 2012, p. 85; Som & Blanckaert, 2015, p. 332). For products offered for sale online, the packaging should be displayed as well given that gift-giving accounts for a large portion of the luxury goods market.

For example, the online product display of the Montblanc 90 Years Meisterstück fountain pen provides high-resolution images from different angles, a video featuring all attributes like the golden nib, rings, or the clip, images of both the packaging and the gift-wrapping, images of the writing of different nib variants, as well as a selection of font types available for a personalized engraving (Montblanc.com, 2015b).

4.2.4 Online add-on services

Luxury goods manufacturers may well supplement their core offerings by online add-on services (Kapferer, 2015, p. 32). Despite or because the lack of touch and feel and the face-to-face interaction with a sales person online services added to luxury goods should meet highest standards to inform and delight the online shopper prior to, during, and after the purchase (Quintavalle, 2012, p. 103). In particular, the manufacturer's delivery and client service policy need to be adapted to the online world (compare Chapter 3.1.3.4 on add-on services in general). If at all committed to any form of online distribution (i.e. directly operated monobrand online store or multibrand online retailers), the online **delivery policy** defines the scope of shipment (i.e. geographical areas served), mode of shipment (i.e. standard versus express delivery), and cost allocation (i.e. retail prices either include or exclude cost of shipping). If we again refer to the example of Montblanc, the scope of shipment of is limited to China, France, Germany, Italy, Japan, Spain, UK, and USA, and in Germany, for example, shoppers can choose between standard (2–3 days) and express delivery and receive free standard delivery for orders above EUR 50 (Montblanc.com, 2015c).

To luxury goods manufacturer, client services have become increasingly important over the last years (König, 2012, p. 263). The exceptional service-level provided in store (compare Chapter 3.4.3.5) should be well replicated online. **Online client services** include customization options, gift-wrapping, online shopping assistance, and offline store information (Kapferer, 2015, pp. 31 & 119; Kollmann, 2013b, p. 78; Wolf, 2007, p. 101). Depending on the product category, online customization options range from engravings (e.g., jewellery or writing instruments), material and colour selection (e.g., fashion, furniture), up to full configuration of products (e.g., cars). However, special orders like made-to-order jewellery at Boucheron or bespoke fragrances at Guerlain are typically completed in person at a stationary point of sale. The online shopping assistance may be either standardized (e.g., Boucheron's care advice, size guide or gift guide; Boucheron.com, 2015a) or personalized in terms of hotlines, call-back options, instant-chat options, inquiry forms, or brand-operated social media platforms (König, 2012, p. 263; Quintavalle, 2012, p. 103). Finally, online client services supplement the offline retail network in terms of providing information on store locations, opening hours, product ranges carried by and merchandise on stock at a given retail store, as well as the possibility to make a personal appointment at a given retail outlet.

4.3 Online price management

In luxury more than in any other segment, the consumer refers to the price as indicator of the overall quality a good is likely to deliver. To reflect the high-end quality and durability of luxury goods, luxury-specific pricing procedures are directed towards two fundamental objectives: prices should be both (1) high-end within a given product category, and (2) stable (see Chapter 3.2 on pricing of luxury goods). In general, the pricing procedures discussed in Chapter 3.2 should equally apply to the online business of a luxury goods manufacturer.

However, the increased transparency of price information through the Internet further complicates managing prices of luxury goods. Kapferer & Bastien (2009a, p. 208) find that the "delicate price management of a luxury product is impossible to carry out correctly on the web, where everything is public". Given the increase in transparency prices should be managed **consistently across channels** and countries. In the following we address three considerations when managing prices of luxury goods online: (1) whether to discriminate prices between online and offline channels, (2) whether to offer price discounts online, and (3) how to communicate prices online.

4.3.1 Cross-channel price discrimination

In general, managing prices of luxury goods should be driven by continuity and consistency (Fassnacht et al., 2013, p. 104; Kapferer & Bastien, 2009a, p. 189; Keller, 2009, p. 292; Kisabaka, 2001, p. 259). As shown in Chapter 3.2 this objective requires a rare-to-no price discrimination policy even though discriminating prices may potentially increase profits.

The rare-to-no price discrimination principle equally applies when managing prices across different channels. Prices for luxury goods ought to be **highly consistent** both across and within offline and online channels (Gastaldi, 2012, p. 115; Manninger, 2012, p. 247; Okonkwo, 2010, p. 251). Any inconsistency of prices across different channels may come at the expense of consumer perceptions of luxury (Fassnacht et al., 2013, p. 106; Keller, 2009, p. 292). Now through the Internet price information and, thus, potential inconsistencies in prices becomes increasingly transparent (Gastaldi, 2012, p. 114; Kapferer & Bastien, 2009a, p. 208).

While managing prices consistently across channels appears to be just "one click" of work, it actually often requires rethinking a luxury firm's distribution network. With rare exceptions like Louis Vuitton and Hermès, the majority of luxury goods manufacturers does not fully control its distribution but relies on a mixed strategy of both retail (e.g., monobrand stores) and wholesale distribution (e.g., department stores, specialty stores; Quintavalle, 2012, p. 88). In 2014, 68 per cent of personal luxury goods sales worldwide was made wholesale (Bain & Company & Fondazione Altagamma, 2014, p. 16). Online, the share of wholesale sales is even higher (compare Figure 28). Retailers have the discretionary power to determine actual retail prices. Luxury goods manufacturers may only recommend retail prices. Aligning multiple offline and online retail partners towards a consistent pricing strategy in fact represents a complex, hardly possible task to luxury goods manufacturers.

4.3.2 Online price discounts

Chapter 3.2.4 reported the need for and reasoning behind a rare-to-no discount policy irrespectively of whether goods are sold offline or online. The Internet, however, is particularly tempting to be used as a discount channel as it has long been considered as a marketplace for bargain hunters looking for better deals (Hennigs, Wiedmann, & Klarmann, 2012, p. 31; Kapferer & Bastien, 2009a, p. 208). And indeed, recent studies show that luxury shoppers do seek for better prices online (Bain & Company & Fondazione Altagamma, 2014, p. 19; Liu et al., 2013, p. 889). From the firm perspective, however, an empirical investigation on 40 luxury monobrand online stores and 20 non-luxury monobrand online stores finds that 87.5 per cent of luxury monobrand online stores do not constantly offer a sales section as opposed to only 20 per cent of non-luxury monobrand online stores (Rosow, 2013, p. 34).

The issue of price discounts particularly applies to fashion brands considering their relatively short innovation cycles. For example, the US fashion label Ralph

Lauren openly communicates end-of-season sales. Once a user arrives at the brand-owned website RalphLauren.de she or he is often confronted with a sales promoting banner like "summer sale" (Ralphlauren.de, 2014). A more discreet alternative refers to selling through closed shopping communities like the German online retailer BestSecret.com. To its suppliers (e.g., Burberry, Fendi, Givnechy, Lanvin, and Mulbuerry; Bestsecret.de, 2014) BestSecret.com offers high levels of discretion in mainly two ways: first, sales offers are not visible for the public but for registered members only. Second, users may only become members upon invitation by other members (Bestsecret.de, 2015a).

4.3.3 Online price communication

As a result of the increased transparency of information the issue of price communication has become "one of the trickiest points on the use of the Internet in luxury" (Kapferer & Bastien, 2009a, p. 192). The open communication of price represents one of the major concerns of luxury goods manufacturers when deciding on whether or not to adopt the Internet as an additional distribution channel (Gastaldi, 2012, p. 112). If a luxury goods manufacturer uses the Internet as a communication channel only, retail prices should not be displayed in order to preserve some price mystery (Kapferer & Bastien, 2009a, p. 192). Clients should become "price-insensitive fans" (Parguel et al., 2014, p. 3) that love the luxury brand not because of its price but because of the high-end functional, emotional, and symbolic value it delivers. The Geneva-based luxury watchmaker Patek Philippe is one good example for pursuing a no price communication strategy online. For example, the online product view of a Patek Philippe Grandes Complications 5078R model in rose gold highlights the product attributes and technical details, but does not display its retail price (Patek.com, 2014a).

If a luxury goods manufacturer actually sells its products online, prices need to be communicated at one point of time during the purchasing process. Then, retail prices should be communicated **as discreetly as possible** in a way that the product and its attributes are communicated first and its retail price appears at subsequent pages only. Particularly when selling discounted products, their online price communication should be as discreet as it would be in an offline retail outlet (Okonkwo, 2010, p. 251). On the website of the Kering-owned haute joaillerie brand Boucheron, for example, products like the Quatre Classique Ring are displayed first along with a brief textual description of the product. Only after clicking on the "More Detail" button, the user accesses the second product view page where, among other details, the price is displayed (Boucheron.com, 2015c).

A recent empirical investigation of 40 luxury monobrand online stores and 20 non-luxury monobrand online stores shows that while 100 per cent of non-luxury monobrand online stores openly communicate prices, 57.5 per cent of luxury monobrand online stores apply a more discreet price communication like mouse-over effects or naming the price under details only (Rosow, 2013, p. 34).

Table 4 – Benefits of and concerns about online brand communication

Benefits	Concerns
▪ Increased reach ▪ Individual-level communication ▪ Interactive communication ▪ Low cost of entry ▪ Measurability of consumer responses	▪ Negative consumer-generated content ▪ Organizational implementation ▪ Consistent communication strategy

Source: author

4.4 Online communication

4.4.1 Online communication and luxury

The Internet has enhanced brand communication in multiple ways. The digital medium allows for an individualized and interactive communication with an increasingly large audience (Fritz, 2001, p. 142; Kollmann, 2013b, p. 43; Kreutzer, 2014, p. 29). Table 4 provides an overview of benefits and concerns associated with online communication. These benefits and concerns as well as the need for luxury goods manufacturers to embrace the Internet as a new medium of brand communication are described in more detail in the following chapters.

4.4.1.1 Benefits of online communication

The Internet first of all serves as an additional, omnipresent consumer touch point through which brand communication initiatives can **reach more consumers** (Kreutzer, 2014, p. 29 & 160). Through the world wide web luxury goods manufacturers can send brand communication messages to virtually any consumer in the world independently of time and space (Stolpmann, 2000, p. 28). As previously shown in Figure 37, in 2014 about four out of five consumers in luxury-savvy markets like France, Germany, Japan, South Korea, United Kingdom and USA have access to the Internet.

Second, this consumer touch point enables luxury goods manufacturers to pursue a **highly individualized** communication throughout different communication instruments (Fritz, 2001, p. 142; Kollmann, 2013b, p. 45; Stolpmann, 2000, p. 55). Like conventional direct marketing initiatives (e.g., mailings, hotlines, in-store etc.; see Chapter 3.3.5.5) the Internet allows for targeting an individual instead of a group of individuals, i.e. communicating on an individual "one-to-one" level instead of a "one-to-many" level (Kreutzer, 2014, p. 12). However, conventional direct marketing initiatives are typically cost-intensive and limited in scale. For example, sending out high-end hard-copy catalogues of a luxury brand's seasonal collection along with a personalized cover letter involves considerable human and financial resources and is mostly limited to the existing client base. The Internet provides the possibility to mass-customize communication messages sent through different communication instruments beyond direct marketing approaches. For example, messages sent through traditional advertising media like TV or print formats reach the masses but are not individualized. Brand communication messages sent through online advertising media (e.g., banner ads on ft.com) also reach an ample amount of consumers. Additionally, these messages can be automatically adapted to an individual's searching and shopping behaviour (e.g., displaying male versus female collection).

Third, next to a mass-customized communication the advance of the Internet has significantly facilitated **interactive communication** between luxury goods manufacturers and their clients (Fritz, 2001, p. 142; Kollmann, 2013b, p. 43; Walter, 1999, p. 7). Clients do not only receive information (one-way communication, e.g., TV or print advertisements) but also send or actively exchange information with the luxury goods manufacturer (interactive communication). While the concept of interactive communication is not new at all – a face-to-face sales talk at a retail store represents one of the purest forms of interactive communication between a luxury goods manufacturer and its client – information technology has significantly accelerated the ways of interactive communication as compared to other media. Typically, there is a time lag between a consumer's perception of and response to a print advertisement, personalized invitation letter or other communication instruments. Today in the digital environment, consumers immediately like, share, and comment on posts on a branded Facebook fanpage, click on banner ads, respond to a personalized e-mail or actively post a question to the instant chat window on a website – either at home on a desktop computer or mobile on a tablet or smartphone.

Fourth, online communication is characterized by relatively **low cost of entry** (Kreutzer, 2014, p. 161; Wolf, 2007, p. 4). As compared to traditional consumer touch points communication through digital consumer touch points starts at relatively lower prices. Of course, however, as for traditional communication there are virtually no upper limits (Kreutzer, 2014, p. 161). For example, operating a branded website or Facebook fanpage comes at lower cost than operating one or more luxury monobrand stores, flagship store, and show rooms. Videos on YouTube are lower priced than TV commercials. And a digital product catalogue at the branded website or send via e-mail is less costly than high-end hard-copy catalogues.

Finally and often underestimated, luxury goods manufacturers can easily and accurately **measure** consumer responses to online brand communication activities (Wolf, 2007, p. 4). Traditionally, the cause-effect-relationship between brand communication initiatives and consumer responses often remains unclear. Marketers can hardly identify the stimuli that caused a luxury shopper to visit a monobrand store and to experience the brand. The individual shopper might be already familiar with the brand, might have seen an advertisement in a glossy magazine, received a secret hint by a friend, been attracted by nicely trimmed shopping windows or for any other plausible reason. Online, marketers can automatically track the websites from which a visitor has been referenced to the branded website, i.e. whether an individual user is directed to the branded website after clicking on a banner ad (e.g., on vogue.com) or a link provided by either a search engine (e.g., Google), a friend (e.g., via Facebook), the firm itself (e.g., via a personalized e-mail) or any unknown other (e.g., blogger) both through desktop or mobile devices. The possibility to easily and accurately measure online consumer behaviour allows for constantly testing (e.g., simple A/B testing) and improving a luxury brand's online communication activities.

4.4.1.2 Concerns about online communication

First, as a consequence of the interactivity of online communication a luxury goods manufacturer cannot fully control what is of highest priority: its brand equity (Keller, 2009, p. 291). Internet users shape a part of a luxury brand's image. They rate products, posts, and videos, write product reviews, comment on posts and post their very subjective opinion of a particular brand on Facebook, Twitter, and other social media. Ever since consumers have shared their opinion about brands and products with significant others. In the digital age, however, user ratings, reviews, comments, and posts have become publicly visible to virtually any other individual in world. Marketers will never control or avoid **consumer-generated content** – whether negatively or positively worded. However, online communication does not only imply proactively conveying a brand communication messages but also dealing with and responding to consumer questions and complaints. This way, online communication activities aim at mitigating negatively worded and reinforcing positively worded consumer-generated content. Also, as will be shown later positively worded user mentions of a brand easily outweigh negatively worded mentions.

Second, when communicating online the instruments used to convey brand communication messages to a targeted audience generally require relatively few financial resources (Wolf, 2007, p. 4). However, managing the content of a branded website and branded social media pages, monitoring and posting in communities and blogs, sending out personalized e-mail newsletters, or initiating viral campaigns is highly labour-intensive. Considering that online communication implies generating more communication content more frequently (e.g., multiple posts a week on a branded Facebook page) even emphasizes the need for additional human resources. Hence, a luxury goods manufacturer should re-think its organizational structure and assign **additional human resources** dedicated to all online brand communication related activities. Given that a post on the Facebook fanpage of a luxury brand quickly reaches a million users, this job is not made for just another 'intern'. Rather it requires a person with an extensive knowledge and keen sense of the luxury brands and its values in order to enhance and preserve the luxury brand's good reputation.

Third, the Internet is by definition a global medium. Any user can access a luxury brand's website, official social media pages, blogs or other websites from anywhere in world and at any time. As consequence online communication should follow a **consistent brand communication strategy** for all digital consumer touch points. Fortunately, as luxury goods manufacturers have usually centralized the brand communication function instead of delegating communication to local entities (Kapferer & Bastien, 2009, p. 219) they can well manage the consistency of brand communication activities across countries and media.

4.4.1.3 *Conclusion: the online communication imperative*

Considering the abovementioned benefits online communication has become daily routine at most luxury goods manufacturers. Today, luxury-savvy consumers consider the online presence of luxury brands as a must-have, a hygiene factor whose absence may cause dissatisfaction among consumers. At the same time the Internet offers a broad range of options to create a high-end brand experience, delight and engage luxury consumers. Online communication has become an **imperative** for luxury goods marketers. Neglecting the Internet as a new medium of brand communication would be an "error" (Kapferer & Bastien, 2009, p. 220). Still, conceptual and empirical literature examining the online communication of luxury goods is scarce with one exception being the book by Okonkwo (2010) titled "Luxury Online".

4.4.2 Online communication instruments

The advance of the Internet has enhanced brand communication. To identify how luxury communication management is affected by the online media, it is helpful to recall the communication process: objectives, audience, message, instruments, budget and control (see Figure 20 and Chapter 3.3). In principle objectives, target audience, or messages of a luxury brand communication strategy remain unchanged. Luxury brand communication still aims at creating awareness, desire, and dreams (cognitive and affective consumer responses) among the targeted clientele rather than pushing sales (behavioural consumer responses). It still targets not only affluent prospects and existing clients but also their significant others. And communication messages should still highlight emotional and symbolic brand attributes using subtle images and abstract descriptions – but never the price. These luxury-specific brand communication principles equally apply to both offline and online communication.

The Internet does, however, affect *how* communication messages can be conveyed to the target audience. The digital medium serves as an additional, omnipresent touch point through which firms can instantly and interactively communicate with the target audience. As mentioned in Chapter 3.3.5 online media do not constitute a new communication *instrument* per se but rather represent an additional channel that mediates the information flow between firms and consumers independently of whichever communication instrument is applied. In essence, with the advancement of the Internet marketers face the challenge how existing communication instruments should be applied to the online world: advertising on websites and social media, public relations with online newspapers, online magazines and blogs, sponsoring of online events, direct marketing via e-mail or social media, and sales promotion through online retailers and directly operated monobrand online stores. The most relevant online brand communication instruments will be described in the following chapters.

4.4.2.1 *Website*

The brand website represents the nucleus of a firm's online marketing strategy (Kreutzer, 2014, p. 95). The term website refers to a set of web pages which are

Figure 39 – Online and offline drivers of website traffic.

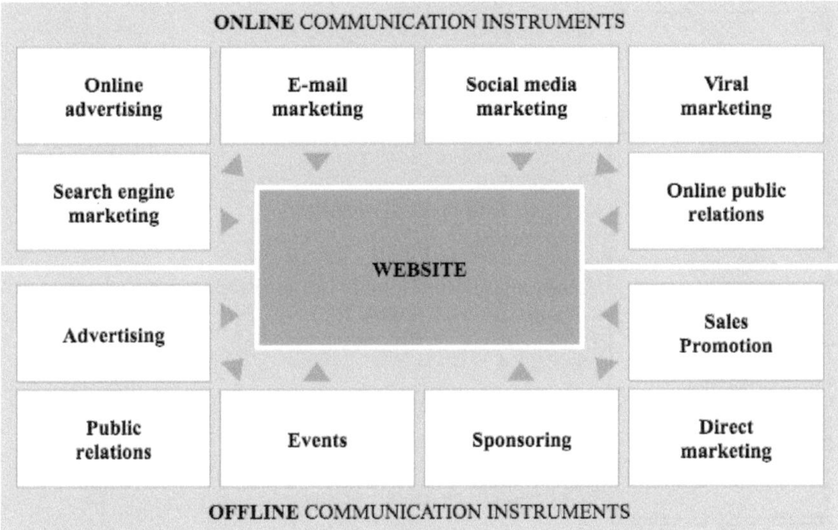

Source: adapted from Gastaldi (2012, p. 111) and Kreutzer (2014, pp. 128 & 133)

interlinked through a common navigation and accessible via a uniform domain (Kreutzer, 2014, p. 95; Okonkwo, 2010, p. 352). Hence, a website like piaget.com comprises multiple integrated web pages like piaget.com/watches or piaget.com/jewelry.

Since the website serves as **central, directly operated medium** for online brand communication and distribution other online and offline communication instruments are frequently designed to direct consumers to the brand website in order to generate website traffic and conversion (see Figure 39). Online communication instruments like search engine marketing, affiliate marketing, banner advertisements or social media marketing (see below) are not only designed to create awareness and interest but particularly to stimulate behavioural consumer responses, i.e. making users click on links and banners that refer to the brand website. Also offline communication instruments like print ads, catalogues, paper mails or product packaging today frequently display the domain of a brand website by name (e.g., Burberry.com, Rolex.com, Tiffany.com) or quick-response code (QR codes).

Luxury website creation. A company's website represents the "company's face to the world" (Nielsen & Tahir, 2001, p. 1). Visiting a branded website and virtually entering the world of a luxury brand often is the very first impression a consumer receives about the brand. Hence, this very first impression of the brand should be visually appealing and evoke consumer perceptions of finest quality, aesthetics, and exclusiveness at first sight. If the website does not appeal at first sight, visitors leave the website immediately. As will be shown in Table 6, about 38 per cent of all visitors to a luxury brand website leave after viewing only one single page of the

Figure 40 – 5C's of luxury website creation.

Concept	Main idea behind the design, e.g.: ▪ Clean and structured vs. experiential ▪ Pagination vs. infinite scrolling ▪ Static elements vs. multimedia content
Competence	User-friendliness in terms of: ▪ Navigation ▪ Functionality (speed, security etc.) ▪ Ease-of-use
Content	Compiling information about the brand that is: ▪ Authentic ▪ Extensive ▪ Compelling ▪ Properly formatted ▪ Relevant
Commerce	▪ High-quality product display and information ▪ Discreet price communication ▪ Excellent online service ▪ Convenient check-out process
Customization	Personalization and customization of: ▪ Content displayed ▪ Products ▪ Services

Source: adapted from the 7C's framework proposed by Okonkwo (2010, pp. 155–181)

website (also known as entrance page) highlighting the importance of creating a visually appealing and engaging luxury brand website.

Okonkwo (2010, pp. 155–181) suggests a 7C's framework for luxury website creation: concept, competence, content, commerce, customization, community, and computing. In the following we concentrate on the first 5C's since they refer to front office at the intersection with users. The latter two C's (community and computing) represent back office activities that are necessary but not directly visible to users (Okonkwo, 2010, p. 156). Figure 40 provides an overview of the **5C's of luxury website creation**.

First, **concept** refers to the main idea behind the design of a luxury brand website (Okonkwo, 2010, p. 156). This first step entails fundamental decisions like applying a clean structure versus an experiential approach, splitting content across discreet pages (pagination) versus having one or few content-loaded pages (infinite scrolling), or using static elements versus experiential 3-D worlds. The concept serves as a guiding principle for consistently defining design elements and content (Stolpmann, 2000, p. 211) and should well reflect a luxury brand's identity.

Second, **competence** refers to the user-friendliness of luxury brand website (Okonkwo, 2010, p. 161). To create an enjoyable online experience users should find the right destination page (navigation) as quickly (functionality) and easily (ease-of-use) as possible (Fritz, 2001, p. 144; Kreutzer, 2014, pp. 121–122; Stolpmann, 2000, p. 217). Visitors may get lost in complex navigation structures or annoyed by long loading times.

Third, based on the concept defined the **content** of the luxury brand website is actually compiled. In fact, compiling and structuring information for a luxury brand website often makes marketers reassess the luxury brand's identity. The information should authentically reflect the identity of the luxury brand, use a compelling wording, be relevant to visitors, extensive and complete, and presented in a legible, pleasing format (Fritz, 2001, p. 143; Okonkwo, 2010, p. 171).

Fourth, whether luxury goods manufacturers should operate a website not only as a mean of brand communication but also as an additional distribution channel will be discussed in detail in Chapter 4.5. If a monobrand online store is integrated into the luxury brand website (**commerce**) it should offer affluent online shoppers a high-quality, multi-angle illustration of products, excellent online service (e.g., style guide, instant chat, hotline), and a convenient checkout process (Okonkwo, 2010, pp. 174–175). As for offline retail stores prices should be communicated discreetly (compare Chapter 4.3.3).

Finally, as stated above the Internet has enabled mass-customized communication. **Customization** can refer to either content shown (e.g., according to the page view history of a returning visitor), or goods and services sold (Fritz, 2001, p. 144; Kreutzer, 2014, p. 122; Okonkwo, 2010, p. 175). The high-end writing instruments brand Montblanc, for example, offers free personalized engraving for each writing instrument purchased.

In order to systematically identify the differences between a conventional and a luxury branded website design Kluge et al. (2013) empirically examine 81 luxury brand websites based on 31 evaluation criteria categorized into typography, graphics and multimedia, navigation, and positioning of elements. Results indicate four main **specificities of luxury homepage design**: colour codes used in the background are darker, stage content covers larger proportions of the screen, the navigation bar is horizontally arranged, and the design concentrates on less elements (Kluge et al., 2013, p. 906). In short: luxury brand websites should be **clean but rich** (Okonkwo, 2010, p. 160). Figure 41 illustrates exemplary schematics of (a) a conventional homepage design and (b) a luxury homepage design.

Figure 41 – Conventional versus luxury-specific homepage design.

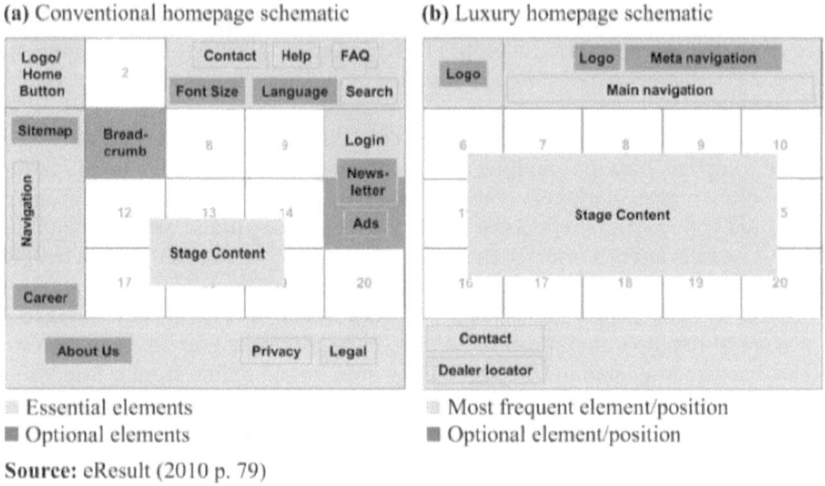

Source: Kluge et al. (2013, p. 908)

Also, the authors test consumer responses to a luxury-specific homepage design. Results of an experimental study show that the identified luxury homepage design evokes higher levels of consumer perceived brand luxury as compared to a conventional homepage design (Kluge et al., 2013, p. 912).

The Richemont-owned haute horlogerie brand Piaget serves as a best practice example for a clean, but rich brand website design (Piaget.com, 2014b). The website is featured with a dark backgroud, a large stage content area highlighting one single piece of jewellery or watchmaking, a horizontal navigation bar with few elements only (i.e. watches, jewellery, haute joaillerie, wedding, boutiques, piaget manufacturers). In contrast, the 2014 version of the website of Swatch-owned watchmaker Breguet used to be heavily loaded with multiple elements and information (Breguet.com, 2014b). For example, the stage content used to be dedicated to the Louvre in Paris, not even to one of Breguet's fine timepieces. The stage was surrounded by multiple smaller images of different product collections. This information overload distracted visitors from what Breguet is actually a master in: producing finest timepieces. As of now, Breguet has fully re-designed its branded website.

Table 5 – Top 5 website performance metrics

Response stage	Metric	Description
Cognitive	**Visitors**	Number of unique visitors to the website per time unit
Affective	**Bounce rate**	Percentage of single-page visits on the website per time unit
	Page views	Average number of web pages visited per visitor on the website per time unit
	Time on site	Average duration of visits to the website
Behavioural	**Conversion rate**	Percentage of visitors who completed a desired action per time unit

Source: adapted from Florès (2014, p. 55–67), KISSmetrics.com (2010), Kreutzer (2014, pp. 139–142), Lammenett (2014, pp. 340–348), Okonkwo (2010, pp. 340–352)

Website performance metrics. The Internet allows for an instant and accurate monitoring website performance in terms of cognitive, affective, and behavioural consumer responses. Programmes like *Google Analytics*, *etracker*, or *Alexa* provide multiple performance metrics indicating the number of individuals visiting the website, which website they are coming from, how much time they spend on average on the website, which pages on the website they discover and exit from, and finally whether they sign up, purchase or complete another action of interest. Depending on how parameters are defined (e.g., time unit, country, ratios etc.) marketers can think of numerous different metrics. Table 5 provides an overview about the five most frequently used website-related metrics corresponding to different stages of the consumer response hierarchy: cognitive, affective, and behavioural (compare Chapter 3.3.2).

Visitors. At the cognitive stage consumers recognize a brand website. Being exposed to the domain of the brand website through any offline or online medium (see Figure 39) they become aware of and attracted to visit the website. The number of unique visitors to (any page of) the website per time unit represents a commonly monitored performance metric to measure the level of reach and attraction (Florès, 2014, p. 57; Kreutzer, 2014, p. 141). Multiple visits to the website by the same visitor within a given time period are counted as one. If enabled through tracking technology, online marketers break this number down to the share of first (versus repeat) visitors in order to identify how many new consumers have been attracted to the website as consequence of a particular communication campaign (Florès, 2014, p. 58). The reference time unit may be defined as per day for mass websites like Facebook or Youtube. For luxury brand websites week or month represents a more relevant time unit considering that luxury goods are rather infrequently purchased.

Bounce rate. Once arrived at the website the visitor becomes either interested or not in the content she or he is confronted with (affective stage). The visitor then either continues browsing different pages of the website (e.g., moving from piaget.com to piaget.com/watches) or exits immediately from the entrance page without further browsing. The latter scenario is measured by the bounce rate, which refers to the percentage of single-page visits to thewebsite, i.e. the share of visitors who arrive at the website, view a single web page of the website and exit from this entrance page (Florès, 2014, p. 61; KISSmetrics.com, 2010; Puri, 2014). Thus, a lower bounce rate is desired.

Table 6 lists the bounce rates of 40 selected luxury brand websites. The average bounce rate for luxury brand websites is **38 per cent** and thus slighty lower than the conventional average bounce rate of **41 per cent** (KISSmetrics.com, 2010). Hence, 38 per cent of all visitors to a luxury brand website exit again after viewing one single page. The bounce rate of luxury brand websites varies considerably, ranging from as low as 16 and 21 per cent for Spykercars.com and Louisvuitton.com respectively up to 77 per cent for Mikimoto.com, i.e. only one in four visitors continues browsing the website.

Page views. Among the visitors who have arrived at the website and decided to visit additional pages of the website, the page view (PV) metric measures the average number of pages visited on the website per visit per given time unit (Florès, 2014, p. 60; Puri, 2014). Page views per visit, also known as page impressions, serve as an indicator of a visitor's interest in the content of the website (affective stage). Thus, online marketers typically aim for a higher number of page views. Luxury brand websites record an average of **4.0 page views** (see Table 6(a)) as opposed to 4.6 page views on conventional websites (KISSmetrics.com, 2010). This figure varies by luxury product categories ranging from a below-average count of 3.5 pages views for cars and jewellery up to 5.2 page views for fashion.

Time on site. Another performance metric commonly used to measure a visitor's interest in the content of the website refers to the time a visitor spends on the website. Time on site, also known as site-stickiness, measures the average duration of visits to the website (Florès, 2014, p. 59; Kreutzer, 2014, p. 141). As for page views, online marketers typically aim at higher figures of time on site.

Table 6 – Website performance metrics of 40 luxury brands

(a) Grand means luxury vs. average website

	BR	PV	Time
Luxury brand websites	**38%**	**4.0**	**3:00**
Average websites	**41%**	**4.6**	**3:10**

(b) Apparel

Website	BR	PV	Time
Louisvuitton.com	21%	2.7	4:28
Ferragamo.com	27%	4.3	4:27
Prada.com	27%	6.7	3:31
Fendi.com	29%	6.9	3:47
Hermes.com	29%	9.1	3:26
Armani.com	30%	5.7	3:28
Versace.com	32%	5.0	3:08
Zegna.com	35%	3.7	2:42
Dior.com	36%	3.4	3:06
Chanel.com	39%	4.7	2:58
Average	**31%**	**5.2**	**3:30**

(c) Cars

Website	BR	PV	Time
Spykercars.com	16%	3.5	2:23
Lamborghini.com	22%	3.8	3:36
Bugatti.com	33%	4.3	2:25
Ferrariworld.com	35%	3.9	3:43
Koenigsegg.com	36%	3.6	2:53
Astonmartin.com	36%	3.3	3:06
Bentleymotors.com	39%	3.5	3:15
Maserati.com	40%	3.1	2:58
Pagani.com	41%	2.9	2:33
Rolls-roycemotorcars.com	48%	2.8	3:20
Average	**35%**	**3.5**	**3:01**

(d) Watches

Website	BR	PV	Time
Audemarspiguet.com	36%	4.5	3:40
Jaeger-lecoultre.com	37%	3.3	3:06
Patek.com	38%	3.1	2:27
Franckmuller.com	38%	4.4	1:54
Rolex.com	38%	4.2	3:02
Breguet.com	42%	5.7	3:04
Blancpain.com	43%	3.4	2:56
Iwc.com	45%	2.9	2:41
Piaget.com	46%	2.6	2:27
Vacheron-constantin.com	65%	1.9	1:54
Average	**43%**	**3.6**	**2:43**

(e) Jewellery

Website	BR	PV	Time
Harrywinston.com	28%	4.9	2:14
Tiffany.com	29%	4.8	4:19
Montblanc.com	31%	3.4	3:38
Bulgari.com	34%	3.3	2:49
Chaumet.com	35%	3.9	3:42
Cartier.com	45%	2.8	2:20
Vancleefarpels.com	46%	3.2	3:00
Boucheron.com	64%	2.2	1:44
Mikimoto.com	77%	3.0	1:02
Kloybateri	n/a	n/a	n/a
Average	**43%**	**3.5**	**2:45**

BR = bounce rate, i.e. percentage of visitors who leave the website after a single page view; PV = daily unique page views per visitor, i.e. daily number of pages visited on a website; Time = average time spent on website; Note: analysis based on Alexa.com competitive intelligence reports retrieved on July 29, 2014 for 40 luxury brands (see Appendix 2).
Source: author

Visitors to luxury brand websites spend on average **3.0 minutes** on the website (see Table 6(a)) as opposed a 3.16 minutes average time on site for conventional websites (KISSmetrics.com, 2010). Louisvuitton.com best engages its visitors yielding a time on site of about 4.5 minutes. The website design of Louisvuitton.com is clean, but rich inviting the visitor to further explore the website. In contrast, the 2014 website design of Mikimoto.com is clean, but old-fashioned and hardly engaging (Mikimoto.com, 2014; as of 2015 Mikimoto has fully re-designed its branded website). Hence, visitors to Mikimoto.com are least engaged spending only about 1 minute on the website. Please note, however, that beyond the design of the website there might be other factors influencing bounce rates, page views, and time on site.

Conversion rates. Finally, marketers are interested in the share of visitors who purchase, register, like, share or complete any other action of interest. These ratios, i.e. percentage of visitors who complete an action, are known as conversion rates (Kreutzer, 2014, p. 142; Lammenett, 2014, p. 143; Okonkwo, 2010, p. 341). If one out of hundred visitors purchases an item, the purchase conversion rate is 1 per cent. This website performance metric is especially relevant for constantly **testing and improving** website parameters. For example, luxury marketers may randomly confront visitors with either image A or image B (simple A/B testing) and compare the average conversion rates for both scenarios. Of course, the issue being tested should comply with ethical and general branding considerations.

As a benchmark, a recent study among more than 1,000 marketing leaders worldwide (not necessarily representing luxury-related firms) reports an **average conversion rate of 2.6 per cent** with the top 20 per cent of firms reporting a conversion rate of 4.5 per cent (Adobe Systems, 2014, p. 1). Slightly different, a recent study by Monetate (2014, p. 9) reports an average conversion rate of 2.8 per cent with the top perfomers yielding a 6.4 per cent rate. Noteably, conversion rates differ by the type of device used for online shopping: 3.4 per cent for desktop computers, 2.9 per cent for tablets, and only 0.9 per cent for smartphones (Monetate, 2014, p. 12) supporting the common saying that "mobile does not convert".

4.4.2.2 Search engine marketing

About 50 per cent of online purchases start with users searching for products on search engines like Google, Bing, Baidu (China) or Yandex (Russia; DoubleClick, 2005, p. 2). Search engine marketing involves all activities directed towards increasing the **visibility** of a branded website on relevant search engine results pages (Kreutzer, 2014, p. 250; Lammenett, 2014, p. 347; Okonkwo, 2010, p. 350). Being visibly listed in search engine results represents an essential pre-requisite for generating user traffic and conversion (e.g., purchases, registrations) on the brand website (Kollmann, 2013b, p. 185). A brand only "exists" in the Internet if its website can be found through search engines (Wolf, 2007, p. 255). Not making a brand website visible on search engines is like having a retail store on a desert island.

Table 7 – Search engine generated website traffic of 40 luxury brands

(a) Apparel

Website	SEGT	Top Keyword
Hermes.com	42%	Hermes
Armani.com	40%	Armani
Fendi.com	38%	Fendi
Louisvuitton.com	36%	Louis Vuitton
Versace.com	35%	Versace
Ferragamo.com	34%	Salvator Ferragamo
Dior.com	33%	Dior
Chanel.com	33%	Chanel
Zegna.com	33%	Ermenegildo Zegna
Prada.com	31%	Prada

(b) Cars

Website	SEGT	Top Keyword
Koenigsegg.com	47%	Koenigsegg
Pagani.com	47%	Pagani
Spykercars.com	44%	Spyker
Bugatti.com	43%	Bugatti
Lamborghini.com	40%	Lamborghini
Astonmartin.com	39%	Aston Martin
Bentleymotors.com	38%	Bentley
Rolls-roycemotorcars.com	35%	Rolls Royce
Maserati.com	30%	Maserati
Ferrariworld.com	27%	Ferrari

(c) Watches

Website	SEGT	Top Keyword
Franckmuller.com	58%	Franck Muller
Patek.com	39%	Patek Philippe
Blancpain.com	38%	Blancpain
Breguet.com	36%	Breguet
Rolex.com	35%	Rolex
Iwc.com	35%	IWC
Jaeger-lecoultre.com	35%	Jaeger LeCoultre
Audemarspiguet.com	31%	Audemars Piguet
Piaget.com	30%	Piaget
Vacheron-constantin.com	27%	Vacheron Constantin

(d) Jewellery

Website	SEGT	Top Keyword
Chaumet.com	51%	Chaumet
Montblanc.com	40%	Mont Blanc
Bulgari.com	32%	Bvlgari
Cartier.com	31%	Cartier
Tiffany.com	30%	Tiffany
Harrywinston.com	29%	Harry Winston
Vancleefarpels.com	27%	Van Cleef & Arpels
Boucheron.com	23%	Boucheron
Mikimoto.com	7%	Mikimoto
Kloybateri	n/a	n/a

Note: figures refer to the percentage of traffic referenced to the website from both organic and paid search result listings. SEGT = search engine generated traffic on the respective website; analysis based on Alexa.com competitive intelligence reports retrieved on July 29, 2014 for 40 luxury brands. Source: author

Figure 42 – Google search results page for Vacheron Constantin.

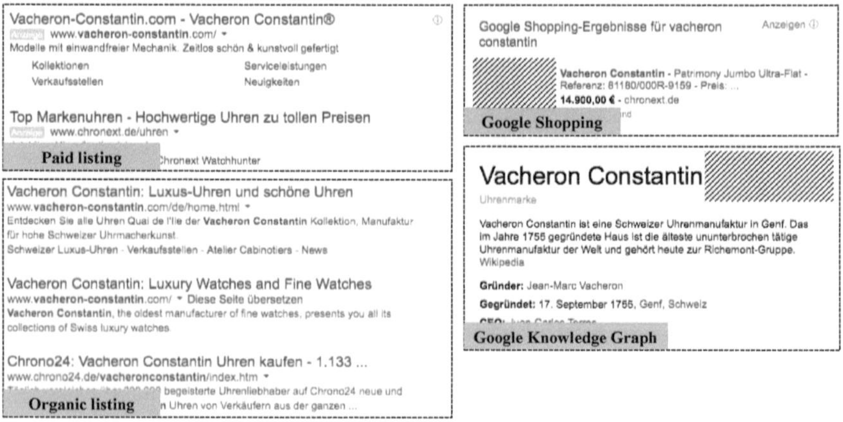

Note: images and logos are blurred for copyright reasons.
Source: Google.de (2015)

In luxury, the thinking behind a brand website's visibility on relevant search engines is comparable to the thinking behind locating a luxury offline store in the city centres of the world's luxury hotspots. Unless it is a connoisseur brand that consciously remains secret, a large proportion of a brand's perceived luxuriousness is attributed to its physical presence in the world's most exclusive locations like London's New Bond Street, Tokyo's Ginza or New York's Fifth Avenue. Luxury brands need to be present in these prime locations in order to be recognized and considered for luxury (gift) shopping (see Chapter 3.4.3.2). Table 7 illustrates the need for luxury goods manufacturers to be present in search engine results pages. On average, about **35 per cent** of website traffic is directly generated by search engine results pages. The brand name itself represents the most frequently searched keyword.

The percentage of website traffic generated by search engine results is even higher (up to 58 per cent) among less well-known brands like Franck Muller, Chaumet, Koenigsegg, or Pagani whose websites are not top-of-mind.

Search engine optimization (SEO). The visibility of a brand website depends on its placement on the search engine results page. We generally differentiate between **organic listing** and non-organic or **paid listing** (also sponsored links or ads; Kreutzer, 2014, p. 250; Lammenett, 2014, p. 347; Okonkwo, 2010, p. 350). As shown in Figure 42, paid listings are typically more visibly placed (i.e. on the top of the search engine results page) than organic listing. Still, organic search results drive considerably more website traffic than paid search results. As shown in Figure 43(a), in 82 per cent of cases users click on an organic search result rather than on a paid search results (9 per cent of cases) or universal search results (e.g., Google Shopping, Google Knowledge Graph, images, videos etc; 9 per cent of cases).

Figure 43 – Share of clicks on search engine results pages.

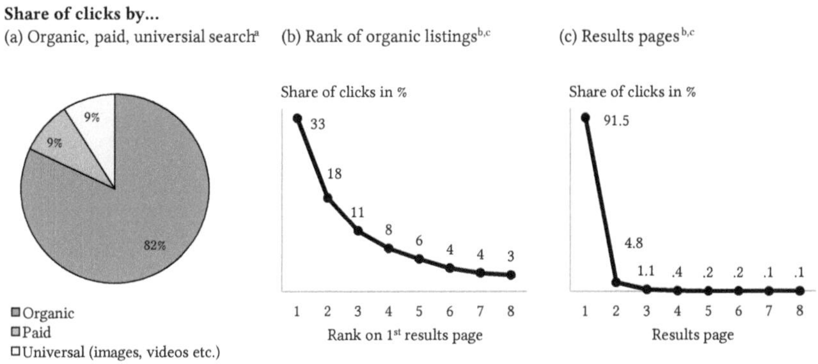

[a]Based on data of 177 online retailers in Germany 2014; [b]Based on 300 m page views in the USA and Canada 2013; [c]Note: numbers do not add up to 100 per cent since the pages/ranks from 9 onwards are not covered.
Source: Aufgesang & Searchmetrics (2014), Chikita Insights (2013)

The **organic** listing includes all textual results (as shown in the example of Figure 42) of a search algorithm that are most relevant to the user's search entry and not paid for by a firm (Kreutzer, 2014, p. 193). In addition to textual results search engines like Google typically display universal search results, i.e. relevant images, videos, maps, or shopping results etc. The term **search engine optimization** (SEO) refers to all activities directed towards increasing the visibility of and ultimately the number of clicks on a link to a brand website by improving its rank in an *organic* search results listing for relevant keywords (Kreutzer, 2014, p. 193; Lammenett, 2014, p. 347). Obviously, the first rank on the first results page generatesthe highest website traffic. A study based on about 300 million page views reports that in 33 per cent of cases users click on the link ranked first on the first results page followed 18 per cent for the second, and 11 per cent for the third rank (see Figure 43(b); Chikita Insights, 2013). The same study reports that 91.5 per cent of search engine generated website traffic is caused by links listed on the first search engine results page followed by 4.8 per cent for the second and 1.1 per cent for the third results page (see Figure 43(c); Chikita Insights, 2013).

Search engine advertising (SEA). Depending on the keyword entered being among the top-ranked organic search results can be very unlikely or complicated to influence. For keywords like "diamond ring" search engines find several million relevant websites ranging from numerous jewelers and retailers to press releases, wikis, communities, or social media posts. To ensure a brand website is listed visibly for relevant keywords firms can pay for a paid search result listing. The term **search engine advertising** (SEA, also keyword advertising) refers to all activities directed towards increasing the visibility of a brand website by placing sponsored advertisements in paid search engine results pages according to relevant keywords (Kreutzer, 2014, p. 193; Lammenett, 2014, p. 346).

Table 8 – Google AdWords: top luxury brands by paid search spending

Keyword categories
(number of keywords measured)

(a) Apparel (559)		(b) Handbags (334)		(c) Beauty (810)		(d) Watches (793)	
Website	**USD spend FY 2013**	**Website**	**USD spend FY 2013**	**Website**	**USD spend FY 2013**	**Website**	**USD spend FY 2013**
Louisvuitton.com	1,316,000	Chanel.com	816,000	Chanel.com	311,000	Rolex.com	149,000
Chanel.com	549,000	Louisvuitton.com	576,000	Lancome-usa.com	122,000	Cartier.us	95,000
Us.burberry.com	323,000	Coach.com	557,100	Us.burberry.com	54,000	Panerai.com	70,000
Hermes.com	265,000	Marcjacobs.com	414,000	Shiseido.com	49,000	Chanel.com	69,000
Armani.com	226,000	Gucci.com	173,000	Gucci.com	38,000	Tagheuer.com	56,000
Us.versace.com	190,000	Michealkors.com	144,000	Dior.com	25,000	Michele.com	37,000
Dior.com	183,000	Hermes.com	102,000	Giorgioarmani[b]	19,000	Movado.com	35,000
Armaniexchange[a]	98,000	Balenciaga.com	76,000	armani.com	7,400	Gucci.com	34,000
Stellamccartney.com	82,000	Jimmychoo.com	54,000	Marcjacobs.com	7,000	Vacheron[c]	29,000
Gucci.com	78,000	Burberry.com	53,000	Biotherm-usa.com	6,000	Bulgari.com	28,000

[a]Armaniexchange.com; [b]Giorgioarmanibeauty-usa.com; [c]Vacheron-constantin.com
Source: AdGooroo (2014)

For example, the luxury goods manufacturers Burberry, Rolex, and Tiffany & Co. invest in Google sponsored ads (paid listing) for the searched keywords "luxury hobo bags", "Swiss watches", or "diamond ring" respectively (Google.de, 2014a, 2014b, 2014c). According to data by AdGooroo (2014), luxury goods firms like Chanel, Kering, LVMH, Prada, and Richemont together spend as much as **USD 22 million** on paid search listing through Google AdWords in 2013. Specifically, Table 8 list the top luxury brands by paid search spending for different segments.

The pricing of placing a sponsored advertisement on search engine results pages typically follows a **cost-per-click** model (**CPC**, pay-per-click), i.e. the advertisers pays a certain amount of money for each click on the sponsored advertisement (Kreutzer, 2014, p. 199; Lammenett, 2014, p. 341; Okonkwo, 2010, p. 341). Hence, in contrast traditional CPM pricing models costs of sponsored ads only incur if users actually recognized and responded to it, i.e. clicking on the ad thereby being referenced to the brand website. The share of users who click on a sponsored ad in a paid search listing is called **click-through-rate (CTR**; Kreutzer, 2014, p. 165). In the European luxury-savvy countries France, Germany, and United Kingdom CPC are EUR 0.34, 0.28, and 0.38 respectively and the **click-through-rate** are 0.9, 2.8, and 2.3 per cent respectively, i.e. about one to three in hundred users click on a paid search result (Kenshoo Social, 2014a).

Still, organic search engine results prevail: organic search results are recognized first in 82 per cent of cases (Jansen & Resnick, 2006, p. 1959), preferred by users in 73 per cent of cases (iProspect, 2004, p. 4), and generate 82 per cent of website traffic (Aufgesang & Searchmetrics, 2014, p. 20). However, both users and established advertisers have become more and more familiar with search engine advertising CTR for single sponsored ads are continuously increasing up 1.9 per cent in Q4 2013 (Kenshoo Social, 2014b).

Luxury goods manufacturers need to make sure they are easily found in the Internet. However, the need for high visibility does not necessarily imply that luxury goods manufacturers should heavily invest in paid listings like Google AdWords (Okonkwo, 2010, pp. 167–168). Rather, Okonkwo (2010, p. 168) recommends further developing a branded social media presence and offline communication linking to the brand website. A consumer's desire for a luxury brand typically develops over a considerable period of time rather than by being exposed to a paid search engine result. In other words, a consumer searches less likely for a "black luxury handbag" than specifically for a Louis Vuitton Speedy or an Hermès Birkin Bag – an item she or he knows and desires for some time (Okonkwo, 2010, p. 168). Having this in mind, the website of a luxury goods manufacturer needs to be highly visible when users search for the brand name itself. As shown in Table 7 the most frequently keyword used to search for the 40 luxury brand websites investigated is the brand name itself.

Figure 44 presents the distribution of luxury branded versus non-branded content on Google.de search engine results pages for searches performed on July 29, 2014 for brand names of 40 luxury goods manufacturers (see list in Appendix 2). Regarding the organic listing, luxury brands enjoy a high visibility. Out of 40 Google searches,

Figure 44 – Google search results analysis for 40 luxury brand names.

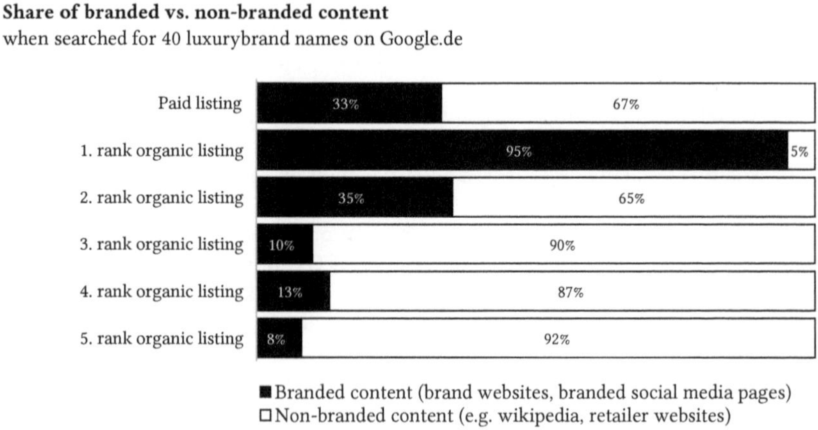

Note: analysis based on Google.de search results pages of searches retrieved on July 29, 2014 for 40 luxury brand names, e.g., "Louis Vuitton" (see full list in Appendix 2).
Source: author

in 95 per cent of cases the respective luxury brand website (e.g., louisvuitton.com) appears first in the organic listing when searching for the brand name (e.g., "Louis Vuitton"). Also, second to fifth organic rank often presents branded content like a luxury brand's official Facebook fan page (e.g., Facebook.com/louisvuitton), Twitter account (e.g., Twitter.com/louisvuitton), or You-Tube channel (e.g., Youtube.com/user/louisvuitton). Non-branded content includes (still rele-vant) Wikipedia articles, official retailers or online press and magazines that report about the luxury brand. Only about 33 per cent of luxury brand websites appear in the paid search results listings right on top of the organic search results listings. None of the luxury brand websites are displayed on the right-hand side paid listing, i.e. 100 per cent non-branded (or no) content. To conclude, luxury brand websites enjoy **high visibility** on Google search engine results pages when search for the respective brand name. Still, luxury goods manufacturers could improve their second to firth rank visibility by further developing and making visitors engage with their official social media pages.

4.4.2.3 Online advertising

Luxury brand advertising through traditional communication media like TV or print formats mainly aims at creating awareness, interest, and desire among the target audience. In addition to these communication objectives online advertising, defined as the paid placement of brand communication material on third-party websites, is directed towards stimulating behavioural consumer responses in the form of generating traffic, leads (e.g., user registration), and conversion (e.g., making a purchase) on the luxury brand website. Today, accounting for **23.5 per cent of**

Figure 45 – Online advertising spendings in EUR million 2011–2013 in Germany.

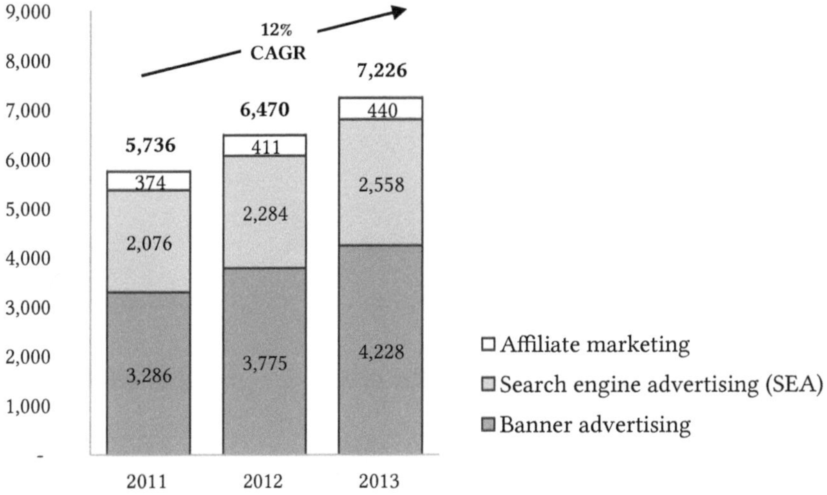

Note: in absence of luxury-specific data general market data is presented here.
Source: OVK & BVDW (2013, p. 7)

advertising spending the Internet ranks third among other advertising media right behind TV (38.8 per cent) and print formats like newspapers and magazines (27.5 per cent; OVK & BVDW, 2013, p. 9). Online advertising spending increases annually by 12 per cent (see Figure 45).

We mainly differentiate **three forms** of online advertising: banner advertising, search engine advertising, and affiliate marketing. About 59 per cent of online advertising budget is allocated to banner advertising, 35 per cent to search engine advertising and 6 per cent to affiliate marketing activities (see Figure 45). Search engine advertising (SEA) has been described above in the context of search engine marketing (see Chapter 4.4.2.2). Banner advertising and affiliate marketing and their relevance to luxury goods manufacturers are described below.

Banner advertising. Banner advertising represents the most commonly applied form of online advertising. It refers to the paid placement of brand communication material on a third-party website in form of static or animated rectangular fields (i.e. banners) intended to create awareness and desire among the targeted audience and to re-direct visitors to the branded website of the sender upon clicking (Kollmann, 2013b, p. 189; Okonkwo, 2010, p. 339; Stolpmann, 2000, p. 147). While for both banner and traditional advertising like print or billboard ads the information flow between sender and receiver is mediated by a third-party partner, banner advertising enhances traditional advertising in two major ways: first, firms can **individualize** communication messages, i.e. displaying the women collection to female users. Second and even more importantly, firms can precisely **measure**

Figure 46 – Banner advertising formats.

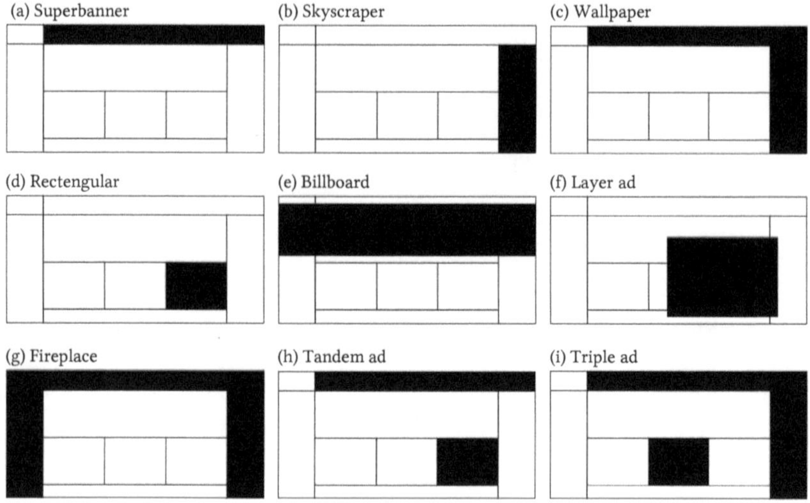

Source: adapted from Kreutzer (2014, pp. 168–172), Lammenett (2014, p. 232)

the effectiveness of banner advertising. Banner ads are typically equipped with a hyperlink redirecting the user to the brand website upon clicking (Fritz, 2001, p. 144; Stolpmann, 2000, p. 147). As for search engine advertising, the number of visitors of the brand website who have been re-directed from a particular banner ad is measured by the **click-through-rate** (CTR) which refers to the ratio of users confronted with a banner ad to those clicking on the banner ad (Kreutzer, 2014, p. 165). For conventional banner ads, the average CTR is about 0.1 per cent, i.e. about one user in 1,000 clicks on a banner ad (Kreutzer, 2014, p. 165). Technology allows for measuring multiple forms of online marketing performance metrics. For more detail we recommend Florès (2014) and Kreutzer (2014, pp. 89–470) as well as the glossaries by Lammenett (2014, pp. 340–349) and Okonkwo (2010, pp. 337–352).

Banner ads differ by size and positioning on the website. Figure 46 illustrates nine commonly used formats of banner advertising highlighted in black color: superbanner, skyscraper, wallpaper, rectangular, billboard, layer ad, fireplace, tandem ad, and triple ad (Kreutzer 2014, pp. 168–172; Lammenett 2014, p. 232). As different banner ad formats generate different user attention and CTR, the mediating third-party websites typically charge different prices for different banner ad formats. Table 9 provides the cost-per-mille (CPM), i.e. the price for 1,000 users being confronted with a banner ad, for selected banner ad formats and luxury-relevant websites. Prices range from EUR 27 cost-per-mille for a superbanner ad on FAZ.net, the website of one of Germany's most respected nationwide newspapers, up to EUR 90 cost-per-mille for a wallpaper banner ad on manager-magazin.de, the website of one of Germany's leading business magazines.

Table 9 – Cost-per-mille for selected banner ad formats and websites 2014

Website	CPM in EUR Superbanner	CPM in EUR Skyscraper	CPM in EUR Wallpaper
Faz.net	27	27	50
Manager-magazin.de	50	70	90
Vogue.com	55	55	75
Wiwo.de	45	45	80
Worldluxuryguide.com	45	55	–

Cost-per-mille (CPM) = the price for 1,000 users being confronted with a banner ad
Source: Axel Springer Mediapilot (2014), FAZ.Nnet (2014), Media Daten Verlag (2014a, 2014b, 2014c)

Affiliate marketing. Affiliate marketing follows a simple principle: an affiliate partner promotes the brand website of a merchant on third-party websites in exchange for a commission per user response (see Figure 47; Duffy, 2005, p. 162; Lammenett, 2014, p. 45; Ryan & Jones, 2012, p. 203). User responses typically refer to completed actions like clicking on the advertisement thereby being referred to the brand website, signing up to the brand website (lead), or ordering a product or service. Different technologies allow for tracking these user actions (Lammenett, 2014, pp. 46–50). A pre-defined commission (e.g., 10 per cent share of sales) only incurs upon completed user action. Thus, the risk of investing in advertising space lies with the affiliate.

As compared to conventional banner advertising affiliate marketing is considered beneficial in two major ways: first, through the affiliate's network the merchant can **reach** more users (Kreutzer, 2014, p. 214). Second, in conventional banner advertising the advertiser pays for visibility only, i.e. a fixed price per 1,000 users being confronted with the advertisement (cost-per-mille; compare Table 9). In an affiliate relationship payments are performance-based, i.e. cost for the merchant only incur if the affiliate's promotion was successful in terms of website traffic, lead generation or conversion into orders (Kollmann, 2013b, p. 201; Kreutzer, 2014, p. 213; Ryan & Jones, 2012, p. 203). These pricing models are commonly known as **cost-per-click (CPC)**, **cost-per-lead (CPL)**, and **cost-per-order (CPO**; Kreutzer, 2014, pp. 224–225; Lammenett, 2014, pp. 56–57). Following a CPC model (also known as pay-per-click) commission incurs when a user has clicked on an advertisement or link to access the promoted website. Following the CPL model (also known as pay-per-lead) commission incurs when a user has clicked on an advertisement, accessed and registered at the promoted website in a way that the merchant receives a qualified consumer contact. Finally and most frequently applied, when following a CPO model (also known as pay-per-sale) commission incurs when a user has placed an order. These most prevailing pricing models may be mixed (e.g., commission per click and additional commission per order) or combined with some fixed fee.

Figure 47 – Affiliate marketing model.

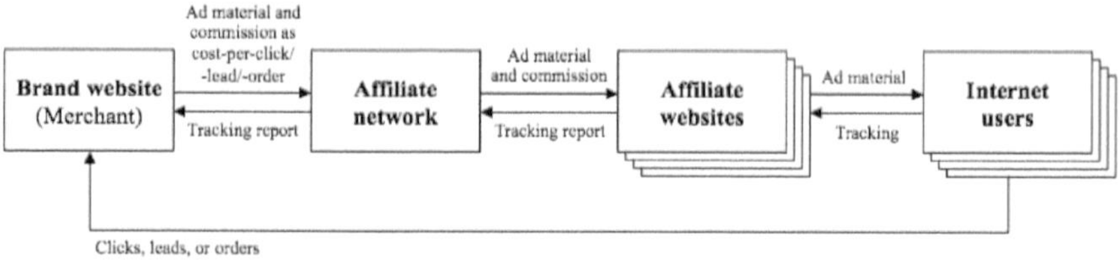

Source: adapted from Kreutzer (2014, p. 222)

In non-luxury markets, affiliate marketing has become a common practice. In Germany, 23 per cent of companies apply affiliate marketing (Deutsche Post, 2014, p. 77). In the United Kingdom, about 6 per cent of online sales is generated by affiliate marketing activities (The Future of Luxury, 2013).

In luxury markets, advertisers have been very reluctant towards affiliate marketing mainly because they are not in full control of the types of affiliate websites their brand is promoted on (G. Lovett, 2014). Protecting a luxury brand's image and how it is communicated is top priority for luxury goods manufacturers (Keller, 2009, p. 291). Affiliate websites, however, often include rather luxury-adverse environments like cashback and price comparison websites targeting price-sensitive, bargain-seeking users (Ryan & Jones, 2012, p. 204). Thus, if at all approaching affiliate marketing luxury goods manufacturers should start with small, carefully selected affiliate networks and consider affiliates like PR partners that talk favorably about the brand – however, not only for brand publicity, but for sales (The Future of Luxury, 2013).

4.4.2.4 Social media marketing (SMM)

Social media refer to Internet-based applications supporting the interactive communication among users with common interests (Grabs & Bannour, 2012, p. 26; Kaplan & Haenlein, 2010, p. 61; Kreutzer, 2014, p. 338; Okonkwo, 2010, p. 43). These applications include social and business networks (e.g., Facebook, Xing, LinkedIn), blogs or microblogs (e.g., Twitter, Wordpress), media-sharing sites (e.g., YouTube, Flickr, Soundcloud), mobile communities (e.g., Foursquare, Instagram), social bookmarking (e.g., Digg, Reddit), open-source platforms (e.g., Wikipedia) and others (Grabs & Bannour, 2012, p. 26; Zarella, 2010, p. 7). The term social media marketing (SMM) refers to the targeted use of social media platforms for brand communication purposes (Kreutzer, 2014, p. 338; Lammenett, 2014, p. 243; Weinberg, 2011, p. 4).

Through social media marketers can increase both **reach and intensity of communication**. As compared to other communication media, marketers can reach an increasingly large audience of users active in social media (Weinberg, 2011, p. 4; Zarella, 2010, p. 6). Social media are increasingly popular among Internet users worldwide. The websites of Facebook, YouTube, Wikipedia, and Twitter are among the top 10 websites in terms of website traffic (Alexa.com, 2014). As shown in Figure 48 the

Figure 48 – Worldwide social media usage.

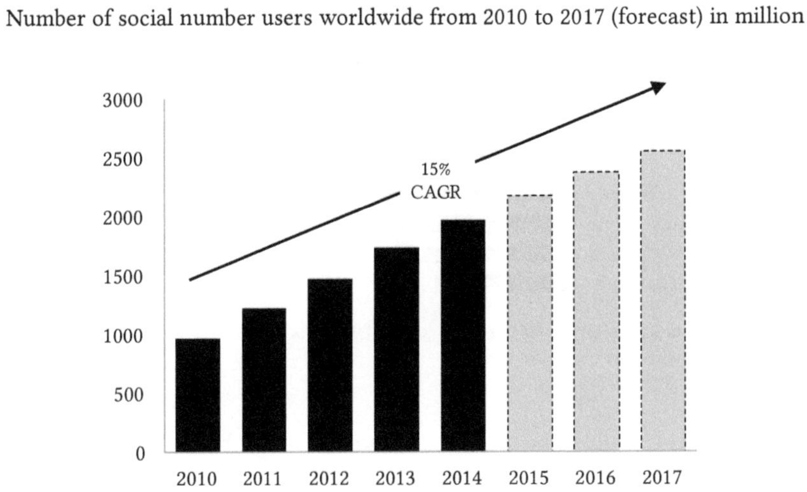

Note: figures refer to Internet users who use social media (e.g., Facebook, Twitter) site via any device at least once per month.
Source: eMarketer (2013)

number of social network users constantly rises by annually 15% up to nearly 2 billion users in 2014 (eMarketer, 2013). Facebook alone counts more than one billion users worldwide (Allfacebook.de, 2014).

Importantly and of interest to luxury goods manufacturers, social networks do not only enjoy high popularity among young, less-affluent users. Around 53 per cent of social network users are 35 years of age or older (Pew Research Center, 2013a). Also, the share of social networks usage is more than 70 per cent among users with an annual income of USD 75,000 or more (Pew Research Center, 2013b).

In addition to higher levels of reach, social media also enhance the intensity of communication. By definition, social media serve as platforms for interactive communication. In contrast to merely confronting users with company-generated content (CGC) on websites, search engine results pages, or banner advertisements, social media allow users to actively communicate with companies and other users and generate own content (user-generated content, UGC; Grabs & Bannour, 2012, pp. 42–43). The traditional one-to-many communication approach has emerged into an interactive many-to-many communication (Kreutzer, 2014, p. 338; Zarella, 2010, p. 5). Users post texts, pictures, music, or videos on their own or other users' social media pages as well as they like, comment, and share other user- or company-generated content. Specifically, social media facilitate sharing information about brands and products. Marketers can use this information as valuable feedback. To luxury shopper opinions and recommendations by family, friends, and colleagues

Figure 49 – Information sources by influence on luxury goods purchase.

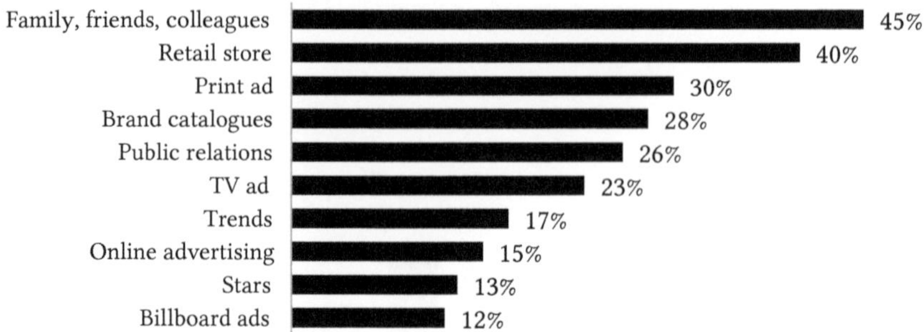

Sample: individuals with a household net income of EUR 60,000 or more from USA, Japan, France, Germany, Italy, Spain, and UK in 2011
Source: Lagardère & Ipsos (2012, p. 17)

represent the most influential source of information (see Figure 49; Lagardère & Ipsos, 2012, p. 17).

In addition to descriptive statistic, scientific research shows that word-of-mouth (WOM) influences demand more than conventional advertising. Specifically, the studies by Chen, Liu, Cheng-Hsi, & Lin (2013, p. 65) and Trusov, Bucklin, & Pauwels (2009, p. 96) report an average long-term WOM elasticity of demand of .43 and .53 respectively which exceeds the long-term elasticity of demand for conventional advertising which is reported to be .24 (Sethuraman, Tellis, & Briesch, 2011, p. 470). For fashion products, WOM elasticity of demand is even higher: an 10 per cent rise in WOM leads comes along with 10.3 per cent increase in sales (Chen et al., 2013, p. 65).

Social media and luxury. Social media facilitate the exchange of information and user-generated content and are thus considered to be "out of control" for marketers (Zarella, 2010, p. 5). In fact, the user community co-creates and distributes the content of brand communications (Jahn, Kunz, & Meyer, 2012, p. 222). In luxury, this user influence contradicts the fundamental necessity to fully control a luxury brand's image (Keller, 2009, p. 291). The lack of control has long caused hesitance among luxury goods manufacturers towards social media (Steel, 2013). The Swiss watchmaker Rolex, for example, has launched its official Facebook fanpage in April 2013 only, which is now counting about 3 million "fans", i.e. users that follow Rolex' Facebook page (Steel, 2013).

However, the phenomenon of consumers sharing opinions about brands and products is **not new** at all. Word-of-mouth (WOM), i.e. the oral exchange of information and opinions about brands and products, has always been an integral part of luxury brand communication – both to its positive and negative ends (Kapferer & Bastien, 2009a, pp. 162 & 178 & 219). Luxury goods are bought as manifestations of special moments in life. They convey a meaning to their owners who often share their stories with significant others both offline and online: the meaning of a Tiffany wedding ring, a Montblanc Meisterstück fountain pen given by a father to his son for graduation, or the Hermès Birkin bag a daughter inherited from her mother.

In principle, the same phenomenon applies to social media. Word-of-mouth has become "**word-of-mouse**" or simply online word-of-mouth (Okonkwo, 2010, p. 251). Consumers do not only orally exchange information but through Internet-based applications like Facebook, Twitter, and Co. These applications, however, have considerably **increased the reach and intensity** of word-of-mouth as they facilitate and accelerate the exchange of information and opinions among users. The president of US upscale retailer Nordstrom Direct refers to word-of-mouse as "word of mouth on steroids" emphasizing the increased volume and speed of information exchange (McCarthy, 2013). On social media user opinions reach more people more quickly.

While the accelerated and amplified diffusion of information is desirable for positive word-of-mouse, it is feared for negative word-of-mouse. However, consumers talk about luxury brands and products independently of whether or not brand owners engage in social media. Actively participating in social media allows luxury goods manufacturers to stimulate positive word-of-mouse and moderate consumer discussion. Hence, today luxury goods manufacturers **cannot afford not being present in social media** (Gastaldi, 2012, p. 122). Otherwise users will represent the luxury brand as stated by Head of Digital for Swiss watchmaker IWC: "But if you are not in those social spaces, then somebody else will be, and they will represent the brand" (Steel, 2013).

This phenomenon was observed for Rolex. As the Swiss watchmaker has long been hesitant to create its official Facebook page (until April 2013) users have generated their own Facebook pages on which they post, share, and discuss Rolex-related content. Combined, the three most prominent user-generated Rolex Facebook pages have collected about 1,800,000 likes (i.e. Facebook users who follow this page) as compared to around 4,200,000 likes the official Rolex fanpage has collected since April 2013 (Facebook.com/Rolex, 2015; Facebook.com, 2015a, 2015b, 2015c; as of April 2015). While these numbers illustrate the strong desirability of the Rolex brand among users worldwide, they also emphasize the need for luxury goods manufacturers to actively participate in social media.

Empirical insights shed a positive light on luxury brands in social media. Kim & Ko (2012, p. 1485) find that social media marketing positively affects luxury brand equity. A recent study by Lovett, Peres, & Shachar (2013, p. 437) reveals that high-end and unique brands enjoy higher levels of word-of-mouth. More importantly, our examination of 40 luxury fashion, car, watch, and jewellery brands using the social media monitoring tool Socialmention.com indicates that all brands enjoy a positive ratio of positive versus negative mentions in social media (see Figure 50). For example, every single negative mention about the British limousine manufacturer Rolls-Royce follows as much as 89 positive mentions.

Figure 50 – Social mentions of 40 luxury brands.

Number and sentiment (positive-to-negative ratio) of mentions of selected luxury brands by other Internet users

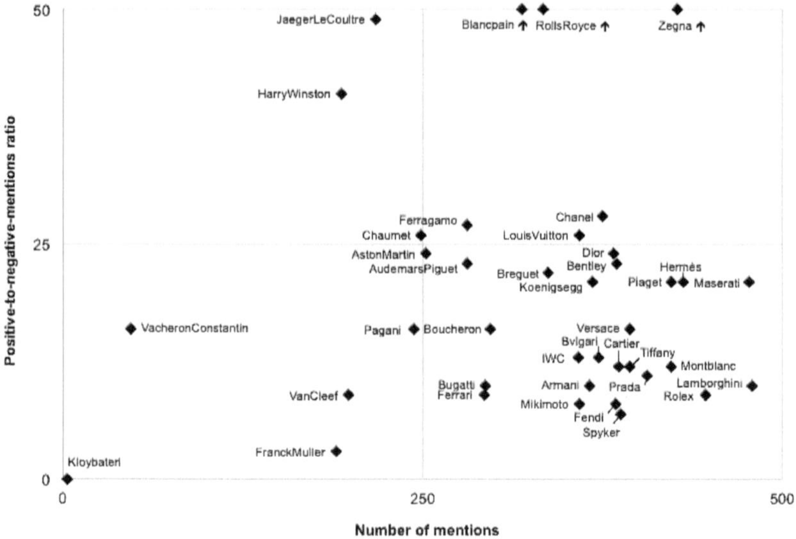

Note: data collected from socialmention.com on July 22, 2014; spelling of brands reflects search terms used.
Source: author

Company-generated content. Social media marketing involves stimulating and moderating interactive communication with users through Internet-based applications like Facebook, Twitter, and Co. Luxury goods manufacturers stimulate interactive communication through company-generated content which can be classified into long-term and short-term content. Long-term company-generated content mainly refers to **social media profiles** through which brands present themselves to other users (Grabs & Bannour, 2012, p. 265; Kollmann, 2013b, p. 196). These profiles include, for example, "fanpages" in Facebook, "channels" on YouTube, or "boards" on Pinterest. Social media allow for branding profiles within a given set of elements, e.g., profile names, pictures and descriptions. These elements typically remain constant for some period of time in order to be easily identifiable for other users.

The British iconic fashion brand Burberry, for example, simply uses "Burberry" as profile name, the equestrian knight Prorsum logo as profile picture, and the seasonal collection as title picture (Burberry.com, 2014b; Facebook.com/Burberry, 2014b; Twitter.com/Burberry, 2014; YouTube.com/user/Burberry 2014). Notably, these elements should be designed consistently across all online channels including the brand website and social media pages.

Users who are interested in a specific luxury brand can follow its branded social media profile, for example, by simply clicking the "like" button on the branded Facebook page, the "follow" button on the branded Twitter account, or the "subscribe" button on the branded YouTube channel. By following a branded social media profile **users subscribe to receiving** the latest company-generated content, i.e. information in the form of text messages, photos, videos, links or other social media enabled tools. Similarly, users can un-follow at any time. Hence, users receive brand communication material only upon subscription.

Short-term content of a branded social media page refers to the information shared with its followers within rather short time intervals, e.g., on a daily basis. Short-term contents are typically listed in "walls" or "boards" and organized by date (latest content appears first). The information shared goes beyond presenting the latest collection. This is typically done in traditional advertising campaigns in order to create awareness and desire among prospects and clients. Followers of a luxury branded social media page are already committed to or at least interested in the luxury brand. Short-term content may reinforce and enhance the positive images users have about a luxury brand (Gastaldi, 2012, p. 123). Hence, company-generated content should be carefully planned and designed according to the following characteristics: authentic, humble, relevant, regularly shared, and consistent across social media channels (Düweke & Rabsch, 2012, p. 159; Kaplan & Haenlein, 2010, pp. 66–67).

A best practice for stimulating consumer engagement refers to Porsche's "Thank You – A 1,000,000 Times" campaign when Porsche's Facebook page reached one million "likes", i.e. users who follow Porsche on Facebook. Porsche allowed one million users to put their name on a Porsche 911 GTS R Hybrid car (Porsche.com, 2014). This campaign was communicated via Facebook only and has gone viral, i.e. the information has diffused as followers shared the information with their respective followers thus multiplying the reach of the campaign (Kreutzer 2014, p. 464). The campaign was a true success: within only ten days one million users entered their names and Porsche's Facebook page gained another 380,000 likes (UDG Consulting, 2012, p. 5). To keep users engaged and make them share the message, Porsche allowed users to search for and precisely locate their names on the Porsche 911.

User-generated content. While social media allow luxury goods manufacturers to simulate user engagement, they also require them to react to or moderate brand-related user-generated content (UCG). Brand-related user-generated content refers to users sharing content on a branded, user-owned or third-party social media page in form of text messages, pictures, videos or links. The content shared conveys positive, neutral, or negative sentiments about the brand (Kreutzer, 2014, p. 71). As shown in Figure 50 positive mentions clearly outweigh negative mentions. Still, luxury goods manufacturers are not immune to negative feedback which eventually emerges as a "shitstorm", i.e. the fast, viral diffusion ("storm") of negative brand-related content ("shit") through social media. To mitigate harmful effects of negative feedbacks or even shitstorms, luxury goods manufacturers need to closely monitor and be prepared to eventually react to user-generated content (Okonkwo, 2010, p. 214).

Figure 51 – Negative user-generated content: Burberry.

Note: logos, images, and names blurred for copyright and privacy reasons.
Source: Facebook.com/Burberry (2014a)

We typically observe three scenarios when a user has shared negative brand-related content: no reaction, company reaction, or other users' reaction. Considering the vast amount of brand-related user-generated content shared on social media marketers cannot react to any user comment or shared content – whether reinforcing positive or mitigating negative feedback. Apart from feasibility considerations, not reacting to negative user-generated content may be a smart tactic as it signals respect for users' opinions and does not provoke further (eventually even more negative) discussion.

Figure 51 shows user reactions to a picture shared by Burberry as part of its "The Burberry Heritage Archive" campaign. The picture displays a worn trench coat with indicates "Made in England". While most followers like the picture and the heritage associated to it, few others criticize that nowadays most Burberry items are produced abroad (Cadwalladr, 2012). User Edmundo argues: "Made in England no more". And another user, Ciprian, writes "Made in Pakistan…".

In serious matters (e.g., severe complaints, false accusations) marketers should friendly and objectively respond. Deleting user-generated content shared on brand-owned social media pages is generally considered a "no-go" (Ceyp & Scupin, 2013, p. 103). Most social media platforms offer a report button through which users can report inappropriate content to the provider of the platform. For example, on August 8, 2014 a user commented on a Facebook post by Hermès by sharing a link referring to dubious website selling fake Hermès products. Some time later this comment has been removed.

Figure 52 – User discussion on Facebook: Chanel.

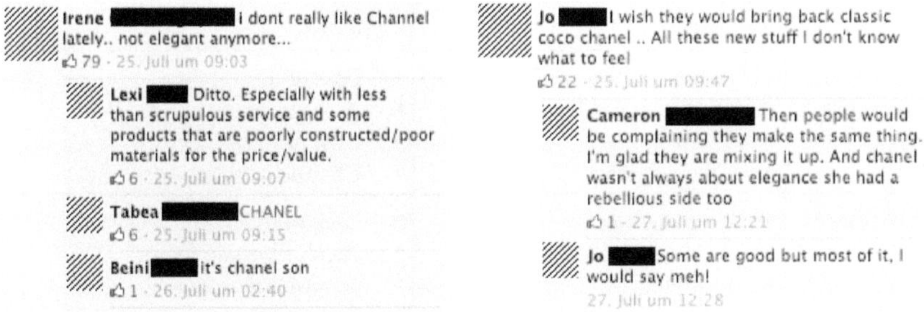

Note: images and names are blurred for copyright and privacy reasons.
Source: Facebook.com/Chanel (2014)

In fortunate cases, luxury goods manufacturers do not have to react as other brand-loyal users vindicate the brand against complaining users (Okonkwo, 2010, p. 53). Figure 52 depicts a user discussion on Chanel's "Coco Coach" Fall/Winter 2014 campaign on Facebook. While nearly 50,000 users express their positive support by "liking" this Chanel campaign, some users (e.g., Irene and Jo) complain about the lack of Chanel's authentic elegance in its new collection and receive support by other users in form of 79 and 22 likes, respectively. However, one brand loyal user, Cameron, vindicates the campaign by expressing his support for the less elegant, but more "rebellious" side of Chanel.

4.5 Online distribution

4.5.1 Online distribution and luxury

Luxury goods manufacturers have long been hesitant to adopt the Internet as a channel of distribution (Chevalier & Mazzalovo, 2008, p. 348; Gastaldi, 2012, p. 112; Okonkwo, 2009, p. 303; Quintavalle, 2012, p. 92). Until today, still 40 to 50 per cent of luxury goods manufacturers do not sell their goods online (Bain & Company & Fondazione Altagamma, 2013, p. 10; L2 Luxury Digital IQ Report 2010 reported by Chevalier & Gutsatz, 2012, p. 68; Roland Berger & Meisterkreis, 2013, p. 16). The suitability of the Internet not only as mean of communication but also as a channel of distribution for luxury goods is still controversially discussed among marketing scholars, practitioners and users (Quintavalle, 2012, p. 75). Due to the apparent incompatibility of the Internet with the aura of luxury the question of whether or not to sell luxury goods online is called the "**Internet dilemma**" (Kapferer & Bastien, 2012, p. 233).

Before assessing whether luxury goods manufacturers should use the Internet not only as a mean of communication but also as a channel of distribution it is important to understand the benefits and concerns associated with the online distribution of luxury goods. Existing literature offers multiple reasons both in favour for or against the online distribution of luxury goods. These benefits and concerns both from a managerial and a consumer perspective are summarized in Table 10.

Table 10 – Benefits of and concerns about direct online distribution

	Benefits	Concerns
Managerial perspective	▪ Additional sales ▪ Higher margin/ profitability ▪ Control ▪ Client contact	▪ Loss of desirability ▪ Transparency ▪ Cost of infrastructure ▪ Channel conflicts
Consumer perspective	▪ Convenience ▪ Product availability ▪ Intimacy	▪ Lack of touch and feel ▪ Lack of human factor ▪ Security concerns ▪ Reduced feelings of exclusiveness

Source: author

4.5.1.1 Benefits of online distribution

Managerial perspective. First, from a managerial perspective **increasing sales volume** represents one of the most obvious motives for firms to sell their goods online. Even though luxury goods manufacturers need to limit the diffusion of their products in order to remain desirable in the eye of the customer (Dubois & Paternault, 1995, p. 69) some healthy growth in sales and profit is required to ensure the long-term success of the firm (Keller, 2009, p. 293; Wetlaufer, 2001, p. 121). Growth in volume sales can be achieved through either acquiring new customers or increasing repeat purchases of existing customers. By offering their products online luxury goods manufacturers can attract new customers that live in geographically distant places or simply prefer an intimate shopping experience at home (Quintavalle, 2012, p. 77 & 93). At the same time luxury goods manufacturers can increase repeat purchases of existing customers – often busy high-income individuals – as they can shop independently of place and time, 24 hours a day, 365 days a year (Hennigs et al., 2012, p. 31; Quintavalle, 2012, p. 77).

Second, by operating a monobrand online store (e.g., a website-integrated online store like on Louisvuitton.com) luxury goods manufacturers may also ensure higher **margins and thus profitability** (Chevalier & Gutsatz, 2012, p. 66). At the one hand, when operating a monobrand online store luxury goods manufacturers do not have to share the margin with third-party distributors. Data from 2008 by Keylens Research Center (reported by Manninger, 2012, p. 245) demonstrate a positive relationship between the share of sales relaized through direct distribution (i.e. monobrand stores) and the firm's EBIT margin. On the other hand, the costs of operating a monobrand online store are lower than the costs of ever-rising rents for operating a stationary monobrand store in the prime locations of the world's metropolitan areas (Kapferer & Bastien, 2012, p. 234).

Third, **control of distribution** represents one of the key characteristics of the luxury business model (Cervellon & Coudriet, 2013, p. 870; Chevalier & Gutsatz,

2012, p. 66). Direct distribution does not only ensure a maximum of control of how a luxury brands' history and aura are communicated to the client (Brun & Moretto, 2012, p. 615; Kapferer & Bastien, 2009a, p. 238), but also how retail prices are set and communicated (Fassnacht et al., 2013, p. 107). Fassnacht et al. (2013, p. 114) empirically find that high-end and stable prices positively affect the rarity value of a luxury brand. Within the online marketplace operating a monobrand online store helps protecting the brand from non-official offers such as resellers or counterfeits (Quintavalle, 2012, p. 93). The official website of a brand serves as a credible source of information and product supply.

Finally, luxury goods manufacturers directly interact with their customers (Quintavalle, 2012, pp. 92–93). Data such as click rates and time spent on site can be automatically collected when users browse the monobrand online store and can be used for **marketing intelligence** purposes in order to constantly improve the firm's market offering. This type of data is considerably more accurate, comprehensive and up-to-date than data *"manually"* collected in stationary monobrand stores.

Consumer perspective. First, consumer motivations to shop online have been found to be fundamentally different from offline shopping motivations (Alba & Lynch, 1997, p. 40; Liu et al., 2013, p. 888; Rohm & Swaminathan, 2004, pp. 752–754). As for non-luxury brands, online shopping motivation for luxury brands is mostly driven by **convenience** considerations (Liu et al., 2013, p. 888; Rohm & Swaminathan, 2004, p. 754; Szymanski & Hise, 2000, p. 317). In a luxury brand's online store consumers can shop independently of opening hours (i.e. 24 hours a day, seven days a week; Hennigs et al., 2012, p. 31; Quintavalle, 2012, p. 94; Riley & Lacroix, 2003, p. 99) and location (i.e. from virtually any place geographically distant from actual stationary store locations; Okonkwo, 2009, p. 304; Quintavalle, 2012, p. 93). For luxury consumers, convenience has been found to rank first among the reason to buy luxury items online (Liu et al., 2013, p. 888).

Second, another motivation for consumers to shop online refers to the **availability of products** (Liu et al., 2013, p. 889). This includes both the actual physical availability of a given product and the variety of products offered. The desired product might be out of stock in the stationary monobrand store nearby or is simply not listed due to limited shelf space (Szymanski & Hise, 2000, p. 312). Also, monobrand online stores can offer a broader variety of products and product variants (e.g., sizes, colours, materials; Liu et al., 2013, p. 889). This is an important benefit for online shoppers since they have been found to exhibit higher levels of variety-seeking behaviour than offline shoppers (Eastman, Iyer, & Randall, 2009, p. 111).

However, the higher perceived product availability offered by online stores mainly refers to the entry or core range of a luxury brand's product portfolio. Limited or one-of-a-kind items (also called "griffe"; Kapferer & Bastien, 2009a, p. 250) are often exclusively sold through stationary flagship or monobrand stores, often to an exclusive, loyal clientele only. The Parisian leather manufacturer Hermès, for example, offers some of its classic bags online like the Jypsiere or Evelyne, but not its iconic Birkin bag (Hermes.com, 2015a, 2015c).

Finally, while some consumers like to celebrate the shopping act for a luxury good walking with conspicuously branded shopping bags through the crowded city centres of the world's metropolitan areas, some consumers might simply prefer the **intimacy** when shopping from home (Quintavalle, 2012, p. 77). Two independent studies by Berger & Ward (2010, p. 558) and Han et al. (2010, p. 17) identify a group of luxury consumers who prefer subtle signals (e.g., brand markers with low visibility) that may be decoded by other insiders only. This is not only to differentiate from the mainstream. Especially in time of economic downturn, a certain clientele prefers not to be seen by others when shopping for luxury goods since it may be regarded as inadequate given the financial suffering of other members of the society. Also, being seen coming out of the most prestigious jeweller in place can attract criminals. In those cases shopping in an online store represents a discreet and rather secure alternative. At the same time the intimate shopping environment provided by online stores enables consumers to purchase a luxury good independently of a sales person's pressure.

4.5.1.2 Concerns about online distribution

Managerial perspective. First, the on-going debate among marketing executives and scholars about the suitability of the Internet as a legitimate channel of distribution has been largely driven by the common belief that making luxury goods accessible online comes at the **expense of brand desirability** (Chevalier & Gutsatz, 2012, p. 67; Hennigs et al., 2012, p. 31; Kapferer & Bastien, 2012, p. 249; Quintavalle, 2012, p. 75). Partly, this belief results from the apparent contradiction between the ubiquity of the mass medium Internet and a luxury brand's concept of exclusiveness (see Figure 36; Gastaldi, 2012, p. 112; Kapferer & Bastien, 2012, p. 247; Kluge et al., 2013, p. 901; Okonkwo, 2009, p. 304). Following the logic of the dream formula (see Figure 21) selling luxury goods online is considered "extremely dangerous" since it increases "penetration too fast" which in turn diminishes the dream value, i.e. the desirability of the brand (Kapferer & Bastien, 2012, p. 249). In addition to this fear of over-diffusion, both executives (as expressed in the quote by Kering-CEO François-Henri Pinault, Daneshkhu, 2012) and marketing scholars (Kapferer & Bastien, 2012, p. 249) are concerned that luxury goods are no longer *hard-to-get* items when sold on the ubiquitous and easily accessible online marketplace. In the offline world consumers are required to invest time and effort to get a luxury product. Consumers are not only required to travel to the location of prestigious luxury retailers, they also need to know the code where to get the most desired items. Since those aspects do not longer hold in the online marketplace, it diminishes consumer feelings of exclusiveness. Thus, the online distribution of luxury goods violates one of the imperatives for marketing luxury brands: "make it difficult for clients to buy" (Kapferer & Bastien, 2009b, p. 318).

Second, another concern refers to the **transparency of information** about both prices and product details (Gastaldi, 2012, p. 112; Hennigs et al., 2012, p. 31; Kapferer & Bastien, 2012, p. 232). Providing detailed information about prices and products in an online store setting is often legally required or simply necessary to make online shoppers buy heavy-ticket items. Kapferer & Bastien (2012, p. 232) consider the communication of price as "one of the trickiest" issues luxury goods manufacturers face when selling their goods online. It represents one main reason why luxury goods manufacturers have long been and still are hesitant to adopt the Internet as channel of distribution (Gastaldi, 2012, p. 112). Transparency of price information is considered undesired for the following three reasons:

(a) Kapferer & Bastien (2009a, pp. 190–191) argue that in luxury the general price level of a brand's product range should be known to a large portion of the population whereas the exact price of a luxury product should be known by the owner only. The expected price as perceived by prospects should always exceed the actual price of a given luxury product. This overestimation of price, they argue, helps justify the purchase of a luxury item or enhances the value of a gift. Now, the likelihood of overestimation decreases considerably with the easy accessibility of exact price information communicated through the online store.

(b) In luxury, a brand is something unique, an identity originated from the vision of its creator, grown over time – something that defies any comparison with competitors (Kapferer & Bastien, 2012, p. 66). However, as a result of the simplified access to information in the online world any luxury product may become subject of price comparisons (Seringhaus, 2005, p. 16).

(c) As price information becomes easily accessible for consumers, luxury goods manufacturers need to rethink and reorganize their pricing strategy towards price consistency across multiple distribution channels. Consistency or stability of high-end prices has been found to positively affect the luxury image of a brand (Fassnacht et al., 2013, p. 112).

Another concern refers to the transparency of information about product details. High-resolution 360-degree views of the product along with a detailed description of product features have become a necessary service for prospects and clients. At the same time, however, the detailed information might help counterfeit suppliers to produce fake products that look highly identical to the originals (Hennigs et al., 2012, p. 31).

Third, directly operating a monobrand online store requires additional financial and organizational resources for installing the **technological and logistical infrastructure**. Launching an online store requires an investment of about EUR 200,000 (Spieler, 2011). Additional resources are needed to re-organize the logistics department in order to cope with the increasingly complex management of stocks and handling of outgoing and incoming deliveries (Gastaldi, 2012, p. 112). While this challenge applies to any business, it becomes particularly tricky for luxury goods manufacturers since, unlike most non-luxury goods manufacturers, they must not excessively boost volume sales while they still need to reach a critical size of sales in order to cover the financial resources involved in running the monobrand online store.

Finally, directly operating a monobrand online store may cause **conflicts with offline channel partners** (Chevalier & Mazzalovo, 2008, p. 348). The monobrand online store is likely not only to expand the customer base (e.g., by attracting new customers who live in geographically distant places) but also to encourage customers who used to shop for a luxury brand's goods at their preferred luxury retailer to switch to the online channel for convenience reasons. This shift from offline to online channels comes at the expense of third-party wholesale partners and might cause severe conflicts.

Consumer perspective. First, while the Internet serves well as a medium for transmitting audio-visual content such as high-resolution product illustrations it **lacks the possibility to touch, smell and feel products** (Chevalier & Mazzalovo, 2008, p. 348; Kapferer & Bastien, 2012, p. 250; Okonkwo, 2009, p. 304; Riley & Lacroix, 2003, p. 98). Two independent studies by Riley & Lacroix (2003, p. 100) and Liu et al. (2013, p. 890) find that the lack of touch and feel ranks as top reason why luxury consumers prefer traditional brick-and-mortar shopping over online shopping. In general, this concern applies to any physical good sold online. However, it becomes more relevant for luxury goods, which are made of finest, extraordinary materials. One might shop for a simple, one-size wristwatch in the Internet. When buying a Vacheron Constantin, however, most clients themselves (especially those buying for the first time and for themselves) as well as the sales personnel wants them to carefully touch the precious metal case and smell the leather strap. Wiedmann, Hennigs, Klarmann, & Behrens (2013, pp. 63–66) stress the importance of a multi-sensory experience of a brand caused by visual, auditory, haptic, olfactory, and gustatory stimuli for a luxury brand's image and distribution strategy. To date electronic devices are not capable of touching this broad range of human senses.

Second, the intimacy and anonymity provided by the Internet comes at the expense of **human interaction** between the shopper and a sales person (Kapferer & Bastien, 2012, p. 250; Okonkwo, 2009, p. 304). However, the one-to-one, "quasi-affective" relationship a sales person should build up with every single shopper plays an important role in the lengthy buying process for luxury goods (Kapferer & Bastien, 2012, pp. 234–235) and has been found to be one of the reasons why some luxury consumers prefer shopping in stationary retail stores (Liu et al., 2013, p. 891). More than for non-luxury products the sales person of luxury brands is a guide of good taste and shares the long-grown passion for the brand and its products. Certainly, providing personalized service via telephone hotline or instant chat has become a common and legitimate practice to compensate for the lack of human interaction. Still, critical elements of human interaction (e.g., gesture, style etc.) cannot be communicated online or via telephone.

Third, as a consequence of the lack of touch and human interaction in an online retailing environment consumers might be concerned about the **security of transactions** (Hennigs et al., 2012, p. 30; Riley & Lacroix, 2003, pp. 99–100; Wu, Chen, & Chaney, 2013, p. 211). Security concerns has been found to rank among the top reasons why consumers do not buy online (Riley & Lacroix, 2003, p. 100) but rather prefer the trusted environment provided by an established brick-and-mortar store (Liu et al., 2013, p. 890). On the one hand, given the heavy price tags of luxury goods consumers might be concerned about the security of their financial transactions (Hennigs et al., 2012, p. 30). On the other hand, consumers might be concerned about complicated return policies for such high-priced items or the risk of receiving a counterfeit product from a fake website (Wu et al., 2013, p. 211).

Finally, knowing that a luxury brand's products are accessible not only to an exclusive clientele but to virtually anyone can **reduce an owner's feelings of exclusiveness**. Thus, the purchase of a luxury good looses parts of its experiential and symbolic value since the effort and connoisseurship needed to find and get an extraordinary item is considerably reduced – for oneself and others (Kapferer & Bastien, 2012, p. 249). Before the rise of the Internet, the affluent consumer was required to know where to get a specific item and not rarely had to travel to cities like Milan, Paris, or London to physically get it. This connoisseurship and effort represents an important part of the associations consumers have with the brand (Kapferer & Bastien, 2012, p. 71). It enhanced the feelings of a self-reward or the gesture of a gift to the beloved ones. This experiential and symbolic value decreases considerably when shopping luxury goods from home just like anybody could.

4.5.1.3 Conclusion: the online distribution challenge

The discussion above reveals a still-existing controversy about the suitability of the Internet as an additional channel of distribution for luxury goods manufacturers. On the one hand, selling luxury goods online increases reach at relatively low cost while providing convenience, product availability, and intimacy to the affluent clientele (compare Table 10). On the other hand, the online distribution lacks in providing the touch and feel and human interaction needed to fully appreciate the sophistication of luxury goods and is commonly believed to dilute a brand's exclusiveness. Consequently, answers to the online distribution challenge of luxury goods vary considerably. Okonkwo (2010) advocates the adoption of online distribution by stating that "it has become crucial to enable this wider client base to not only interact with the products and services, but also to be able to purchase them" (p. 173). In contrast, Kapferer & Bastien (2012) argue that luxury goods "**should not be sold**" (p. 248) via the Internet (with few exceptions being entry range products and the case of young luxury brands aiming for initial growth (pp. 249 & 253)) in order to preserve the luxury brand's exclusiveness.

Yet, to date the question how the online accessibility of luxury goods actually affects consumer perceptions of scarcity and brand desirability remains unanswered. This question, i.e. the third research question of this manuscript, will be examined in more detail both theoretically and empirically in the Chapters 5 to 8, which will follow below.

4.5.2 Online store formats

Online distribution should be considered as an integral part of a manufacturer's overall distribution strategy (compare Chapter 3.4) rather than being an independent, isolated decision. Online and offline distribution channels complement rather than substitute each other. As a part of a manufacturer's channel-mix online distribution extends the reach of supply from a local supply of affluent locals and travellers in major cities, tourist destinations, and airports to a nationwide supply of the affluent clientele in selected countries. In accordance with the overall distribution strategy, online distribution strategy is first of all about defining objectives (e.g., which countries to serve at which cost, share of margin, and level of control) and designing an integrated channel structure in terms of channel length (i.e. how many tiers of intermediaries) and width (i.e. how intermediaries per tier; compare Chapter 3.4.2). For both offline and online alike, luxury distribution strategy typically aims at a rather low channel length (i.e. few, preferably no tiers of intermediaries) and width (i.e. selective or exclusive distribution). While distribution-strategic considerations similarly apply to both offline and online distribution, with the advance of the Internet new store formats have developed like **monobrand online stores, multibrand online retailers** and **outlet stores** (see Figure 33). These online store formats will be described in the following.

4.5.2.1 Monobrand online store

The monobrand online store is typically integrated into the main brand website (e.g., Louisvuitton.com) and carries goods of one brand only that are usually offered at full prices and directly sold and delivered to end consumers. Similar to offline monobrand boutiques, monobrand online stores are operated either directly by the manufacturer or indirectly by a franchise partner. The Yoox Group, for example, has specified in managing the monobrand online stores of luxury brands like Armani, Bottega Veneta, Lanvin, Missoni, or Pomellato in about 100 countries based on a revenue-sharing model (Yooxgroup.com, 2015). While a franchise operated store model leaves the manufacturer with a relatively lower share of margin, it benefits from the expertise of franchise partner in terms of e-commerce processes, technology, and logistics while keeping control over brand communication, assortment, and service levels. Similar to offline store design, planning a monobrand online store involves deciding on the domain name, store layout, assortment, product display and service level.

Domain name. The domain name (e.g., Louisvuitton.com) can be referred to as the "location" of an online store. Basically, the monobrand online store can be either **integrated into** or **separated from** the major brand website (Quintavalle, 2012, p. 94), i.e. the online store can be accessed either through the major brand domain "brand.com" or a separate domain like "brand-estore.com". Today, the majority of monobrand online stores are integrated into brand websites with intuitive, credible domain names, e.g., Hermes.com, Montblanc.com, or Piaget.

com. A website-integrated online store facilitates navigation of online shopping and increases the credibility of the online store. However, brands like Bugatti and Tag Heuer used to experiment with operating a monobrand online store separate from their core domains in order to sell branded accessories only. In addition to the main domains Bugatti.com and Tagheuer.com, which were dedicated to communicating the brand and its core products (i.e. supercars and watches, respectively), they used to operate online stores under the domains Bugatti-collection.com and Tagheuereboutique.com.

Layout. Similar to the layout of a brick-and-mortar retail outlet (compare Chapter 3.4.3.3), the layout of the online store navigates user through product categories and products (Manganari, Siomkos, & Vrechopoulos, 2009, p. 1143). As for offline stores, we may mainly differentiate between a **grid layout** and a **freeform layout** (Vrechopoulos, O'Keefe, Doukidis, & Siomkos, 2004, p. 14; Zentes et al., 2011, p. 275). The grid layout is characterized by an easy-to-use, hierarchical structure (e.g., product category > collection > product), where products are displayed in lines and columns, whereas the less structured freeform layout allows for a more entertaining discovery of products (Vrechopoulos et al., 2004, pp. 17 & 20). In luxury, the online store layout should be in line with the overall website concept (compare Chapter 4.4.2.1) and allow for both an experiential discovery of the brand and its products and for an easy-to-use navigation along logical, hierarchical structures. For example, the main navigation of Montblanc's website consists of "Show Collections", "Meet Montblanc", and "Shop Online" (Montblanc.com, 2015a). While "Show Collections" links to an area of the website, where user may discover different collections and products in a enjoyable informative manner (freeform layout), "Shop Online" links to a dedicated shopping area, where products are displayed in lines and columns and may be sorted by multiple criteria (grid layout). However, an experiential design applies to the pre-purchase, product-discovery phase only. Once a product has been put to the shopping basket the checkout process should be as convenient as possible.

Assortment, product display, and service level. Defining which products the monobrand online store should carry, how they should be displayed, and which add-on services should be provided is closely linked to online product management considerations. First, while Kapferer & Bastien (2012) explicitly state luxury goods manufacturers should sell a limited number of entry-range products only, but "no core products" (p. 253), the assortment of a monobrand online store typically covers both entry- and core-range products, but not the limited, high-end collections (compare Chapter 4.2.2). Second, products, product details, packaging, and gift-wrapping should be displayed using high-resolution images from multiple angles, videos, zooming, and configuration options (compare Chapter 4.2.3). Third, online add-on services include delivery, customization, shopping assistance, gift-wrapping, and offline-store information (compare Chapter 4.2.4).

4.5.2.2 Multibrand online retailers

Other than directly serving end consumers through a monobrand online store, luxury goods manufacturers may sell their merchandise wholesale to carefully selected multibrand online retailers. These online retailers buy and resell the merchandise of multiple, competing brands under their own domain name. As opposed to direct distribution via monobrand online stores in selected countries, luxury goods manufacturers benefit from a wholesale distribution model via multibrand online retailers in terms of both supply-based and economic objectives (compare Figure 30 and Figure 33): in terms of supply multibrand online retailers help manufacturers quickly increase **reach** and thus generate a critical level of sales. Multibrand retailers like Net-a-porter.com or Yoox.com offer a nearly worldwide delivery and record higher website traffic than websites of single brands like Armani.com, Gucci.com, or Prada.com (Alexa.com, 2015a, 2015b, 2015c, 2015d, 2015e). In terms of economic considerations the manufacturer benefits from secured **up-front orders** on the one hand and **low cost** on the other, i.e. neither capital investments in setting up the technological and logistical infrastructure of the online store (requires about EUR 200,000; Spieler, 2011) nor fixed costs of operating the store incur.

These benefits, however, come at the expense of a lower **share of margin**, lowered levels of **exclusiveness**, a lack of direct **client interaction** as well as lower levels of **control**. Hence, like for their offline counterparts, multibrand online retailers should be carefully selected based on the quality and price level of assortment, online store atmosphere, product display, pricing policies, and service levels. In general, we may differentiate multibrand online retailers along three dimensions: breadth of assortment (broad versus narrow), pricing policy (full-price versus off-price channels), and channel strategy (online pure-player versus multi-channel players).

Online department store. Like its brick-and-mortar counterpart (compare Chapter 3.4.3.1), the online department store is characterized by offering a broad variety of product categories and SKUs within each category (i.e. a broad and deep assortment) primarily sold at full prices. Online department stores are either online pure-players like the Richemont-owned Net-a-porter.com or Yoox.com, primarily online players with stationary store roots like Mytheresa.com or Luisaviaroma.com, or the online stores of traditional stationary department stores like Harrods.com, Kadewe.de, or Nordstrom.com. Their assortment typically ranges from ready-to-wear, leather goods, accessories, perfume & cosmetics, to jewellery & watches and home design. These online department stores carry the merchandise of well-respected luxury brands like Bottega Veneta, Chloé, Fendi, Lanvin, or Prada.

Online specialty store. In contrast to the online department store, online specialty stores offer a broad variety of products within few product categories (i.e. a narrow, but deep assortment), which are primarily sold at full prices. The category foci of online specialty stores range from **beauty** (e.g., pure-player like Flaconi.de or multi-channel retailers like Douglas or Sephora carrying all major beauty brands), **fashion** (e.g., the Yoox-owned Thecorner.com authorized to carry brands like Bottega Veneta, Burberry Prorsum, or Jil Sander; Thecorner.com, 2015), **jewellery** (e.g., Hamiltonjewelers.com authorized to carry brands like Mikimoto, and Pomellato; Hamiltonjewelers.com, 2015), **furniture** (e.g., Cairo.de authorized to carry brands like USM Haller, Thonet, and Vitra; Cairo.de, 2015), to **wine & spirits** (e.g., Hawesko.de authorized to carry wines like Château Lafite-Rothschild, Château Latour, or Château Margaux and champagnes like Krug and Dom Perignon; Hawesko.de, 2015a, 2015b).

Online outlet store. In contrast to online department and specialty stores, an online outlet store refers to an **off-price** online store format that offers a limited amount of original merchandise at discounted prices (Fassnacht et al., 2012, p. 129; Quintavalle, 2012, p. 95; Wiedmann, Hennigs, & Klarmann, 2011, p. 38). Often, online outlet stores are organised as so called shopping communities (also shopping clubs) whose offering is limited to registered members only and either time-limited like on Vente-privee.com or Westwing.de (also called sales events or flash sales) or continuous like on Bestsecret.de. Other online outlet stores like Outnet.com (a subsidiary of the Net-a-Porter Group) do not require prior member registration. Prices are discounted up to 70 per cent of original retail prices (Quintavalle, 2012, p. 95).

Particularly ready-to-wear, leather goods, and home design manufacturers make use of online shopping communities in order to sell overstock, end-of-season, or second choice items through channels separate from their full-price monobrand outlets. However, since excessive price discounts may dilute a luxury brand's appeal of exclusiveness (compare Chapter 3.2), online shopping communities should be carefully selected based on criteria like **exclusiveness** of membership, **discretion** of brand communication, and **assortment**. For example, while users can freely register to become a member of Amazon's Buyvip.com or Vente-privee.com, you need to be invited by existing members and apply for the limited membership in the community of Bestsecret.de (Bestsecret.de, 2015a; Buyvip.com, 2015; Vente-privee.com, 2015). Also, online outlets differ in terms of discretion of brand communication. While online outlets like Outnet.com or Vente-privee.com openly communicate brands for sale without previous member login, brand communication at Bestsecret.com is more discreet allowing only logged in members to browse brands and products (Bestsecret.de, 2015c; Outnet.com, 2015b; Vente-privee.com, 2015). Finally, the average quality and price level of the assortment should be considered. For example, while the outlet stores of Bestsecret.de and Vente-privee.com also feature mass-market brands like Adidas, Desigual, Nike, and Tommy Hilfiger, the assortment of Outnet.com combines young, talented fashion designers with established labels like Balenciaga, Chloé, Fendi, Lanvin or Versace (Bestsecret.de, 2015b; Outnet.com, 2015a; Vente-privee.com, 2015).

4.5.2.3 Multi-channel integration

Having discussed multiple store formats separately (both offline and online, monobrand and multibrand) it is important to note that luxury goods manufacturers should manage all elements of the channel-mix in an integrated, rather than isolated, manner (Arrigo, 2014, p. 272). An integrated multi-channel strategy implies **aligning** different distribution channels in terms of brand communication, assortment, prices, service levels, and customer relationship management in order to create consistency across all relevant consumer touch points and enhance the customer-brand-relationship (Chevalier & Gutsatz, 2012, p. 226; Manninger, 2012, p. 252). Offline and online channels should be considered as complementing rather than substituting each other. More than consistently aligning multiple channels, offline and online channels should be **interlinked**. Offline elements linking to online content include but are not limited to web addresses printed on shopping bags, QR-codes linking to specific online content, and in-store screens displaying a brand's online content. Vice versa, online elements linking to offline consumer touch points include but are not limited to information on store locations, opening hours, product categories available, availability of specific SKUs as well as the possibility to make an appointment at a specific outlet.

Burberry, for example, has designed a seamless multi-channel strategy. On its website, Burberry provides detailed information about its points of sales like Regent Street flagship store, i.e. location, opening hours, a list of product categories carried and services offered, the possibility to make an appointment, the possibility to pick up online-ordered products in-store (also called "click-and-collect") as well as the store's heritage and events hosted (Burberry.com, 2015a, 2015c). The flagship store itself is equipped with around 100 screens and 500 speakers displaying fashion shows and other events, digital screens that may turn into mirrors, iPads allowing sales people to access individual customer data, and a bespoke fitting room featuring large screens and iPads allowing clients to access the digital trench coat configurator (Burberry.com, 2015b; Lamb, 2012).

5. Expert Interviews – Online Distribution

The issue of selling luxury goods online has been controversially discussed both in business press (Chapter 1.1) and literature (Chapter 4.5). To identify the current state of the managerial discussion on the online distribution challenge for luxury goods we conducted a series of individual interviews with luxury industry experts from July to September 2013. The purpose of this pre-study is twofold: first, re-confirming the managerial relevance of the research question before actually testing it using experimental studies with luxury consumers. More specifically, expert interviews help identify whether selling luxury goods online has become common practice or whether it is still controversially discussed among luxury industry experts and thus represents a relevant subject for further research. Second, expert interviews help identify managerial approaches to preserve consumer perceptions of brand luxury within the ubiquitous mass medium Internet.

Individual interviews represent a qualitative research technique of exploring fundamental dimensions and elements of a research topic through an open, oral, and usually personal one-to-one dialogue (Berekhoven, Eckert, & Ellenrieder, 2009, p. 89). Rather than confronting the participant with a standardized set of questions and answer options as done with surveys, the interviewer acts as a rather passive but interested listener leaving room for the interviewee's own thoughts and focus on particular issues (Kepper, 2008, p. 181). Still, interviewers usually guide the dialogue to some extent using a semi-structured interview guideline (as opposed to a fully-structured guideline in surveys; Homburg & Krohmer, 2008, p. 26; Kepper, 2008, p. 180). The exploratory approach of qualitative interviews often serves as a pilot or pre-study to gain some basic insights into a problem and derive first hypotheses, which are tested in subsequent quantitative research (Aaker, Kumar, Leone, & Day, 2013, p. 149; Churchill & Iacobucci, 2005, p. 75).

In the field of research on luxury goods, qualitative research methods have been frequently applied either as a pre-study interviewing managers, sales personnel, consumers, consultants, and scholars (Mohr, 2013, pp. 53–54; Monkhouse, Barnes, & Stephan, 2012, p. 653; Wieseke, Alavi, et al., 2013, p. 133) or as main study interviewing millionaires (Heine & Phan, 2011, p. 110), thought-leaders on luxury brands (Roper, Caruana, Medway, & Murphy, 2013, p. 383), managers of luxury retailers (Brun et al., 2008, p. 558; Fionda & Moore, 2009, p. 353; Moore et al., 2010, p. 145) or winemakers and wine consumers (Beverland, 2006, p. 252). Similarly, we interviewed luxury industry experts, i.e. senior managers, consultants, and scholars, on their thoughts about luxury in general and the online distribution of luxury goods in particular. In the following, our methodological approach is described first. In a second step, the results of this qualitative pre-study are presented.

Table 11 – Pre-study: sample characteristics

Expert ID	Position	Segment	Luxury qualification	Job experience in years	Interview duration in minutes
A	Managing Director	Low-involvement luxury goods	Member of Comité Colbert and Meisterkreis	16	40
B	Managing Director	Low-involvement luxury goods	Member of Comité Colbert and Meisterkreis	29	46
C	CEO	High-involvement luxury goods	Member of Meisterkreis	14	48
D	Digital Marketing Manager	High-involvement luxury goods	Sportscar manufacturer (prices > EUR 100,000)	12	65
E	Practice Leader Luxury	Consultancy	Luxury practice	28	35
F	CEO	Consultancy	Luxury practice	28	55
G	Professor, CEO	Academia/ Consultancy	Teaching/ Luxury practice	10	118

Source: author

5.1 Method

We conducted seven interviews with luxury industry experts using a semi-structured interview guideline that comprised three parts: first, we asked for general information, i.e. name, institution, position, job experience, as well as the expert's personal Internet usage and shopping behavior. Second, as an introduction we asked for the expert's personal understanding of luxury, its constituting characteristics and the importance of exclusiveness and scarcity for luxury goods. Third, we narrowed the dialogue down to marketing luxury goods online. Specifically, we asked for the opportunities and challenges the expert associates with marketing luxury goods online, whether or not luxury goods should be sold online and if so how. The complete semi-structured interview guideline is shown in **Error! Reference source not found.** and 4.

The sample consists of seven experts who hold senior positions at luxury goods manufacturers or consultancies specialized in luxury goods (see Table 11). The manufacturers qualify as luxury goods manufacturers as they are members of the

French luxury goods association Comité Colbert and/or the German equivalent Meisterkreis. The remaining firm is a luxury car manufacturer with annual unit sales of less than 10,000 cars and new car prices beyond EUR 100,000.

On average, interviewees indicated a job experience of 20 years, privately browse the Internet multiple times a day, and make online purchases once a month. Three interviews were conducted face-to-face, four interviews were conducted via telephone. All interviews were audiotaped and transcribed verbatim. On average, we recorded a net duration of 58 minutes per expert interview.

5.2 Results[4]

5.2.1 Attitudes towards online distribution

The experts generally agree on the characteristics that constitute luxury goods including craftsmanship, heritage, and exclusiveness. However, the interviews also reveal a considerable controversy among luxury experts in multiple aspects. Most evidently, luxury experts have differing opinions on whether or not a luxury goods manufacturer should adopt the Internet as a channel of distribution.

Both expert F, CEO of a consulting firm, and expert B, managing director at multibrand low-involvement luxury goods manufacturer, refer to the fundamental trade-off between growth in sales and preserving a luxury brand's exclusiveness (as shown by quotes 1 and 2 (Q1 and Q2)). Hence, if not facing the pressure to increase sales figures, expert G, CEO of a consulting firm, would rather avoid selling luxury goods online or at least limit the availability of goods in order to protect a luxury brand's image (Q3).

> *Q1:* *"...a strong trade-off between uhm... creating barriers, creating borders to preserve the attractiveness of the brand and delivering highest increase in sales possible."*

> *Q2:* *"Of course it is the exclusiveness of distribution. I must not have a luxury product everywhere. And that's the art of luxury brands: finding the balance between optimizing sales... [and exclusiveness; author] [...] the thin line between self-restraint and optimization within that self-restraint."*

> *Q3:* *"If my financial and economic situation allows it I would go without e-commerce. [...] I would recommend participating in e-commerce, in the Internet. Consumers are online. Still uhm... I would rather restrain the availability as I believe that uhm... the image of the brand suffers in the long run."*

Common concerns about online distribution of luxury goods include the loss of desirability, the lack of human interaction, and the lack of touch. In particular, expert

4 Note: for reasons of reading convenience English translations of non-English quotes are presented here. Original language quotes are listed in Appendix 5 in the order of appearance.

F, CEO of a consulting firm, emphasizes the **loss of desirability** of luxury brands caused by the increasing accessibility through online distribution:

> *Q4: "Limited accessibility is a characteristic of luxury brands. In other words, if it is available on every street corner – and this includes online – then it loses parts of its desirability."*

Other experts rather emphasize their concern about the **lack of human interaction**. Expert C, CEO of a high-involvement luxury goods manufacturer, considers the interaction with the client essential for communicating a luxury brand's aura (Q5). Similarly, expert D, digital marketing manager at a high-involvement goods manufacturer, refers to the lack of human interaction as a major obstacle towards online distribution (Q6).

> *Q5: "Of course you don't have... in an online distribution channel you don't have the interaction with the client, which is necessary to fine-tune your business and transmit this... this brand world."*

> *Q6: "I don't believe we will go through an online selling experience considering the products we have. I think human mediation will be always important in our case."*

Another concern refers to the **lack of touch** when buying online. In particular, considering the high price level of luxury goods consumers need to touch and feel the product as expert C, CEO at a high-involvement luxury goods manufacturer, mentions (Q7). However, the need to touch might vary depending on consumer shopping preferences and spending power as expert E, Luxury Practice Leader at a consulting firm, argues (Q8).

> *Q7: "I believe, in these price levels uhm... I don't buy before having actually seen it somewhere else."*

> *Q8: "I know some jewellery brands that sell single pieces at more than 100,000 US Dollar online during Christmas trade. Personally, this would probably make me want to physically encounter that piece in-store. But there are just different uhm... preferences and different spending power."*

Other experts (particularly managers of low-involvement luxury goods) advocate the Internet as a channel of distribution. They consider the Internet simply as another part of a firm's channel mix as pointed out by expert E, Luxury Practice Leader at a consulting firm (Q9). From their perspective, luxury goods manufacturers must not shy away from a medium which has become an essential part of consumers' everyday lives as confirmed by expert B, managing director at multibrand low-involvement luxury goods manufacturer (Q10).

> *Q9: "Well, from my perspective the Internet today belongs to a channel mix one cannot and should not refuse to accept."*

> *Q10: "I think it is our job to go where our consumers are."*

One major benefit refers to the **increase in reach**. Expert A, managing director at a multibrand high- and low-involvement luxury goods firm, refers to those numerous geographically distant areas where individuals are exposed to luxury brand communication through online channels but lack a point of sale close by. In these cases the Internet represents an additional sales channel that allows reaching virtually anyone (Q11). Still, she admits that luxury goods manufacturers are very careful in approaching the issue of online distribution (Q12).

> *Q11: "Through our communication, through our advertising we go to every single, small household in any one-horse town. However, we are not available there in the stationary retail. And today, through the Internet, it is actually the only alternative for many, many consumers to acquire luxury brands."*

> *Q12: "We do see [the Internet as; author] an opportunity – admittedly we have been somewhat forced to do so. The luxury industry did not used to be very open-minded and proactive towards e-commerce. We are very, very careful."*

5.2.2 Preserving brand luxury online

Luxury industry experts have different approaches in mind how to preserve consumer perceptions of luxury when selling online. Expert F emphasizes the importance of compensating for the increased accessibility resulting from online distribution:

> *Q13: "Knowing where to get something is also part of the luxury buying process, i.e. consumers need to master the code where to access this or that product. [...] If I reduce barriers – that's what I am doing by selling online – I need to create even higher barriers elsewhere."*

In essence, these barriers refer to the efforts consumers need in order to access a luxury item. The experts mention different approaches to create these "barriers" online ranging from (1) dedicating a detached area on the website for the online store which is separate from the traditional product view, (2) giving access to the online store upon invitation only, (3) offering a dedicated "online only" collection, to (4) accepting online orders upon request only. For example, expert C, CEO at a high-involvement luxury goods manufacturer, recommends selling a limited selection of entry and core range products only (Q14) while a luxury brand's high-end, iconic items should rather not be sold online. In this context, expert G, CEO of a consulting firm, refers to the example of the Parisian fashion and leather manufacturer Hermès (Q15).

> *Q14: "We have a 'product area' and a 'buy area'. In the 'buy area' are about 25, 30 articles which you can buy online. [...] The classics."*

> *Q15: "For example, Hermès does offer those small scarves there [online; author]. But not, for example, the Kelly bag. No way. Never."*

Apart from installing some kind of barriers, expert B (Q16) and expert A (Q17) recommend keeping the online buying process as convenient as possible for online shoppers:

Q16: "For the consumer e-commerce needs to be accessible, simple, and convenient."

Q17: "One must have a balance between appealing and convenient."

The necessity of these barriers as mentioned by the experts well corresponds to the commodity theory by Brock (1968, p. 249), which will be described below in Chapter 6.3. Accordingly the desirability of any commodity increases as the effort needed to obtain the commodity increases. Perceptions of being hard-to-get nurture scarcity perceptions and the desirability of the brand.

5.3 Conclusion

Overall, the interviews show a still-existing controversy among luxury industry experts on whether or not to sell luxury goods online and if so how consumer perceptions of brand luxury may be preserved or created. This controversy calls for further research on how a luxury goods manufacturer should market its brand online while preserving its fragile perception of exclusiveness. Expert F, CEO of a consulting firm, calls for future research:

Q18: "In the field of luxury, research and experiments are still needed to develop brand-appropriate [online; author] shops. They are all quite at the beginning. And they all do not really know how to manage it. Hence, research studies make sense a lot."

Both managerial practice and literature show mixed results on whether or not to sell luxury goods online. In the following Chapter 6 we rely on both socio-economic and social-psychological theory in order to derive hypotheses about the effects of online accessibility on consumer perceived scarcity, brand desirability, convenience, and willingness-to-buy. In Chapters 7 and 8 we then empirical test how the online accessibility of luxury goods affects consumer perceptions of scarcity, desirability, convenience, and ultimately willingness-to-buy. More specifically, as expressed by the expert interview we do not only test the simple effects of online accessibility (i.e. buy vs. cannot buy online) but also the effects of incorporating "barriers" to online shopping, i.e. users may not directly click on a "buy now" button but are required to (a) sign in first before being able to shop online or (b) to fill in a purchase request form which is being sent to the luxury goods manufacturer for approval.

6. Theory and Hypotheses – Effects of Online Accessibility

6.1 Introduction

The marketing of luxury goods is directed towards balancing sales growth against the brand's fragile perception of exclusiveness. In particular, while selling luxury goods online represents a potential source of additional sales it is generally believed to harm a luxury brand's appeal of being reserved for the happy few. Business press (Chapter 1.1), literature (Chapter 4.5), and interviews with luxury industry experts (Chapter 5) leaves us with **mixed results** on whether or not and, if so, how to sell luxury goods online. In the following Chapters 6 to 8 we are interested in deepening our understanding of the effects of online accessbility of luxury goods. Specifically, we address the third research question (see Chapter 1.2):

RQ3: How does the online accessibility and price display of luxury goods affect consumer perceived scarcity, desirability, convenience, and willingness-to-buy?

Providing neither theory nor empirical evidence some authors have argued against the online distribution of luxury goods (Kapferer & Bastien, 2012, pp. 220 & 248; Seringhaus, 2005, p. 15) and some in favour of it (Chevalier & Gutsatz, 2012, p. 64; Hennigs et al., 2012, p. 34; Okonkwo, 2010, p. 173; Quintavalle, 2012, p. 77). The benefits and concerns about the online distribution of luxury goods have been conceptually discussed in Chapter 4.5.1. Most of the benefits and concerns described apply to both luxury and non-luxury goods manufacturers alike (e.g., lack of touch, lack of human interaction, or conflicts with third-party distributors). In luxury, however, marketers additionally fear that making luxury goods accessible online comes at the expense of perceived scarcity and thus a brand's desirability (Chevalier & Gutsatz, 2012, p. 67; Seringhaus, 2005, p. 15). The online accessibility reduces the effort and know-how needed to buy a luxury item that used to be reserved for the happy few connoisseurs (Kapferer & Bastien, 2012, p. 249). Making luxury goods accessible online jeopardizes the fragile perception of scarcity. Scarcity perceptions, however, represent a pre-requisite of brand desirability.

In the following chapters the **phenomenon of scarcity** will be discussed first drawing on socio-economic and social-psychological theory. Socio-economic theory (Chapter 6.2) introduces scarcity as a fundamental phenomenon of economic activity in a society. Due to limited resources quantity demanded exceeds quantity supplied and prices go up (Lavoie, 1992, p. 45). Some members of the society desire scarce goods as the number of co-owners is limited (snobbism) and their high price serves as a signal of wealth and social status (Veblenian theory; see Chapter 6.2; Leibenstein, 1950, p. 189).

Table 12 – Theory of scarcity

Domain	Theory	Main proposition
Socio-economic theory	**(Neo-) classical economic theory** (Marshall, 1890; Smith, 1776)	Society has limited resources. Quantities demanded and supplied of resources and goods are regulated by price. The desirability of any good is enhanced by its scarcity.
	Snobbism (Leibenstein, 1950)	Demand for any good decreases as the number of others consuming the same good increases.
	Veblenian theory (Veblen, 1899)	The conspicuous consumption of high-priced goods signals wealth and thus social status. Hence, demand for any good decreases as its price decreases.
Social-psychological theory	**Commodity theory** (Brock, 1968)	The desirability of any good (or commodity) increases as it is unavailable.
	Uniqueness theory (Snyder & Fromkin, 1977, 1980)	Individuals crave for a moderate level of self-differentiation from peers in order to enhance one's self-concept. Scarce goods serve as a source of self-differentiation.
	Naïve economic theories (Lynn, 1992a)	Scarce goods are believed to be more expensive. More expensive goods are associated with higher quality and status and thus more desired than goods low in quality and status.
	Reactance theory (Brehm, 1966)	Scarcity threatens an individual's freedom to possess a good. Scarce goods increase in attractiveness since reactance motivates the individual to restore this threatened freedom.

Source: author

While socio-economic theory is used to describe *how* the phenomenon of scarcity affects economic behaviour, social-psychological theory (Chapter 6.3) is used to explain *why* individuals desire scare goods more than commodities. The desirability for scarce goods may be explained by (a) an individual's inherent need to be moderately dissimilar to peers (uniqueness theory by Snyder & Fromkin, 1977, 1980), (b) an individual's naïve economic beliefs that scarce goods confer higher levels of quality and status (naïve economic theories by Lynn, 1992a), and (c) an individual's motivation to regain things that have become unavailable (reactance theory by (Brehm, 1966)).

Table 12 provides an overview of scarcity-related theory from both domains socio-economic and social-psychological theory and reports their main propositions. Socio-economic theory as presented here examines *how* consumer demand changes in response to scarcity and price. Social-psychological theory provides different motives *why* consumers desire scarce goods more than available ones.

Next, hypotheses will be derived on how these scarcity perceptions of luxury goods are possibly affected by their **online accessibility** (Chapter 6.4). Perceived scarcity is driven by numerous antecedents like rarity of material and human resources, limited production, high-end prices, and a limited distribution, which is typically about constraining the accessibility of its products, i.e. the extent to which consumers may easily obtain a luxury item (Catry, 2003, p. 16; Fassnacht et al., 2013, p. 114; Lynn, 1989, p. 267114). All these antecedents of perceived scarcity being equal, the following chapters examine whether or not the online accessibility affects the overall scarcity perception of a luxury brand as it extends rather than limits the access to its goods. In addition to this potential dilution-effect of online accessibility on a luxury brand's perceived scarcity, more "positive" effects of online distribution are examined. Chapter 4.5.1 has shown that online distribution potentially drives sales as – among other benefits – it makes shopping luxury goods more convenient. Hence, hypotheses about the effect of online accessibility on consumer perceived transaction convenience and thus willingness-to-buy are derived in Chapter 6.4.2.

6.2 Socio-economic theory

6.2.1 (Neo-) classical economic theory

Scarcity is a fundamental phenomenon of economics. A society suffers from scarcity in that it does not have sufficient resources to produce all the goods demanded by its members. In essence, economic activity is about the optimal allocation of a society's limited resources (Lavoie, 1992, p. 45). In cases quantity demanded exceeds quantity supplied (also referred to as **shortage of supply** or demand excess) suppliers typically raise prices until quantity demanded drops to a level that can be sufficiently supplied. The British neoclassical economist Alfred Marshall (1920[1890], p. 288) notes that the "scarcity of the amount supplied, relatively to the demand, will raise the price".

Mankiw & Taylor (2011, pp. 80–82) provide a graphical explanation of shortage of supply, i.e. demand exceeds supply. Figure 53 illustrates the relationship between the quantity q demanded and supplied of a good as function of price p. According to the law of demand, the market demand curve denoted by Dhas a negative slope indicating that, all other things being equal (ceteris paribus (c.p.)) market demand for a given good decreases as price goes up (Varian, 2010, p. 147). In contrast, the supply curve denoted by S has a positive slope indicating that c.p. the quantity supplied of a given good increases as price increases (law of supply; Mankiw & Taylor, 2011, p. 76).

Figure 53 – Shortage of supply.

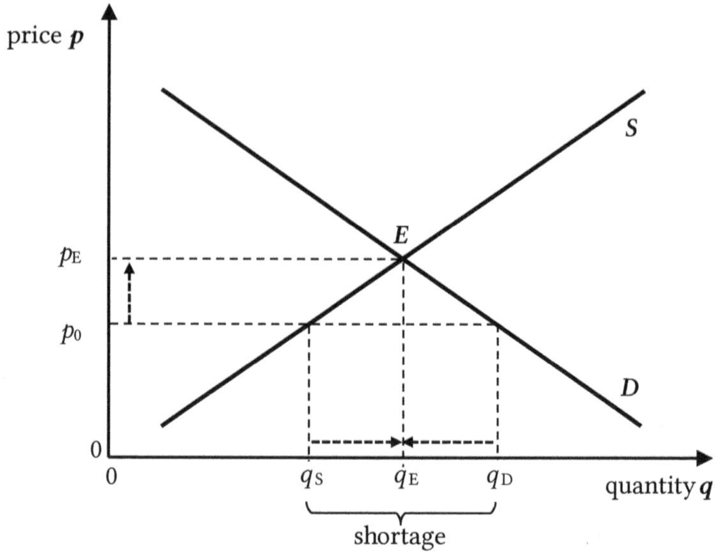

D = demand curve; *E* = equilibrium; *S* = supply curve
Source: Mankiw & Taylor (2011, p. 82)

A shortage of supply occurs when at a given price p_0 the quantity supplied q_S does not meet the quantity demanded q_D by the buyers. Since quantity demanded exceeds the quantity supplied suppliers are increasing prices. As a result, market demand falls and quantity supplied increases. Suppliers raise prices up to the equilibrium price p_E at which the quantity supplied equals the quantity demanded (q_E).

Lynn (1992a, p. 67) argues that classical economic theory disregards the effect of scarcity on the psychological value or desirability of a good. The increase in price for a scarce good is driven by an increase in competition rather than desirability for that good (Lynn, 1992a, p. 67). However, the Scottish philosopher and pioneer in modern economics Adam Smith has already argued in favour for a positive effect of scarcity on the desirability of anything of use. Smith (2005[1766], p. 147) states: **"the merit of an object, which is in any degree either useful or beautiful, is greatly enhanced by its scarcity, or by the great labour which it requires to collect any considerable quantity of it"**.

Considering this statement, Adam Smith explicitly differentiates between a functional ("useful") and a non-functional ("beautiful") utility component of a good. Specifically, he cites the example of precious stones that are "of no use" to the owner but demanded simply because of their "beauty" which is enhanced by the fact that they are scarce (Smith, 2005[1766], p. 148). Individuals desire goods or anything of use that is scarce even if alternative goods of equal quality are readily available as

Smith (2005[1766], p. 190) confirms: "**In times of wealth and luxury, what is rare, with only nearly equal merit, is always preferred to what is common**".

Also, Adam Smith differentiates **two forms of scarcity: limited diffusion** ("rare" versus "common") and **effort** ("great labour which it requires"). Diffusion refers to the perceived number of co-possessors of a given good. Individuals desire goods whose perceived number of co-possessors is low (also known as snobbism as described below; Leibenstein, 1950). Effort refers to the "difficulty and expense" of acquiring anything of use (Smith, 2005[1766], p. 148). Individuals desire goods that are "hard-to-get". Effort includes anything a buyer needs to invest in order to acquire a good, e.g., money, knowledge, or physical effort. The price or monetary effort represents one of the most prominent signals of being hard-to-get. Hence, some individuals prefer expensive goods over more affordable ones (as described in the Veblenian theory below; Veblen, 1960[1899]).

6.2.2 Snobbism

In socio-economic theory, snobbism refers to the "extent to which the demand for a consumers' good is decreased owing to the fact that others are consuming the same commodity" (Leibenstein, 1950, p. 189). A snob's individual demand decreases as total market demand increases (Amaldoss & Jain, 2005, p. 30). Hence, snobbish consumer behaviour is characterized by the desire and consumption of goods that are unavailable to others in terms of scarcity or limited diffusion. This premise provides a possible explanation for Smith's notion of a positive scarcity-desirability relationship and is supported by social-psychological theory as described below.

The negative correlation of a snob's individual demand with total market demand is the exact opposite of the "bandwagon" consumption behaviour according to which a bandwagon consumer's demand increase as total market demand increases in order to conform with a reference group, i.e. being "one of the boys" (Kastanakis & Balabanis, 2012, p. 1401; Leibenstein, 1950, p. 189; Vigneron & Johnson, 1999, p. 6). However, "even though snobs and followers buy luxury products for apparently opposite reasons, their basic motivation is really the same; whether through differentiation or group affiliation, they want to enhance their self-concept" (Dubois & Duquesne, 1993, p. 37).

Leibenstein (1950, pp. 199–202) provides a graphical explanation of the snob effect. Figure 54 illustrates the demand curve of a snob D_{Snob} relative to the market demand curves D_a and D_c. The market demand curve D_a (D_c) signifies the quantity q demanded at price p given that all consumers assume that the total quantity demanded is a units (c units) (Leibenstein, 1950, p. 94). According to the law of demand the market demand curve is negatively sloped, i.e. quantity q decreases as price p goes up and vice versa.

In the virtual equilibrium E_a, at a given price p_a the quantity demanded is q_a. In absence of snobs, given a change in price from p_a to p_b quantity demanded increases from q_a to q_b (price effect of q_aq_b). At price p_b the quantity demanded would be q_b given that every consumer assumes that the total quantity demanded does not increase. However, some snobs will leave the market in response to an anticipated increase in quantity demanded. Hence, in presence of snobs, the price effect q_aq_b is reduced by the snob effect q_bq_c yielding a net effect of q_aq_c.

Figure 54 – Snob effect.

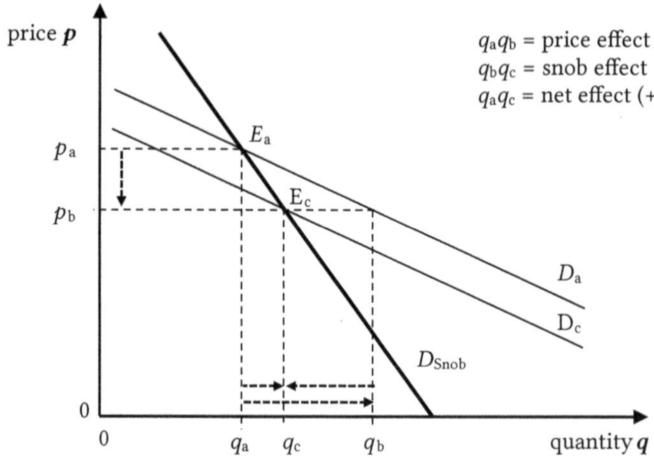

D = demand curve; *E* = market equilibrium
Source: Leibenstein (1950, p. 201)

Empirical findings support the negative relationship between a snobbish consumer's demand for a good and total market demand for the same good. Pantzalis (1995, pp. 67–70) finds for both wristwatches and wine that a limited supply positively affects product desirability and that this positive relationship is mediated by consumer perceptions of exclusiveness. Similarly, Verhallen (1982, p. 310) shows that product preferences increase due to limited supply. Dubois & Paternault (1995, p. 73) report that the desirability for a luxury brand negatively associates with high levels of diffusion. The more people own a luxury brand, the less desirable it becomes. And Kastanakis & Balabanis (2012, p. 1405) empirically prove that snobs (consumers high in need for uniqueness) engage less in bandwagon consumption behaviour, i.e. they avoid mainstream consumption patterns.

6.2.3 Veblenian theory

The Veblenian theory deals with the conspicuous consumption of expensive goods as a signal of wealth in order to achieve social status. Named after the American economist and sociologist Thorstein Bunde Veblen (1960) the Veblenian theory refers to the "extent to which the demand for a consumers' good is increased because it bears a higher rather than a lower price" (Leibenstein, 1950, p. 189). Hence, Veblenian consumer behaviour is characterized by the desire and consumption of goods that are unavailable to others in terms financial effort in order to obtain higher perceived levels of status.

A high price serves as a surrogate of status. Consumers associate high prices with higher levels of prestige (Lichtenstein, Ridgway, & Netemeyer, 1993, p. 241).

Figure 55 – Veblen effect.

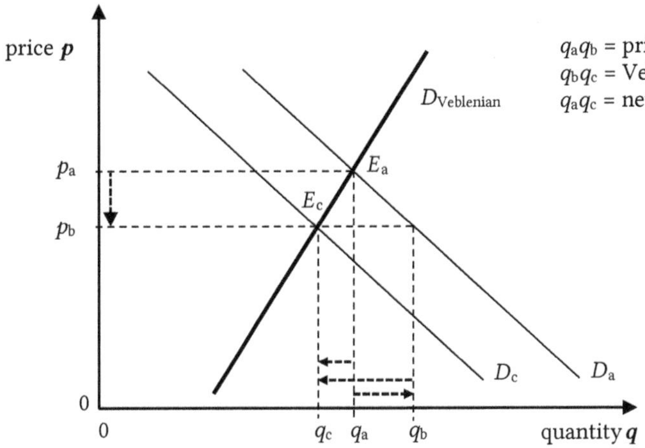

D = demand curve; E = market equilibrium
Source: Leibenstein (1950, p. 202)

Consequently, the Veblenian consumers enhances his or her self-concept by buying goods that he or she considers to cause desired reactions from a reference group (Bearden & Etzel, 1982, p. 183; Grubb & Grathwohl, 1967, p. 25; Kotler, 1965, p. 43; R. Mason, 1984, p. 26). Leibenstein (1950, pp. 202–205) provides a graphical explanation of the Veblen effect. Figure 55 illustrates the demand curve of a Veblenian consumer $D_{Veblenian}$ relative to the market demand curves D_a and D_c. Leibenstein (1950, p. 203) distinguishes between real prices and conspicuous prices. The real price refers to the money amount a consumer pays for a given commodity. The conspicuous price refers to the price that other consumers believe a given consumer has paid for a given commodity. Accordingly, the market demand curve D_a (D_c) signifies the quantity q demanded at a real price p for an expected conspicuous price of a monetary unit (c units). Again, the market demand curve is negatively sloped, i.e. quantity q decreases as price p goes up and vice versa. In contrast, the Veblenian demand curve $D_{Veblenian}$ is positively sloped, i.e. demand increases as price goes up and vice versa. The existence of upward-sloping demand curves among conspicuous consumers is supported by Amaldoss & Jain (2005, p. 40) and Corneo & Jeanne (1997a, p. 56). In the virtual equilibrium E_a, at a given price p_a the quantity demanded is q_a assuming that consumers have accurate information about the market, i.e. real price equals conspicuous price. In absence of Veblenian consumers, given a decrease in price from p_a to p_b quantity demanded increases from q_a to q_b (price effect of q_aq_b). At price p_b the quantity demanded would be q_b given that consumers do not expect a change in conspicuous price. However, some Veblenian consumers will leave the market in response to the decreased conspicuous utility of the commodity. Hence, the price effect q_aq_b is reduced by the Veblen effect q_bq_c yielding a negative net effect of q_aq_c.

6.3 Social-psychological theory

Theory and empirical research in the field of social psychology appear to support the notion of a positive scarcity-desirability effect as shown by (neo-) classical economic theory (Lynn, 1992b, p. 4). In social-psychological theory, commodity theory (Brock, 1968) provides the fundamental assumption that individuals desire scarce goods more than available ones. This premise may be explained by (a) an individual's inherent need to be moderately dissimilar to peers (uniqueness theory by Snyder & Fromkin, 1977, 1980), (b) an individual's naïve economic beliefs that scarce goods confer higher levels of quality and status (naïve economic theories by Lynn, 1992a), and (c) an individual's motivation to regain things that have become unavailable (reactance theory by Brehm, 1966).

6.3.1 Commodity theory

Commodity theory is based on the assumption that the desirability of a good varies as a function of its availability. Goods that are perceived as unavailable enjoy higher levels of desirability. More formally, the American psychologist Timothy C. Brock (1968, p. 246) states that "**any commodity will be valued to the extent that it is unavailable**". The term "commodity" refers to anything "that can be possessed, is useful to its possessor, and is transferable from one person to another" (Lynn, 1991, p. 43). While Brock (1968, p. 248) uses valuable information as example of a commodity that is possessed by one person and eventually transferred to another person in form of a message he explicitly states that the reasoning behind commodity theory can be equally applied to the possession of physical goods. The term "unavailability" is defined as (a) the extent to which it is scarce and (b) the extent of effort needed to obtain a good as perceived by an individual (Brock, 1968, p. 246).

Brock's commodity theory is "reminiscent of Smith's observations" (Lynn, 1992b, p. 4) in two major ways: first, commodity theory similarly posits that individuals desire scarce goods more than available ones. Second, Brock (1968, p. 246) similarly differentiates between two forms of unavailability namely scarcity in terms of a limited availability to others and effort in terms of being hard-to-obtain. Both of these forms and how they apply to the context of marketing luxury goods are described in more detail below.

Scarcity-based unavailability. Scarcity refers to the **perceived number of co-possessors**, i.e. other individuals possessing or potentially receiving the same commodity (Brock, 1968, p. 248). Accordingly the desirability of any good increases as the perceived number of co-possessors or co-receivers decreases. The more people own a specific good the less attractive it becomes. In economic literature, this assumption is also known as "snob effect" which refers to the extent to which the demand for any consumer good decreases as the level of its diffusion among other consumers increases (Leibenstein, 1950, p. 189).

Empirical studies published prior to the work by Brock (1968) provide support for this positive scarcity-desirability effect. Based on the results of two experimental studies Brehm, Stires, Sensenig, & Shaban (1966, p. 313) conclude that the attractiveness of a choice alternative increases as it becomes unavailable. Similarly, another experimental study by Mischel & Masters (1966) reveals that "the unavailability of a positive outcome enhances its perceived desirability" (p. 395). Also Lynn (1991, p. 52) reports a meta-analysis of 41 empirical studies published from 1968 to 1989 (i.e. subsequent to the work by Brock (1968)) that shows strong support for the positive effect of perceived scarcity on the desirability of a commodity.

In luxury, manufacturers enhance the desirability of their brand by nurturing consumer perceptions of scarcity. They operate exclusive distribution networks, limit sales volumes and set high-end prices in order to limit the number of clients (Lynn, 1991, p. 44). These marketing activities are antecedents of perceived scarcity. Following this logic, selling luxury goods online and thus making them accessible to virtually everyone can be assumed to decrease consumer perceptions of unavailability and thus to dilute a brand's desirability. Perceived unavailability may be assumed to be lower among individuals being confronted with a luxury brand website featuring a "Buy online" button next to a product displayed as compared to individuals not being confronted with a "Buy online" button.

Effort-based unavailability. Another form of perceived unavailability refers to the effort needed to transfer or obtain a commodity (Brock, 1968, p. 249). Accordingly the desirability of any good increases as the effort involved for the possessor to transfer the commodity or the effort involved for the receiver to obtain the commodity increases. Again, empirical findings support this assumption. Experimental studies by Becker & Brock (1966, p. 152) and Brock & Becker (1965, p. 657) show that withholding a commodity increases its desirability to potential receivers. Similarly, Giebelhausen, Robinson, & Cronin (2011, p. 901) show through a series of experiments that while waiting in line is generally considered as source of anger and frustration, it positively influences consumers perception about quality. Other experimental studies by Wicklund, Cooper, & Linder (1967, pp. 421 & 425) reveal that individuals more positively change their attitudes when high levels of efforts are involved rather than when low levels of effort are involved.

Walster, Walster, Piliavin, & Schmidt (1973, p. 113) more specifically differentiate between (a) the effort the individual him or herself needs to invest, and (b) the effort others need to invest as perceived that individual. In the context of the selection of romantic partners, they find that "playing hard-to-get" is not a generally effective strategy women should pursue (Walster, Walster, & Berscheid, 1971, p. 76). Rather, men fell more attracted to woman they perceive as being hard-to-get for others but as easy-to-get for themselves (Walster et al., 1973, p. 120). In a similar manner, Koo & Fishbach (2010, p. 722) find that when an individual is waiting in line to get a product the presence of other individuals behind (versus ahead) increases the perceived value of that product. Thus, the desirability of good increases as an individual perceives it as being hard-to-obtain for others but easy-to-obtain for him- or herself.

Making it "**difficult for clients to buy**" represents one of the fundamental anti-laws of luxury goods marketing (Kapferer & Bastien, 2009a, p. 67). In contrast to traditional marketing practices that are designed to facilitate access to goods, parts of the luxury shopping experience originate from the financial efforts (working for and saving money), cultural efforts (education in and appreciation of heritage and craftsmanship, e.g., mechanical movements of wristwatches or hand-stitched leather bags), logistical efforts (finding and visiting a store), and time efforts involved (searching and waiting for a purchase, e.g., waiting time of several months for a Ferrari sportscar; Kapferer & Bastien, 2009, p. 67). Accordingly, making luxury goods accessible online reduces the efforts needed to access luxury (Kapferer & Bastien, 2012, p. 249) and can thus be assumed to negatively affect consumer perceptions of scarcity and desirability.

Commodity theory may be considered a **meta-theory** as it posits an enhancing effect of scarcity on the desirability of a good but does not provide an explanation *why* this positive relationship occurs (Lynn, 1992a, p. 68). In the following, three social-psychological theories are presented that add to explaining the positive scarcity-desirability effect, namely: uniqueness theory (Snyder & Fromkin, 1977, 1980), naïve economic theories (Lynn, 1992a), and reactance theory (Brehm, 1966).

6.3.2 Uniqueness theory

Snobbish consumer behaviour is motivated by an individual's need for uniqueness (Vigneron & Johnson, 1999, p. II). Uniqueness theory provides a social-psychological explanation of snobbism and the positive scarcity-desirability relationship as proposed by commodity theory (see Chapter 6.3.1). The social psychologists Snyder and Fromkin (1977, 1980) refer to the fundamental assumption that **individuals crave for a moderate extent of uniqueness, i.e. being different from peers, in the pursuit of enhancing one's self-concept.** Potential sources of self-distinctiveness include memberships to groups, experiences or material possessions (Lynn & Snyder, 2002, pp. 398–399).

Self-concept. According to self-theory (see Sirgy (1982) for a review) an individual's concept of the self refers to an "object which is perceived by the individual" (Grubb & Grathwohl, 1967, p. 24). The self-concept of an individual represents the "totality of the individual's thoughts and feelings having reference to himself as an object" (Rosenberg, 1979, p. 7). Individuals engage in actions that either preserve or eventually enhance one's self-concept (Snyder, 1992, p. 10).

Moderate extent of uniqueness. To enhance one's self-concept individuals aim at a moderate level of differentiation from peers. The notion of a "moderate" extent of uniqueness refers to the assumption that individuals strive for both dissimilarity and similarity to peers at the same time (see Figure 56; Brewer, 1991, p. 477; Lynn & Snyder, 2002, p. 395). Individuals maintain a certain level of similarity in order to fuel feelings of affiliation and to prevent isolation from the relevant peer group. Hence, as shown in Figure 56 the relationship between the extent of similarity and an individual's satisfaction with one's self-concept can be thought of as an inverted u-shaped curve whose optimum represents the equilibrium of the extent of similarity and dissimilarity (Brewer, 1991, p. 477; Snyder, 1992, p. 12).

Figure 56 – Self-concept satisfaction as a function of similarity.

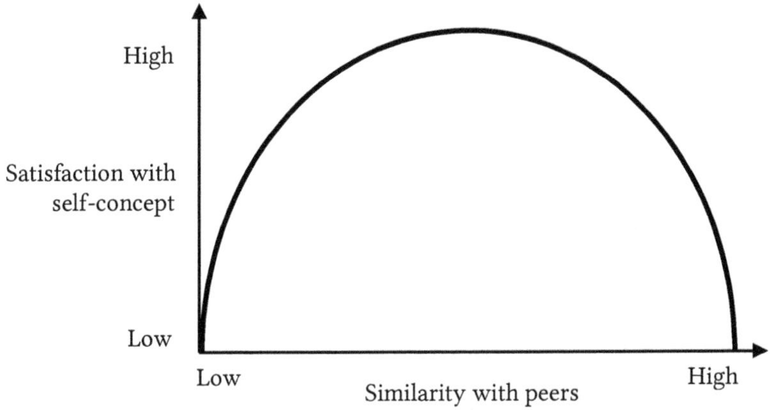

Source: Snyder (1992, p. 12)

Goods as symbols. Goods can serve as means of self-differentiation. Individuals seek for differentiation from peers through the acquisition, possession, and consumption of goods in order to cater one's self-concept (Tian, Bearden, & Hunter, 2001, p. 52). In general, goods have the potency to enhance a consumer's self-concept as they are material displays of who the consumer is (Belk, 1988, p. 139).

Individuals use goods as a material display to convey a particular meaning to significant others (Grubb & Grathwohl, 1967, p. 24). As shown in Figure 57, through the acquisition, possession, or consumption of symbols like goods and brands an individual enhances his or her self-concept in two ways: first, the consumer believes that the symbolic meaning of the goods supports his or her desired self-concept (effect a). Second, the symbolic meaning of the good causes significant others to react in a desired manner (indirect effect through b and c).

Scarce goods as source of differentiation. Scarce goods represent a valuable source of differentiation. An empirical study by Lynn & Harris (1997, p. 610) shows that the desire for scarce consumer goods is higher among consumers high in need for uniqueness. Individuals enhance their self-concept through the acquisition, possession, or consumption of goods that becomes commonplace among peers the snobbish consumers becomes less interested and starts searching for new goods meeting his or her need for uniqueness (Snyder, 1992, p. 21).

Figure 57 – Self-concept: goods as symbols.

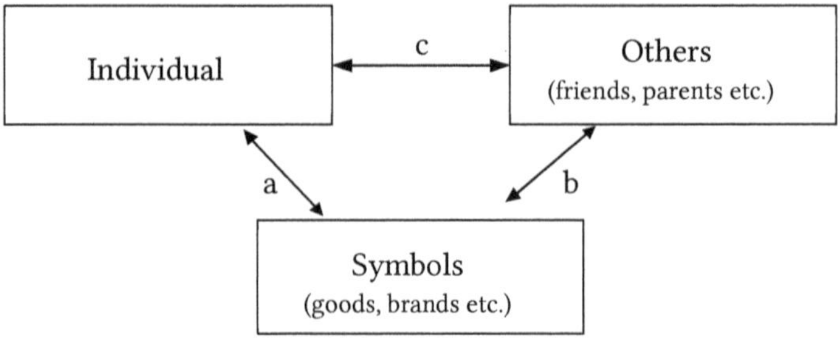

Source: Grubb & Grathwohl (1967, p. 25)

Luxury goods are typically unavailable to most individuals and thus serve as a potential mean of differentiation (Vigneron & Johnson, 1999, p. 3). Luxury goods are desired by many, but possessed by the happy few only (Dubois & Paternault, 1995, p. 73). Both of these aspects are critical: first, in the pursuit of dissimilarity, consumers desire luxury goods due to their unavailability to peers. Second, both the owner and his peers should desire the luxury good. This way, the owner and his or her peers are similar in their desire for a luxury good but dissimilar in their ownership status.

Now, since selling luxury goods online gives access too easily to too many individuals (Kapferer & Bastien, 2012, p. 249) it might be considered to reduce the perceived potency of the luxury branded good to differentiate the owner from his or her peers. Not only the scarce good itself, but also the point of sale represents a potential source of differentiation (Lynn & Harris, 1997, p. 605; Lynn & Snyder, 2002, p. 400). The exclusive knowledge of *where* to obtain scarce, desired goods adds to the uniqueness of one's self-concept. A large-scale study by Gutman & Mills (1982, p. 82) shows that consumers high in need of being different and standing out of the crowd prefer exclusive specialty stores over mass merchandisers that are commonly known to everyone. Exclusive and mass retailers largely differ in terms of assortment, quality- and price level. These differences equally exist online (e.g., Amazon versus Net-a-Porter). However, due to the increased transparency of information provided by the Internet the knowledge where to get scarce goods becomes less exclusive.

6.3.3 Naïve economic theories

The social psychologist and Brock's disciple Michael Lynn (1992a) explains the positive scarcity-desirability effect as proposed by commodity theory through naïve economic theories. He refers to the term naïve economic theories as "people's beliefs and expectations about the relationships among economic variables" like demand, supply, utility and price (Lynn, 1992a, p. 68). Examples of those market beliefs include "smaller stores charge more for the same brands than larger stores" or "price is a reliable indicator of quality" (Duncan, 1990, pp. 729–730). Individuals have a number of these naïve market beliefs that they have learned from experience or instruction, that may be salient or unconscious and that affect their attitudes and shopping behaviour (Duncan, 1990, p. 730; Lynn, 1992a, pp. 68–69).

A common market belief refers to the relationship of between scarcity, expensiveness, and desirability, also known as S-E-D model (Lynn, 1992a, p. 70). According to the S-E-D model the positive scarcity-desirability relationship is mediated by assumed expensiveness. As learned from experience (e.g., increased prices for sold-out tickets) or formal economic theory (e.g., prices increase as demand exceeds supply) individuals believe that scarce goods are more expensive than available ones.

Expensiveness, in turn, is assumed to be positively related to the desirability of a good. Lynn (1992a, p. 69) cites two arguments explaining the positive expensiveness-desirability relationship: first, consumers attribute higher quality to high-priced products than low-priced products and higher quality is more desired than lower quality (Dodds, Monroe, & Grewal, 1991, p. 312; Monroe, 1973, p. 72; A. R. Rao & Monroe, 1989, p. 351). Second, higher levels of price confer higher levels of status to the owner of the good and higher status is more desired than lower status (Leibenstein, 1950, p. 189; Veblen, 1960, p. 62). Previously, Lynn (1989, p. 271) has reported empirical support that positive effect of scarcity on desirability is mediated by assumed expensiveness. More recently, an empirical study by Wu & Hsing (2006, p. 130) similarly supports the relationships between perceived scarcity, assumed expensiveness, perceived value, and willingness-to-buy as proposed by the S-E-D model.

Over time consumers have also developed naïve market beliefs concerning the Internet as a digital marketplace. First, the Internet is generally considered a mass medium providing availability of and effortless access to goods to virtually anyone rather than being an exclusive marketplace for exchanging scarce goods among a limited number of sellers and buyers (Gastaldi, 2012, p. 108; Kapferer & Bastien, 2012, p. 247; Seringhaus, 2005, p. 15). Second, the Internet is generally considered a low-price shopping channel (Curtis, 2000; Kapferer & Bastien, 2009a, p. 208). As learned from price-comparison websites and the strong presence of cheap, low-quality counterfeits (e.g., on eBay or spam e-mails) consumers often argue "I can get a better deal online". Considering these market beliefs the Internet appears to be an inappropriate market place for selling luxury goods. Consumer associations with mass consumption and low-end prices diminish perceptions of scarcity, assumed expensiveness and thus desirability of luxury brands.

Figure 58 – S-E-D model.

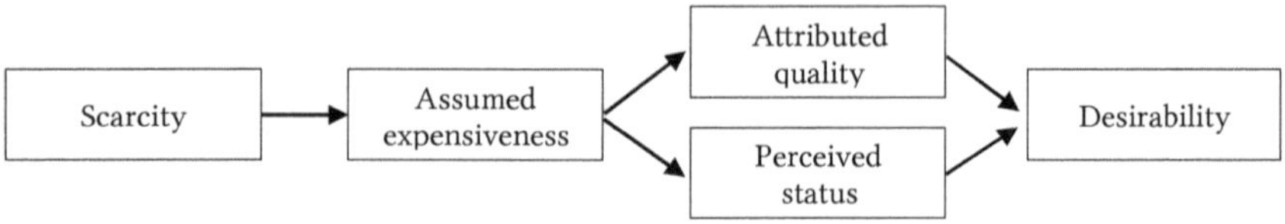

Source: Lynn (1992a, p. 70)

6.3.4 Reactance theory

In psychology, reactance refers to an individual's emotional reaction to external threats. Reactance theory as first introduced by the American social-psychologist Jack W. Brehm in 1966 posits: "when a person's freedom to engage in a particular behavior is eliminated or threatened with elimination, the individual will experience psychological reactance, a motivation direct toward the re-establishment of the lost or threatened freedom" (Brehm, 1968, pp. 277–278). In a choice situation an individual has the freedom to choose from a range of alternatives. Reactance occurs when another person or another external condition eliminates or threatens to eliminate one of these alternatives (Hammock & Brehm, 1966, pp. 546–547). As a motivational state psychological reactance drives individuals to regain the eliminated alternative, i.e. to engage in "freedom-restoration behaviors" (Miron & Brehm, 2006, p. 4).

Reactance theory implies that the **attractiveness of a choice alternative increases as it becomes unavailable** to an individual (Brehm et al., 1966, pp. 301–302; Hammock & Brehm, 1966, p. 547; Worchel, 1992, p. 81). A common example of psychological reactance refers to a child's opposite reaction to what his or her parents advise him or her what to do or not to do. Teenagers often feel attracted to forbidden actions like consuming alcoholic beverages or smoking cigarettes.

Scarcity threatens an individual's freedom to possess a commodity (Lynn, 1992b, p. 5; Verhallen & Robben, 1995, p. 374). Several sources of scarcity can cause this threat including physical unavailability and higher levels of effort needed to obtain the commodity (Worchel, 1992, p. 81). Scarce goods are those eliminated from an individual's range of alternatives. Hence, following the logic of psychological reactance theory, if scarcity is a threat to an individual's freedom to possess a good this **scarce good increases in attractiveness** since psychological reactance motivates the individual to restore this threatened freedom (Lynn, 1992b, p. 5).

Empirical findings support the positive scarcity-desirability relationship as explained by reactance theory. An experimental study by Worchel, Lee, & Adewole (1975, p. 910) shows that individuals feel more attracted to cookies scarce in supply than to cookies that are abundantly available. Similarly, experiments by Hammock & Brehm (1966, p. 553) and Brehm et al. (1966, p. 313) find that when one choice alternative is eliminated this choice alternative increases in attractiveness. The positive scarcity-desirability effect holds particularly true if a commodity is unavailable to the individual but available to others (Worchel, 1992, pp. 89–90).

Now, when shopping for luxury goods selecting the point of purchase implies choosing from a set of alternatives, i.e. purchasing either in-store or online at either a directly operated monobrand store or a multibrand retailer. Since not selling luxury goods increases the effort needed to obtain the luxury good it can be considered as a source of scarcity and as an elimination of one of the individual's set of alternatives. This elimination would then represent a threat to the individual's freedom, cause psychological reactance and motivate the individual restore her or his threatened freedom. Hence, the possibility to shop the luxury brand online would increase its attractiveness.

6.4 Hypotheses development

Based on socio-economic and social-psychological theory related to the phenomenon of scarcity hypotheses can be derived about the effects of selling luxury goods online on consumer brand evaluations. In particular, we are interested in the effects of online accessibility of a luxury good (i.e. whether or not it can be purchased online) on consumer perceptions of scarcity and thus brand desirability (Chapter 6.4.1). In addition, we are interested in potentially "positive" effects of online accessibility, specifically in consumer evaluations of convenience and thus willingness-to-buy (Chapter 6.4.2).

6.4.1 Online accessibility, scarcity, and desirability

Business press (Chapter 1.1), literature (Chapter 4.5), and expert interviews (Chapter 5) leave us with mixed results on whether or not and, if so, how to sell luxury goods online. In particular, managers, marketing scholars, and luxury industry experts express concerns about a potentially diluting effect of online accessibility of luxury goods on perceptions of scarcity and, thus, brand desirability (Daneshku, 2012; Experts F & G; Kapferer & Bastien, 2012, pp. 220 & 248; Seringhaus, 2005, p. 15). Perceptions of scarcity, i.e. perceptions of being hard-to-get and unfrequently diffused, are inherent to the concept of luxury (Chapter 2.1.3). Limited diffusion is one of the key reasons why consumers are dreaming of luxury goods (Dubois & Paternault, 1995, p. 73). Keeping the brand exclusive is top-of-mind among luxury brand marketers (see Chapter 1.1) as scarcity is considered a necessary ingredient of the concept of luxury (see Chapter 2.1.3). Much of a luxury brand's desriability is accounted for by the fact that its products are scarce and hard-to-get. Now, the online accessibility of luxury goods is often considered as a potential threat to a luxury brand's fundamental image of scarctiy and thus brand desirability. In following, we derive hypotheses about (1) the fundamental effect of perceived scarcity on brand desirability, and (2) how the online accessibility of luxury goods affects perceptions of scarcity.

First, we are interested in the relationship between perceived scarcity and brand desirability. As shown in Chapters 6.1 and 6.2, both socio-economic and social-psychological theory proposes a **positive effect of scarcity on desirability**. Smith

(2005[1766]) argues: "the merit of an object [...] is greatly enhanced by its scarcity" (p. 147). For anything that is useful and scarce – whether naturally or virtually (Catry, 2003, p. 11) – demand exceeds supply and prices increase. To dissociate from the mass, snobbish individuals desire scarce goods since the number of co-owners is limited (see Chapter 6.2.2; Leibenstein, 1950, p. 189). And the Veblenian individual desires scarce goods as their high price serves as a signal of wealth and social status (see Chapter 6.2.3; Leibenstein, 1950, p. 189).

Similarly, according to social-psychological theory individuals prefer scarce goods to readily available commodities. Brock (1968) states: "any commodity will be valued to the extent that it is unavailable" (p. 246). An individual's preference for goods that are unavailable or hard-to-obtain to others may be explained by the individual's need for a moderate level of distinctiveness from others (uniqueness theory; Snyder & Fromkin, 1977, 1980), by the individual's naïve economic beliefs that scarce goods are more expensive and thus confer higher levels of quality and social status (naïve economic theories; Lynn, 1992a), as well as by an individual's motivation to regain things that have become unavailable to him or her (reactance theory; Brehm, 1966). Empirically, the enhancing effect of scarcity on the desirability of anything of use has been supported by a meta-analysis of 41 studies (Lynn, 1991; also compare Chapter 6.3). Hence, we may hypothesize:

H1. Perceived scarcity positively affects brand desirability.

Second, we are interested in how the **online accessibility of luxury goods might affect perceived scarcity**. Luxury goods are generally perceived as scarce, i.e. as being unavailable or hard-to-obtain to others. A luxury brand's aura of scarcity or unavailability may be driven by multiple antecedents including limited supply (Lynn, 1989, p. 271; Pantzalis, 1995, pp. 67–68; Verhallen, 1982, p. 310), waiting time (Giebelhausen et al., 2011, p. 901; Koo & Fishbach, 2010, p. 722), price (Cervellon, De Barnier, & Laurent, 2014, p. 19), and level of diffusion (adverse effect; Dubois & Paternault, 1995, p. 73).

An exclusive distribution contributes to consumer perceptions of a luxury brand's goods as not being easily accessible to everyone. Traditionally, the (offline) purchase of luxury goods does not only involve financial effort (e.g., paying high-end prices) but also cultural effort (e.g., knowing where to get it), logistical effort (e.g., visiting the store), and time effort (e.g., searching or waiting for it). This effort is considered fundamental to perceived scarcity (Brock, 1968, p. 246; Smith, 2005[1766], p. 147).

In the Internet, however, information about *where* to get a unique item is more readily available to everyone (lowered cultural effort). Also, the naïve economic belief prevails that the online marketplace serves as a low-price distribution channel (lowered financial effort). And, instead of travelling to the prime locations of large cities like Paris, London, or New York, consumers may quickly shop online at home (lowered logistical and time effort). Hence, **online distribution** decreases the effort needed to obtain a luxury good and thus **diminishes consumer perceptions of scarcity**.

Kapferer & Bastien (2012) consider the online distribution of luxury goods as "extremely dangerous" as "it very quickly reduces the 'dream value' of the brand by increasing penetration too fast, giving too easy an access to the product to too many non-qualified people" (p. 249). Seringhaus (2005) states: "since the Internet democratizes information access, it diminishes the isolation and exclusivity of luxury brands" (p. 15). The mass medium Internet apparently contradicts with the exclusive distribution of luxury goods (Curtis, 2000).

As online distribution lowers the effort for others to obtain a luxury good it loses parts of its potency to differentiate the owner from others. In the pursuit of some extent of self-differentiation snobbish consumers (i.e. those being high in need for uniqueness) prefer goods that are unavailable or hard-to-obtain for others (Snyder & Fromkin, 1977, 1980). Here, not only the scarce good itself but also the point of sale represents a potential source of differentiation (Lynn & Harris, 1997, p. 605; Lynn & Snyder, 2002, p. 400). The exclusive knowledge of where to obtain scarce, desired goods adds to the uniqueness of one's self- and social image.

In contrast, not selling luxury goods online may be considered as an eliminated choice alternative, a limitation of an individual's freedom to instantly order a luxury good while goods of similar quality are readily available online. In the pursuit to restore this lost freedom the eliminated choice alternative might actually increase in attractiveness (psychological reactance; Brehm, 1966). An individual might desire a particular luxury good not despite its inaccessibility online but because of it. Taking theory and conceptual considerations together it may be hypothesized:

H2. Online accessibility of luxury goods negatively affects perceived scarcity.

To mitigate the negative effect of online accessibility on perceived scarcity luxury marketers might think about increasing the effort needed to order a product online. For example, instead of a simple "Buy online" button commonly featured on e-commerce websites luxury brand websites could feature buttons like "Sign in for online store" (i.e. consumers get access to the online store only upon prior registration) or "Order upon request" (i.e. consumer are required to fill in and submit a purchase request to receive further order information). These alternative purchase processes increase the effort involved for consumers to purchase the product online and are empirically examined in one of the experimental studies presented later.

6.4.2 Online accessibility, transaction convenience, and willingness-to-buy

The issue of selling luxury goods online is controversially discussed with multiple pros and cons (compare Chapters 4.5.1 and 5). Above, we addressed one of the most promiment concerns: a potential dilution-effect of online accessbility on a luxury brand's fragile image of scarcity and thus brand desirability (Chapter 6.4.1). Yet, there are several arguments in favour of selling luxury goods online both from a consumer and a managerial perspective (Chapter 4.5.1). One of the most frequently cited pros of online distribution refers to convenience. Online shopping motivation for luxury goods is mainly driven by convenience considerations like being able to shop whenever and from wherever a consumer wants (Liu et al., 2013, p. 888). Complementing the existing offline distribution network by the possibility to shop online might increase consumers' willingness-to-buy. Ultimately, like any other business, luxury goods manufacturers intend to generate sales in excess of costs incurred. Hence, we are not only interested in potential threats of online accessibility but also in potential benefits of selling luxury goods online. In the following, we derive hypotheses about (1) the effects of online accessbility of luxury goods on transaction convenience and (2) how convenience affects consumers' willingness-to-buy.

First, we are interested in the effect of online accessbility on transaction convenience. **Transaction convenience** refers to savings in "time and effort costs associated with finalizing the transaction" (Seiders, Voss, Godfrey, & Grewal, 2007, p. 145), i.e. the speed and ease of making a purchase. Multiple authors agree upon the convenience of online shopping in terms of saving time and effort as compared to offline shopping (Childers, Carr, Peck, & Carson, 2001, p. 517; Forsythe, Liu, Shannon, & Gardner, 2006, p. 60; Grewal, Iyer, & Levy, 2004, p. 706; Rohm & Swaminathan, 2004, p. 750). Similarly, consumer quotes refer to the savings in time and effort provided by online shopping channels: "Why leave the house, waste gas, wait at red lights, stand in line and have to go to five places just to find what you're looking for" (Wolfinbarger & Gilly, 2001, p. 41).

In the field of research on luxury goods, authors similarly agree that the possibility to shop online makes shopping luxury goods more convenient and independent of constraints in terms of time and place (Hennigs et al., 2012, p. 31; Quintavalle, 2012, p. 94; Riley & Lacroix, 2003, p. 99). As compared to in-store purchases, the Internet allows consumers to easily search for and discover luxury items that used to be known among few connoisseurs only (lowered cultural effort). And instead of investing time and effort to travel to one of the few selected retailers typically located in large cities like Paris, London, and New York shopping luxury goods online requires few clicks only (lowered time and logistical effort). These convenience aspects are well summarized by a consumer quote: "I can order the product at any time where ever I am. It is easy to find what you are looking for" (Liu et al., 2013, p. 888). Hence, an individual given the possibility to shop online might perceive general shopping conditions as more convenient as compared to those not given that possibility. Hence we may hypothesize:

H3. Online accessibility positively affects perceived transaction convenience.

Second, we are interested in the effect of transaction convenience on a consumer's **willingness-to-buy**, i.e. the likelihood a consumer considers to purchase a luxury good (Dodds et al., 1991, p. 318). If a consumer values convenience, he or she should be more likely to consider to make the purchase the higher he or she perceives the savings in time and effort to be (Li, Kuo, & Rusell, 1999). Convenience of shopping has generally been found to contribute to consumer satisfaction (Park & Kim, 2003,

p. 23; Szymanski & Hise, 2000, p. 317), a positive attitude towards online shopping (Childers et al., 2001, pp. 524–525), consumer preferences (Mathwick, Malhotra, & Rigdon, 2001, p. 50; Overby & Lee, 2006, p. 1164) and behavioural intentions like willingness-to-buy (Seiders et al., 2007, p. 153).

In luxury, a purchase often represents an once-in-a-lifetime event. As a result of the low purchase frequency of luxury goods some first-time shoppers attach more importance to experiencing a luxury good in-store rather than getting it as quickly and easily as possible online (Riley & Lacroix, 2003, p. 103). At the same time, however, purchasing a luxury good represents a "lengthy act" (Kapferer & Bastien, 2009a, p. 200) which often involves multiple encounters with the brand both offline and online. From a consumer perceptive, offline and online channels complement rather than substitute each other. A consumer might discover and experience a particular wristwatch at a monobrand store during a trip to Zurich, take some time to think about and ask peers for opinions, and finally buy online to save the time and effort of travelling to the next retail store. "I purchase luxury products online because there is not a retailer nearby for the product," as one consumer argues (Liu et al., 2013, p. 889). Among consumers who shop for luxury goods online convenience proves to be the most relevant motivational factor for shopping online (Liu et al., 2013, p. 888).

Considering both the relevance of convenience for shopping luxury goods online and the effects of convenience on consumer responses empirically shown in multiple non-luxury settings as reported above, we may hypothesize:

H4. Transaction convenience positively affects willingness-to-buy.

Finally, we are interested in whether a consumer's desirability for a luxury brand translates into a higher willingness-to-buy. Following the generic hierarchy-of-effects model (Bruhn, 2013, pp. 49 & 189; Homburg, 2012, p. 751; Kotler & Keller, 2012, p. 503) affective consumer responses like desirability are likely to be positively related to behavioural consumer responses like willingness-to-buy. Obviously not all consumers who desire a particular luxury good can actually afford buying it. However, those consumers high in desirability for a particular luxury good are more likely to at least consider buying it once they have the money readily at hand.

In a non-luxury context, various studies have empirically shown that behavioural intentions like willingness-to-buy, usage and purchase intention are positively affected by affective consumer responses like consumer perceived value (Dodds et al., 1991, p. 315; Sweeney & Soutar, 2001, p. 215), perceived brand equity and consumer preferences (Cobb-Walgren, Ruble, & Donthu, 1995, pp. 35–36), and brand attitude (Hansen, 2005, p. 431). This positive relationship should equally hold true for luxury goods. In particular, Reich (2005, p. 185) has empirically shown that consumers high in desire for a particular luxury good are more willing to buy than those consumers low in desire for that good. Similarly, we may hypothesize:

H5. Brand desirability positively affects willingness-to-buy.

Figure 59 – Conceptual model.

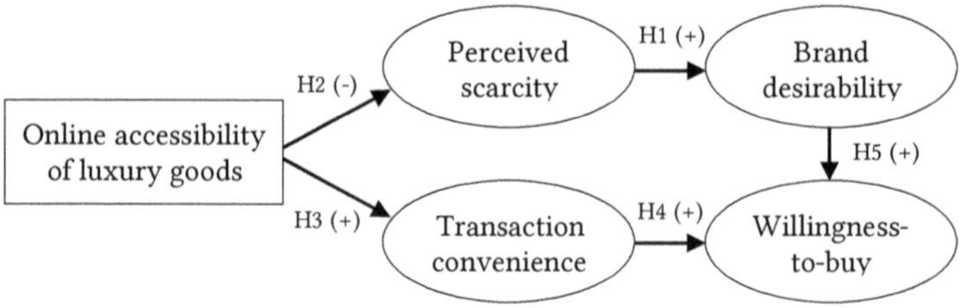

Source: author

6.4.3 Conclusion

To conclude, drawing on socio-economic and social-psychological theory and conceptual considerations a dilution-effect of selling luxury goods online on brand desirability may be hypothesized. This negative relationship may be explained by the assumption that online accessibility decreases the effort needed to obtain a luxury good and thus diminishes consumer perceptions of scarcity (H2) with perceived scarcity being a positive determinant of brand desirability (H1). At the same time, lowering efforts potentially enhances consumer perceived convenience of shopping (H3). Convenience and brand desirability, in turn, are assumed to increase willingness-to-buy (H4 and H5). An overview of all hypothesized effects is provided in the conceptual as shown in Figure 59.

In the following chapters we test these hypotheses. Two experiments are presented: first, we conduct experiment 1 (Chapter 7) using 183 high-income individuals from Germany to test for the effects of online accessibility on consumer perceived scarcity, desirability, convenience, and willingness-to-buy. Second, we conduct experiment 2 (Chapter 8) using 142 qualified luxury insiders from the US to test consumer responses to the online accessibility and price display of luxury goods.

7. Experiment 1 – Online Accessibility

The suitability of the Internet as a channel of distribution for luxury goods is controversially discussed in business press (Chapter 1.1), among scholars (Chapter 4.5) and luxury industry experts (Chapter 5). The ubiquitous accessibility of the mass medium Internet is seemingly incompatible with the fragile perception of exclusiveness of luxury brands. In particular, based on conceptual und theoretical considerations (Chapter 6) we hypothesize that the online accessibility of luxury goods negatively affects consumer perceptions of scarcity (H2), which, in turn, are assumed to be a fundamental driver of a luxury brand's desirability (H1). Apart from this hypothesized dilution-effect of online accessibility on perceived scarcity, we assume that the possibility to shop online actually increases perceived transaction convenience (H3) and thus willingness-to-buy (H4). Finally, we hypothesize a positive relationship between brand desirability and willingness-to-buy (H5; see Chapter 6 and Figure 59 for a detailed hypotheses development).

We empirically test these hypotheses in the following Chapters 7 and 8. In the first experiment (Chapter 7) we examine how consumer perceptions of scarcity and convenience vary depending on whether or not consumers are given the possibility to shop online. In addition to testing consumer responses to the two extremes "can shop online" and "cannot shop online", we are also interested in testing alternatives that might potentially mitigate the hypothesized dilution-effect of online accessibility on perceived scarcity. More specifically, in our series of expert interviews (Chapter 5) we identified approaches designed to create "barriers" to access luxury goods online. These barriers are intended to increase the effort needed to obtain a luxury good with effort being considered to be a fundamental source of scarcity perceptions (compare Chapters 6.1.1 and 6.2.1). In particular, we additionally examine two alternatives: (1) giving access to the online store area of a branded website upon prior user registration only and (2) allowing orders upon request only.

Similar appraoches are increasinly found in practice. For example, on Louisvuitton.com a prospect consumer can instantly order the classic Speedy 30 by clicking on the "place in cart" button while she is required "call to purchase" the more expensive SC bag PM (Louisvuitton.com, 2015b, 2015c). Similarly, in the monobrand online stores of the haute horlogerie brands Jaeger-LeCoultre and Piaget (both Richemont-owned) a prospect watch client can instantly order core-range watches, i.e. "add to cart" a Grande Reverso and "add to bag" an Altiplano watch, respectively (Jaeger-lecoultre.com, 2015b; Piaget.com, 2015b). Yet, interested clients need to "call our concierge" or "shop by phone" first to order limited, more sophisticated timepieces like the Reverso Gyroturbillon 2 or the Altiplano Skeleton watch, respecitively (Jaeger-lecoultre.com, 2015c; Piaget.com, 2015a).

Hence, for experiment 1 we apply a single-factor (i.e. online accessibility), randomized between-subject design with four levels of online accessibility: (1) find a jeweller nearby (i.e. cannot buy online), (2) order upon request, (3) sign in for online store, or (4) buy online. In this first experiment, we test consumer responses of 183 high-income individuals from Germany to levels of online accessibility of a high-involvement luxury product, i.e. wristwatch. In the second experiment reported below (Chapter 8 on experiment 2), responses of 142 US luxury insiders to the online accessibility of a relatively lower-involvement product, i.e. fountain pen, are tested. In the following the first experimental study is described in more detail in terms of methodological approach applied, results, and conclusion.

7.1 Method

7.1.1 Sample: 183 high-income individuals from Germany

Luxury consumers are "notoriously hard to access" for research purposes (Heine, 2010, p. 132). At the same time, the representativeness of student samples for luxury consumer surveys remains questionable (Kapferer, 2014, p. 2). Thus, to make findings more generalizable for the luxury clientele we avoid both student and convenience samples (Kapferer & Laurent, 2014, p. 9). Instead, we apply two different **approaches of approximation** for identifying participants: the identification of (1) high-income individuals (experiment 1), and (2) luxury insiders, i.e. consumers with some knowledge of and a positive attitude towards luxury (experiment 2, see below Chapter 8.1.1).

Participants in this first experimental study are **183 high-income individuals** from Germany. High income serves as an approximation for identifying participants in luxury consumer surveys (Heine, 2010, p. 135). Dubois & Duquesne (1993, p. 42) find that income is a positive and significant determinant of luxury penetration.

Participants are recruited from the Norstat (formerly ODC Services) online panel. Individuals participating in this panel (i.e. panellists) are registered with basic socio-demographic information including income levels. We apply a quota sampling approach, i.e. only individuals with a household net income of at least **EUR 5,000** per month qualify as participants in this first experimental study. When defining this income level two major aspects are considered: first, the income level should be reasonably high in order to best represent the luxury clientele. In Germany, a household net income of at least EUR 5,000 per month represents the top 14 per cent of the total population (Statistisches Bundesamt, 2014, p. 39). For comparison, Kapferer & Laurent (2014, p. 9) apply an income level representing the top 50 per cent of a country's total population.

Second, the income level should be reasonably low to allow a sufficient sample size. Applying a filter of EUR 5,000 monthly household net income to the Norstat online panel results in around 200 panellists. This potential number of participants is sufficient considering the experimental design with four cells. According to rule of thumb, the minimum acceptable sample size for a four-cell experimental design is 120 subjects, i.e. four cells 30 subjects each.

Table 13 – Experiment 1: sample characteristics

Characteristic	Relative frequency (n=183)	Characteristic	Relative frequency (n=183)
Age		**Internet usage**	
18–29	.12	Multiple times a day	.77
30–39	.13	Once a day	.22
40–49	.23	Multiple times a week	.01
50–59	.24	Once a week	.00
≥ 60	.28	Once a month	.01
Gender		Less than monthly	.00
Female	.37	**Education**	
Male	.63	Secondary education	.18
Monthly household income		University entrance diploma	.20
EUR 5,000–7,499	.66	University degree	.52
EUR 7,500–9,999	.30	Doctoral degree or higher	.09
≥ EUR 10,000	.05	No degree	.02
		Prefer not to say	.00

Note: individual values are rounded and might not total 1.00
Source: authors

Only panellists with a registered monthly household net income of at least EUR 5,000 are invited to participate in the study. To crosscheck for income, we first confront participants with a set of questions about some socio-demographic information including gender, age, education level, Internet usage, and income level. Individuals with a self-reported income level of less than EUR 5,000 were automatically screened out from the questionnaire. In order to mitigate the possibility of providing spurious income information, the instructions do not indicate the actual purpose of the study (i.e. selling luxury goods online). Also, participants are not only asked for income but for multiple socio-demographic data.

Sample characteristics are reported in Table 13. On average, participants are 49 years old, 37 per cent are female, 99 per cent browse the Internet for private use at least once per day and 61 per cent hold an university degree or higher.

7.1.2 Procedure: self-administered online survey

7.1.2.1 Scenario: website of high-end watch brand Vaupré

Panellists who qualified as high-income individuals are invited to participate in a self-administered online survey. Following a brief textual instruction, participants are asked to provide socio-demographic information including gender, age, education level, income level, and Internet usage. Next, participants were asked to imagine the **fictitious scenario** of dreaming of and treating themselves to a high-end wristwatch some day. In this scenario the individual shops for her- or himself rather than for a gift for a significant other. We consciously differentiate between these two shopper types as shopping motives for luxury goods differ depending on who is the indented owner of the item, i.e. the shopper her- or himself or a significant other (compare Chapter 2.2). The gift-shopper, for example, might attach relatively less importance on feelings of exclusiveness and relatively more importance on convenience.

A fictitious scenario is applied in order to control for effects resulting from a consumer's previous brand familiarity and associations. We chose the product category of **wristwatches** for the following four reasons: first, wristwatches represent an established segment of the luxury goods industry. Wristwatches account for around 16 per cent of the worldwide personal luxury goods market (Bain & Company & Fondazione Altagamma, 2014, p. 36). Second, wristwatches are not gender-specific (Kastanakis & Balabanis, 2012, p. 1404). Other than for categories like jewellery (rather female category) or cars (rather male category) both female and male participants can imagine shopping for a wristwatch for themselves. Third, wristwatches are typically one-size products. Wristwatches with a leather strap mostly fit any wrist size. Consequently, other than for most fashion items consumers do not necessarily need to test the fit of the product in-store. Lastly, luxury watch manufacturers are particularly reluctant to adopt online distribution formats while non-luxury wristwatches are generally sold online (e.g., Casio watches on Amazon). To date specialist watchmakers like A. Lange & Söhne, Breguet, Patek Philippe, Rolex and Vacheron Constantin do not operate monobrand online stores. Launching an online store in 2013 only, the Swiss brands Jaeger-LeCoultre and Piaget (both Richemont subsidiaries) are among the first watchmakers to directly sell online (Jaeger-lecoultre.com, 2015d; Piaget.com, 2015b).

Subjects are further asked to imagine that they incidentally arrive at the website of the **high-end wristwatch producer Vaupré** when occasionally browsing the Internet for wristwatches. Instructions inform subjects that the brand name Vaupré is fictitious but that the information given is representative for an existing high-end wristwatch manufacturer. The characteristics used to describe the brand well reflect the generic characteristics of a luxury brand (see Chapter 2.1) as well as the category-specific characteristics of a high-end watch manufacturer. For comparison, Table 14 lists the top 10 high-end watch manufacturer according to the World Luxury Association (2012) and their characteristics in terms of ownership, country-of-origin, year of foundation, types of movements, estimated annual production capacity in timepieces, and the estimated retail price range in EUR. Specifically, the brand Vaupré is described using the following characteristics:

- **Ownership:** to emphasize the heritage and longevity of the brand Vaupré is described as a still privately owned, family-run business. Originating from small, specialized manufacturers (e.g., Hermès making saddles, Louis Vuitton making suitcases) the luxury industry has become highly consolidated over the past decades. In the case of high-end wristwatches, most brands are now owned by the three leading watchmaking groups: Swatch Group (brands like Blancpain, Breguet, and Glashütte Original; Swatchgroup.com, 2015), Richemont (brands like IWC, Piaget, and Vacheron Constantin; Richemont.com, 2014), and LVMH (brands like Hublot, Tag Heuer and Zenith; LVMH.com, 2014ag, 2014ba, 2014bf). To date, Audemars Piguet, Patek Philippe, and Rolex are rare examples of high-end wristwatch manufacturers that are still privately owned.
- **Country-of-origin:** the scenario indicates that Vaupré wristwatches are made in Switzerland. As Switzerland is well known for its rich heritage in haute horlogerie, i.e. the art of finest watchmaking, it is considered as positive country-of-origin effect (COO). A meta-analysis of 964 independent studies by Peterson & Jolibert (1995, p. 890) shows that a positive country-of-origin effect (e.g., watches from Switzerland, cars from Germany) increases consumer perceptions of quality and thus purchase intentions. From a consumer perspective, the importance of a positive country-of-origin effect is even increased for luxury goods (Godey et al., 2012, p. 6). In the case of watches, "Swiss made" watches enjoy a considerable price premium vis-á-vis non-swiss watches. For examples, the average price of swiss watch is 200 times the price of a Chinese watch (Fédération de l'Industrie Horlogère Suisse FH, 2014, p. 3). This price premium explains why Swiss watches account for more than 40 per cent of worldwide value exports of watches (UN Comtrade, 2012) while accounting for only about 2.5 per cent of unit exports (Fédération de l'Industrie Horlogère suisse FH, 2012, p. 3).
- **Year of foundation:** the scenario states that the brand Vaupré is built upon a rich tradition and a heritage of 150 years. In 2013 (i.e. the year of examination), the heritage of real high-end watch brands ranges from 278 years (Blancpain.com, 2014) and 258 years (Vacheron-constantin.com, 2015) to 105 years (Rolex.com, 2015b) and 16 years (Franckmuller.com, 2014).
- **Movement:** Vaupré is said to produce primarily mechanical movements. As opposed to watches with electronic movements like quartz movements, watches with mechanical movements are more complicated to produce and, thus, priced about 10 times higher (Fédération de l'industrie horlogère suisse FH, 2015). Still, high-end watch manufacturers partly rely on the less complicated quartz movements, e.g., for ladies watches.
- **Annual production:** Vaupré is said to produce less than 100,000 timepieces per year which well reflects the production capacity of real high-end watchmakers like Patek Philippe, Vacheron Constantin, and Jeager-LeCoultre with 45,000, 20,000, and 50,000 timepieces p.a. respectively (Braun, 2013, pp. 202, 272 & 338).

Table 14 – Experiment 1: characteristics of top 10 high-end wristwatch manufacturers

Brand	**Ownership**	**Country of origin**	**Year of foundation**	**Movement focus[a]**	**Estimated production p.a.**	**Estimated retail price range in EUR**
Audemars Piguet	Private	Switzerland	1875	mechanical	26,000	12,000–210,000
Blancpain	Swatch	Switzerland	1735	mechanical	n.a.	12,000–300,000
Breguet	Swatch	Switzerland	1775	mechanical	17,000	10,000–175,000
Franck Muller	Private	Switzerland	1997	mechanical	n.a.	7,300–2,000,000
IWC	Richemont	Switzerland	1868	mechanical	30,000	3,600–190,000
Jaeger-Le Coultre	Richemont	Switzerland	1833	mechanical	50,000	7,300–190,000
Patek Philippe	Private	Switzerland	1839	mechanical	45,000	20,000–600,000
Piaget	Richemont	Switzerland	1874	mechanical	20,000	15,000–45,000
Rolex	Private	Switzerland	1908	mechanical	1,000,000	3,600–36,000
Vacheron Constantin	Richemont	Switzerland	1755	mechanical	20,000	15,000–220,000
Vaupré (fictitious)	Private	Switzerland	1864	mechanical	< 100,000	five-digit

[a]Applies to core range timepieces. Entry range timepieces may be equipped with quartz movements.

Source: Audemarspiguet.com (2014), Blancpain.com (2014), Braun (2013), Breguet.com (2014a), Franckmuller.com (2014), IWC.com (2014), Jaeger-lecoultre.com (2014), Patek.com (2014b), Piaget.com (2014a), Rolex.com (2015b), Vacheron-constantin.com (2015), Watchuseek.com (2011), and World Luxury Association (2012)

- **Price range:** retail prices for Vaupré watches were said to range around the five-digit Euro range on average. This price range well reflects that of high-end watchmakers like Patek Philippe (about EUR 20,000 to 600,000; Braun, 2013, pp. 272–275), Vacheron Constantin (about EUR 15,000 to 220,000; Braun, 2013, pp. 338–341), and Piaget (about EUR 15,000 to 45,000; Braun, 2013, pp. 282–284).
- **Manufacturing:** the scenario indicates that Vaupré watches are crafted by hand using precious metals only. As shown in Chapter 2.1 some degree of natural scarcity in terms of limited human resources (i.e. craftsmanship and designers) and rare material (e.g., precious metals) represents an essential element of a luxury brand's concept of exclusiveness.
- **Distribution:** in addition to natural scarcity, a highly selective distribution is needed to preserve consumer perceptions of being hard-to-get. Patek Philippe, for example, operates only three monobrand boutiques in the most prestigious places, i.e. Rue de Rhône (Geneva, Switzerland), Place Vendôme (Paris, France), and New Bond Street (London, United Kingdom; Patek.com, 2015c). Similarly, Vaupré watches are said to be available at few, selected retailers in the prime locations of major cities only.

7.1.2.2 Manipulation: online accessibility

On the next page, the scenario asks the participants to further imagine to clicking on a wristwatch of interest to access the product view, which shows a series of product images, primary product information and a set of buttons. Subjects are randomly confronted with one of four sets of buttons as shown in Figure 60: (a) group 1 is confronted with two buttons only, namely 'More details' and 'Find a jeweller nearby'. In addition to these two buttons (b) group 2 is confronted with a 'Order upon request' button, (c) group 3 with a 'Sign in for online store' button, and (d) group 4 with a 'Buy online' button. Each button is complemented with a brief textual explanation of what subjects could expect as a next step when clicking on a particular button. For example, by clicking on the 'Order upon request' button subjects are said to arrive at an order request form, which they could submit to Vaupré.

The two alternatives 'sign in for online store' and 'order upon request' are tested as they increase the effort needed to obtain a luxury good and thus potentially mitigate the expected negative effect of online accessibility (i.e. the 'buy online' alternative) on consumer perceptions of scarcity. As shown above, these alternatives are also observed in practice.

To control for effects of price information as shown by Lynn (1989) the scenario does not include any explicit price information. Subsequent to the scenario participants are asked to evaluate the brand described in terms of perceived scarcity, desirability, transaction convenience and willingness-to-buy as well as to perform a manipulation check.

Figure 60 – Experiment 1: stimuli for online accessibility.

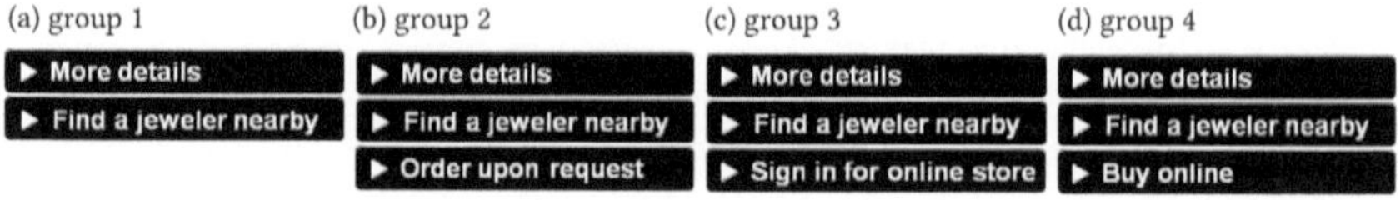

Source: authors

7.1.2.3 Measurement scales

All constructs are measured using established scales. Table 15 shows the original German scales used in this first experimental study among German high-income individuals. The English equivalent version used in the second experimental study among luxury insiders from the US is presented below in Chapter 8.1.2.3.

Perceived scarcity is measured using three items drawn from the uniqueness dimension of the well-established brand luxury index by Vigneron & Johnson (2004, p. 502): "To me Vaupré is (1) exclusive, (2) rare, (3) unique". In its original form Vigneron & Johnson (2004, p. 502) apply a seven-point semantic differential scale, i.e. the following pairs: "(1) fairly exclusive... (7) extremely exclusive", "(1) uncommon... (7) rare", and "(1) unusual... (7) unique". However, both discussions with other academics and the pre-testing using a student sample reveal considerable difficulties in differentiating these pairs. Consequently, we apply a seven-point Likert-type scale anchored with "does not apply at all" and "does fully apply".

To measure **brand desirability** we apply an adapted version of Dubois & Paternault's (1995, p. 70) luxury-specific dream value measure which asks respondents: "Imagine you are given the possibility of choosing a beautiful present because you won a contest. Which are the five brands [to be selected from a list] you would like the best?"

By using this formulation the dream value basically asks for a respondent's desire for a luxury brand independently of prices to be paid (Kapferer & Bastien, 2009a, p. 129; Kastanakis & Balabanis, 2012, p. 1404). Since we are interested in measuring a respondent's desire for one brand only (i.e. Vaupré), we re-formulate the question as follows: "Now, let's assume you won a contest. As a reward you receive any luxury wristwatch of your choice. How likely would you choose a Vaupré product?" Similar to Kastanakis & Balabanis (2012, p. 1404), we measure brand desirability on a seven-point rating scale anchored "very unlikely" and "very likely".

Transaction convenience is measured using three items drawn from the multidimensional SERVCON (service convenience) scale by Seiders et al. (2007, p. 148). Respondents are asked to indicate to which extend they agree or disagree with statements like "It takes little time to pay for my purchase at Vaupré" on a seven-point Likert-type scale anchored with "strongly disagree" and "strongly agree".

Finally, to measure a respondent's **willingness-to-buy** we use three items drawn from the original scale by Dodds et al. (1991, p. 348) which has been previously applied to the context of research on marketing luxury brands by Bian & Forsythe (2012, p. 1447). Consequently, respondents are asked to indicate to which extend they agree

Table 15 – Experiment 1: measurement scales (German)

	Measurement			
Construct	**Question**	**Items**	**Scale**	**Source(s)**
Perceived scarcity	Wie sehr treffen Ihrer Meinung nach folgende Eigenschaften auf die Marke Vaupré zu?	Für mich ist Vaupré (a) exklusiv (b) rar (c) einzigartig	(1) Überhaupt nicht zutreffen … (7) Voll zutreffend	Vigneron & Johnson (2004, p. 502)
Brand desirability	Angenommen Sie erhalten als Preis für Ihren Erfolg bei einem Wettbewerb eine Armbanduhr Ihrer Wahl. Mit welcher Wahrscheinlichkeit würden Sie eine Armbanduhr der Marke Vaupré wählen?	n.a.	(1) Sehr unwahrscheinlich … (7) Sehr wahrscheinlich	Dubois & Paternault (1995, p. 70); Kastanakis & Balabanis (2012, p. 1404)
Transaction convenience	Wie schätzen Sie die Kaufabwicklung für eine Armbanduhr der Marke Vaupré generell ein?	(a) Es würde mich wenig Zeit kosten, eine Armbanduhr von Vaupré zu kaufen. (b) Vaupré macht es mir einfach, meinen Einkauf abzuwickeln. (c) Der Kauf einer Armbanduhr von Vaupré ginge schnell.	(1) Stimme überhaupt nicht zu … (7) Stimme voll zu	Seiders, Voss, Godfrey, & Grewal (2007, p. 148)
Willingness-to-buy	Angenommen Sie würden eine hochwertige Armbanduhr kaufen wollen. Wie sehr würden Sie den Kauf einer Armbanduhr der Marke Vaupré in Erwägung ziehen?	(a) Wenn ich mir eine hochwertige Armbanduhr kaufen würde, würde ich in Betracht ziehen, eine Armbanduhr von Vaupré zu kaufen. (b) Meine Bereitschaft eine Armbanduhr von Vaupré zu kaufen wäre hoch, wenn ich planen würde, eine hochwertige Armbanduhr zu kaufen. (c) Es ist sehr wahrscheinlich, dass ich erwägen würde, eine Armbanduhr von Vaupré zu kaufen.	(1) Stimme überhaupt nicht zu … (7) Stimme voll zu	Bian & Forsythe (2012, p. 1447); Dodds, Monroe, & Grewal (1991, p. 318)

Note: an English version is provided in Table 24.

Source: authors

or disagree with statements like "If I were going to buy a luxury writing instrument, I would consider buying a Vaupré product" on a seven-point Likert-type scale anchored with "strongly disagree" and "strongly agree". This hypothetic formulation is preferred over asking for a concrete purchase intention (e.g., "how likely would buy a Vaupré watch") since luxury goods are typically infrequently bought considering their heavy price tag. The complete list of items in English is displayed below in Chapter 8.1.2.3.

7.1.2.4 Pre-testing

The scenario and measurement scales were developed and tested in two subsequent steps. First, we conducted a series of qualitative interviews with both other marketing scholars and uninvolved consumers. The iterative process resulted in three major modifications: (a) narrowing down the description of the brand Vaupré to the key characteristics as described above (Chapter 7.1.2.1), (b) using graphical cues (i.e. the set of buttons, see Chapter 7.1.2.2) as stimuli for different levels of online accessibility, and (c) changing the scale format for measuring perceived scarcity from its original semantic differential format as applied by Vigneron & Johnson (2004, p. 502) into a Likert-type scale format (see Chapter 7.1.2.3). The latter modification resulted from reported problems in understanding some of the bipolar pairs, e.g., "rare" as opposed to "uncommon".

Second, after having developed and iteratively refined the scenario and measurements scales, we tested the complete survey using 46 students recruited through an online student career forum. Both qualitative feedback and participation statistics suggested the following two modifications: (a) shortening some of scales to a minimum of three items, and (b) adding brief textual descriptions to each of graphical buttons displayed as some few respondents asked for more information on what they could expect as a next step when clicking on, for example, the 'Order upon request' button.

7.2 Results

Before testing the hypotheses on the effects of online accessibility on consumer brand evaluations using analysis of variance (ANOVA) and structural equation modeling (SEM) we perform some preliminary analyses to test the effectiveness of the manipulation of online accessibility as well as the validity and reliability of the measurement model.

7.2.1 Preliminary analyses

7.2.1.1 Manipulation check

Before testing whether the manipulation of the independent variable online accessibility causes some of the variance in the dependent variables we first assess the effectiveness of the manipulation. If, for example, online accessibility fails to significantly affect the desirability of the brand, there are two alternative explanations:

Table 16 – Experiment 1: manipulation check

	Manipulation present	Manipulation absent	*t*-test results			
Group	*M*(*SE*)	*M*(*SE*)	*Mean difference*	*t*-statistic	*df*	*p*
"Buy online"	.46 (.073)	.24 (.037)	.22	2.821	181	.005
"Sign in for online store"	.45 (.072)	.08 (.024)	.37	6.272	181	.000
"Order upon request"	.46 (.073)	.13 (.029)	.33	4.960	181	.000

M = mean scores of aided recall; *SE* = standard error; *df* = degrees of freedom; *p* = significance (two-tailed)
Source: authors

firstly, variation in the levels of online accessibility does in fact not explain any of the variation in desirability, i.e. there is neither a positive nor a negative effect and the variation in desirability is explained by variables other than online accessibility. Secondly, variation in the levels of online accessibility was not manipulated successfully, e.g., subjects confronted with the 'Buy online' condition were actually not aware of the opportunity to directly buy online when evaluating the desirability of the brand. Consequently, it is important to know whether subjects sufficiently recognized the manipulated variable, i.e. whether the manipulation was successful.

To assess the effectiveness of the manipulation we performed a series of independent *t*-tests. As summarized in Table 16, the manipulation can be considered successful: aided recall of the 'Buy online' button is significantly higher among subjects who were confronted with this button ($M_{buy}(SE)$=.46 (.073)) than among subjects who were not confronted with this button ($M_{non\text{-}buy}(SE)$=.24 (.037); $t(181)=2.821$; $p = .005$). Similarly, we find a significantly higher aided recall of the 'Sign in for online store' button ($M_{sign}(SE)$=.45 (.072) vs. $M_{non\text{-}sign}(SE)$ =.08 (.024); $t(181)=6.272$; p=.000) and the 'Order upon request button' ($M_{order}(SE)$=.46 (.073) vs. $M_{non\text{-}order}(SE)$=.13 (.029); $t(181)=4.960$; p=.000) among subjects who were confronted with the respective button. These results indicate that the online accessibility was successfully manipulated between groups.

7.2.1.2 Confirmatory factor analysis

A confirmatory factor analysis using Mplus is performed to assess the validity of the measurement model, i.e. whether the observed variables adequately measure the latent variables of perceived scarcity, brand desirability, transaction convenience, and willingness-to-buy. CFA results yield a satisfactory model fit with $\chi^2(30)=39$ (p=.121),

Table 17 – Experiment 1: evaluation of measurement validity

Indicator	*M*	*SD*	λ^*	*t*	ρ_{IR}	ρ_{CR}	ρ_{AVE}
Perceived scarcity							
To me Vaupré is exclusive.	5.951	1.268	.777*	19.68	.604	.836	.632
To me Vaupré is rare.	5.399	1.379	.877*	25.11	.770		
To me Vaupré is unique.	5.000	1.367	.719*	15.99	.517		
Transaction convenience							
It takes little time to pay for my purchase at Vaupré.	4.295	1.899	.804*	24.43	.646	.882	.714
Vaupré makes it easy for me to conclude my transaction.	4.656	1.692	.889*	33.04	.790		
I am able to complete my purchase quickly at Vaupré.	4.475	1.709	.850*	29.04	.722		
Willingness-to-buy							
If I were going to buy a luxury wristwatch, I would consider buying a Vaupré product.	4.557	1.750	.921*	57.97	.848	.928	.812
My willingness to buy a Vaupré product would be high if I were shopping for a luxury wristwatch.	4.623	1.685	.941*	66.28	.886		
The probability I would consider buying a Vaupré wristwatch is high.	4.060	1.849	.847*	35.58	.718		

*significant at $p < .001$ (two-tailed); *M* = mean; *SD* = standard deviation; λ^* = standardized factor loading; *t* = *t*-value; ρ_{IR} = indicator reliability; ρ_{CR} = composite reliability; ρ_{AVE} = average variance extracted
Source: authors

CFI =.99, RMSEA=.04, and SRMR=.04 (Bagozzi & Yi, 1998, p. 82; Hu & Bentler, 1999, p. 27) and support the reliability and validity of measurement scales (see Table 17). Indicator reliability scores for all items exceed .50 (Bagozzi & Yi, 2012, p. 17). Convergent validity of perceived scarcity, transaction convenience, and willingness-to-buy proves to be satisfactory as composite reliability scores are .84, .88, and .93 respectively, i.e. greater than .70 (Bagozzi & Yi, 2012, p. 17) and scores of average variance extracted are .63, .71, and .81 respectively, i.e. greater than .50 (Bagozzi & Yi, 1998, p. 82). Finally, discriminant validity can be assumed since for each construct the average variance extracted is greater than the squared correlation with any other construct (Fornell & Larcker, 1981, p. 46).

7.2.2 Hypotheses testing

First, we perform structural equation modeling (SEM) to simultaneously test the hypothesized relationships between online accessibility, perceived scarcity, brand desirability, transaction convenience, and willingness-to-buy (H1 to H5). Second, the four experimental groups are tested for mean differences in perceptions of scarcity and transaction convenience using analysis of variance (ANOVA). ANOVA allows both testing the overall experimental effect of online accessibility as well as the differences between the four factor levels of online accessibility.

7.2.2.1 Structural equation modeling

We perform SEM in Mplus to test the hypothesized relationships between online accessibility, perceived scarcity, brand desirability, transaction convenience, and willingness-to-buy (H1 to H5). SEM results are displayed in Table 18. First, based on socio-economic and social-psychological theory we expected perceived scarcity to be a fundamental driver of brand desirability (H1). The data supports this hypothesis as the standardized path coefficient β of the structural path between perceived scarcity and brand desirability is both positive and statistically significant (β=.380; p<.001). Next, we are interested in whether perceived scarcity is negatively affected by online accessibility (H2). The path coefficient of the relationship between online accessibility and perceived scarcity is indeed negative, however, not statistically significant (β=-.017; p=.832). Hence, we reject H2.

Furthermore we hypothesized that individuals who are given the possibility to shop online perceive higher levels of transaction convenience (H3). SEM results show that the relationship between online accessibility and transaction convenience is positive, though non-significant (β=.101; p=.194). Hence, we reject H3. Finally, we expected that parts of the variation in willingness-to-buy are explained by variation in both transaction convenience and brand desirability (H4 and H5). Supporting both H4 and H5, the estimated path coefficients for both transaction convenience (β=.265; p<.001) and brand desirability (β=.642; p<.001) on willingness-to-buy are positive and statistically significant.

7.2.2.2 Analysis of variance

In addition to testing the overall model using SEM as shown in Table 18, we perform two one-way ANOVA using SPSS. This procedure allows us not only to test the overall experimental effect of the manipulated variable online accessibility but also the potential differences between the four levels of online accessibility through pairwise comparisons.

First, descriptive statistics (see Figure 61(a)) report only marginal differences in perceived scarcity between subjects who were confronted with either 'Find a store close to you' only (M=5.28; SD=1.38), 'Order upon request' (M=5.54; SD=.84), 'Sign in for online store' (M=5.68; SD=1.15), or 'Buy online' (M=5.35; SD=.95). Indeed, results of the one-way ANOVA indicate that the overall experimental effect of online accessibility on perceived scarcity is statistically non-significant (F(3,179)=1.29; p=.280). Similar to the SEM results, this finding supports the rejection of H2.

Table 18 – Experiment 1: results of structural equation modeling

Structural relationship	Path coefficient β	Two-tailed *p*–value	Evaluation of hypothesis
H1: Perceived scarcity → Brand desirability	.380	***	not rejected
H2: Online accessibility → Perceived scarcity	-.017	.832 *ns*	rejected
H3: Online accessibility → Transaction convenience	.101	.194 *ns*	rejected
H4: Transaction convenience → Willingness-to-buy	.265	***	not rejected
H5: Brand desirability → Willingness-to-buy	.642	***	not rejected

***significant at $p < .001$; *ns* = non-significant
Source: authors

Figure 61 – Experiment 1: descriptive statistics

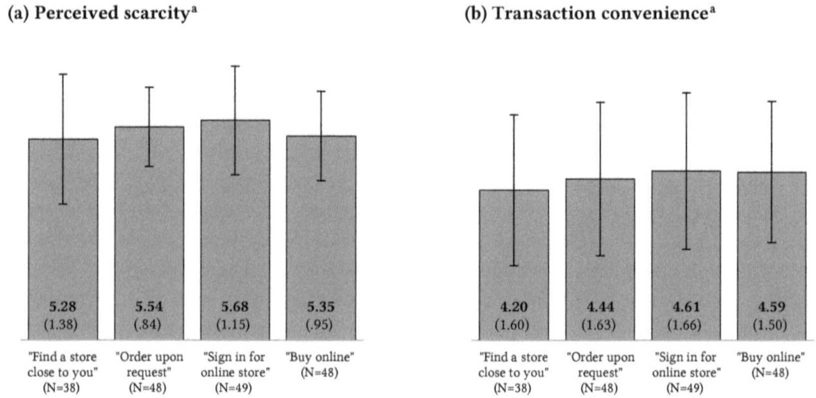

[a]measured on a seven-point Likert-type scale; mean scores are reported with standard deviations in parenthesis
Source: authors

Similarly, descriptive statistics (see Figure 61(b)) show only a slight tendency that evaluations of transaction convenience decrease as the effort needed to obtain the luxury good increases. Still, the overall experimental effect of online accessibility on transaction convenience is non-significant ($F(3,179)=.567$; $p=.637$). This finding confirms the rejection of H3 as previously shown by our SEM analysis. Overall, the variation in consumer evaluations of scarcity and transaction convenience is not explained by the manipulation of online accessibility.

Table 19 – Experiment 1: pairwise comparisons

		Mean differences[a]									
		Perceived scarcity					Transaction convenience				
Groups	*N*	*M*	**1.**	**2.**	**3.**	**4.**	*M*	**1.**	**2.**	**3.**	**4.**
1. Find a jeweller close to you	38	5.28	0				4.20	0			
2. Order upon request	48	5.54	.26	0			4.44	.24	0		
3. Sign in for online store	49	5.68	.40	.14	0		4.61	.41	.17	0	
4. Buy online	48	5.35	.07	-.19	-.33	0	4.60	.40	.16	-.01	0

[a]all mean differences are non-significant applying Bonferroni-adjusted levels of significance; *N* = group size; *M* = means
Source: author

Second, we perform *post hoc* tests to examine pairwise differences between the means of the four levels of online accessibility: (1) 'Find a jeweler close to you', (2) 'Order upon request', (3) 'Sign in for online store', and (4) 'Buy online'. Rather than testing the overall effect of the variation in online accessibility, we are interested in whether one single alternative of the four levels yields significantly higher or lower scores of perceived scarcity and transaction convenience than any other alternative. In total we perform $m=6$ pairwise comparisons since $m=k(k-1)/2$ with k being the number of factor levels. As we test these 6 pairwise comparisons simultaneously we adjust the critical significance level of $\alpha=.05$ using the conservative Bonferroni method, which yields a modified value of $\alpha/m=.05/6=.00833$. Results show that groups confronted with any of the four levels of online accessibility do not significantly differ from each other in terms of perceived scarcity or transaction convenience (see Table 19). Consequently, contrary to our expectations the two options 'Order upon request' and 'Sign in for online store' do not prove to evoke significantly higher perceptions of scarcity.

7.3 Conclusion

According to socio-economic and social-psychological theory anything is desired to the extent to which it is unavailable. Both Smith (2005[1766], p. 190) and Brock (1968, p. 246) argue that individuals feel more attracted to goods that are scarce. The data supports this positive scarcity-desirability relationship. The desirability of the high-end watch brand Vaupré is higher when being perceived as scarce. However, in contrast to the prevailing hesitance towards the online distribution of luxury goods (e.g., Kapferer & Bastien, 2012, p. 249; Seringhaus, 2005, p. 15) online accessibility does not prove to be a statistically significant antecedent of perceived scarcity. Differences in consumer perceptions of scarcity are not explained by the presence or absence of online distribution. Hence, selling luxury goods online per se does not diminish consumer perceptions of scarcity and desirability. We refer to this finding as "no-dilution" finding.

In addition to the general research question of whether or not the possibility to shop luxury goods online dilutes the fragile perception of exclusiveness, we were interested in the differences between the four levels of online accessibility: (1) ‚Find a jeweller close to you' (no online accessibility), (2) ‚Order upon request', (3) ‚Sign in for online store', and (4) ‚Buy online'. In particular, since the two alternatives ‚Order upon request' and ‚Sign in for online store' require more effort to shop for a luxury good than the easy-to-obtain option ‚Buy online' they were assumed to evoke relatively higher levels of perceived scarcity. Yet, none of the two alternatives yielded significantly higher scores on perceived scarcity than the mere ‚Buy online' option. Hence, artificially increasing the effort needed to obtain a luxury good by complicating the shopping process does not evoke higher levels of perceived scarcity than a simple and convenient ‚Buy online' button. There may be other circumstances, however, that require the (non-artificial) use of an ‚Order upon request' button (e.g., the product is in fact limitedly available or difficult to ship).

At the same time, making luxury goods accessible online was expected to increase consumer perceptions of transaction convenience since it reduces the effort needed to obtain a luxury good as compared to visiting a brick-and-mortar store. In particular, we expected that individuals in the ‚Find a jeweller close to you' condition (i.e. no possibility to shop online) would perceive shopping that brand less convenient than individuals given the possibility to shop through either way ‚Buy online', ‚Sign in for online store', or ‚Order upon request'. This hypothesis is not supported by the data. This might be possibly explained by the assumption that individuals place less importance on convenience aspects when shopping for an extraordinarily expensive good (EUR > 10,000) they have been dreaming of for a long time. It might be assumed that the majority of individuals would have gone to the shop anyway to touch and feel the product. In contrast, convenience aspects might become more important when shopping for gifts for significant others rather than shopping for oneself as imagined in the scenario presented here.

8. Experiment 2 – Online Accessibility and Price Display

Results of experiment 1 provide a first indication that selling luxury goods online does not dilute a luxury brand's fragile image of exclusiveness. This "no-dilution" finding contradicts the concerns raised in previous conceptual work (e.g., Kapferer & Bastien, 2012, p. 249; Seringhaus, 2005, p. 15; see Chapters 4.5.1). Experiment 2 is designed to (1) replicate the effects of online accessibility and (2) additionally test for effects of price display, which was controlled for in experiment 1. We conduct another experimental study using a 2 (online accessibility: yes vs. no) by 2 (price display: yes vs. no) randomized between-subject design. The factor online accessibility was reduced from four to two levels since the four levels did not prove to cause significant differences (see Chapter 7.2.2.1). Hence, participants in experiment 2 are confronted with either the possibility to shop online or not and the retail price for the product shown is either displayed or not.

Price information influences consumer evaluations of brands (Dodds et al., 1991, p. 316). The price to be paid in exchange for any good or service is not only a monetary sacrifice but serves as a global indicator of the functional, experiential, and symbolic value, the good is likely to deliver (Fassnacht et al., 2013, p. 104; Völckner, 2006, p. 474). The role of price as quality indicator should become even more salient when shopping for a luxury good since consumers typically have less prior knowledge about price and quality levels than for convenience goods they shop every day.

Luxury goods manufacturers typically pursue a discreet-to-no price communication policy (Fassnacht et al., 2013, p. 106; Kapferer & Bastien, 2009a, p. 70). Ten out of 24 luxury brand boutiques located on the prestigious Place Vendôme in Paris do not show retail prices at all (Parguel, Delécolle, & Valette-Florence, 2014, p. 28). And also online some luxury brand websites do not disclose retail prices at first sight but rather postpone the display of price information to a later phase of the online shopping process.

For example, if users browse products on Montblanc.com under "Show Collections" no prices are displayed. They need click on the "Buy now" button first to access the online store area where also prices are displayed (Montblanc.com, 2014c). Similarly, Boucheron.com products like the Quatre Classique Ring are displayed first along with a brief textual description of the product. Only after clicking on the "More Detail" button, the user accesses the second product view page where, among other details, the price is displayed (Boucheron.com, 2015c).

As a consequence price knowledge among consumers is highly heterogeneous (Kapferer & Laurent, 2014, p. 10). However, individuals tend to overestimate the actual price (Kapferer & Bastien, 2012, p. 74). This overestimation is desirable given the dual role of price as monetary sacrifice and quality indicator. If the assumed price is higher than the actual price consumers can be expected to attribute higher levels of functional, experiential, and symbolic value to the brand.

The Internet, however, has made price information more transparent. Consumers are less likely to overestimate prices and thus quality. Consequently, Kapferer & Bastien (2012, p. 212) state that the "price communication is one of the trickiest points regarding the use of the Internet in luxury". Similarly, Gastaldi (2012, p. 112) argues that one reason of many luxury goods manufacturers' "reluctance to adopt an e-commerce strategy lies in the issue of price display".

In this second experimental study we manipulate both online accessibility (as in experiment 1) and price display in order to test whether price display itself affects consumer perceptions of scarcity (main effect of price display) and whether the no-dilution effect of online accessibility as shown in experiment 1 persists even when retail prices are explicitly communicated (interaction effect between online accessibility and price display). Other than for the first experimental study, a relatively lower-involvement luxury good (i.e. fountain pen) is used and the sample consists of luxury insiders from the US. In the following this second experimental study is described in more detail in terms of methodological approach applied, results, and conclusion.

8.1 Method

8.1.1 Sample: 142 luxury insiders from USA

Participants in experiment 2 were **142 luxury insiders** from the US selected through a **qualification test among 1,022 US consumers**. Similar to Heine (2010, p. 134) we define *luxury insiders* as consumers with some knowledge of and a positive attitude towards luxury brands.

As in experiment 1 selecting an adequate sample of participants in a survey about luxury goods requires specific approaches since the actual target group of affluent, luxury consuming individuals is "notoriously hard to access" and the appropriateness of students as participants in luxury consumer surveys remains "questionable" (Heine, 2010, p. 132). Consequently, in experiment 1 we selected individuals based on their household income, which serves as a good proxy for being a (potential) luxury consumer (see Chapter 7.1.1). In addition to this approach of approximation, Heine (2010, pp. 135–138) introduces more sophisticated approaches based on an individual's luxury consumption history ("luxury consumption scale") or her or his cognitive and affective statements about luxury ("luxury affection scale") which are intended to further refine the sample of luxury consumers. Only the luxury affection scale allows identifying the "genuine" luxury consumer who has some knowledge of and a positive attitude towards luxury (Heine, 2010, p. 138).

Consequently, in experiment 2 subjects are luxury insiders, i.e., that have acquired some knowledge of luxury brands and generally hold a more positive attitude towards luxury as compared to the general population. As will be shown below luxury insiders do enjoy higher income levels than those who are not luxury insiders.

In the following, we describe in more detail the procedure of the qualification test, the qualification criteria applied and the resulting sample of luxury insiders.

8.1.1.1 Procedure of qualification test

In order to identify luxury insiders we performed a qualification test with 1,022 US consumers recruited from the cloud-computing platform Amazon Mechanical Turk (AMT). On AMT registered users (*workers*) perform human intelligence tasks (HIT) provided by other users (*requesters*) in exchange for a pre-defined dollar reward. Those HITs typically include but are not limited to surveys and experiments for both market and academic research purposes. For more information on AMT as a tool for consumer research please see Crump, McDonnell, & Gureckis (2013) and Mason & Suri (2012).

In February 2013 we posted a three-minute HIT titled "Guess the Brand!" rewarded with USD 0.36 reflecting an hourly wage of USD 7.20, which is generally considered an above-average pay on AMT. Only workers meeting each of the following three requirements were able to access our HIT: (1) workers with residence in the US, (2) workers with a registered track record of at least 100 completed HITs, and (3) workers with an approval rate of 95 per cent or higher i.e. the rate of the number of HITs completed and approved by the respective HIT requester divided by the number of HITs started.

All of these requirements are automatically and continuously tracked by AMT. The latter two requirements are commonly applied to ensure some minimum level of quality and credibility of the workers performing the HITs. Workers who had accepted the HIT were forwarded to a survey containing personal information questions first followed by questions about their attitude towards luxury and six product-to-brand assignment tasks, which are described in the following.

8.1.1.2 Qualification criteria

Two qualification criteria were applied to identify luxury insiders: (1) **attitude towards luxury** and (2) **actual knowledge** of luxury brands. Only individuals proving to have both a more positive attitude towards luxury than the general population (i.e. the top 25 per cent) and a higher level of actual knowledge about luxury brands (i.e. at least three correct out of six given product-to-brand assignments) qualified as luxury insiders. Liu et al. (2013, p. 887) apply a similar approach: individuals qualify as luxury consumers only if they have both purchased a luxury good within the past three years and scored higher than four on the seven-point conspicuous consumption motive scale.

Attitude towards luxury. An individual's attitude towards luxury was measured using a self-reported measurement scale with items drawn from Dubois, Czellar, & Laurent (2005, p. 117). The ten items are reported in Table 20. Importantly, as the attitude towards luxury scale is a self-reported measure, individuals may be tempted to provide responses, which they believe would comply with researcher's expectations.

Table 20 – Experiment 2: items of attitude towards luxury

(1)	In my opinion, luxury is good taste.
(2)	In general, luxury products are better quality products.
(3)	I don't know much about the luxury world.*
(4)	All things considered, I rather like luxury products.
(5)	Luxury makes me dream.
(6)	In my opinion, luxury is too expensive for what it is.*
(7)	Luxury products make life more beautiful.
(8)	Some education is needed for appreciating luxury products.
(9)	I almost never buy luxury products.*
(10)	One buys luxury goods primarily for one's pleasure.

*reversed scoring; all items were measured on a seven-point Likert-type scale
Source: Dubois et al. (2005, p. 117)

To mitigate the probability of subjects providing spurious responses, they were manipulated in two ways: first, the HIT was not officially declared as qualification test (which is common practice on AMT) but as a research study on consumers' general knowledge of brands titled "Guess the Brand!". Consequently, participants were not aware of a follow-up HIT and thus were not tempted to provide answers that would increase their personal likelihood of being invited to another (paid) HIT. Second, we instructed participants that they were **randomly** assigned to one of multiple product segments. In fact, we told all participants to have been randomly assigned to the product segment of luxury goods. This way, we may assume that participants did not necessarily have a specific incentive to state their attitude towards luxury different than their actual attitude.

Actual knowledge of luxury brands. Additionally to the self-reported measure of attitude towards luxury we tested the subjects' actual knowledge of luxury brands. Subjects were given the task to assign the correct brand name to each of six images of branded luxury products from different luxury product categories. We applied an aided recall (multiple choice) format and a balanced number between rather female (e.g., shoes) and rather male products (e.g., cars) as well as between rather conspicuously (e.g., Lamborghini Aventador) and rather subtly branded products (e.g., Bottega Veneta intrecciato handbag). The six product-to-brand assignments are reported in Table 21.

8.1.1.3 Results of qualification test

Out of the 1,022 participants in the qualification test 202 individuals qualified as luxury insiders. Those 202 individuals met each of the two qualification criteria, i.e.

Table 21 – Experiment 2: product-to-brand assignment tasks

Product shown[a]	**Choice options**[b,c]
(a) Jewellery Blue/turquoise gift box with silver pendant, no logo shown	**Tiffany's,** Harry Winston, Cartier, Bulgari
(b) Cars Sportscar, orange, open gull-wing doors, slightly visible logo, front view	**Lamborghini** Ferrari Corvette Porsche
(c) Leather goods Woven leather hobo bag, dark brown, no logo shown	**Bottega Veneta** Louis Vuitton Hermès Prada
(d) Watches Watch with rectangular dial with Roman numerals, rounded angels and exposed screws, yellow gold, alligator-skin strap, no logo shown	**Cartier** Rolex Patek Philippe IWC
(e) Fashion Patent leather shoe with high heels, black, red soles, no logo shown	**Christian Louboutin** Jimmy Choo Manolo Blahnik Alexander Wang
(f) Writing instruments A set of pens (fountain and ballpoint), black resin, golden nib and ring, visible logo	**Montblanc** S.T. Dupont Montegrappa Caran d'Ache

[a]Product descriptions are reported only; images originally shown to participants are not reported due to copyright reasons; [b]Brand in bold is the correct answer; [c]The order of the choice options was randomized.
Source: authors

being among the top 25 per cent in terms of attitude towards luxury (i.e. having a more positive attitude towards luxury than general population) and providing at least three correct out of six given product-to-brand assignment tasks (i.e. exhibiting higher levels of actual knowledge about luxury brands than general population).

Attitude towards luxury. On average, the US consumers surveyed did neither hold a positive nor a negative attitude towards luxury. Attitude towards luxury (measured on a seven-point Likert-type scale) was normally distributed with M=4.02, SD=.95, $z_{skewness} < 1.96$, and $z_{kurtosis} < 1.96$ as shown in Figure 62. By definition, luxury insiders hold a more positive attitude towards luxury, i.e. scores of at least 4.625 (75 percentile). As noted above, the purpose of the survey (i.e. a luxury insider

Figure 62 – Experiment 2: histogram of attitude towards luxury.

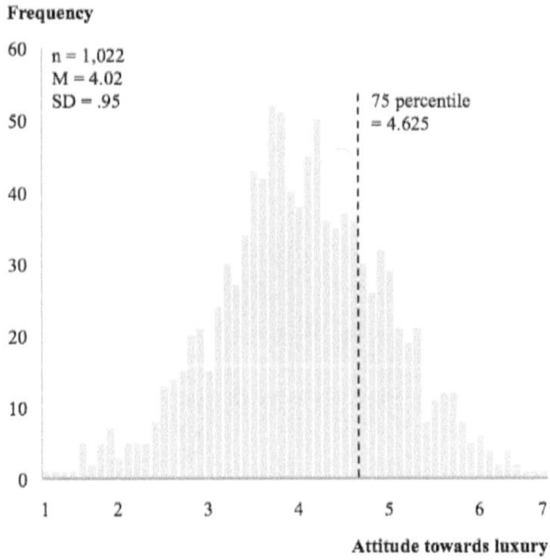

Source: authors

qualification test) was deliberately disguised in order to prevent participants from providing responses, which they believe would comply with the researcher's expectations and lead to an invitation to an additional (paid) study.

This kind of spurious response behaviour can be assumed to produce a negatively skewed distribution, i.e. participants would spuriously indicate a more positive attitude towards luxury than their actual attitude. However, since in fact attitude towards luxury is not negatively skewed but rather normally distributed, it may be assumed that the probability of spurious response behaviour has been successfully lowered.

Actual knowledge of luxury brands. On average, the US consumers surveyed assigned the correct brand name to the product shown in three out of six cases. By definition, to qualify as luxury insider individuals were required to perform a minimum of three correct product-to-brand assignments, which reflects the top 50 per cent of all 1,022 participants. The relative frequency for each choice option is displayed in Figure 63. Not surprisingly, the relative frequency of correct assignments was found to be higher for rather conspicuously branded products ($f_{Tiffany}$=.83; $f_{Lamborghini}$=.78; $f_{Montblanc}$=.67) than for rather subtly branded products ($f_{Bottega\ Veneta}$=.16; $f_{Louboutin}$=.39; $f_{Cartier}$=.43).

Figure 63 – Experiment 2: results of product-to-brand assignment tasks.

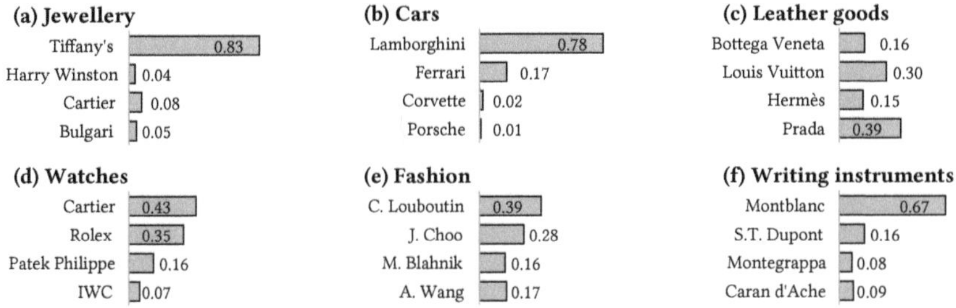

Note: relative frequencies are reported; numbers might not add add up to 1.00 due to rounding; the first option in each category refers to the correct choice.
Source: authors

Comparing luxury insiders and non-luxury insiders. The sample of luxury insiders was selected based on the individuals' attitude towards luxury and their actual knowledge of luxury brands. These luxury insiders are not necessarily high-income individuals. However, a comparison between the group of individuals who has qualified as luxury insiders with the group of individuals that have not qualified as luxury insiders reveals that luxury insiders indeed enjoy relatively higher levels of household income while they do not significantly differ in terms of age, gender, education and Internet usage (see Table 22). To test whether this difference in income is statistically significant, income is interpreted as interval scaled variable and log transformed as the assumption of homogeneity of variances was violated (Field, 2009, p. 155). The results of a *t*-test analysis indicate that luxury insiders enjoy a statistically significant higher level of income than non-luxury insiders ($t(1020)=3.725$; $p=.000$).

Table 22 – Experiment 2: comparison of luxury insiders and non-luxury insiders

Relative frequency			Relative frequency		
Characteristic	**Luxury insiders (n=202)**	**Others (n=820)**	**Characteristic**	**Luxury insiders (n=202)**	**Others (n=820)**
Age			**Employment status**		
18-29	.55	.55	Employed full time	.60	.43
30-39	.28	.28	Employed part time	.14	.18
40-49	.10	.08	Homemaker	.05	.06
50-59	.04	.07	Student	.13	.16
≥ 60	.02	.02	Retired	.00	.02
Gender			Unemployed	.07	.15
Female	.35	.40	**Income**		
Male	.65	.60	Less than $20,000	.15	.23
Prefer not to say			$20,000 – $39,999	.23	.26
Education	.01	.01	$40,000 – $59,999	.22	.23
Some high sch., no degree	.09	.12	$60,000 – $79,999	.17	.14
High school degree	.27	.32	$80,000 – $99,999	.06	.07
Some college, no degree	.11	.11	$100,000 or more	.16	.07
Associate's degree	.43	.43	**Internet usage**		
Bachelor's degree	.08	.07	Multiple times a day	.96	.96
Graduate degree	.55	.55	Once a day	.02	.02
			Multiple times a week	.01	.02
			Once a week	.00	.00
			Once a month	.00	.00
			Less than monthly	.00	.00

Note: numbers might not add up to 1.00 due to rounding.
Source: author

8.1.1.4 *Final sample*

Each of the 202 qualified individuals was invited to participate in the follow-up, eight-minute HIT rewarded with USD 1.00 reflecting an hourly wage of USD 7.50, which is again considered an above-average pay on AMT. We sent out two rounds of personalized invitation e-mails. 151 individuals started the questionnaire, 142 completed it. On average, subjects are 32 years of age, 37 per cent are female, 61 per cent are full time employed, 53 per cent hold at least a bachelor's degree, 38 per cent report an annual household income of at least USD 60,000, and 94 per cent browse the Internet at least once per day. All sample characteristics are reported in Table 23.

8.1.2 Procedure: self-administered online survey

8.1.2.1 *Scenario: website of high-end writing instruments brand Vaupré*

Individuals who have qualified as luxury insiders were invited to participate in a self-administered online survey. The scenario is very similar to that of experiment 1. Instead of a high-involvement good as used in experiment 1 the scenario describes a relatively lower-involvement good, i.e. writing instruments. Similarly to the product category of wristwatches **writing instruments** (e.g., fountain pens, ballpoint pens, and mechanical pencils) are not gender-specific and typically available in one size only. Thus, both women and men might be able to imagine buying a high-end writing instrument for themselves (i.e. not as a gift for their beloved ones) and do not necessarily need to test different sizes in-store (as opposed to fashion products, for example).

Again, we asked the participants to imagine the **fictitious scenario** of dreaming of and treating themselves to a high-end writing instrument some day. Subjects are further asked to imagine that they incidentally arrive at the website of the high-end writing instruments manufacturer Vaupré when occasionally browsing the Internet for writing instruments. Instructions inform subjects that the brand name Vaupré is fictitious but that the information given is representative for an existing high-end writing instruments manufacturer whose name is not disclosed.

For reasons of comparison, most of the characteristics used to describe the brand are identical to those used to describe the watchmaker Vaupré in experiment 1 (see Chapter 7.1.2.1). Only the category-specific characteristics (i.e. technical product attributes) are adjusted. Again, to emphasize the rich tradition of the brand Vaupré is described as a Geneva-based, family-owned writing instruments manufacturer with a heritage of 150 years. Other than for wristwatches, we are not aware of a positive country-of-origin association for the product category of writing instruments. The leading, Richemont-owned writing instruments brand Montblanc claims to have a European heritage (Montblanc.com, 2014a). Other brands like Montegrappa and Omas are from Italy (Montegrappa.com, 2014; Omas.com, 2014), S.T. Dupont from France (ST-Dupont.com, 2014), Caran d'Ache from Switzerland (Carandache.com, 2014), Graf von Faber-Castell from Germany (Graf-von-Faber-Castell.com, 2014), and Jack Row from the United Kingdom (JackRow.com, 2014).

Table 23 – Experiment 2: sample characteristics

Characteristic	Relative frequency (n=142)	Characteristic	Relative frequency (n=142)
Age		**Employment status**	
18–29	.53	Employed full time	.61
30–39	.29	Employed part time	.12
40–49	.11	Homemaker	.06
50–59	.06	Student	.12
≥ 60	.02	Retired	.01
Gender		Unemployed	.09
Female	.37	**Annual household income**	
Male	.62	Less than $20,000	.14
Prefer not to say	.01	$20,000 – $39,999	.24
Education		$40,000 – $59,999	.24
Some high school, no degree	.01	$60,000 – $79,999	.15
High school degree	.08	$80,000 – $99,999	.08
Some college, no degree	.27	$100,000 or more	.15
Associate's degree	.10	**Internet usage**	
Bachelor's degree	.45	Multiple times a day	.94
Graduate degree	.08	Once a day	.00
		Multiple times a week	.01
		Once a week	.01
		Once a month	.01
		Less than monthly	.02

Note: numbers might not add up to 1.00 due to rounding.
Source: authors

Vaupré writing instruments are said to be crafted by hand using precious metals only. Consequently, the production capacity of Vaupré writing instruments is naturally limited. In addition to this natural scarcity, Vaupré writing instruments are said to be available at few, selected retailers in the prime locations of major cities only. The price range is indicated to start from a three-digit USD amount with virtually no upper limit. The core ranges of Montblanc pens like "Meisterstück" and "Starwalker", for example, are priced at the three-digit USD range while selected limited editions may easily exceed USD 10,000 (Montblanc.com, 2014b).

8.1.2.2 Manipulation: online accessibility and price display

On the next page, the scenario asks participants to imagine that they have clicked on a fountain pen of interest to access the online product view. We randomly confront the participants with one of four illustrative mock-ups of an online product view for the Vaupré 1864 Fountain Pen (fictitious branded product) as shown in Figure 64. The four mock-ups are identical in terms of layout, product image, and product information presented (i.e. product name and the product characteristics "handcrafted gold nib", "stainless steel body", and "geometric pattern"). However, the four mock-ups differ in terms of online accessibility ('Buy online' button: present versus absent) and price display ('$ 150' retail price: present versus absent). To determine the price level, we conducted a pre-test (see details below in Chapter 8.1.2.4) resulting a median consumer estimated retail price of USD 150 for a Vaupré fountain pen as described in the scenario above. Overall, the following four conditions apply (see Figure 64): (a) both the 'Buy online' button and the retail price of '$150', (b) 'Buy online' is present, '$150' is absent, (c) 'Buy online' is absent, '$150' is present, (d) both 'Buy online' and '$150' are absent.

8.1.2.3 Measurement scales

The scales used to measure perceived scarcity, brand desirability, transaction convenience and willingness-to-buy are identical to that used in experiment 1 except for language differences. Since the sample comprises luxury insiders from the US all scales are translated back from German (see Chapter 7.1.2.3) into English as shown in Table 24. Again, **perceived scarcity** is measured by asking respondents to indicate to which extent they believe the attributes (a) exclusive, (b) rare, and (c) unique apply to Vaupré products. The items are drawn from Vigneron & Johnson (2004, p. 502) and measured on a seven-point Likert-type scale anchored with "does not apply at all" and "does fully apply". To measure **brand desirability** respondents are asked how likely they would choose a Vaupré product if they were free to choose, i.e. if money is not an issue (Kastanakis & Balabanis, 2012, p. 1404). We apply a seven-point rating scale anchored with "very unlikely" and "very likely".

Figure 64 – Experiment 2: stimuli for online accessibility and price display.

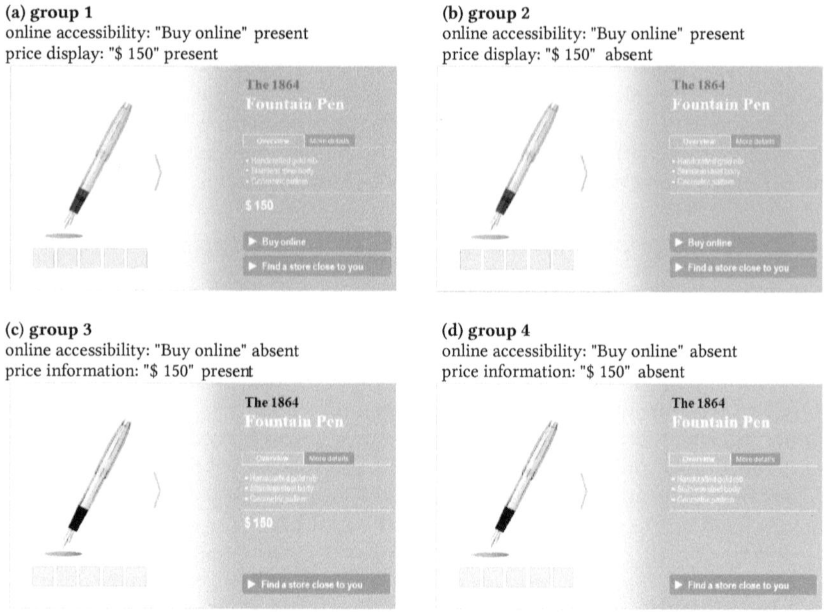

© image of fountain pen by Foeock Kannilc (2012; retrieved from flickr.com under a CC BY 2.0)
Source: authors

Drawing on the SERVCON scale by Seiders et al. (2007, p. 148), **transaction convenience** is measured by asking respondents to which extent they agree or disagree to three statements like "It takes little time to pay for my purchase at Vaupré" measured on seven-point Likert-type scale anchored with "strongly disagree" and "strongly agree". Finally, to measure willingness-to-buy we rely on the scale by Dodds et al. (1991, p. 318) which was previously applied to the context of luxury marketing research by Bian & Forsythe (2012, p. 1447). We ask respondents to which extent they agree or disagree to statements like "If I were going to buy a luxury writing instrument, I would consider buying a Vaupré product" on a seven-point Likert-type scale anchored with "strongly disagree" and "strongly agree".

8.1.2.4 Pre-testing

We are interested in the sole effect of the presence vs. absence of price information, not its amount. Prices that consumers perceive as disproportionately high or low might influence consumer evaluation of the brand. Kapferer & Laurent (2014, p. 10) find that price perceptions for luxury goods are highly heterogeneous across consumers and more heterogeneous as compared to everyday products. To mitigate these potential effects we identify the median consumer estimated retail price for

Table 24 – Experiment 2: measurement scales

	Measurement			
Construct	**Question**	**Items**	**Scale**	**Source(s)**
Perceived scarcity	In your opinion, to which extent do the following attributes apply to Vaupré products?	To me Vaupré is (a) exclusive (b) rare (c) unique	(1) does not apply at all ... (7) does fully apply	Vigneron & Johnson (2004, p. 502)
Brand desirability	Now, let's assume you won a contest. As a reward you receive any luxury writing instrument of your choice. How likely would you choose a Vaupré product?	n.a.	(1) very unlikely ... (7) very likely	Dubois & Paternault (1995, p. 70); Kastanakis & Balabanis (2012, p. 1404)
Transaction convenience	How do you perceive the convenience of purchasing a Vaupré product?	(a) It takes little time to pay for my purchase at Vaupré. (b) Vaupré makes it easy for me to conclude my transaction. (c) I am able to complete my purchase quickly at Vaupré.	(1) strongly disagree ... (7) strongly agree	Seiders et al. (2007, p. 148)
Willingness-to-buy	Let's assume you are about buying a luxury writing instrument (e.g., fountain pen or ballpoint pen). How likely would you consider buying a Vaupré product?	(a) If I were going to buy a luxury writing instrument, I would consider buying a Vaupré product. (b) My willingness to buy a Vaupré product would be high if I were shopping for a luxury writing instrument. (c) The probability I would consider buying a Vaupré writing instrument is high.	(1) strongly disagree ... (7) strongly agree	Bian & Forsythe (2012, p. 1447); Dodds, Monroe, & Grewal (1991, p. 318)

Source: author

Figure 65 – Experiment 2: consumer estimated retail price.

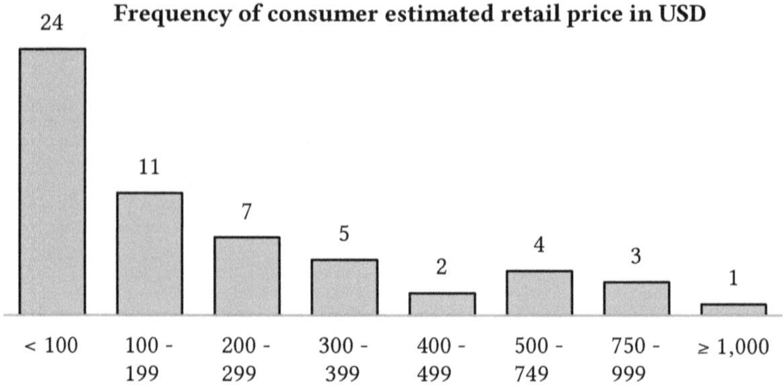

Source: authors

a Vaupré fountain pen (as described in Chapter 8.1.2.1) using a pre-test with 57 US consumers. Consumer estimated retail prices range from USD 5 up to USD 1,350 with a median retail price of USD 150 (see Figure 65). Previous literature indicates a minimum price for a luxury pen ranging from USD 100 (Dubois & Duquesne, 1993, p. 39) to EUR 100 (about USD 130; Heine, 2010, p. 137).

Also, participants in the pre-test attested an easy understanding of the scenario. On average, respondents indicated that the scenario was "easy to understand" (*M*=6.42; *SD*=.82) and that they "could well imagine" the scenario (*M*=6.33; *SD*=1.04; both items were measured on a 7-point Likert-type scale from "1 = strongly disagree" to "7 = strongly agree"). Furthermore, the description of the fictitious brand Vaupré successfully evoked consumer perceptions of scarcity (*M*=6.04; *SD*=.90; measured on a 7-point Likert-type scale). None of the participants associated a real brand with the image of a pen shown.

8.2 Results

Before examining the effects of online accessibility and price display on consumer brand evaluations using analysis of variance (ANOVA) and structural equation modeling (SEM) we perform some preliminary analyses to test the effectiveness of the manipulation of online accessibility and price display as well as the validity and reliability of the measurement model.

8.2.1 Preliminary analyses

8.2.1.1 Manipulation check

We first assess the effectiveness of the manipulation using a series of independent *t*-tests (see Table 25; for more information on the importance of manipulation checks

Table 25 – Experiment 2: manipulation check

	Manipulation present	**Manipulation absent**	***t*-test results**			
Group	*M*(*SE*)	*M*(*SE*)	*Mean difference*	*t*-statistic	*df*	*p*
"Buy online" button (online accessibility)	.81 (.046)	.26 (.053)	.55	3.869	140	.000
"$ 150" (price display)	.77 (.049)	.12 (.039)	.65	13.349	140	.000

M = mean scores of aided recall; *SE* = standard error; *df* = degrees of freedom; *p* = significance (two-tailed)
Source: authors

please see Chapter 7.2.1.1). Aided recall of the 'Buy online' button is significantly higher among subjects who were confronted with this button (M_{buy}(*SE*)=.81 (.046)) than among subjects who were not confronted with this button ($M_{non\text{-}buy}$(*SE*)=.26 (.053); *t*(140)=3.869; *p*=.000). Similarly, we find a significantly higher aided recall of the retail price of '$ 150' (M_{price}(*SE*)=.77 (.049) vs. $M_{non\text{-}price}$(*SE*)=.12 (.039); *t*(140)=13.349; *p*=.000) among subjects who were confronted with the explicit display of price information. Thus, both online accessibility and price display prove to be manipulated successfully between subjects.

Overall, subjects attest a very good understanding of the scenario. On average, respondents indicate that the scenario was "easy to understand" (*M*=6.61; *SD*=.63) and that they "could well imagine" the scenario (*M*=6.57; *SD*=.62; both items were measured on a 7-point Likert-type anchored with "strongly disagree" (1) to "strongly agree" (7).

8.2.1.2 Confirmatory factor analysis

To test the psychometric properties of the latent variables of perceived scarcity, brand desirability, transaction convenience, and willingness-to-buy we perform a confirmatory factor analysis (CFA) using Mplus. CFA results indicate a satisfactory model fit with $\chi^2(30)=42$ (*p*=.070), CFI=.98, RMSEA=.05, and SRMR=.05 (Bagozzi & Yi, 1998, p. 82; Hu & Bentler, 1999, p. 27). Also, results approve the reliability and validity of the measurement of transaction convenience and willingness-to-buy with indicator reliability scores for all items being greater than .50, composite reliability scores of .92 and .88 respectively, and scores of average variance extracted of .79 and .71 respectively (see Table 26; Bagozzi & Yi, 2012, p. 17). Convergent validity of perceived scarcity does not prove satisfactory with a composite reliability of .63 (<.70) and average variance extracted of .38 (<.50). However, for reasons of comparison with experiment 1 the measure of perceived scarcity is retained in its original form. Finally, we may assume discriminant validity since for each construct the average variance extracted is greater than the squared correlation with any other construct (Fornell & Larcker, 1981, p. 46).

Table 26 – Experiment 2: evaluation of measurement validity

Indicator	*M*	*SD*	λ^*	*t*	ρ_{IR}	ρ_{CR}	ρ_{AVE}
Perceived scarcity							
To me Vaupré is exclusive.	6.338	.807	.791*	8.52	.517	.643	.382
To me Vaupré is rare.	5.732	1.260	.644*	8.00	.415		
To me Vaupré is unique.	5.852	1.117	.517*	5.74	.268		
Transaction convenience							
It takes little time to pay for my purchase at Vaupré.	5.162	1.569	.787*	22.62	.619	.918	.790
Vaupré makes it easy for me to conclude my transaction.	5.437	1.451	.934*	50.63	.873		
I am able to complete my purchase quickly at Vaupré.	5.394	1.483	.950*	54.66	.903		
Willingness-to-buy							
If I were going to buy a luxury wristwatch, I would consider buying a Vaupré product.	5.775	1.296	.916*	34.96	.839	.878	.712
My willingness to buy a Vaupré product would be high if I were shopping for a luxury wristwatch.	6.042	.967	.839*	25.95	.704		
The probability I would consider buying a Vaupré wristwatch is high.	5.472	1.457	.784*	20.22	.614		

*significant at $p < .001$ (two-tailed); *M* = mean; *SD* = standard deviation; λ^* = standardized factor loading; *t* = *t*-value; ρ_{IR} = indicator reliability; ρ_{CR} = composite reliability; ρ_{AVE} = average variance extracted
Source: authors

8.2.2 Hypotheses testing

To replicate the findings of experiment 1 (Chapter 7.2.2), we first perform structural equation modeling (SEM) to test the overall model (H1 to H5) as shown in Figure 59. Second, to additionally test for effects of price display we conduct two two-way analyses of variance (ANOVA). Specifically, we test the 2 (online accessibility: 'buy online' present versus absent) by 2 (price display: '$ 150' present versus absent) experimental groups for mean differences in perceptions of scarcity and transaction convenience (H2 and H3).

Table 27 – Experiment 2: results of structural equation modeling

Structural relationship	**Path coefficient β**	**Two-tailed p-value**	**Evaluation of hypothesis**
H1: Perceived scarcity → Brand desirability	.216	*	not rejected
H2: Online accessibility → Perceived scarcity	.015	.881 *ns*	rejected
H3: Online accessibility → Transaction convenience	.373	***	not rejected
H4: Transaction convenience → Willingness-to-buy	.359	***	not rejected
H5: Brand desirability → Willingness-to-buy	.446	***	not rejected

*significant at $p < .05$; **significant at $p < .01$; ***significant at $p < .001$; *ns* = non-significant
Source: authors

8.2.2.1 Structural equation modeling

In a first step we are interested whether the results previously found in experiment 1 are replicated by the data of experiment 2. Hence, we perform SEM using Mplus to simultaneously test the hypothesized relationships between online accessibility, perceived scarcity, brand desirability, transaction convenience, and willingness-to-buy (H1 to H5). Table 27 provides an overview of SEM results for experiment 2.

Similar to the findings of experiment 1, the data again supports a positive scarcity-desirability relationship (H1). The standardized path coefficient β of the structural path between perceived scarcity and brand desirability is both positive and statistically significant (β=.216; p<.05). Next, we are interested in whether perceptions of scarcity are negatively affected by online accessibility (H2). The path coefficient for the structural relationship between online accessibility and perceived scarcity does not prove to be statistically significant (β=.015; p=.881). Again, the data support the "no-dilution" finding and thus the rejection of H2.

In contrast to the findings in experiment 1, SEM results show that the relationship between online accessibility and transaction convenience is positive and significant (β=.373; p<.001). Consumers who are not given the possibility to shop online but instead to locate a store nearby evaluated the shopping process for a Vaupré product as less convenient. Hence, we do not reject H3 this time.

Finally, we expected that parts of the variation in willingness-to-buy are explained by variation in both transaction convenience and brand desirability (H4 and H5). Similar to the findings of experiment 1, the results of experiment 2 support both H4 and H5 since estimated path coefficients for both transaction convenience (β=.359; p<.001) and brand desirability (β=.446; p<.001) on willingness-to-buy are positive and statistically significant.

Figure 66 – Experiment 2: descriptive statistics.

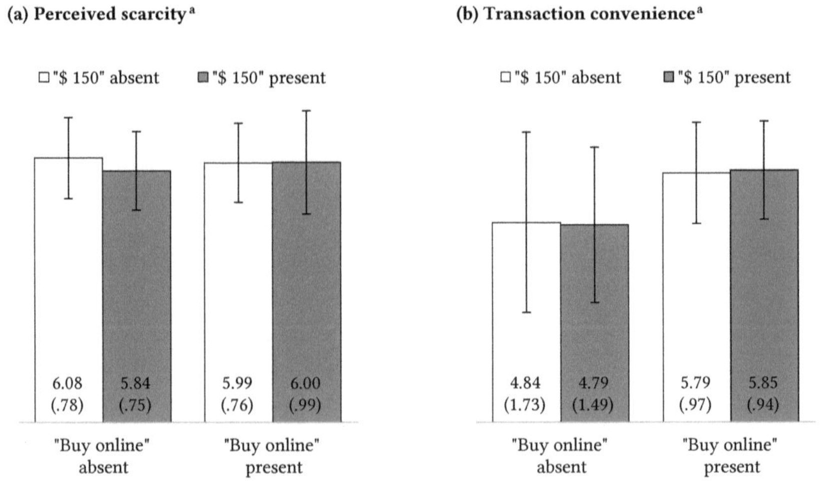

[a]measured on a seven-point Likert-type scale; mean scores are reported with standard deviations in parenthesis
Source: author

8.2.2.2 *Analysis of variance*

In a second step we are interested in the potential effects of price display. The issue of price display is considered to be one of the major obstacles towards the online distribution of luxury goods (Gastaldi, 2012, p. 112; Kapferer & Bastien, 2012, p. 212). Hence, we test whether the "no-dilution" of online accessibility on perceived scarcity persists even if prices are displayed. To assess both the main effects of online accessibility and price display as well as their interaction effect on consumer perceived scarcity and transaction convenience we additionally perform two two-way analyses of variance (ANOVA) in SPSS.

First, we are interested in the effects of online accessibility and price display on **perceived scarcity**. Similar to our previous findings, mean scores of perceived scarcity differ only marginally between different groups of online accessibility (see Figure 66(a)). Subjects confronted with ‚Buy online' button do not perceive different levels of scarcity as compared to subjects who were not confronted with this button (F(1,138)=.063; p=.802; see Table 28). The data again supports the rejection of H2.

Interestingly, this "no-dilution" effect of online accessibility on perceived scarcity persists independently of whether or not retail price is explicitly displayed. Perceptions of scarcity are not affected by the explicit display of the '$ 150' price information. Both the main effect of price display on perceived scarcity (F(1,138)=.726; p=.396) as well as the interaction effect of online accessibility and price display on perceived scarcity are non-significant (F(1,138)=.844; p=.360; see Table 28).

Table 28 – Experiment 2: two-way ANOVA results

	Perceived scarcity			Transaction convenience		
Factor	*df*	*F*	*p*	*df*	*F*	*p*
Constant term	1	7438.820	.000	1	2331.559	.000
Online accessibility	1	.063	.802	1	20.550	.000
Price display	1	.726	.396	1	.000	.984
Online accessibility * price display	1	.844	.360	1	.063	.802
Residual	138			138		

df = degrees of freedom; *F* = *F*-statistic; *p* = significance (two-tailed);
Source: authors

Second, we are interested in whether subjects who are given the possibility to shop online perceive higher levels of **transaction convenience** as compared to those not given that possibility (H3). Results of experiment 2 yield a significant main effect of online accessibility on perceived transaction convenience ($F(1,138)=20.550$; $p<.001$; see Table 28). At the same time, perceptions of transaction convenience are not at all affected by the explicit display of price ($F(1,138)=.000$; $p=.984$). If price is not displayed, individuals need to proceed further in the shopping process to obtain price information. Still, this does not influence consumer evaluations of convenience. Also, the interaction effect of online accessibility and price display on transaction convenience is non-significant ($F(1,138)=.063$; $p=.802$).

8.3 Conclusion

In experiment 1 we found empirical support for the hypothesized positive scarcity-desirability relationship while at the same time consumer perceptions of scarcity are independent of whether or not consumers are given the possibility to shop online (see Chapter 7). The purpose of this second experimental study was (1) to replicate these findings and (2) additionally test for potential effects of price display. Experiment 2 differs from experiment 1 in the following four major aspects: first, instead of testing the effects of one factor (i.e. online accessibility) with four levels we applied a 2 (online accessibility: 'buy online' present versus absent) x 2 (price display: '$ 150' present versus absent) factorial design. Second, to enhance external validity we confronted individuals with a more realistic mock-up of a complete web page (including product image, description etc.; see Chapter 8.1.2.2) instead of merely a set of buttons along with textual descriptions (e.g., a 'Buy online' button; see Chapter 7.1.2.2). Third, instead of a high-involvement luxury good (i.e. wristwatch) we used a relatively lower-involvement luxury good in experiment 2 (i.e. writing instrument). Fourth, instead of high-income individuals from Germany the sample of experiment 2 consists of luxury insiders from the US, i.e. consumers with a positive attitude towards and some prior knowledge of luxury brands. Aside from these differences, experiment 1 and 2 are very similar in terms of scenario description and measurement scales used.

Similar to the findings of experiment 1, results of experiment 2 provide support for the hypothesized **positive effect of scarcity on desirability** (H1) as proposed by socio-economic and social-psychological theory (e.g., Brock (1968, p. 246) and Smith (2005[1766], p. 190)). Even more interestingly, the empirical findings again give reason to contradict the prevailing hesitance towards the online distribution of luxury goods (e.g., Kapferer & Bastien, 2012, p. 249; Seringhaus, 2005, p. 15). Contrary to our hypothesis (H2), **online accessibility** has not been found to be a significant determinant of perceived scarcity. Consumer perceptions of scarcity are independent of whether or not individuals are given the possibility to shop online. Variables other than online accessibility possibly explain variation in perceived scarcity. Selling luxury goods online per se does not dilute a luxury brand's fragile image of exclusiveness.

This **"no-dilution" finding** persists independently of whether or not retail prices are explicitly displayed. In contrast to mass-market manufacturers, luxury goods manufacturers pursue a discreet-to-no price communication policy as to preserve the myth of price. In luxury, it is desirable that individuals hardly know exact prices and tend to overestimate actual prices (Kapferer & Bastien, 2012, p. 74). The Internet, however, makes price information easily accessible for everyone. Hence, the issue of online price communication represents one of the major obstacles towards the online distribution of luxury goods (Gastaldi, 2012, p. 112; Kapferer & Bastien, 2012, p. 212). Our empirical results, however, show that the explicit display of price does not at all affect consumer perceptions of the brand being exclusive, rare, and unique.

In contrast to the findings of experiment 1, results of experiment 2 support the hypothesis that making luxury goods accessible online positively affects consumer perceptions of **convenience**. The data shows that consumers who are not given the possibility to shop online evaluate the shopping process as less convenient. One explanation for the difference between the findings of experiment 1 (H3 rejected) and experiment 2 (H3 not rejected) might refer to the different levels of product involvement used in the two experiments. It can be assumed that consumers place less importance on convenience when shopping for an extraordinarily expensive high-involvement good (e.g., wristwatch priced beyond EUR 10,000) than for a relatively lower-involvement product (e.g., fountain pen priced USD 150). Another explanation refers to cultural differences in the shopping behaviour of the two samples. Given the assumption that US consumers value convenience more than Germans do, responses of US consumers to different levels of online accessibility might vary more significantly.

Not surprisingly, both studies confirm the hypothesis that consumers who perceive the shopping process as more convenient express higher levels of willingness-to-buy than those who perceive the shopping process as relatively less convenient.

Similarly, the data from both studies support the positive influence of brand desirability on consumers' willingness-to-buy.

Overall, the data of both studies give reason to conclude that selling luxury goods online does not affect consumer perceptions of scarcity and thus brand desirability. This "no-dilution" finding has been found for both high- and relatively lower-involvement luxury goods, among both German and US consumers, and independently of whether prices are displayed or not.

9. Conclusion

The present manuscript contributes to the current practice and research on marketing luxury goods in three major ways: first, the manuscript conceptually examines the specificities of marketing luxury goods in terms of product management, pricing, communication, and distribution management (RQ1). Second, the manuscript conceptually examines the benefits and concerns about marketing luxury goods online and how the marketing-mix for luxury goods can be adapted to the possibilities provided by the Internet (RQ2). Third, the manuscript advances the on-going debate about the suitability of the Internet as a channel of distribution for luxury goods by empirically testing the effects of selling luxury goods online on consumer perceived scarcity, brand desirability, convenience, and willingness-to-buy (RQ3). Throughout the following chapters we discuss major conceptual and empirical findings, identify limitations and directions for future research and derive implications for managerial practice.

9.1 Conceptual findings

9.1.1 Specificities of marketing luxury goods

Traditional marketing practices do not equally apply to luxury goods. The marketing of luxury goods necessitates a delicate balance between growing sales and profit on the one hand and preserving the brand's fragile image of being hard-to-get on the other (Kastanakis & Balabanis, 2012, p. 1399; Keller, 2009, p. 293; Wetlaufer, 2001, p. 121). In order to create and preserve consumer perceived scarcity and desirability marketing luxury goods requires specific procedures that may be counterintuitive to conventional marketing approaches (Kapferer & Bastien, 2009a, p. 61). Identifying the specificities of marketing luxury goods was subject to this manuscript as stated by the first research question (compare Chapter 1.2):

RQ1: What are the specificities of marketing luxury goods in terms of product management, pricing, communication, and distribution management?

Figure 67 provides an overview of the most eminent specificities of marketing luxury goods as conceptually examined in Chapter 3. In the following, we briefly highlight the specificities for each marketing-mix element.

Product management. Luxury goods are designed beyond mere function. Like art, a luxury good is aesthetically appealing; something extraordinary whose sophistication is appreciated by the educated clientele only. To the happy few owners luxury goods serve as a mean of pleasure, self-reward, and signalling status to significant others. Luxury product management is directed towards satisfying these needs and characterized by the following specificities (compare Chapter 3.1): first, luxury goods manufacturers consistently deliver product excellence in terms of function,

Figure 67 – Conclusion: marketing-mix of luxury goods.

Product	Price	Communication	Distribution
▪ Product excellence in terms of function, aesthetics, durability, packaging, and add-on services ▪ Heritage of craftsmanship ▪ Consistent brand signature ▪ Pyramidal product-mix ▪ Designer-driven, long-term strategy	▪ High-end, stable prices ▪ Continuous increase of the average price of the product-mix ▪ Rare-to-no discount policy ▪ Rare-to-no use of price discrimination ▪ Discreet-to-no price communication	▪ Focus on awareness and desire (do not "sell") ▪ Target audience is beyond target clientele ▪ Focus on aesthetic and symbolic rather than functional product attributes ▪ Selective mix of communication instruments (print, PR, events, direct marketing, sponsoring)	▪ Targeting affluent locals and tourists ▪ Retaining high levels of control ▪ Preferably low channel length and width (exclusive distribution) ▪ Monobrand and carefully selected multibrand store formats ▪ Prestige locations in major cities, tourist destinations, and airports ▪ Exceptional service level

Source: author

aesthetics, durability, packaging, and add-on services. Second, design and manufacturing involves a human element, i.e. the craftsmanship, aim for perfection, and attention to detail of a skilled artisan. Third, luxury goods are marked with an identifiable and differentiated brand signature, which is consistent across products and over time. Fourth, the product-mix typically takes on a pyramidal form with a limited number of griffe and high-end range products at the top to create awareness and desire, core range products in the middle to generate sales and profit, and more broadly diffused entry-range products at the bottom to generate trial (see Figure 8). Finally, luxury product strategy is strongly driven by the genuine, creative independence and long-term vision of the creative director rather than by systematic market research.

Pricing. In luxury more than in any other segment consumers refer to the price as an indicator for the overall value a luxury good may be expected to deliver. To enhance and preserve a luxury brand's image of finest quality, aesthetic appeal, and prestige, the price of a luxury good should be both high-end in the given category and stable. In the pursuit of high-end, stable prices, pricing luxury goods (compare Chapter 3.2) includes first defining objectives and the price positioning for each product both vis-à-vis category competitors and within the brand's product-mix. This typically entails inaccessible price-positioning for griffe and high-end range products, intermediate price-positioning for core range products, and accessible price-positioning for entry-range products. Second, the average price of the product-mix should be continuously raised in the long run in order to recreate the gap between the mass and the class. Third, in the short run luxury goods manufacturers should pursue a rare-to-no discount policy and limit price discounts to end-of-season items, if needed. Fourth, a continuity-driven pricing strategy also implies a rare-to-no use of price discrimination, i.e. prices should be highly consistent across retail outlets and countries when accounted for differences in consumption taxes. Finally, the communication of exact retail prices should be as discreet as possible in-store and ideally avoided in advertisements and media releases.

Communication. In luxury, brand communication does not "sell" (Kapferer & Bastien, 2009a, p. 68). It primarily aims at creating awareness, desire and dreams among the targeted audience. Hence, luxury brand communication is first of all directed towards triggering cognitive and affective rather than behavioural consumer responses. Second, the target audience does not only include prospect and existing clients but also their significant others. After all, the potency of a luxury good to confer social status to its owner largely depends on the extent to which it is recognised by significant others. Third, the message of a luxury brand communication campaign is typically designed to emphasize the aesthetic beauty of products and the emotional and symbolic attributes of the brand rather than communicating purely informative and functional aspects. Fourth, rather than communicating to the masses through television, luxury goods manufacturers carefully select a mix of relevant, and economically viable communication instruments, e.g., in particular print media, public relations, events, sponsoring, direct marketing and nowadays branded website, search engines, selective online advertising, and social media.

Distribution. In luxury, distribution strategy aims at making goods available to affluent locals and tourists at relevant places in a profitable and highly selective manner. Also, more than making goods available, luxury distribution is about brand communication (Kapferer & Bastien, 2009a, p. 198). To shoppers the store often represents the first physical point of contact, a place where the brand comes to life. Hence, luxury goods manufacturers typically aim at high levels of control over location, assortment, store atmosphere, prices, and service levels of any point of sale carrying its products. In order to retain high levels of control and margin the channel structure of luxury distribution is characterized by preferably no-to-few tiers of intermediaries (low channel length considering the ongoing "retailization" of the luxury goods industry (see Chapter 3.4.2)) and a limited number of intermediaries per tier (low channel width), i.e. a selective or exclusive distribution network. Depending on the product category and a firm's objectives regarding supply, economics, and control, luxury goods manufacturers typically pursue a mixed-channel strategy consisting of both directly operated monobrand store formats like flagship, monobrand, or concession stores and multibrand store formats like duty-free, department, and specialty stores. These points of sales are typically located in prestige locations in major cities, tourist destinations, and airports. Finally, an exceptional service in-store is inherent to the luxury experience. The salesperson acts as a brand and product expert, who welcomes any client with courtesy and no pressure.

9.1.2 Online marketing-mix for luxury goods

In addition to identifying the specificities of marketing luxury goods in general, we were interested into how the marketing-mix for luxury goods may be adapted to the online world. Specifically, in Chapter 4 we addressed the second research question:

RQ2: What are the specificities of marketing luxury goods online in terms of product management, pricing, communication, and distribution management?

The present manuscript intends to illustrate that the suitability of the Internet for marketing of luxury goods can be thought of as **love at second sight**. At first sight, the Internet is commonly associated with mass availability, off-price sales, and transparency of information whereas luxury goods are characterized by exclusiveness, high-end prices, and discretion. Yet at second sight, the Internet has become an omnipresent companion in consumers' everyday lives, which allows for increasing reach and intensity of brand communication and selling to clients who live in geographically distant places. Hence, online marketing has long become an **imperative** to luxury goods manufacturers. Figure 68 provides an overview of the online marketing-mix for luxury goods in terms of product management, pricing, communication, and distribution management.

Product management. While the Internet has fundamentally affected product categories like media, banking, and travel services, luxury goods cannot be fully digitized and remain physical in nature for both off- and online channels (low e-potential; compare Chapter 4.2). Yet, online-specific product management considerations include deciding on product ranges offered for sale, online product display, and online add-on services. While the full product range should be communicated online, sales should be limited to entry and core range products. Accessing limited, high-end range products typically requires prior contact in-store or via a service hotline. To compensate for a lack of touch and feel, the online product display should feature high-resolution images from multiple angles, close-ups of product details, zooming options, configuration options, videos or even augmented reality like virtual fitting rooms. Finally, the exceptional service level in-store should be replicated online. Online add-on services include delivery policies and client services like customization options, gift-wrapping, online shopping assistance, and offline store information.

Pricing. The online price management of luxury goods follows the same luxury-specific pricing principles as outlined before. Both offline and online, managing prices of luxury goods should be driven by continuity and consistency. More specifically, in accordance with the general rare-to-no price discrimination policy prices of luxury goods should be highly consistent across off- and online channels. For consumers, any inconsistency of prices across different retail outlets (both offline and online) along the consumer decision journey may dilute perceptions of excellent quality, exclusiveness, and timelessness (Fassnacht et al., 2013, p. 106; Keller, 2009, p. 292). Similarly, even though the Internet is commonly perceived as an off-price sales channel, online price discounts should be avoided at all or limited to few selected end-of-season items. Finally, online retail prices in general and online price discounts in particular should be communicated as discreetly as possible. The luxury product and its details should always be presented more visibly than any price information.

Figure 68 – Conclusion: online marketing-mix of luxury goods.

Product	Price	Communication	Distribution
▪ Focus on entry- and core-range products for sale ▪ High-quality product display ▪ High-quality add-on services	▪ Price consistency across offline and online channels ▪ Discreet-to-not price discounts ▪ Discreet-to-no price communication	▪ Clean, but rich website design ▪ High visibility through search engines ▪ Selective use of online advertising ▪ Engage with users through selected social media	▪ Monobrand online stores in selected, economically viable countries ▪ Low-cost reach through selected multibrand online retailers ▪ No or careful use of selected online outlets

Source: author

Communication. The advance of the Internet has enhanced brand communication as it enables luxury goods manufacturers to communicate with consumers in an instant, interactive, and measurable way. The brand website represents the nucleus of a firm's online marketing strategy (Kreutzer, 2014, p. 95). It is the central, fully controlled point of communication linked to by other means of communication. Luxury website design should be clean and simple and feature rich media content allowing users to experience the sophistication of the brand and its products. Common means of generating visibility and website traffic include search engine marketing, banner advertising on selected media sites, and social media marketing. Embracing these means of online brand communication has become an imperative to luxury goods manufacturers.

Distribution. The suitability of the Internet as an additional channel of distribution is still controversially discussed: on the one hand, selling luxury goods online increases reach at relatively low cost while providing convenience, product availability, and intimacy to the affluent clientele. On the other hand, the online distribution lacks in providing the touch and feel and human interaction needed to fully appreciate the sophistication of luxury goods and is commonly believed to dilute a brand's exclusiveness appeal (compare Chapter 4.5 for detailed discussion). Depending on the product category and the firm's objectives regarding supply, economics, and control, luxury goods manufacturers pursue a mixed-channel strategy consisting of both monobrand online stores (whether directly or franchise operated) in selected, economically viable countries and multibrand online retailers allowing for a broader reach at lower cost and risk of distribution. Like their offline counterparts, multibrand online retailers in general and online outlet stores in particular should be carefully selected based on the quality of assortment, online store atmosphere, product display, pricing policies, service levels, discretion and exclusiveness.

9.2 Empirical findings

Selling luxury goods online has long been expected to come at the expense of a luxury brand's desirability. A luxury brand's concept of exclusiveness is seemingly incompatible with the ubiquitous accessibility provided by the mass medium Internet. The present manuscript empirically addresses this apparent contradiction. We conducted two experiments in order to test for effects of selling luxury goods online on different consumer brand evaluations. On the one hand, we were interested in the effect of scarcity perceptions on brand desirability and whether or not the possibility to shop online dilutes the fragile perceptions of scarcity. On the other hand, we were interested in whether the possibility to shop online evokes higher levels of perceived transaction convenience and thus willingness-to-buy. Specifically, we were intersted in empirically examining the research question:

RQ3: How does the online accessibility and price display of luxury goods affect consumer perceived scarcity, desirability, convenience, and willingness-to-buy?

Scarcity and desirability. First, we were interested in the importance of consumer percieved scarcity for a brand's desirability. Socio-economic and social-psychological theory proposes a positive scarcity-desirability relationship. Both Smith (2005[1766], p. 190) and Brock (1968, p. 246) argue that individuals desire scarce goods more than available ones. An individual's preference for goods that are unavailable or hard-to-obtain to others can be attributed to the individual's need for uniqueness (Snyder & Fromkin, 1977, 1980), the individual's naïve economic beliefs that scarce goods are more expensive and thus of higher value (Lynn, 1992a), as well as to an individual's motivation to regain things that have become unavailable (Brehm, 1966). Results of both experiments support this hypothesis. Individuals were more attracted to the brand when they perceived it as something exclusive, rare, and unique.

Online accessibility and scarcity. Considering the desirability-enhancing effect of scarcity, we were interested in whether or not the possibility to shop online influences consumer perceptions of scarcity. While online distribution represents a source of additional sales both marketing scholars and executives show considerable hesitance towards the Internet as a channel of distribution. Leading scholars in the field of marketing luxury goods like Jean-Noël Kapferer & Vincent Bastien (2012, p. 248) argue that luxury goods "should *not* be sold" via the Internet. Indeed, according to recent data about 40 to 50 per cent of luxury goods manufacturers do not sell online despite the fact that consumers rank the possibility to shop online as the second most important feature of a luxury brand website (Bain & Company & Fondazione Altagamma, 2013, p. 10; Roland Berger & Meisterkreis, 2013, pp. 8 & 16). The prevailing hesitance towards the online distribution of luxury goods has been partly explained by the common assumption that the possibility to shop online might dilute consumer perceptions of scarcity (Curtis, 2000; Kapferer & Bastien, 2012, p. 249; Seringhaus, 2005, p. 15).

The empirical findings presented here give reason to disagree with this assumption. Results of both experiments do not support the concern that the online accessibility of luxury goods negatively affects consumer perceptions of scarcity. In fact, the possibility to shop online does not at all affect consumer evaluations of scarcity – neither negatively nor positively. This "**no-dilution**" finding was found for both high- and relatively lower-involvement luxury goods, among both German and US luxury consumers, and independently of whether or not price information is explicitly displayed.

Also, we found that artificially increasing the effort needed to obtain a luxury good by complicating the online shopping process does not prove to be an effective mean to enhance consumer perceptions of scarcity. In particular, we tested the following four alternatives in order of decreasing effort needed to obtain the luxury good: "Find a jeweller close to you" (i.e. no possibility to shop online), "Order upon request", "Sign in for online store", and "Buy online". Results of experiment 1 show that groups confronted with any of these alternatives do not significantly differ from each other in terms of perceptions of scarcity.

Online accessibility and convenience. Apart from the (disproved) assumption that selling luxury goods online dilutes perceptions of scarcity, we were also interested in positive effects of online accessibility. In particular, we tested how the possibility to shop online affects consumer perceptions of transaction convenience, i.e. the speed and ease of making a purchase. Online shopping is generally considered to save time and effort as compared to brick-and-mortar store shopping in crowded city centres. Not surprisingly, convenience has been found to be the dominant motivation for luxury consumers to shop online (Liu et al., 2013, p. 888). Hence, we expected that consumers who are given the possibility to shop online perceive shopping as more convenient than consumers not given that possibility.

Yet, our two experimental studies yield differing results. While results of experiment 2 show a positive, significant effect of online accessibility on transaction convenience, results of experiment 1 are non-significant. Possible explanations for the difference between the findings of experiment 1 (H3 rejected) and experiment 2 (H3 not rejected) include but are not limited to the difference in product involvement or cultural differences in the shopping behaviour of the two samples. More specifically, it can be assumed that consumers place less importance on convenience when shopping for an extraordinarily expensive, high-involvement good (e.g., wristwatch priced beyond EUR 10,000 as used in experiment 1) than for a relatively lower-involvement product (e.g., fountain pen priced USD 150 as used in experiment 2). Also, if we may assume that US shoppers (participants in experiment 2) attach relatively more importance on convenience than Germans (participants in experiment 1), evaluations of convenience might differ more significantly between US shoppers who are given the possibility to shop online and those who are not.

Willingness-to-buy. Finally, we were interested in whether cognitive and affective consumer responses to online accessibility translate into behavioural intentions. In particular, we tested how perceived transaction convenience and brand desirability affect an individual's willingness-to-buy, i.e. the likelihood he or she considers to actually purchase a luxury good.

Convenience has generally been found to affect behavioural intentions like willingness-to-buy (e.g., Seiders et al., 2007, p. 153). In luxury, however, goods are less frequently bought than conventional goods. The purchase often represents an once-in-a-lifetime event. Especially first-time shoppers usually take some time to decide on the brand, model, and product attributes. Hence, intuitively a luxury goods purchase is less about speed and ease of purchase, more about time and experience.

At the same time, however, a consumer often experiences multiple encounters with the brand both offline and online along his or her consumer decision-making journey. A consumer might discover and experience a particular wristwatch at a monobrand store during a trip to Zurich, take some time to think about and ask peers for opinions, and finally buy online to save the time and effort of travelling to the next retail store. Hence, to those consumers, who quite clearly know what they want but do not have the time or mood to travel to the closest brick-and-mortar store, a monobrand online store represents a convenient alternative. Previous empirical work by Liu et al. (2013) identifies convenience as the most important driver for luxury online shopping.

Our empirical work indicates that consumer perceptions of transaction convenience are positively related to his or her willingness-to-buy. Consumers high in perceived convenience are more likely to consider buying than consumers low in perceived convenience. Considering this finding we may agree with the notion by some of the experts interviewed (see Chapter 5) that, also in luxury, online shopping needs to be convenient for the user. And as shown above, the additional convenience of a monobrand online store does not necessarily come along with a loss in perceived scarcity or desirability since other elements of perceived scarcity remain unchanged (e.g., scarce material, scarce human resources, high-end price, and a selective offline distribution).

Finally, we were interested in whether a consumer's desirability for a luxury brand translates into a higher willingness-to-buy. Obviously not all consumers who desire a particular luxury good, can actually afford buying it. However, those consumers high in desirability for a particular luxury good are more likely to at least consider buying it (Reich, 2005, p. 185) and may turn into actual consumers once they have the money readily at hand. Indeed, both of our experimental studies reveal a positive relationship between brand desirability and willingness-to-buy.

9.3 Limitations and future research directions

Despite the growing importance of the Internet for the luxury goods market, scientific literature on marketing luxury goods online remains scarce (see Figure 2). Future research is needed to advance the ongoing debate among executives and marketing scholars on how firms should position a luxury brand in the ubiquitous mass medium Internet while preserving its fragile image of exclusiveness. This complexity becomes particularly salient in the context of online distribution of luxury goods. The present manuscript empirically examines consumer responses to the online accessibility of luxury goods. However, the empirical studies presented are not without limitations.

First, participants in the experiments were confronted with a fictitious brand to control for pre-existing brand associations. However, while the scenario was carefully designed to describe the brand as genuinely as possible, future research should test the effects of online accessibility using a **real luxury brand** in order to enhance the external validity of the findings. A consumer's dream of a specific luxury brand typically evolves over time rather than when spontaneously browsing the Internet.

Second, the scenario asks subjects to make an immediate buying decision. In luxury, however, the buying process often represents a lengthy journey including multiple interactions with the brand. A consumer may first encounter a desired luxury good during a city trip to Paris, London or Milan, ask significant others for their opinion, reconfirm his or her decision online and finally buy at the monobrand store close by – or vice versa. Future research should attempt to account for this **consumer decision-making journey**.

Third, the experimental studies presented are limited to prospect clients. However, existing clients who feel as members of an exclusive brand clientele might be concerned that launching a monobrand online store provides access to the brand for too many, non-qualified individuals. Snobbish individuals desire things they have access to but that are unavailable to others. The existing clientele might fear that the brand does no longer serve as source of self-differentiation from others. Future research should empirically test how the **existing clientele** responds to the online accessibility of luxury goods.

Fourth, the scenario asks subjects to imagine that they are about buying a luxury item for themselves, i.e. shopper and consumer are identical. In luxury, however, about half of sales are made with **gifts**, i.e. shopper and consumer are different individuals. When shopping for gifts shoppers might place more importance on convenience and product availability than when shopping for oneself. During the busy pre-Christmas season individuals might prefer shopping online for luxury goods than travelling to crowded city centers. Future research should test for differing channel preferences and brand evaluations depending on whether an individual shops for himself or his beloved ones.

Fifth, the fictitious scenario is described using text form and static graphical stimuli as shown in Figure 60 (experiment 1) and Figure 64 (experiment 2). To increase the external validity of the findings, future research should manipulate stimuli using a **real website setting** and measure actual consumer responses like click rates, time spent on site and actual purchases.

Sixth, the scenario incorporated one product only. Luxury brands typically offer a range of products from entry products to high-end, one-of-a-kind items but do not sell all of them online. For example, the French leather goods specialist Hermès does offer only a very limited range of products on its website. On Louisvuitton.com a prospect client can easily order the iconic Speedy 30 Damier Canvas, but has to call the hotline for requesting the high-end models. Future research should explore these different **online assortment strategies**. Consumers can be disappointed when not given a chance at all to shop online. However, when consumers are given the possibility to shop entry and classic iconic products online, the presence of high-end one-of-a-kind products that are not for sale might actually increase brand desirability.

Seventh, the present manuscript examines direct online distribution only, i.e. selling luxury goods via a monobrand online store, which is typically operated by the luxury goods manufacturer and integrated into the official brand website like Louisvuitton.com or Prada.com. Through a monobrand online store a luxury goods manufacturer does not only realize full margins but also fully controls prices and brand communication. By applying a luxury-specific website design (see Kluge et al., 2013) luxury marketers can evoke and maintain consumer perceptions of exclusiveness. Selling **wholesale** to multibrand online retailers like Net-a-porter.com or Mytheresa.com implies that multiple luxury brands are more or less uniformly communicated and become easily comparable. Future research should explore the effects of online wholesale distribution of luxury goods on consumer brand evaluations.

Finally, throughout this manuscript the perspective of the brand-owning luxury goods manufacturer was applied. While luxury goods sales through direct distribution formats are constantly gaining share, wholesale distribution formats like department or multibrand specialty stores still account for two third of the personal luxury goods market (Bain & Company & Fondazione Altagamma, 2014, p. 16). Similar to the current situation among luxury goods manufacturers, some retailers do not yet follow an online distribution strategy (e.g., multibrand specialty store chains like Bucherer and Wempe, which merely sell their own branded products online). Future research should examine the issue of online distribution from the **retailer perspective** – both for pure online retailers (e.g., Net-a-porter.com) or traditional retailers adopting the Internet as an additional distribution channel (e.g., mytheresa.com or harrods.com).

9.4 Managerial implications

Marketing luxury goods online can be thought of as **love at second sight.** At first sight, the Internet contradicts the concept of luxury. Distribution for luxury goods is highly selective while the mass medium Internet provides availability of goods to anyone at any time and anyplace. While touch and feel are fundamental ingredients of the luxury experience, the Internet is virtual and intangible. While in luxury prices are communicated as discreetly as possible the Internet makes price information transparent to virtually everyone. While luxury is aristocratic, the Internet is democratic.

At second sight, however, the Internet allows luxury goods manufacturers to reach a much broader audience and prospect clients who were previously not aware of the brand or lived in distant places. The time has gone when the Internet was merely a shopping channel for bargain hunters. The affluent clientele browses the Internet for brand and product information and increasingly shops for luxury goods online – whether from home or via a mobile device. For many consumers, a luxury brand's online communication and distribution has become a hygiene factor: online communication and distribution per se does not excite most consumers, but their absence disappoints them. Hence, **online marketing has become an imperative** for luxury goods manufacturers. If a luxury brand marketer shies away from online marketing, the brand does not only fall short of consumer expectations but also risks that other (uncontrolled) people represent the brand online in an undesirable way and eventually resell its products without authorization.

Online product and price management. The advancement of the Internet particularly affects brand communication and distribution issues. Product and price management issues should not largely differ between offline and online channels. Unlike non-luxury brands whose online market offering sometimes deviates from offerings in stationary retail, a luxury brand's offering should be characterized by **consistency**. While the range of products offered for sale via the Internet might differ from the range offered in stationary retail, the products as such should remain identical. However, the brand and its products must be described and illustrated in much more detail. While luxury marketers have been more or less consciously aware of the identity of the brand, communicating what the brand and its products stands for can require some re-thinking and structuring.

Like prices for offline channels, online prices should be consistent across channels and retailers, communicated as discreetly as possible, and hardly ever discounted. However, creating a consistent price structure throughout the entire product range and across offline and online, retail and wholesale distribution channels represents a complex task.

Online communication. Online brand communication has become daily routine of most luxury goods marketers. The Internet has enhanced brand communication as it allows for an individualized and interactive communication with an increasingly large audience as well as for measuring the effectiveness of communication initiatives. Luxury-specific brand communication principles concerning objectives, audience, and message more or less equally apply to both offline and online brand communication. Luxury brand communication aims at creating awareness and desire among the target audience rather than pushing sales. It does not only target prospects and existing clients but also their significant others. And, communication messages highlight emotional and symbolic brand attributes using subtle images and abstract descriptions – but never the price. However, the advancement of the Internet has affected *how* communication messages can be conveyed to the target audience. The Internet can be thought of as an **additional, omnipresent touch point** through which marketers can instantly and interactively communicate with the target audience.

The official brand website (e.g., Chanel.com) builds the nucleus of a luxury brand's online marketing strategy. Other online communication initiatives like search engine marketing, banner advertising, and social media marketing typically link to a luxury brand's official website. The design of a luxury **brand website** can follow a "5C's" framework, which includes defining the main idea behind the design (concept), the user-friendliness of the website (competence), relevant and authentic content (content), assortment, price, and process of an integrated online store (commerce), and levels of personalization (customization; see Chapter 4.4.2.1; adapted from Okonkwo, 2010, pp. 155–181). In total, the design of a luxury brand website should be **rich but clean**.

About 35 per cent of traffic on luxury brand websites is generated through search engines like Google, Baidu, or Yandex. For a luxury brand to be found in the Internet, it must be highly visible on search engine result pages. Not making a brand website visible on search engines is like having a retail store on a desert island. Hence, the purpose of **search engine marketing** is to increase the visibility of the brand on search engine results pages – either through improving the rank in organic listings for relevant keywords (search engine optimization or SEO) or through placing advertisements in paid listings (search engine advertising or SEA).

Other forms of online advertising refer to **banner advertising** (i.e. paid placement of brand communication material on third-party websites) and **affiliate marketing** (i.e. an affiliate partner promotes the brand website of a merchant on third-party websites in exchange for a commission per user response). Unlike traditional above-the-line advertising, online advertising is not only directed towards creating awareness and desire but also behavioural consumer responses like traffic on website, leads (e.g., user registrations), or conversion (e.g., finally making a purchase). Additionally, online advertising has two advantages over traditional advertising: first, marketers can **individualize** communication messages, i.e. displaying the women collection to female users. Second and more importantly, marketers can accurately **measure the effectiveness** of online advertising by tracking online marketing metrics like click-through-rates (CTR). In any case, luxury marketers should carefully select third-party websites and (if at all) affiliate partners that fit the luxury brand's image. Affiliate marketing should be approached very cautiously as the luxury marketer does not fully control where the affiliate partner place brand communication material.

Finally, luxury marketers can increase both reach and intensity of communication through the use of **social media**, i.e. Internet-based applications supporting the interactive communication among users with common interests. Social media are becoming increasingly popular not only among young users but also among the grown-up, affluent clientele. Facebook, YouTube, Wikipedia, and Twitter are among the top 10 websites in terms of website traffic (Alexa.com, 2014). Still, luxury brands like Rolex have long been hesitant to engage in social media. Social media have been commonly believed to be out of control for marketers and prone to negative word-of-mouth (WOM). However, consumers talk about luxury brands and products independently of whether or not brand owners engage in social media. Actively participating in social media allows luxury goods manufacturers to stimulate positive word-of-mouse and moderate consumer discussion. Hence, today luxury goods manufacturers cannot afford not being present in social media.

Online distribution. While stationary retail represents the major source of sales in the luxury goods industry, online sales are constantly gaining share. Despite this growth opportunity about every second luxury goods manufacturer is still hesitant to adopt the Internet as a channel of distribution. Whether or not to sell luxury goods online represents a multi-faceted business question. Multiple benefits and concerns apply both from a consumer (e.g., convenience versus lack of touch) and a managerial perspective (e.g., sales growth versus loss in exclusiveness). While most concerns equally apply to luxury and non-luxury goods, luxury managers additionally face the dilemma that online distribution may come at the expense of a brand's appeal of exclusiveness and desirability. The empirical findings of the present manuscript show that offering luxury goods online does not affect consumer perceptions of scarcity and, thus, does not dilute a brand's desirability. This **"no-dilution" finding** applies to both high- and low-involvement goods, among luxury consumers from both Germany and the US, and independently of whether retail prices are explicitly communicated or not. Consequently and in absence of other concerns luxury goods manufacturers should not shy away from seizing the growth opportunity of selling their goods online. In fact, we find partial support that consumers perceive shopping convenience to be higher when given the possibility to order luxury goods online in addition to merely locating a store nearby. After all, even in luxury consumers are more willing to buy when shopping is considered convenient.

In particular, the integration of a monobrand online store into the official brand website allows marketers to **fully control** prices, assortment, and how the brand is communicated to the audience. Here, shoppers should be given the opportunity to order at least selected **entry range and classic iconic products** like a Montblanc Meisterstück fountain pen, a Louis Vuitton Speedy 30 Canvas bag, a Tiffany & Co. Return to Tiffany necklace, or the Clara Rhinoceros by Porzellanmanufaktur Nymphenburg. A luxury brand's entry range and iconic pieces are often purchased as gifts for significant others as manifestation of meaningful moments in life. The educated affluent clientele is well aware of these luxury products, has often encountered them in store or at other familiar places, and does not necessarily want to travel to the busy, sometimes distant city centres to purchase a desired item.

After all, however, deciding on whether or not to sell online in a given country through either a mono- or multibrand store represents a separate business case that needs to be economically viable. Considering that online sales still account for about only 5 per cent of the total luxury market (Bain & Company & Fondazione Altagamma, 2014, pp. 10–19), some countries might be simply too small to generate a critical mass of sales needed to cover the expenses of setting up (about EUR 200,000; Spieler, 2011) and operating a monobrand online store.

References

Aaker, D.A., Kumar, V., Leone, R.P., & Day, G.S. (2013): Marketing Research, 11th ed., Singapore: John Wiley & Sons.

Achenbaum, A.A. (1993): The Mismanagement of Brand Equity, presented at the ARF Fifth Annual Advertising and Promotion Workshop (February 1, 1993).

Adams, A. (2009): Rolex Buys Rolex Watches To Prevent Price Drops, retrieved March 30, 2015, from http://rss2.com/feeds/Luxist/885/.

AdGooroo (2014): The Luxury Market and Paid Search: An AdGooroo Special Report, retrieved March 30, 2015 from http://intelligence.adgooroo.com/Luxury_Paid_Search.

Adobe Systems (2014): 2014 Digital Marketing Optimization Survey Results, retrieved May 20, 2015 from http://offers.adobe.com/content/dam/offer-manager/en/na/marketing/Target/50825_target_Q214_optimization_survey_whitepaper_ue_v3.pdf.

Ahlert, D., & Kenning, P. (2007): Handelsmarketing: Grundlagen der marktorientierten Führung von Handelsbetrieben [Retail Marketing: Fundamentals of the Market-Oriented Management of Retail Firms], 1st ed., Berlin, Heidelberg: Springer.

Ahrendts, A. (2013): Burberry's CEO on Turning An Aging British Icon into a Global Luxury Brand, in: Harvard Business Review, Vol. 91, No. 1, pp. 39–42.

Alba, J., & Lynch, J. (1997): Interactive Home Shopping: Consumer, Retailer, and Manufacturer Incentives to Participate in Electronic Marketplaces, in: Journal of Marketing, Vol. 61, No. 3, pp. 38–53.

Albers, S., Bachem, C., Clement, M., & Peters, K. (1998): Produkte und Inhalte [Products and Content], in: Albers, S., Clement, M, & Peters, K. (Eds.): Marketing mit Interaktiven Medien: Strategien zum Markterfolg [Marketing in Interactive Media: Strategies for Market Success], 1st ed., Frankfurt am Main: IMK, pp. 267–282.

Albers, S., & Herrmann, A. (2007): Ziele, Aufgaben und Grundkonzept des Produktmanagement [Objectives, Tasks, and Concept of Product Management], in: Albers, S. & Herrmann, A. (Eds.): Handbuch Produktmanagement [Handbook of Product Management], 3rd ed., Wiesbaden: Gabler, pp. 1–18.

Alexa.com (2014): The Top 500 Sites on the Web, retrieved August 3, 2014 from http://www.alexa.com/topsites.

Alexa.com (2015a): Armani.com, retrieved March 20, 2015 from http://www.alexa.com/siteinfo/armani.com.

Alexa.com (2015b): Gucci.com, retrieved March 20, 2015 from http://www.alexa.com/siteinfo/gucci.com.

Alexa.com (2015c): Net-a-porter.com, retrieved March 20, 2015 from http://www.alexa.com/siteinfo/net-a-porter.com.

Alexa.com (2015d): Prada.com, retrieved March 20, 2015 from http://www.alexa.com/siteinfo/prada.com.

Alexa.com (2015e): Yoox.com, retrieved March 20, 2015 from http://www.alexa.com/siteinfo/yoox.com.

Allfacebook.de (2014): Facebook Nutzerzahlen [Number of Facebook Users], retrieved July 21, 2014 from http://allfacebook.de/nutzerzahlen.

Amaldoss, W., & Jain, S. (2005): Pricing of Conspicuous Goods: A Competitive Analysis of Social Effects, in: Journal of Marketing Research, Vol. 42, No. 1, pp. 30–42.

American Marketing Association (2015a): Dictionary: Letter B, retrieved February 10, 2015 from https://www.ama.org/resources/Pages/Dictionary.aspx?dLetter=B.

American Marketing Association. (2015b): Dictionary: Letter M, retrieved March 6 from https://www.ama.org/resources/Pages/Dictionary.aspx?dLetter=M.

Arrigo, E. (2014): Luxury Brands Enter the Online Market, in: Berghaus, B, Müller-Stewens, G. & Reinecke, S. (Eds.), The Management of Luxury: A Practitioner's Handbook, 1st ed., London et al.: Kogan Page, pp. 259–273.

Astonmartin.com (2014a): 007 & Aston Martin, retrieved July 16, 2015 from http://www.astonmartin.com/bond.

Astonmartin.com (2014b): Histroy: The ONE 77, retrieved October 6, 2014 from http://history.astonmartin.com/2010-one-77/secondary.

Astonmartin.com (2015): Dealers, retrieved February 25, 2015 from http://www.astonmartin.com/en/dealers.

Audemarspiguet.com (2014): Established in 1875, retrieved September 22, 2014 from http://www.audemarspiguet.com/en/about#established-1875.

Audemarspiguet.com (2015): Royal Oak Tourbillon, retrieved February 12, 2015 from http://www.audemarspiguet.com/en/watch-collection/royal-oak/tourbillon-1/26560IO.OO.D002CA.01.

Audi.de (2015): Händlersuche, retrieved February 25, 2015 from http://www.audi.de/de/brand/de/haendlersuche.html.

Aufgesang & Searchmetrics. (2014): SEO, SEA und Social-Media bei deutschen Online-Shops 2014 [SEO, SEA, and Social Media of German Online Stores 2014], retrieved May 20, 2015 from http://www.sem-deutschland.de/Downloads/ecommerce-studie-2014/Aufgesang_E-Commerce_Studie2014_final.pdf.

Ausschuss für Definitionen aus Handel und Distribution (2009): Katalog E – Definition of Terms in Trade and Distribution, 5th ed., Cologne.

Axel Springer Mediapilot (2014): Key Facts Online / Mobil / Video 2014, retrieved July 27, 2014 from http://www.axelspringer-mediapilot.de/artikel/Medien-Key-Facts-Key-Facts-Online-Mobil-Video-2014_782002.html.

Bagozzi, R.P., & Yi, Y. (1998): On the Evaluation of Structural Equation Models, in: Journal of the Academy of Marketing Science, Vol. 16, No. 1, pp. 74–94.

Bagozzi, R.P., & Yi, Y. (2012): Specification, Evaluation, and Interpretation of Structural Equation Models, in: Journal of the Academy of Marketing Science Journal, Vol. 40, No. 1, pp. 8–34.

Bagwell, L.S., & Bernheim, B.D. (1996): Veblen Effects in a Theory of Conspicuous Consumption, in: The American Economic Review, Vol. 86, No. 3, pp. 349–373.

Bain & Company (2014): Luxury Goods Worldwide Market Study Fall-Winter 2014: The Rise of the Boarderless Consumer, retrieved May 27, 2015 from http://www.bain.com/ bainweb/PDFs/Bain_Worldwide_Luxury_Goods_Report_2014.pdf.

Bain & Company, & Fondazione Altagamma. (2008): Luxury Goods Worldwide Market Study: Key Findings, 7th Edition.

Bain & Company, & Fondazione Altagamma. (2013): 2013 Luxury Goods Worldwide Market Study, 12th Edition.

Bain & Company, & Fondazione Altagamma. (2014): Altagamma 2014 Worldwide Markets Montior.

Banks, S.K. (1979): Gift-Giving: A Review and an Interactive Paradigm, in: Advances in Consumer Research, Vol. 6, No. 1, pp. 319–324.

Bastien, V., & Kapferer, J.-N. (2013): More on Luxury Anti-Laws of Marketing. In Wiedmann, K.-P. & Hennigs, N. (Eds.): Luxury Marketing, 1st ed., Wiesbaden: Gabler, pp. 19–34.

Bearden, W.O., & Etzel, M.J. (1982): Reference Group Influence on Product and Brand Purchase Decisions, in: Journal of Consumer Research, Vol. 9, No. 2, pp. 183–194.

Becker, J. (1990): Marketing-Konzeption: Grundlagen des strategischen Marketing-Managements [Marketing Concept: Fundamentals of Strategic Marketing Management], 3rd ed., München: Franz Vahlen.

Becker, L.A., & Brock, T.C. (1966): Prospective Recipients' Estimates of Withheld Evaluation, in: Journal of Personality and Social Psychology, Vol. 4, No. 2, pp. 147–154.

Belch, G.E., & Belch, M.A. (2012): Advertising and Promotion: An Integrated Marketing Communications Perspective, 9th ed., New York: MCGraw-Hill.

Belk, R.W. (1976): It's the Thought that Counts: A Signed Digraph Analysis of Gift-Giving, in: Journal of Consumer Research, Vol. 3, No. 3, pp. 155–162.

Belk, R.W. (1977): Gift-Giving Behavior (Part A), Faculty Working Paper, College of Commerce and Business Administration, University of Illinois at Urbana-Champaign.

Belk, R.W. (1988): Possessions and the Extended Self, in: Journal of Consumer Research, Vol. 15, No. 2, pp. 139–168.

Berekhoven, L., Eckert, W., & Ellenrieder, P. (2009): Marktforschung: Methodische Grundlagen und praktische Anwendung [Market Research: Methodological Foundations and Practical Application], 12th ed., Wiesbaden: Gabler.

Berger, J., & Ward, M. (2010): Subtle Signals of Inconspicuous Consumption, in: Journal of Consumer Research, Vol. 37, No. 4, pp. 555–569.

Bernstein Research. (2009): LVMH: King of the Luxury Jungle, retrieved September 15, 2014 from http://www.luxesf.com/wp-content/uploads/2009/10/LVMH-King-of-the-luxury-jungle.pdf.

Berry, C.J. (1994): The Idea of Luxury: A Conceptual and Historical Investigation. Cambridge et al.: Cambridge University Press.

Berthon, P., Pitt, L., Parent, M., & Berthon, J.-P. (2009): Aesthetics and Ephemerality: Obeserving and Preserving the Luxury Brand, in: California Management Review, Vol. 52, No. 1, pp. 45–66.

Bestsecret.de (2014): Home, retrieved July 1, 2014 from android app of bestsecret.de

Bestsecret.de (2015a): About, retrieved March 23, 2015 from https://www.bestsecret.com/about.htm.

Bestsecret.de (2015b): Designer, retrieved March 23, 2015 from https://www.bestsecret.com/designer.htm?gender=MALE.

Bestsecret.de (2015c): Home, retrieved March 23, 2015 from https://www.bestsecret.com/home.htm.

Beverland, M. (2006): The "Real Thing": Branding Authenticity in the Luxury Wine Trade, in: Journal of Business Research, Vol. 59, No. 2, pp. 251–258.

Bian, Q., & Forsythe, S. (2012): Purchase Intention for Luxury Brands: A Cross Cultural Comparison, in: Journal of Business Research, Vol. 65, No. 10, pp. 1443–1451.

Bicestervillage.com (2015): Brands, retrieved March 5, 2015 from http://www.bicestervillage.com/en/brands/brands.

Bijmolt, T.H.A., van Heerde, H.J., & Pieters, R.G.M. (2005): New Empirical Generalizations on the Determinants of Price Elasticity, in: Journal of Marketing Research, Vol. 42, No. 2, pp. 141–156.

Blancpain.com (2014): History, retrieved September 22, 2014 from http://www.blancpain.com/en/history.

Blattberg, R.C., & Neslin, S.A. (1989): Sales Promotion: The Long and the Short of It, in: Marketing Letters, Vol. 1, No. 1, pp. 81–97.

Bliemel, F., & Fassott, G. (2000): Produktpolitik mit E-Share [Product Policy with E-Share], in: Bliemel, F., Fassot, G., & Theobald, A. (Eds.): Electronic Commerce: Herausforderungen, Anwendungen, Perspektiven [Electronic Commerce: Challenges, Applications, Perspectives], 3rd ed., Wiesbaden: Gabler, pp. 191–204.

Bloch, P.H. (1995): Seeking the Ideal Form: Product Design and Consumer Response, in: Journal of Marketing, Vol. 59, No. 3, pp. 16–29.

BMW.de (2015): BMW Partner, retrieved February 25, 2015 from http://www.bmw.de/de/fastlane/bmw-partner.html.

BMWGroup.com (2009): Annual Report 2009, retrieved February 18, 2015 from http://www.bmwgroup.com/annualreport2009/_downloads/BMW_Group_2009.pdf.

BMWGroup.com (2011): Annual Report 2011, retrieved February 18, 2015 from http://www.bmwgroup.com/e/0_0_www_bmwgroup_com/investor_relations/corporate_events/hauptversammlung/2012/BMW-Annual-Report-2011.pdf.

BMWGroup.com (2013): Annual Report 2013, retrieved February 18, 2015 from http://www.bmwgroup.com/e/0_0_www_bmwgroup_com/investor_relations/finanzberichte/geschaeftsberichte/2013/_pdf/report2013.pdf.

Bottegaveneta.com (2015a): Clutch, retrieved February 11, 2015 from http://www.bottegaveneta.com/gb/clutch_cod45210890gr.html.

Bottegaveneta.com (2015b): Knot Eau de Parfum 30 ml, retrieved February 11, 2015 from http://www.bottegaveneta.com/gb/fragrance_cod62000742ld.html.

Bottegaveneta.com (2015c): New Bronze Intrecciato Calf Metal Sandal, retrieved February 11, 2015 from http://www.bottegaveneta.com/gb/flat_cod44673327ew.html#itemPage=9.

Bottegaveneta.com (2015d): Oro Giallo Intrecciato Burnished Silver Earring, retrieved February 11, 2015 from http://www.bottegaveneta.com/us/earrings_cod50153415qj.html.

Bottegaveneta.com (2015e): Our History, retrieved February 11, 2015 from http://www.bottegaveneta.com/experience/en/pages/about-us/our-history/.

Boucheron.com (2015a): Expertise: Advice, retrieved March 16, 2015 from http://eu.boucheron.com/en_eu/expertise/advice.html.

Boucheron.com (2015b): Gold, retrieved February 7, 2015 from http://eu.boucheron.com/en_eu/expertise/advice/gold.html.

Boucheron.com (2015c): Quatre Classique Large Ring, retrieved April 9, 2015 from http://eu.boucheron.com/en_eu/the-creations/jewelry/quatre/quatre-classique-large-diamond-ring.html#details.

Bourdieu, P. (1984): Distinction: A Social Critique Of The Judgement Of Taste, 1st ed., Cambridge, MA: Harvard University Press.

Bourne, F.S. (1957): Group Influence in Marketing and Public Relations, in: Likert, R. & Hayes, S.P. (Eds.): Some Applications Of Behavioural Research, 1st ed., New York: UNESCO.

Braun, P. (2013): Wristwatch Annual 2014: The Catalog of Producers, Prices, Models, & Specifications, New York: Abbeville Press.

Breguet.com (2014a): History, retrieved September 22, 2014 from http://www.breguet.com/en/History.

Breguet.com (2014b): Screenshot of Breguet Website, retrieved July 24, 2014 from http://www.breguet.com/en/.

Breguet.com (2015): Breuguet Boutiques, retrieved February 25, 2015 from http://www.breguet.com/en/Boutiques-Breguet.

Brehm, J.W. (1966): A Theory of Psychological Reactance, 1st ed., New York & London: Academic Press.

Brehm, J.W. (1968): Attitude Change from Threat to Attitudinal Freedam, in: Greenwald, A.G., Brock, T.C, & Ostrom, Thomas M. (Eds.): Psychological Foundations of Attitudes, 1st ed., New York & London: Academic Press, pp. 277–296.

Brehm, J.W., Stires, L.K., Sensenig, J., & Shaban, J. (1966): The Attractiveness of an Eliminated Choice Alternative, in: Journal of Experimental Social Psychology, Vol. 2, No. 3, pp. 301–313.

Brewer, M.B. (1991): The Social Self: On Being the Same and Different at the Same Time, in: Personality & Social Psychology Bulletin, Vol. 17, No. 5, pp. 475–482.

Brock, T.C. (1968): Implications of Commodity Theory for Value Change, in: Greenwald, A.G., Brock, T.C, & Ostrom, Thomas M. (Eds.): Psychological Foundations of Attitudes, 1st ed., New York & London: Academic Press, pp. 243–275.

Brock, T.C., & Becker, L.A. (1965): Ineffectiveness of "Overheard" Counterpropaganda, in: Journal of Personality and Social Psychology, Vol. 2, No. 5, pp. 654–660.

Bruhn, M. (2013): Kommunikationspolitik: Systematischer Einsatz der Kommunikation für Unternehmen [Communication Management: Systematic Use of Communication for Enterprises], 7th ed., München: Vahlen.

Bruhn, M. (2014): Marketing: Grundlagen für Studium und Praxis [Marketing: Fundamentals for Students and Practitioners],12th ed., Wiesbaden: Springer Gabler.

Bruhn, M., & Batt, V. (2012): Der Einfluss von Sponsoring auf den Erfolg von Luxusmarken [The Effect of Sponsoring on the Performance of Luxury Brands], in: Marketing Review St. Gallen, Vol. 29, No. 1, pp. 38–41.

Bruhn, M., & Homburg, C. (Eds., 2004): Gabler Lexikon Marketing [Gabler Encyclopaedia Marketing], 2nd ed., Wiesbaden: Gabler.

Brun, A., Caniato, F., Caridi, M., Castelli, C., Miragliotta, G., Ronchi, S., Sianesi, A., & Spina, G. (2008): Logistics and Supply Chain Management in Luxury Fashion Retail: Empirical Investigation of Italian Firms, in: International Journal of Production Economics, Vol. 114, No. 2, pp. 554–570.

Brun, A., & Castelli, C. (2013): The Nature of Luxury: A Consumer Perspective, in: International Journal of Retail & Distribution Management, Vol. 41, No. 11/12, pp. 823–847.

Brun, A., & Moretto, A. (2012): Contract Design and Supply Chain Management in the Luxury Jewellery Industry, in: International Journal of Retail & Distribution Management, Vol. 40, No. 8, pp. 607–628.

Bulgari.com (2015): Serpenti Secret Watches, retrieved February 5, 2015 from http://www.bulgari.com/de-de/alpencatalog/print/index/product/51074/lat/49.468451111748884/lng/11.173857208766707.

Burberry.com (2014): Screenshot of Website, retrieved July 21, 2014 from uk.burberry.com.

Burberry.com (2015a): Press: Regent Street, retrieved March 23, 2015 from http://press.burberry.com/regentstreet/#/index.

Burberry.com (2015b): Press: Regent Street / Bespoke, retrieved March 23, 2015 from http://press.burberry.com/regentstreet/#/bespoke/1.

Burberry.com (2015c): Regent Street Store, retrieved March 23, 2015 from http://de.burberry.com/storesuche/regent-street-store/.

Buyvip.com (2015): Anmelden [Register], retrieved March 23, 2015 from https://www.amazon.de/ap/signin?openid.ns=http%3A%2F%2Fspecs.openid.net%2Fauth%2F2.0&pageId=quarterdeck&openid.identity=http%3A%2F%2Fspecs.openid.net%2Fauth%2F2.0%2Fidentifier_select&clientContext=278-0295680-4480918&openid.claimed_id=http%3A%2F%2Fspecs.openid.net%2Fauth%2F2.0%2Fidentifier_select&openid.mode=checkid_setup&marketPlaceId=A38GABX06X24K&openid.assoc_handle=quarterdeckde_buyvip_xd&openid.return_to=https%3A%2F%2Fde.buyvip.com%2Fsignin&openid.pape.max_auth_age=0&siteState=http%3A%2F%2Fde.buyvip.com%2Fhomepage%3Fhash%3D%26features%3DSigninAlternateImage%2FC%3B.

Cadieux, D. (2005): De Beers and The Global Diamond Industry, in: Ivey Business Cases.

Cadwalladr, C. (2012): The Hypocrisy of Burberry's "Made in Britain" Appeal, in: The Guardian, retrieved August 8, 2014 from http://www.theguardian.com/commentisfree/2012/jul/16/burberry-china-british-carole-cadwalladr.

Cailleux, H., Mignot, C., & Kapferer, J.-N. (2009): Is CRM for Luxury Brands?, in: Journal of Brand Management, Vol. 16, No. 5/6, pp. 406–412.

Cairo.de (2015): Hersteller [Manufacturers], retrieved March 20, 2015 from http://www.cairo.de/Hersteller/#A-D.

Carandache.com (2014): La Maison, retrieved May 13, 2015 from http://www1.carandache.com/m/la-maison/index.lbl.

Carr, T. (2012): Cartier Extends L'Odyssée Campaign Through Multichannel Efforts, in: Luxurydaily.com, retrieved January 11, 2015 from http://www.luxurydaily.com/cartier -extends-its-lodyssee-campaign-through-multiple-channels/.

Catry, B. (2003): The Great Pretenders: The Magic of Luxury Goods, in: Business Strategy Review, Vol. 14, No. 3, pp. 10–17.

Cervellon, M.-C., & Coudriet, R. (2013): Brand Social Power in Luxury Retail: Manifestations of Brand Dominance Over Clients in the Store, in: International Journal of Retail & Distribution Management, Vol. 41, No. 11/12, pp. 869–884.

Cervellon, M.-C., De Barnier, V., & Laurent, G. (2014): Playing Hard to Get, Signaling Status and Enhancing The Social Influence of Luxury Brands, in: Proceedings of the 2014 Monaco Symposium on Luxury, April 10th- 11th, 2014, Monaco.

Ceyp, M., & Scupin, J.-P. (2013): Erfolgreiches Social Media Marketing: Konzepte, Maßnahmen und Praxisbeispiele [Successful Social Media Marketing: Concepts, Tactics, and Best Practices], 1st. ed.,Wiesbaden: Gabler Verlag.

Chaffey, D., & Ellis-Chadwick, F. (2012): Digital Marketing: Strategy, Implementation, and Practice, 5th ed., Harlow et al.: Pearson.

Chandon, P. (1995): Consumer Research on Sales Promotions: A State-of-the-Art Literature Review, in: Journal of Marketing Management, Vol. 11, No. 5, pp. 419–441.

Chanel.com (2015a): Classic Flap Bag, retrieved February 12, 2015 from http://www.chanel.com/en_US/fashion/products/handbags/g/s.classic-flap-bag-in-quilted-lambskin.0V.A58600Y01480C3906.sto.ico.html.

Chanel.com (2015b): Store Locator, retrieved March 6, 2015 from http://www.chanel.com/en_GB/Jewellery#storelocator_wfj.

Chen, Y., Liu, F., Cheng-Hsi, F., & Lin, T.M.Y. (2013): Understanding the Effectiveness of Word-of-Mouth: An Elasticity Perspective, in: Journal of Research in Interactive Marketing, Vol. 7, No. 1, pp. 57–77.

Chevalier, M., & Gutsatz, M. (2012): Luxury Retail Management: How the World's Top Brands Provide Quality Product and Service Support, 1st ed., Singapore: John Wiley & Sons.

Chevalier, M., & Mazzalovo, G. (2008): Luxury Brand Management: A World of Privilege, 1st ed., Singapore: John Wiley & Sons.

Chevalier, M., & Mazzalovo, G. (2012): Luxury Brand Management: A World of Privilege, 2nd ed., Singapore: John Wiley & Sons.

Chikita Insights (2013): The Value of Google Result Positioning, retrieved May 20, 2015 from http://chitika.com/google-positioning-value.

Childers, T.L., Carr, C.L., Peck, J., & Carson, S. (2001): Hedonic and Utilitarian Motivations for Online Retail Shopping Behavior, in: Journal of Retailing, Vol. 77, No. 4, pp. 511–535.

Chiu, S. (2014): North American Trend: Concessions Within Department Stores, in: Retail-Insider.com, retrieved May 21, 2015 from http://www.retail-insider.com/retail-insider/2014/3/trend-in-luxury-retailing-concessions-within-department-stores.

Cho, Y.-S. (2012): Rolls-Royce Sells Out Dragon Phantom in China, retrieved January 31, 2012, from http://www. bloomberg.com/news/2012-01-11/rolls-royce-sells-out-dragon-phantom-in-china.html.

Christodoulides, G., Michaelidou, N., & Ching Hsing Li. (2009): Measuring Perceived Brand Luxury: An Evaluation of the BLI Scale, in: Journal of Brand Management, Vol. 16, No. 5/6, pp. 395–405.

Churchill, G.A.J., & Iacobucci, D. (2005): Marketing Research: Methodological Foundations, 9th ed., Mason, OH: South-Western.

Cobb-Walgren, C.J., Ruble, C.A., & Donthu, N. (1995): Brand Equity, Brand Preference, and Purchase Intent, in: Journal of Advertising, Vol. 24, No. 3, pp. 25–40.

Coca-colacompany.com (2015): Our Company, retrieved March 9, 2015 from http://www.coca-colacompany.com/our-company/.

Comtesse.com (2015a): Craftsmanship, retrieved February 3, 2015 from http://www.comtesse.de/en/house-of-comtesse/craftsmanship.

Comtesse.com (2015b): Materials, retrieved February 5, 2015 from http://www.comtesse.de/en/materials.

Cornell, A. (2002): Cult of Luxury: The New Opiate of the Masses, in: Australian Financial Review, April 27, 2002, p. 47.

Corneo, G., & Jeanne, O. (1997a): Conspicuous Consumption, Snobbism and Conformism, in: Journal of Public Economics, Vol. 66, No. 1, pp. 55–71.

Corneo, G., & Jeanne, O. (1997b): Snobs, Bandwagons, and the Origin of Social Customs in Consumer Behavior, in: Journal of Economic Behavior & Organization, Vol. 32, No. 3, pp. 333–347.

Crump, M.J.C., McDonnell, J.V., & Gureckis, T.M. (2013): Evaluating Amazon's Mechanical Turk as a Tool for Experimental Behavioral Research, in: PLoS ONE, Vol. 8, No. 3, pp. 1–18.

Curtis, J. (2000): Not Taking Luxury for Granted, in: Marketing, August 24, 2000, pp. 26–27.

Dacre, K. (2013): Lift-Off for Louis Vuitton in Selfridges: 'Store-Within-a-Store' Contains Willy Wonka-Like Glass Elevator, in: Standard, retrieved May 21, 2015 from http://www.standard.co.uk/news/london/liftoff-for-louis-vuitton-in-selfridges-storewithinastore-contains-willy-wonkalike-glass-elevator-8925882.html.

Dahm, J.-M. (2013): Luxury Brand Advertising: An Empirical Investigation of Luxury-Specific Characteristics of Print Advertisements, unpublished thesis at the WHU – Otto Beisheim School of Management, Vallendar.

Daneshkhu, S. (2012): François-Henri Pinault: Mix of Form and Function Is Raison d'Être, in: Financial Times, May 30, 2012, retrieved November 20, 2013 from http://www.ft.com/intl/cms/s/0/71179b18-a33d-11e1-ab98-00144feabdc0.html#axzz2lBogbWJe.

Davies, A. (2013): Analysts Say Bugatti Loses $6.24 Million For Every Veyron Supercar It Sells, in: Business Insider, October 3, 2013, retrieved February 18, 2015, from http://www.businessinsider.com/bugatti-may-lose-6-million-per-veyron-2013-10.

De Barnier, V., Falcy, S., & Valette-Florence, P. (2012): Do Consumers Perceive Three Levels of Luxury? A Comparison of Accessible, Intermediate and Inaccessible Luxury Brands, in: Journal of Brand Management, Vol. 19, No. 7, pp. 623–636.

De Pelsmacker, P., Geuens, M., & Van den Bergh, J. (2013): Marketing Communications: A European Perspective, 5th ed., Harlow et al.: Pearson.

Deutsche Post (2014): Dialogmarketing Deutschland 2014: Dialog Marketing Monitor Studie 26 [Dialogue Marketing Germany 2014: Dialogue Marketing Monitor Study 26], retrieved August 2, 2014 from https://www.dialogmarketing-shop.de/studien-national/.

Dion, D., & Arnould, E. (2011): Retail Luxury Strategy: Assembling Charisma through Art and Magic, in: Journal of Retailing, Vol. 87, No. 4, pp. 502–520.

Dior.com (2015): The Dior Boutiques, retrieved March 6, 2015 from http://www.dior.com/couture/en_gb/store/search_result?univers[horlogerie]=pla_watches&univers[joaillerie]=pla_fine_jewelry&continent=3715&pays=3738&region=&ville=3739&node_id=581.

Dodds, W.B., Monroe, K.B., & Grewal, D. (1991): Effects of Price, Brand, and Store Information on Buyers' Product Evaluations, in: Journal of Marketing Research, Vol. 28, No. 3, pp. 307–319.

Dodes, R., & Passariello, C. (2011): Luxury Brands Stake Out New Department Store Turf, in: The Wall Street Journal, retrieved May 21, 2015 from http://www.wsj.com/articles/SB10001424052748704740604576301113906906234.

Dolbec, P.-Y., & Chebat, J.-C. (2013): The Impact of Flagship vs. a Brand Store on Brand Attitude, Brand Attachment and Brand Equity, in: Journal of Retailing, Vol. 89, No. 4, pp. 460–466.

DoubleClick (2005): Search Before The Purchase: Suchaktivitäten der Online-Käufer [Search Before The Purchase: Search Activities of Online Shoppers], retrieved July 29, 2014 from http://www.lammenett.de/fileadmin/PDFs/DE_search_0502_rv2.pdf.

Doyle, P., & Hooley, G.J. (1992): Strategic Orientation and Corporate Performance, in: International Journal of Research in Marketing, Vol. 9, No. 1, pp. 59–73.

Dubois, B. (1992): Comment Surmonter les Paradoxes du Marketing du Luxe [How to Master the Paradoxes of Marketing Luxury Goods], in: Revue Française de Gestion, February 1992, No. 87, pp. 30–37.

Dubois, B., Czellar, S., & Laurent, G. (2005): Consumer Segments Based on Attitudes Toward Luxury: Empirical Evidence from Twenty Countries, in: Marketing Letters, Vol. 16, No. 2, pp. 115–128.

Dubois, B., & Duquesne, P. (1993): The Market for Luxury Goods: Income versus Culture, in: European Journal of Marketing, Vol. 27, No. 1, pp. 35–44.

Dubois, B., & Laurent, G. (1994): Attitudes Towards the Concept of Luxury: an Exploratory Analysis, in: Cote, J.A. & Leong, S.M. (Eds.): Asia Pacific Advances in Consumer Research, Vol. 1, pp. 273–278.

Dubois, B., & Laurent, G. (1996): The Functions of Luxury: A Situational Approach to Excursionism, in: Advances in Consumer Research, Vol. 23, pp. 470–477.

Dubois, B., Laurent, G., & Czellar, S. (2001): Consumer Rapport to Luxury: Analyzing Complex and Ambivalent Attitudes, Working Paper 736, HEC School of Management, Jouy-En-Josas, France.

Dubois, B., & Paternault, C. (1995): Observations: Understanding the World of International Luxury Brands: The "Dream Formula", in: Journal of Advertising Research, Vol. 35, No. 4, pp. 69–76.

Duffy, D.L. (2005): Affiliate Marketing and Its Impact On E-Commerce, in: Journal of Consumer Marketing, Vol. 22, No. 3, pp. 161–163.

Duncan, C.P. (1990): Consumer Market Beliefs: A Review of the Literature and an Agenda for Future Research, in: Advances in Consumer Research, Vol. 17, No. 1, pp. 729–736.

Düweke, E., & Rabsch, S. (2012): Erfolgreiche Websites: SEO, SEM, Online-Marketing, Usability [Successful Websites: SEO, SEM, Online Marketing, Usability] 2nd ed., Bonn: Galileo Press.

Eastman, J.K., Iyer, R., & Randall, C. (2009): Understanding Internet Shoppers: An Exploratory Study, in: Marketing Management Journal, Vol. 19, No. 2, pp. 104–117.

eMarketer (2015a): Digital Accounts for Over 50% of Time Spent with Media in China, retrieved July 19, 2015 from http://www.emarketer.com/Article/Digital-Accounts-Over-50-of-Time-Spent-with-Media-China/1012618.

eMarketer (2015b): UK Adults Spend More Time on Mobile Devices than on PCs, retrieved July 19, 2015 from http://www.emarketer.com/Article/UK-Adults-Spend-More-Time-on-Mobile-Devices-than-on-PCs/1012356.

eMarketer (2015c): US Adults Spend 5.5 Hours with Video Content Each Day, retrieved July 19, 2015 from http://www.emarketer.com/Article/US-Adults-Spend-55-Hours-with-Video-Content-Each-Day/1012362.

eMarketer (2013): Number of Social Network Users Worldwide from 2010 to 2017 (in Billion), retrieved July 22, 2014 from http://www.statista.com/statistics/278414/number-of-worldwide-social-network-users/.

Euromonitor.com (2015): Top 100 City Destinations Ranking, retrieved March 9, 2015 from http://blog.euromonitor.com/2015/01/top-100-city-destinations-rank ing.html.

Facebook.com (2015a): User-Generated Facebook Page for Rolex (A), retrieved April 9, 2015 from https://www.facebook.com/TheRolexForYou.

Facebook.com (2015b): User-Generated Facebook Page for Rolex (B), retrieved April 9, 2015 from https://www.facebook.com/pages/Rolex/38345699073.

Facebook.com (2015c): User-Generated Facebook Page for Rolex (C), retrieved April 9, 2015 from https://www.facebook.com/pages/Rolex-Passion/498531100186609.

Facebook.com/Burberry (2014a): Burberry: A Badge of Origin Since the 1920s, the Iconic Burberry Check First Appeared on the Lining of Trench Coats, retrieved August 8, 2014 from https://www.facebook.com/burberry/photos/ms.c.eJxlzME

NACAIQ9GNDMUWZP~;FjCcTuL78Fga5yitJD7oWvqShiXaXOKNh~;6G6BMZq NNRrLkf9IIU~-.bps.a.10152514684046425/10152592974701425/?type=1&theater.

Facebook.com/Burberry (2014b): Burberry Branded Facebook Page, retrieved July 21, 2014 from https://www.facebook.com/burberry.

Facebook.com/Chanel (2014): "Coco Coach", The Fall-Winter 2014 campaign, retrieved July 27, 2014 from https://www.facebook.com/chanel/photos/a.10150605473904235.3986 57.10109514234/10152558638834235/.

Facebook.com/Ferrari (2015): Ferrari Official Facebook Page, retrieved March 30, 2015 from https://www.facebook.com/Ferrari.

Facebook.com/Rolex (2015): Rolex Branded Facebook Page, retrieved April 9, 2015 from https://www.facebook.com/rolex?fref=ts.

Falke.com (2015): Vicuña, retrieved February 4, 2015 from http://www.falke.com/de/specials/falke-vicuna.html.

Fassnacht, M. (1996): Preisdifferenzierung bei Dienstleistungen: Implementationsformen und Determinanten [Price Discrimination for Services: Implementation and Determinants], 1st ed., Wiesbaden: Gabler Verlag.

Fassnacht, M., Kluge, P.N., & Mohr, H. (2013): Pricing Luxury Brands: Specificities, Conceptualization and Performance Impact, in: Marketing ZFP – Journal of Research and Management, Vol. 35, No. 2, pp. 104–117.

Fassnacht, M., Kluge, P.N., & Mohr, H. (2012): Do Luxury Pricing Decisions Create Price Continuity?, in: Burmann, C., König, V., & Meurer, J. (Eds.): Identitätsbasierte Luxusmarkenführung: Grundlagen – Strategien – Controlling [Identity-Based Luxury Brand Management: Fundamentals – Strategies – Control], 1st ed., Wiesbaden: Springer Gabler, pp. 121–137.

Fassnacht, M. & Königsfeld, J.A. (2015): Sales Promotion Management in Retailing: Tasks, Benchmarks, and Future Trends, in: Marketing Review St. Gallen, Vol. 32, No. 3, pp. 67–77.

FAZ.net (2014): FAZ.net – Preisliste (Gültig ab 01.04.2014) [FAZ.net – Pricing (valid from April 1, 2014)], retrieved July 27, 2014 from https://filebox.faz.de/public/505F4B6E505D5D56545C54585F/Mediaportal/FAZ%20Digital%20Preise%202014.pdf.

FCAGroup.com (2013): Annual Report 2013, retrieved February 18, 2015 from http://www.fcagroup.com/en-US/investor_relations/financial_reports/FiatDocuments/Bilanci/2013/2013_annual_report.pdf?redirectFromFiatspa=1.

Fédération de l'Industrie Horlogère Suisse FH (2012): The Swiss and World Watchmaking Industry in 2012, retrieved March 30, 2015 from http://www.fhs.ch/file/59/Watchmaking_2012.pdf.

Fédération de l'Industrie Horlogère Suisse FH. (2014): The Swiss and World Watchmaking Industry in 2014, retrieved March 30, 2015 from http://www.fhs.ch/file/59/Watchmaking_2014.pdf.

Fédération de l'Industrie Horlogère Suisse FH (2015): Exports of Swiss Watches Electronic and Mechanical, retrieved March 30, 2015 from http://www.fhs.ch/scripts/getstat.php?file=histo_elec_mec_150202_a.pdf.

Fendi.com (2015): Baguette: The Icon, retrieved February 12, 2015 from http://baguette.fendi.com/the-icon/.

Ferrari.com (2015): Find a Dealer, retrieved February 25, 2015 from http://auto.ferrari.com/en_EN/car-dealers/.

Field, A. (2009): Discovering Statistics Using SPSS (And Sex And Drugs And Rock "N" Roll), 3rd ed., London et al.: Sage.

Fionda, A.M., & Moore, C.M. (2009): The Anatomy of the Luxury Fashion Brand, in: Journal of Brand Management, Vol. 16, No. 5/6, pp. 347–363.

Fleishmann Hillard, & Harris Interactive (2012): Understaning The Role of the Internet In The Lives of Consumers, retrieved July 29, 2014 from http://www.harrisinteractive.com/vault/HI_UK_Corp_Insights-Fleishman-Hillard-DDI-2012.pdf.

Flett, G.L., & Hewitt, P.L. (2002): Perfectionism and Maladjustment: An Overview of Theoretical, Definitional, and Treatment Issues, in: Flett, G.L. & Hewitt, P.L (Eds.), Perfectionism: Theory, Research, and Treatment, 1st ed., Washington DC: American Psychological Association, pp. 5–31.

Florès, L. (2014): How To Measure Digital Marketing: Metrics For Assessing Impact And Designing Success, 1st ed., Basingstoke: Palgrave Macmillan.

Focus Medialine (2008): Der Markt für Luxusgüter: Daten, Fakten, Trends zu Mode, Accessoires, Uhren, Düften [Luxury Goods Market: Figures, Facts, Trends on Fashion, Accessories, Watches, Perfumes], retrieved September 15, 2014 from http://www.medialine.de/media/uploads/projekt/medialine/docs/bestellung_download/marktanalysen/2008/foc_ma_luxusgueter_200807.pdf.

Focus Medialine (2009): Der Markt für Luxusgüter: Daten, Fakten, Trends zu Mode, Accessoires, Uhren, Düften [Luxury Goods Market: Figures, Facts, Trends on Fashion, Accessories, Watches, Perfumes], retrieved September 15, 2014 from http://www.medialine.de/media/uploads/projekt/medialine/docs/bestellung_download/marktanalysen/2009/foc_ma_luxusgueter_200908.pdf.

Foeock Kannilc. (2012): mont banc pen_6, retrieved September 22, 2014 from https://www.flickr.com/photos/foeock/7892594054/sizes/o/in/photolist-d2rBeQ-d2rBdw-d2rB3m-d2rBrE-d2rAR1-d2rBbS-d2rAYb-d2rBoh-6ET7LM-b4neP2-b4nf3z-b4nebT-8wbwTV-7p8478-7p84ST-7pbUyS-7pbWYu-7pWvQL-589Emq-585sQ6-7pSxcB-7pSxB4-7pWuRL-7pSy3X-7pSzZa-4DXqro-4DTesa-4DXtKb-4DTcTp-4DXt2S-4DT9nz-4DXrKC-4DXpxb-4DXp5d-4DTdnZ-4DXrju-4DXsyo-4DTcxD-4DXrwW-4DTa4M-4DTd2g-4DXr5b-4DTc7H-4DT9Ni-4DTebP-4DXttu-4DTaTD-4DTeJc-4DXsbu-w5Zki-w5Zy9/.

Fondazione Altagamma & SDA Bocconi (2014): Fashion & Luxury Insight: FY 2013 Results, retrieved May 27, 2015 from http://www.primaonline.it/wp-content/uploads/2014/10/1210251456146841830file.pdf.

Forbes (2012): Cost of Living Extremely Well Index: Our Annual Consumer Price Index-Billionaire Style, retrieved September 19, 2012, from http://www.forbes.com/sites/scottdecarlo/2012/09/19/cost-of-living-extremely-well-index-our-annual-consumer-price-index-billionaire-style/.

Fornell, C., & Larcker, D.F. (1981): Evaluating Structural Equation Models with Unobservable Variables and Measurement Error, in: Journal of Marketing Research, Vol. 18, No. 1, pp. 39–50.

Forsythe, S., Liu, C., Shannon, D., & Gardner, L.C. (2006): Development of a Scale to Measure the Perceived Benefits and Risks of Online Shopping, in: Journal of Interactive Marketing, Vol. 20, No. 2, pp. 55–75.

France-galop.com (2014): All the Races, retrieved July 16, 2014 from http://www.france-galop.com/All-the-races.233+M52087573ab0.0.html?&course_id=9149&no_cache=1&numero_id=12.

Franckmuller.com (2014): History, retrieved September 22, 2014 from https://www.franckmuller.com/en/franck-muller/history.

Frazier, G.L., & Lassar, W.M. (1996): Determinants of Distribution Intensity, in: Journal of Marketing, Vol. 60, No. 4, pp. 39–51.

Freitag, M. (2013): Wie Ferrari Millionen mit dem Marken-Mythos macht [How Ferrari Makes Millions Through Its Brand Myth], in: Manager-magazin.de, retrieved January 9, 2015 from http://www.manager-magazin.de/unternehmen/autoindustrie/fanartikel-und-merchandising-bei-ferrari-a-903666.html.

Freitag, M., & Katzensteiner, T. (2013): Interview mit Ferrari-Lenker Luca Cordero di Montezemolo [Interview With Ferrari-Head Luca Cordero di Montezemolo], in: Manager-magazin.de, retrieved January 13, 2014, from http://www.manager-magazin.de/unternehmen/autoindustrie/interview-mit-ferrari-lenker-luca-cordero-di-montezemolo-a-909387.html.

Fritz, W. (2001): Internet-Marketing und Electronic Commerce: Grundlagen – Rahmenbedingen – Instrumente [Internet-Marketing and Electronic Commerce: Fundamentals – Business Conditions – Instruments], 2nd ed., Wiesbaden: Gabler.

Frontier Economics, & ECCIA (2012): The Value of the Cultural and Creative Industries to the European Economy: A Report Prepared for the ECCIA, retrieved January 13, 2014 from http://www.comitecolbert.com/assets/files/paragraphes/fichiers/20/ Thevalueoftheculturalandcreative.PDF.

Frost, R.O., Marten, P., Lahart, C., & Rosenblate, R. (1990): The Dimensions of Perfectionism, in: Cognitive Therapy and Research, Vol. 14, No. 5, pp. 449–468.

Gastaldi, F. (2012): Internet, Social Media and Luxury Strategy, in: Hoffmann, J. & Coste-Manière, I. (Eds.): Luxury Strategy in Action, 1st ed., Basingstoke: Palgrave Macmillan, pp. 108–143.

Gedenk, K. (2002): Verkaufsförderung [Sales Promotion], 1st ed., München: Vahlen.

Gedenk, K., Neslin, S.A., & Ailawadi, K.L. (2010): Sales Promotion, in: Krafft, M., & Mantrala, M.K. (Eds.): Retailing in the 21st Centruy: Current and Future Trends. 1st ed., Berlin, Heidelberg: Springer, pp. 393–407.

Giebelhausen, M., Robinson, S., & Cronin, J. (2011): Worth Waiting For: Increasing Satisfaction by Making Consumers Wait, in: Journal of the Academy of Marketing Science, Vol. 39, No. 6, pp. 889–905.

Gierke, S. (2011): Aston Martin als Sponsor von 1860 München: Luxuswagen für den Arbeiterverein [Aston Martin Sponsor 1860 Munich: Luxury Cars for the Workers' Club], in: Sueddeutsche.de, September 16, 2011, retrieved July 16, 2014 from http://www.sueddeutsche.de/sport/aston-martin-ist-neuer-sponsor-von-muenchen-luxuswagen-statt-grosse-liebe-1.1145073.

Gierl, H., & Huettl, V. (2010): Are Scarce Products Always More Attractive? The Interaction of Different Types of Scarcity Signals with Products' Suitability for Conspicuous Consumption, in: International Journal of Research in Marketing, Vol. 27, No. 3, pp. 225–235.

Godey, B., Pederzoli, D., Aiello, G., Donvito, R., Chan, P., Oh, H., Singh, R., Skorobogatykh, I.I., Tsuchiya, J., & Weitz, B. (2012): Brand and Country-of-Origin Effect on Consumers' Decision to Purchase Luxury Products, in: Journal of Business Research, Vol. 65, No.10, pp. 1461–1470.

Google.de (2014a): Google Search for "Diamond Ring", retrieved July 29, 2014 from https://www.google.de/?gfe_rd=cr&ei=RcfXU_maG8Pjsgb-qYEI&gws_rd=ssl#q=diamond+ring.

Google.de (2014b): Google Search for "Luxury Hobo Bag", retrieved July 29, 2014 from https://www.google.de/?gfe_rd=cr&ei=RcfXU_maG8Pjsgb-qYEI&gws_rd=ssl#q=luxury+hobo+bag.

Google.de (2014c): Google Search for "Schweizer Uhren", retrieved July 29, 2014 from https://www.google.de/?gfe_rd=cr&ei=BcrXU4qOEsjisgb1s4DQDA&gws_rd=ssl#q=schweizer+uhren.

Google.de (2015): Google Search for "Vacheron Constantin", retrieved January 12, 2015 from https://www.google.de/#q=vacheron+constantin.

Grabs, A., & Bannour, K.-P. (2012): Follow me! Erfolgreiches Social Media Marketing mit Facebook, Twitter und Co. [Follow Me! Successful Social Media Marketing Using Facebook, Twitter & Co.], 2nd ed., Bonn: Galileo Press.

Graf-von-Faber-Castell.com (2014): Tradition, retrieved September 22, 2014 from http://www.graf-von-faber-castell.com/tradition.

Grewal, D., Iyer, G.R., & Levy, M. (2004): Internet Retailing: Enablers, Limiters and Market Consequences, in: Journal of Business Research, Vol. 57, No. 7, pp. 703–713.

Groth, J.C., & Mcdaniel, S.W. (1993): The Exclusive Value Principle, in: Journal of Consumer Marketing, Vol. 10, No. 1, pp. 10–16.

Grubb, E.L., & Grathwohl, H.L. (1967): Consumer Self-Concept, Symbolism and Marketing Behavior: A Theoretical Approach, in: Journal of Marketing, Vol. 31, No. 4, pp. 22–27.

Grüger, M. (2007): Die Vertikalisierung der Textilwirtschaft durch Handelsmarken-Produktdesignteams, Shop-in-Shop- und Concession-Konzepte: Überlegungen zur Variation der Arbeitsteilung zwischen Bekleidungsindustrie und Handel [Vertical Forward Integration of the Textile Industry through Retailer Brand Product Design Teams, Shop-in-Shop and Concession Concepts: Considerations of Variations in the Division of Labour Between the Textile Industry and Retailers], doctoral dissertation, University of Cologne, retrieved May 25, 2015 from http://core.ac.uk/download/pdf/12009927.pdf.

Gucci.com (2015): New Bamboo, retrieved March 13, 2015 from http://www.gucci.com/uk/category/f/new_bamboo.

Guerlain.com (2015): Bespoke Fragrances, retrieved February 9, 2015 from http://www.guerlain.com/uk/en-uk/sur-mesure-page-2.

Gutman, J., & Mills, M.K. (1982): Fashion Life Style, Self-Concept, Shopping Orientation, and Store Patronage: An Integrative Analysis, in: Journal of Retailing, Vol. 58, No. 2, pp. 64–86.

Hagtvedt, H., & Patrick, V.M. (2009): The Broad Embrace of Luxury: Hedonic Potential as a Driver of Brand Extendibility, in: Journal of Consumer Psychology, Vol. 19, No. 4, pp. 608–618.

Hamiltonjewelers.com (2015): Designers, retrieved March 20, 2015 from http://www.hamiltonjewelers.com/categories/Designers/.

Hammock, T., & Brehm, J.W. (1966): The Attractiveness of Choice Alternatives When Freedom to Choose is Eliminated by A Social Agent, in: Journal of Personality, Vol. 34, No. 4, pp. 546–554.

Handelsblatt (2011): Deutsche trinken mehr Billig-Biere [German Consumers Drinking More Low-Price Beers], retrieved July 17, 2014, from http://www.handelsblatt.com/unternehmen/industrie/statistik-2011-deutsche-trinken-mehr-billig-biere/6126862.html.

Hansen, A.-K., Joseph, K., & Krafft, M. (2008): Price Delegation in Sales Organizations: An Empirical Investigation, in: Business Research, Vol. 1, No. 1, pp. 94–104.

Hansen, J., & Wänke, M. (2011): The Abstractness of Luxury, in: Journal of Economic Psychology, Vol. 32, No. 5, pp. 789–796.

Hansen, T. (2005): Perspectives on Consumer Decision Making: An Integrated Approach,in: Journal of Consumer Behaviour, Vol. 4, No. 6, pp. 420–437.

Han, Y.J., Nunes, J.C., & Drèze, X. (2010): Signaling Status with Luxury Goods: The Role of Brand Prominence, in: Journal of Marketing, Vol. 74, No. 4, pp. 15–30.

Hawesko.de (2015a): Champagner, retrieved March 20, 2015 from http://www.hawesko.de/cgi-bin/WebObjects/FrontApp.woa/wo/13.0.0.0.0.109.7.1.1.3. 5.0.3.1.9.1.1.

Hawesko.de (2015b): Rotwein [Red Wine], retrieved March 20, 2015 from http://www.hawesko.de/cgi-bin/WebObjects/FrontApp.woa/wo/4.0.0.109.7.3.1.0.3.0.3.1.9.1.1.

Heine, K. (2010): Identification and Motivation of Participants for Luxury Consumer Surveys Through Viral Participant Acquisition, in: The Electronic Journal of Business Research Methods, Vol. 8, No. 2, pp. 132–145.

Heine, K. (2012): The Concept of Luxury Brands, 2nd ed., Lyon & Berlin: www.conceptofluxurybrands.com.

Heine, K., & Phan, M. (2011): Trading-Up Mass-Market Goods to Luxury Products, in: Australasian Marketing Journal, Vol. 19, No. 2, pp. 108–114.

Hennigs, N., Wiedmann, K., & Klarmann, C. (2012): Luxury Brands in the Digital Age – Exclusivity versus Ubiquity, in: Marketing Review St. Gallen, Vol. 29, No. 1, pp. 30–35.

Hermes.com (2015a): Evelyne, retrieved January 13, 2015 from http://uk.hermes.com/leather/bags-and-luggage/women/handbag-1/rouge/evelyne-iii-bag-1.html?color_hermes=ROUGE%20CASAQUE&nuance=35.

Hermes.com (2015b): Hermès Zürich, retrieved February 25, 2015 from http://de.stores.hermes.com/Europa/Schweiz/Zuerich/Hermes-Zuerich.

Hermes.com (2015c): Jypsiere, retrieved January 13, 2015 from http://usa.hermes.com/leather/bags-and-luggage/for-day/jypsiere-31/jypsiere-34.html.

Hermes.com (2015d): Le Monde d'Hermès, retrieved January 11, 2015 from http://monde.hermes.com/index.php?lang=EN.

Herrmann, A. (1998): Produktmanagement [Product Management], 1st ed., München: Vahlen.

Herrmann, A., & Huber, F. (2013): Produktmanagement: Grundlagen, Methoden, Beispiele [Product Management: Fundamentals, Methods, Examples], 3rd ed., Wiesbaden: Springer Gabler.

Hirschman, E.C., & Holbrook, M.B. (1982): Hedonic Consumption: Emerging Concepts, Methods and Propositions, in: Journal of Marketing, Vol. 46, No. 3, pp. 92–101.

Hoffmann, M. (2014): "Festival des Métiers" von Hermès: So geht Luxus ["Festival des Métiers" by Hermès: How Luxury is crafted], in: Manager-magazin.de, retrieved July 15, 2015 from http://www.manager-magazin.de/lifestyle/mode/festival-des-metiers-in-hamburg-hermes-zeigt-wie-luxus-entsteht-a-969131.html.

Holland, H. (2009): Direktmarketing: im Dialog mit dem Kunden [Direct Marketing: The Dialogue With The Customer], 3rd ed., München: Vahlen.

Hollensen, S., & Opresnik, M. (2010): Marketing: A Relationship Perspective, 1st ed., München: Vahlen.

Homburg, C. (2012): Marketingmanagement: Strategie – Instrumente – Umsetzung – Unternehmensführung [Marketing Management: Strategy – Instruments – Implementation – Corporate Management], 4th ed., Wiesbaden: Gabler.

Homburg, C. (2015): Marketingmanagement: Strategie – Instrumente – Umsetzung – Unternehmensführung [Marketing Management: Strategy – Instruments – Implementation – Corporate Management], 5th ed., Wiesbaden: Springer Gabler.

Homburg, C., & Krohmer, H. (2008): Der Prozess der Marktforschung: Festlegung der Datenerhebungsmethode, Stichprobenbildung und Fragebogengestaltung [The Process of Market Research: Methods of Data Collection, Sampling, and Survey Design], in: Herrmann, A., Homburg, C. & Klarmann, M. (Eds.): Handbuch Marktforschung: Methoden – Anwendungen – Praxisbeispiele [Handbook of Market Research: Methods – Applications – Examples], 3rd ed., Wiesbaden: Gabler, pp. 21–51.

Homburg, C., Kuester, S., & Krohmer, H. (2013): Marketing Management: A Contemporary Perspective, 2nd ed., Maidenhead: McGraw-Hill.

Homburg, C., & Totzek, D. (2011): Preismanagement auf B2B-Märkten: Zentrale Entscheidungsfelder und Erfolgsfaktoren [Price Management for B2B Markets: Key Decisions and Success Factors], in: Homburg, C., & Totzek, D. (Eds.): Preismanagement auf Business-to-Business-Märkten: Preisstrategie – Preisbestimmung – Preisdurchsetzung [Pricing for Business-to-Business Markets: Strategy – Price Setting – Implementation], 1st ed., Wiesbaden: Gabler, pp. 13–69.

Homer, P.M. (2009): Product Placements, in: Journal of Advertising, Vol. 38, No. 3, pp. 21–31.

Hudders, L. (2012): Why the Devil Wears Prada: Consumers' Purchase Motives for Luxuries, in: Journal of Brand Management, Vol. 19, No. 7, pp. 609–622.

Hudson, B.T. (2011): Brand Heritage and The Renaissance of Cunard, in: European Journal of Marketing, Vol. 45, No. 9/10, pp. 1538–1556.

Hu, L., & Bentler, P.M. (1999): Cutoff Criteria for Fit Indexes in Covariance Structure Analysis: Conventional Criteria Versus New Alternatives, in: Structural Equation Modeling: A Multidisciplinary Journal, Vol. 6, No. 1, pp. 1–55.

hypo.physe (2010): Rolex Datejust II 116334, retrieved March 25, 2015 (under CC BY-SA 2.0 license) from https://www.flickr.com/photos/hypophyse/4788440734/in/photolist-8i91B1-6kHHhi-q13aSc-ReJNP-9gnCX4-eYCMRQ-ag1WBM-71Emno-5zLvxV-4JiwFb-f3phWZ-5ukjzc-6djBvp-9R71iF-9WHNJB-nzEnSZ-9yEvaX-4W1f4R-kEwSJ9-dxnNpb-9bm12M-6kyo6x-bmjDsQ-bmjCFQ-9bp8NG-g7vGFG-fvJNq-Bhmv3-948TzB-ac8ebS-agZED6-jwLUfp-bzAVCV-pTHDQB-8MDWGM-65ESuQ-8uRtKS-7A8dDj-bzewdP-bmjCN5-9cWH25-gf9bDZ-6u1F7Z-bzevmv-bmjD7W-7awmrq-qMdoNE-9iUUgF-bRLLhR-dxGW9T.

Interbrand (2011): Interview with Thomas Patrick, CEO Hermès, in: Best Global Brands 2011, retrieved January 13, 2014 from http://www.interbrand.com/de/

best-global-brands/previous-years/Best-Global-Brands-2011/Hermes-Patrick-Thomas.aspx.

International Skating Union (2002): ISU Grand Prix of Figure Skating Trophée Lalique Medal Winners, retrieved July 16, 2014 from http://ww2.isu.org/historical/fsgpfranames.html.

Internet Live Stats (2014a): Internet Users, retrieved July 22, 2014 from http://www.internetlivestats.com/internet-users/.

Internet Live Stats (2014b): Internet Users by Country, retrieved July 22, 2014, from http://www.internetlivestats.com/internet-users-by-country/.

iProspect (2004): Search Engine User Attitudes, retrieved July 29, 2014 from http://c.ymcdn.com/sites/www.sempo.org/resource/resmgr/docs/iprospectsurveycom plete.pdf.

Irisvonarnim.com (2015): Store Locator, retrieved February 24, 2015 from http://www.irisvonarnim.de/en/store-locator/.

IWC.com (2014): Our Story, retrieved September 22, 2014 from http://www.iwc.com/en/about/our-story/.

JackRow.com (2014): About, retrieved September 22, 2014 from http://www.jackrow.com/about.htm.

Jaeger-lecoultre.com (2014): Manufacture: Our History, retrieved September 22, 2014 from http://www.jaeger-lecoultre.com/DE/en/luxury-watches/history#55click=megamenu.

Jaeger-lecoultre.com (2015a): Grande Reverso Taille, retrieved January 19, 2015 from http://www.jaeger-lecoultre.com/GB/en/watches/reverso-grande-taille/2708410#/t1.

Jaeger-lecoultre.com (2015b): Grande Reverso Ultra Thin, retrieved January 19, 2015 from http://www.jaeger-lecoultre.com/US/en/watches/grande-reverso-ultra-thin/2782520#/t1.

Jaeger-lecoultre.com (2015c): Reverso Gyrotourbillon 2, retrieved January 19, 2015 from http://www.jaeger-lecoultre.com/GB/en/watches/reverso-gyrotourbil lon-2/2332420#/t1.

Jaeger-lecoultre.com (2015d): Watch Finder: Master Control, retrieved March 31, 2015 from http://www.jaeger-lecoultre.com/DE/en/watch-finder/master/1.

Jahn, B., Kunz, W., & Meyer, A. (2012): The Role of Social Media for Luxury Brands—Motives for Consumer Engagement and Opportunities for Business, in: Burmann, C. König, V., & Meurer, J. (Eds.): Identitätsbasierte Luxusmarkenführung [Identity-Based Luxury Brand Management], 1st ed., Wiesbaden: Springer Gabler, pp. 221–236.

Jansen, B.J., & Resnick, M. (2006): An Examination of Searcher's Perceptions of Nonsponsored and Sponsored Links During Ecommerce Web Searching, in: Journal of the American Society for Information Science and Technology, Vol. 57, No. 14, pp. 1949–1961.

Jardine, A. (2012): Behind the Work: “Odysee de Cartier”, in: Adage.com, retrieved January 11, 2015 from http://adage.com/article/news/work-odyssee-de-cartier/233232/.

Jerath, K., & Zhang, Z.J. (2010): Store Within a Store, in: Journal of Marketing Research, Vol. 47, No. 4, pp. 748–763.

Jones Lang LaSalle. (2011): Glanz & Glamour in Europas Luxusmeilen: Die 100 renommiertesten Luxusmarken und ihre Präsenz in Europas Metropolen [Glamour on Europe’s Luxury Shopping Miles: The Top 100 Luxury Brands and Their Presence in Europe’s Major Cities], retrieved February 24, 2015 from http://www.jll.de/germany/de-de/Research/Advance_Luxusmeilen_2011.pdf.

Kadewe.de (2015): Brand Overview: Luxury Boulevard, retrieved March 4, 2015 from http://www.kadewe.de/en/contextual_pages/statische_seiten/overview_of_brands/#/division/6#/item/6152.

Kapferer, J.-N. (1997): Managing Luxury Brands, in: Journal of Brand Management, Vol. 4, No. 4, pp. 251–259.

Kapferer, J.-N. (2012): Abundant Rarity: The Key to Luxury Growth, in: Business Horizons, Vol. 55, No. 5, pp. 453–462.

Kapferer, J.-N. (2014): What Research Themes For The Future, presented at the 2014 Monaco Symposium on Luxury, April 10th–11th, 2014, retrieved September 8, 2014 from http://monaco-symposium-on-luxury.com/?page=programme10.

Kapferer, J.-N. (2015): Kapferer on Luxury: How Luxury Brands Can Grow yet Remain Rare, 1st ed., London: Kogan Page.

Kapferer, J.-N., & Bastien, V. (2009a): The Luxury Strategy: Break the Rules of Marketing to Build Luxury Brands, 1st ed., London et al.: Kogan Page.

Kapferer, J.-N., & Bastien, V. (2009b): The Specificity of Luxury Management: Turning Marketing Upside Down, in: Journal of Brand Management, Vol. 16, No. 5/6, pp. 311–322.

Kapferer, J.-N., & Bastien, V. (2012): The Luxury Strategy: Break the Rules of Marketing to Build Luxury Brands, 2nd ed., London et al.: Kogan Page.

Kapferer, J.-N., & Laurent, G. (2014): The Minimum Price of Luxury: Modeling Consumers’ Highly Heterogeneous Perceptions, in: Proceedings of the 2014 Monaco Symposium on Luxury, April 10th–11th, 2014, Monaco.

Kaplan, A.M., & Haenlein, M. (2010): Users of the World, Unite! The Challenges and Opportunities of Social Media, in: Business Horizons, Vol. 53, No. 1, pp. 59–68.

Kastanakis, M.N., & Balabanis, G. (2012): Between the Mass and the Class: Antecedents of the “Bandwagon” Luxury Consumption Behavior, in: Journal of Business Research, Vol. 65, No. 10, pp. 1399–1407.

Keller, K.L. (1998): Strategic Brand Management – Building, Measuring, and Managing Brand Equity, 1st ed., Upper Saddle River, NJ: Prentice-Hall.

Keller, K.L. (2009): Managing the Growth Tradeoff: Challenges and Opportunities in Luxury Branding, in: Journal of Brand Management, Vol. 16, No. 5/6, pp. 290–301.

Kenshoo Social (2014a): Europe, Africa & Middle East (EMEA) Search Advertising Trends Q1/2014, retrieved August 1, 2014 from http://www.kenshoo.com/digitalmarketingtechnology/wp-content/uploads/2014/04/Kenshoo-Search-Ad-Trends-Q1-2014-EMEA.pdf.

Kenshoo Social (2014b): Globale Trends in der Suchmaschinenwerbung Q4/2013 [Global Trends in Search Engine Advertising Q4/2013], retrieved August 1, 2014 from http://www.kenshoo.com/digitalmarketingtechnology/wp-content/uploads/2013/03/Kenshoo-Global-Search-Ad-Trends-Q4-2013-DE.pdf.

Kepper, G. (2008): Methoden der qualitativen Marktforschung [Methods of Qualitative Market Research], in Herrmann, A., Homburg, C., & Klarmann, M. (Eds.): Handbuch Marktforschung: Methoden – Anwendungen – Praxisbeispiele [Handbook of Market Research: Methods – Applications – Examples], 3rd ed., Wiesbaden: Gabler, pp. 175–212.

Kim, A.J., & Ko, E. (2012): Do Social Media Marketing Activities Enhance Customer Equity? An Empirical Study of Luxury Fashion Brand, in: Journal of Business Research, Vol. 65, No. 10, pp. 1480–1486.

Kisabaka, L. (2001): Marketing für Luxusprodukte [Marketing of Luxury Products], 1st ed., Köln: Fördergesellschaft Produkt-Marketing.

KISSmetrics.com (2010): Bounce Rate Demystified, retrieved July 30, 2014, from http://blog.kissmetrics.com/bounce-rate/.

Kluge, P.N., & Fassnacht, M. (2014): Selling Luxury Goods Online? Effects of Making the Inaccessible Accessible, in: Proceedings of the 2014 Monaco Symposium on Luxury, April 10th–11th, 2014, Monaco.

Kluge, P.N., & Fassnacht, M. (2015): Selling Luxury Goods Online: Effects of Online Accessbility and Price Display, in: International Journal of Retailing & Distribution Management, *forthcoming*.

Kluge, P.N., Fassnacht, M., Stich, A., Königsfeld, J.A., & Mitschke, F. (2013): Preserving Brand Luxury Online? An Examination of Luxury Homepage Design, in: Proceedings of the 42th European Marketing Academy Conference, June 4–7, 2013, Istanbul.

Kluge, P.N., Königsfeld, J.A., Fassnacht, M., & Mitschke, F. (2013): Luxury Web Atmospherics: An Examination of Homepage Design, in: International Journal of Retail & Distribution Management, Vol. 41, No. 11/12, pp. 901–916.

Kollmann, T. (2013a): E-Business: Grundlagen elektronischer Geschäftsprozesse in der Net Economy [E-Business: Fundamentals of Electronic Business Processes in the Net Economy], 5th ed., Wiesbaden: Springer Gabler.

Kollmann, T. (2013b): Online-Marketing: Grundlagen der Absatzpolitik in der Net Economy [Online Marketing: Fundamentals of Marketing in the Net Economy], 2nd ed., Stuttgart: Kohlhammer.

König, V. (2012): Externe Call Center Agents als Luxusmarkenbotschafter am Telefon und in Sozialen Netzwerken [External Call Center Agents as Luxury Brand Ambassadors on the Phone and in Social Networks], in: Burmann, C., König, V., & Meurer, J. (Eds.): Identitätsbasierte Luxusmarkenführung [Identity-Based Luxury Brand Management], 1st ed., Wiesbaden: Springer Gabler, pp. 259–276.

Koo, M., & Fishbach, A. (2010): A Silver Lining of Standing in Line: Queuing Increases Value of Products, in: Journal of Marketing Research, Vol. 47, No. 4, pp. 713–724.

Koppelmann, U. (1997): Produktmarketing [Product Marketing], 5th ed., Berlin et al.: Springer.

Koppelmann, U. (2006): Marketing: Einführung in Entscheidungsprobleme des Absatzes und der Beschaffung [Marketing: Introduction to Decisions in Marketing and Sourcing], 8th ed., Stuttgart: Lucius & Lucius.

Kotler, P. (1965): Behavioral Models for Analyzing Buyers, in: Journal of Marketing, Vol. 29, No. 4, pp. 37–45.

Kotler, P., & Armstrong, G. (2012): Principles of Marketing, 14th ed., Upper Saddle River, NJ: Pearson.

Kotler, P., & Keller, K.L. (2012): Marketing Management, 14th global ed., Harlow et al.: Pearson.

Kozinets, R.V., Sherry, J.F., DeBerry-Spence, B., Duhachek, A., Nuttavuthisi, K., & Storm, D. (2002): Themed Flagship Brand Stores in the New Millenium: Theory, Practice, Prospects, in: Journal of Retailing, Vol. 78, No. 1, pp. 17–29.

Kreutzer, R.T. (2014): Praxisorientiertes Online-Marketing: Konzepte – Instrumente – Checklisten [Practitioners' Guide to Online Marketing: Concepts – Instruments – Checklists], 2nd ed., Wiesbaden: Gabler.

Lagardère, & Ipsos (2012): Welche Informationsquellen beeinflussen Ihren Kauf von Luxusprodukten? [Which Information Sources Do Influence Your Luxury Goods Purchase?], in: Horizont, Vol. 19, retrieved January 12, 2015 from http://de.statista.comlogin.bibproxy.whu.edu/statistik/daten/studie/224387/umfrage/einfluss-von-informationsquellen-beim-kauf-von-luxusprodukten-je-einkommen/.

Lamb, R. (2012): Burberry Unleashes Tech Expertise, Heritage with Most-Advanced Brand Flagship, in: Luxurydaily.com, retrieved March 23, 2015 from http://www.luxurydaily.com/burberry-unleashes-tech-savvy-heritage-with-new-flagship-launch/.

Lamb, R. (2012): Swarovski St. Valentine's Day Discounts Could Harm Jeweler's luxury Status, in: Luxurydaily.com, retrieved January 31, 2012, from http://

www.luxurydaily.com/swarovski-drives-online-transactions-through-st-valentine%e2%80%99s-day-promotion/.

Lammenett, E. (2014): Praxiswissen Online-Marketing: Affiliate- und E-Mail-Marketing, Suchmaschinenmarketing, Online-Werbung, Social Media, Online-PR [Practitioners' Guide to Online Marketing: Affiliate Marketing, E-Mail Marketing, Search Engine Marketing, Online Advertising, Social Media, Online Public Relations], 4th ed., Wiesbaden: Gabler.

Lasslop, I. (2005): Identitätsorientierte Führung von Luxusmarken [Identity-Oriented Luxury Brand Management], in: Meffert, H., Burmann, C., & Koers, M. (Eds.): Markenmanagement: Identitätsorientierte Markenführung und praktische Umsetzung [Brand Management: Identity-Oriented Branding And Implementation], 2nd ed., Wiesbaden: Gabler, pp. 469–494.

Lavoie, M. (1992): Towards a New Research Programme for Post-Keynesianism and Neo-Ricardianism, in: Review of Political Economy, Vol. 4, No. 1, pp. 37–78.

Leibenstein, H. (1950): Bandwagon, Snob, and Veblen Effects in the Theory of Consumers' Demand, in: Quarterly Journal of Economics, Vol. 64, No. 2, pp. 183–207.

Lévi-Strauss, C. (1965): The Principle of Reciprocity, in Coser, L.A. & Rosenberg, B. (Eds.): Sociological Theory, 1st ed., New York: Macmillan.

Levy, M., & Weitz, B.A. (2009): Retailing Management, 7th ed., Boston: McGraw-Hill.

Lichtenstein, D.R., Ridgway, N.M., & Netemeyer, R.G. (1993): Price Perceptions and Consumer Shopping Behavior: A Field Study, in: Journal of Marketing Research, Vol. 30, No. 2, pp. 234–245.

Li, H., Kuo, C., & Rusell, M.G. (1999): The Impact of Perceived Channel Utilities, Shopping Orientations, and Demographics on the Consumer's Online Buying Behavior, in: Journal of Computer-Mediated Communication, Vol. 5, No. 2.

Liu, X., Burns, A.C., & Hou, Y. (2013): Comparing Online and In-Store Shopping Behavior Towards Luxury Goods, in: International Journal of Retail & Distribution Management, Vol. 41, No. 11/12, pp. 885–900.

Loropiana.com (2014): Loro Piana e La Vicuña, retrieved October 6, 2014 from http://www.loropiana.com/flash.html#/lang:en/panel:section/Loro_Piana_e_la_Vicuna.

Loropiana.com (2015): Zürich, retrieved February 25, 2015 from http://www.loropiana.com/flash.html#/lang:en/panel:store/CITY%7CZÜRICH.

Louisvuitton.com (2014): Website, retrieved July 30, 2014 from http://eu.louisvuitton.com/eng-e1/homepage.

Louisvuitton.com (2015a): Locate a Store, retrieved February 25, 2015 from http://eu.louisvuitton.com/eng-e1/stores.

Louisvuitton.com (2015b): SC Bag PM, retrieved January 19, 2015 from http://us.louisvuitton.com/eng-us/products/sc-bag-pm-006818#M48888.

Louisvuitton.com (2015c): Speedy 30, retrieved January 19, 2015 from http://us.louisvuitton.com/eng-us/products/speedy-30-monogram-008784.

Louisvuitton.com (2015d): Stories: Monogram Icons, retrieved March 13, 2015 from http://uk.louisvuitton.com/eng-gb/stories/monogram-icons.

Lovett, G. (2014): High-Class Performance: Luxury Brands Find New Confidence in Affiliate Marketing, retrieved August 2, 2014, from http://www.thedrum.com/news/2014/03/25/high-class-performance-luxury-brands-find-new-confidence-affiliate-marketing.

Lovett, M.J., Peres, R., & Shachar, R. (2013): On Brands and Word of Mouth, in: Journal of Marketing Research, Vol. 50, No. 4, pp. 427–444.

Luxury Institute (2012): High-Income Shoppers Talk Openly About Luxury Salespeople; Relationships With Wealthy Customers Blossom When Staff Shows Knowledge, Professionalism and Courtesy, in: The Luxury Institute News, retrieved May 25, 2015 from http://luxuryinstitute.com/blog/?p=2212.

LVMH.com (2015): 2014 Consolidated Financial Statements, retrieved May 27, 2015 from http://r.lvmh-static.com/uploads/2015/03/lvmh_consolidated-financial-statements-2014-va.pdf.

LVMH.com (2014a): Acqua di Parma, retrieved October 3, 2014 from http://www.lvmh.com/the-group/lvmh-companies-and-brands/perfumes-cosmetics/acqua-di-parma.

LVMH.com (2014b): Ardbeg, retrieved October 3, 2014 from http://www.lvmh.com/the-group/lvmh-companies-and-brands/wines-spirits/ardbeg.

LVMH.com (2014c): Belvedere, retrieved October 3, 2014 from http://www.lvmh.com/the-group/lvmh-companies-and-brands/wines-spirits/belvedere.

LVMH.com (2014d): BeneFit Cosmetics, retrieved October 3, 2014 from http://www.lvmh.com/the-group/lvmh-companies-and-brands/perfumes-cosmetics/benefit-cosmetics.

LVMH.com (2014e): Berluti, retrieved October 3, 2014 from http://www.lvmh.com/the-group/lvmh-companies-and-brands/fashion-leather-goods/berluti.

LVMH.com (2014f): Bodega Chandon Argentina, retrieved October 3, 2014 from http://www.lvmh.com/the-group/lvmh-companies-and-brands/wines-spirits/bodega-chandon-argentina.

LVMH.com (2014g): Bulgari, retrieved October 3, 2014 from http://www.lvmh.com/the-group/lvmh-companies-and-brands/watches-jewelry/bulgari.

LVMH.com (2014h): Cape Mentelle, retrieved October 3, 2014 from http://www.lvmh.com/the-group/lvmh-companies-and-brands/wines-spirits/cape-mentelle.

LVMH.com (2014i): Céline, retrieved October 3, 2014 from http://www.lvmh.com/the-group/lvmh-companies-and-brands/fashion-leather-goods/celine.

LVMH.com (2014j): Chateau Cheval Blanc, retrieved October 3, 2014 from http://www.lvmh.com/the-group/lvmh-companies-and-brands/wines-spirits/chateau-cheval-blanc.

LVMH.com (2014k): Chateau d'Yquem, retrieved October 3, 2014 from http://www.lvmh.com/the-group/lvmh-companies-and-brands/wines-spirits/chateau-d-yquem.

LVMH.com (2014l): Chaumet, retrieved October 3, 2014 from http://www.lvmh.com/the-group/lvmh-companies-and-brands/watches-jewelry/chaumet.

LVMH.com (2014m): Cheval des Andes, retrieved October 3, 2014 from http://www.lvmh.com/the-group/lvmh-companies-and-brands/wines-spirits/cheval-des-andes.

LVMH.com (2014n): Christian Dior Parfums, retrieved October 3, 2014 from http://www.lvmh.com/the-group/lvmh-companies-and-brands/perfumes-cosmetics/parfums-christian-dior.

LVMH.com (2014o): Cloudy Bay, retrieved October 3, 2014 from http://www.lvmh.com/the-group/lvmh-companies-and-brands/wines-spirits/cloudy-bay.

LVMH.com (2014p): De Beers, retrieved October 3, 2014 from http://www.lvmh.com/the-group/lvmh-companies-and-brands/watches-jewelry/de-beers.

LVMH.com (2014q): Domaine Chandon Australia, retrieved October 3, 2014 from http://www.lvmh.com/the-group/lvmh-companies-and-brands/wines-spirits/domaine-chandon-australia.

LVMH.com (2014r): Domaine Chandon California, retrieved October 3, 2014 from http://www.lvmh.com/the-group/lvmh-companies-and-brands/wines-spirits/domaine-chandon-california.

LVMH.com (2014s): Domaine Chandon China, retrieved October 3, 2014 from http://www.lvmh.com/the-group/lvmh-companies-and-brands/wines-spirits/domaine-chandon-china.

LVMH.com (2014t): Domaine Chandon India, retrieved October 3, 2014 from http://www.lvmh.com/the-group/lvmh-companies-and-brands/wines-spirits/domaine-chandon-india.

LVMH.com (2014u): Dom Perignon, retrieved October 3, 2014 from http://www.lvmh.com/the-group/lvmh-companies-and-brands/wines-spirits/dom-perignon.

LVMH.com (2014v): Donna Karan, retrieved October 3, 2014 from http://www.lvmh.com/the-group/lvmh-companies-and-brands/fashion-leather-goods/don na-karan.

LVMH.com (2014w): Edun, retrieved October 3, 2014 from http://www.lvmh.com/the-group/lvmh-companies-and-brands/fashion-leather-goods/edun.

LVMH.com (2014x): Emilio Pucci, retrieved October 3, 2014 from http://www.lvmh.com/the-group/lvmh-companies-and-brands/fashion-leather-goods/emilio-pucci.

LVMH.com (2014y): Fendi, retrieved October 3, 2014 from http://www.lvmh.com/the-group/lvmh-companies-and-brands/fashion-leather-goods/fendi.

LVMH.com (2014z): Fendi Perfumes, retrieved October 3, 2014 from http://www.lvmh.com/the-group/lvmh-companies-and-brands/perfumes-cosmetics/fendi-perfumes.

LVMH.com (2014aa): FRED, retrieved October 3, 2014 from http://www.lvmh.com/the-group/lvmh-companies-and-brands/watches-jewelry/fred.

LVMH.com (2014ab): Fresh, retrieved October 3, 2014 from http://www.lvmh.com/the-group/lvmh-companies-and-brands/perfumes-cosmetics/fresh.

LVMH.com (2014ac): Givenchy, retrieved October 3, 2014 from http://www.lvmh.com/the-group/lvmh-companies-and-brands/fashion-leather-goods/givenchy.

LVMH.com (2014ad): Glenmorangie, retrieved October 3, 2014 from http://www.lvmh.com/the-group/lvmh-companies-and-brands/wines-spirits/the-glenmo rangie-company.

LVMH.com (2014ae): Guerlain, retrieved October 3, 2014 from http://www.lvmh.com/the-group/lvmh-companies-and-brands/perfumes-cosmetics/guerlain.

LVMH.com (2014af): Hennessy, retrieved October 3, 2014 from http://www.lvmh.com/the-group/lvmh-companies-and-brands/wines-spirits/hennessy.

LVMH.com (2014ag): Hublot, retrieved October 3, 2014 from http://www.lvmh.com/the-group/lvmh-companies-and-brands/watches-jewelry/hublot.

LVMH.com (2014ah): Kenzo, retrieved October 3, 2014 from http://www.lvmh.com/the-group/lvmh-companies-and-brands/fashion-leather-goods/kenzo.

LVMH.com (2014ai): Kenzo Parfums, retrieved October 3, 2014 from http://www.lvmh.com/the-group/lvmh-companies-and-brands/perfumes-cosmetics/kenzo-parfums.

LVMH.com (2014aj): Krug, retrieved October 3, 2014 from http://www.lvmh.com/the-group/lvmh-companies-and-brands/wines-spirits/krug.

LVMH.com (2014ak): Loewe, retrieved October 3, 2014 from http://www.lvmh.com/the-group/lvmh-companies-and-brands/fashion-leather-goods/loewe.

LVMH.com (2014al): Loro Piana, retrieved October 3, 2014 from http://www.lvmh.com/the-group/lvmh-companies-and-brands/fashion-leather-goods/loro-piana.

LVMH.com (2014am): Louis Vuitton, retrieved October 3, 2014 from http://www.lvmh.com/the-group/lvmh-companies-and-brands/fashion-leather-goods/louis-vuitton.

LVMH.com (2014an): LVMH Letter to the Shareholders March 2014, retrieved January 26, 2015 from http://www.lvmh.com/uploads/assets/Com-fi/Documents/fr/Lettre_aux_actionnaires/Letter_to_shareholders_March_2014_-_e-accessible_version.pdf.

LVMH.com (2014ao): MAKE UP FOR EVER, retrieved October 3, 2014 from http://www.lvmh.com/the-group/lvmh-companies-and-brands/perfumes-cosmetics/make-up-for-ever.

LVMH.com (2014ap): Marc Jacobs, retrieved October 3, 2014 from http://www.lvmh.com/the-group/lvmh-companies-and-brands/fashion-leather-goods/marc-jacobs.

LVMH.com (2014aq): Mercier, retrieved October 3, 2014 from http://www.lvmh.com/the-group/lvmh-companies-and-brands/wines-spirits/mercier.

LVMH.com (2014ar): Moët Chandon, retrieved October 3, 2014 from http://www.lvmh.com/the-group/lvmh-companies-and-brands/wines-spirits/moet-chandon.

LVMH.com (2014as): Newton Vineyard, retrieved October 3, 2014 from http://www.lvmh.com/the-group/lvmh-companies-and-brands/wines-spirits/newton-vineyard.

LVMH.com (2014at): Nicholas Kirkwood, retrieved October 3, 2014 from http://www.lvmh.com/the-group/lvmh-companies-and-brands/fashion-leather-goods/nicholas-kirkwood.

LVMH.com (2014au): NOWNESS, retrieved October 3, 2014 from http://www.lvmh.com/the-group/lvmh-companies-and-brands/fashion-leather-goods/nowness.

LVMH.com (2014av): Nude, retrieved October 3, 2014 from http://www.lvmh.com/the-group/lvmh-companies-and-brands/perfumes-cosmetics/nude.

LVMH.com (2014aw): Numanthia, retrieved October 3, 2014 from http://www.lvmh.com/the-group/lvmh-companies-and-brands/wines-spirits/numanthia.

LVMH.com (2014ax): Parfums Givenchy, retrieved October 3, 2014 from http://www.lvmh.com/the-group/lvmh-companies-and-brands/perfumes-cosmetics/parfums-givenchy.

LVMH.com (2014ay): Perfumes Loewe, retrieved October 3, 2014 from http://www.lvmh.com/the-group/lvmh-companies-and-brands/perfumes-cosmetics/perfumes-loewe.

LVMH.com (2014az): Ruinart, retrieved October 3, 2014 from http://www.lvmh.com/the-group/lvmh-companies-and-brands/wines-spirits/ruinart.

LVMH.com (2014ba): Tag Heuer, retrieved October 3, 2014 from http://www.lvmh.com/the-group/lvmh-companies-and-brands/watches-jewelry/tag-heuer.

LVMH.com (2014bb): Terrazas de los Andes, retrieved October 3, 2014 from http://www.lvmh.com/the-group/lvmh-companies-and-brands/wines-spirits/terrazas-de-los-andes.

LVMH.com (2014bc): Thomas Pink, retrieved October 3, 2014 from http://www.lvmh.com/the-group/lvmh-companies-and-brands/fashion-leather-goods/thomas-pink.

LVMH.com (2014bd): Veuve Clicquot, retrieved October 3, 2014 from http://www.lvmh.com/the-group/lvmh-companies-and-brands/wines-spirits/veuve-clicquot.

LVMH.com (2014be): Wenjun, retrieved October 3, 2014 from http://www.lvmh.com/the-group/lvmh-companies-and-brands/wines-spirits/wenjun.

LVMH.com (2014bf): Zenith, retrieved October 3, 2014 from http://www.lvmh.com/the-group/lvmh-companies-and-brands/watches-jewelry/zenith.

Lynn, M. (1989): Scarcity Effects on Desirability: Mediated by Assumed Expensiveness?, in: Journal of Economic Psychology, Vol. 10, No. 2, pp. 257–274.

Lynn, M. (1991): Scarcity Effects on Value: A Quantitative Review of the Commodity Theory Literature, in: Psychology & Marketing, Vol. 8, No. 1, pp. 43–57.

Lynn, M. (1992a): Scarcity's Enhancement of Desirability: The Role of Naive Economic Theories, in: Basic and Applied Social Psychology, Vol. 13, No. 1, pp. 67–78.

Lynn, M. (1992b): The Psychology of Unavailability: Explaining Scarcity and Cost Effects on Value, in: Basic & Applied Social Psychology, Vol. 13, No. 1, pp. 3–7.

Lynn, M., & Harris, J. (1997): The Desire for Unique Consumer Products: A New Individual Differences Scale, in: Psychology & Marketing, Vol. 14, No. 6, pp. 601–616.

Lynn, M., & Snyder, C. R. (2002): Uniqueness Seeking, in: Snyder, C.R. & Lopez, S.J. (Eds.): Handbook of Positive Psychology, 1st ed., New York, NY: Oxford University Press.

Manganari, E.E., Siomkos, G.J., & Vrechopoulos, A.P. (2009): Store Atmosphere in Web Retailing, in: European Journal of Marketing, Vol. 43, No. 9/10, pp. 1140–1153.

Mankiw, N.G., & Taylor, M.P. (2011): Economics, 2nd ed., Andover et al.: South-Western.

Manlow, V., & Nobbs, K. (2013): Form and Function of Luxury Flagships, in: Journal of Fashion Marketing and Management, Vol. 17, No. 1, pp. 49–64.

Manninger, K. (2012): Herausforderung "Multi-Channel-Management" – Luxusvermarktung im Spannungsfeld traditioneller Kanäle und digitaler Revolution [The Challenge of Multi-Channel-Managament – Luxury Brand Management Between Traditional Channels and Digital Revolution], in: Burmann, C., König, V., & Meurer, J. (Eds.): Identitätsbasierte Luxusmarkenführung [Identity-Based Luxury Brand Management], 1st ed., Wiesbaden: Springer: Gabler, pp. 237–257.

Manriquez, C. (2014): Snobby Salespeople Sell More Luxury Goods, in: Marketplace.org, retrieved May 25, 2015 from http://www.marketplace.org/topics/your-money/ask-money/snobby-salespeople-sell-more-luxury-goods.

Marn, M.V., & Rosiello, R.L. (1992): Managing Price, Gaining Profit, in: Harvard Business Review, Vol. 70, No. 5, pp. 84–94.

Marshall, A. (1920): Principles of Economics, 8th ed., London: Macmillan.

Mason, R. (1984): Conspicuous Consumption: A Literature Review, in: European Journal of Marketing, Vol. 18, No. 3, pp. 26–39.

Mason, R. (1998): The Economics of Conspicuous Consumption – Theory and Thought since 1700, 1st ed., Cheltenham: Edward Elgar.

Mason, W., & Suri, S. (2012): Conducting Behavioral Research on Amazon's Mechanical Turk, in: Behavior Research Methods, Vol. 44, No. 1, pp. 1–23.

Mathwick, C., Malhotra, N., & Rigdon, E. (2001): Experiential Value: Conceptualization, Measurement and Application in the Catalog and Internet Shopping Environment, in: Journal of Retailing, Vol. 77, No. 1, pp. 39–56.

Mauss, M. (1967): The Gift: Forms and Functions of Exchange in Archaic Societies, 1st ed., New York, NY: W.W. Norton & Company.

McCarthy, E.J. (1964): Basic Marketing: A Managerial Approach, 2nd ed., Homewood, IL: Richard D. Irwin.

McCarthy, J. (2013): Nordstrom Direct President: Social Media is Word of Mouth on Steroids, in: Luxurydaily.com, retrieved August 4, 2014 from http://www.luxurydaily.com/its-not-about-channels-nordstrom-direct-president/.

McKinsey & Co. (1990): The Luxury Goods Industry: An Asset for France, unpublished study, Paris.

Media Daten Verlag (2014a): Manager Magazin Online, retrieved July 27, 2014 from https://www.mediadaten-online.com/mediadaten/popup/datenblatt/online/alledaten.do?tenantId=00021&werbetraegerId=53033.

Media Daten Verlag (2014b): VOGUE.COM, retrieved July 27, 2014 from https://www.mediadaten-online.com/mediadaten/tarife/online/mann_frau_mode_beauty_lifestyle/v/vogue_com/titel_w_23386.html.

Media Daten Verlag (2014c): WirtschaftsWoche Online, retrieved July 27, 2014 from https://www.mediadaten-online.com/mediadaten/tarife/online//wirtschaftswoche_online/titel_w_21441.html.

Meffert, H., Burmann, C., & Kirchgeorg, M. (2008): Marketing: Grundlagen Marktorientierter Unternehmensführung: Konzepte – Instrumente – Praxisbeispiele [Marketing: Fundamentals of Market-Oriented Management: Concepts – Instruments – Examples], 10th ed., Wiesbaden: Gabler.

Mikimoto.com (2014): Screenshot of Mikimoto Website, retrieved July 30, 2014 from http://www.mikimoto.com.

Miller, K.W., & Mills, M.K. (2012): Probing Brand Luxury: A Multiple Lens Approach, in: Journal of Brand Management, Vol. 20, No. 1, pp. 41–51.

Miron, A.M., & Brehm, J.W. (2006): Reactance Theory – 40 Years Later, in: Zeitschrift Für Sozialpsychologie, Vol. 37, No. 1, pp. 9–18.

Mischel, W., & Masters, J.C. (1966): Effects of Probability of Reward Attainment on Responses to Frustration, in: Journal of Personality and Social Psychology, Vol. 3, No. 4, pp. 390–396.

Mohr, H. (2013): Der Preismanagement-Prozess für Luxusmarken: Gestaltung und Erfolgsauswirkungen [The Pricing Process for Luxury Brands: Conceptualization and Performance Impact], 1st ed., Frankfurt am Main: Peter Lang.

Monetate (2014): Ecommerce Quarterly EQ4 2014: The Gift of Personalization, retrieved May 20, 2014 from http://www.monetate.com/resources/research/#ufh-i-48179143-ecommerce-quarterly-q4-2014.

Monkhouse, L.L., Barnes, B.R., & Stephan, U. (2012): The Influence of Face and Group Orientation on the Perception of Luxury Goods, in: International Marketing Review, Vol. 29, No. 6, pp. 647–672.

Monroe, K.B. (1973): Buyers' Subjective Perceptions of Price, in: Journal of Marketing Research, Vol. 10, No. 1, pp. 70–80.

Monroe, K.B. (2003): Pricing: Making Profitable Decisions, 3rd ed., New York, NY: McGraw-Hill Irwin.

Montblanc.com (2014a): About Us, retrieved August 28, 2014 from http://www.montblanc.com/en-gb/flash/default.aspx/#/corporate/about-us.

Montblanc.com (2014b): Browse All Writing Instruments, retrieved September 22, 2014 from http://www.montblanc.com/en-gb/shop/writing-instruments/browse.aspx.

Montblanc.com (2014c): Meisterstück 90 Years 149 Fountain Pen, retrieved September 22, 2014 from http://www.montblanc.com/en-gb/flash/default.aspx/#/collections/writing-instruments/unisex/meisterstck/meisterstueck-90-years/meisterstuck-90-years-149-fountain-pen-111062.

Montblanc.com (2015a): Homepage, retrieved March 19, 2015 from http://www.montblanc.com/en-gb/default.aspx.

Montblanc.com (2015b): Meisterstück 90 Years 149 Fountain Pen, retrieved February 12, 2015 from http://www.montblanc.com/en-gb/shop/writing-instruments/meisterstck/meisterstueck-90-years/meisterstuck-90-years-149-fountain-pen-111062.aspx.

Montblanc.com (2015c): Shop, retrieved March 16, 2015 from http://www.montblanc.com/de-de/shop/default.aspx?sc_lang=de-de.

Montegrappa.com (2014): About Montegrappa, retrieved September 22, 2014 from http://www.montegrappa.com/about_montegrappa.html.

Moore, C.M. & Birtwistle, G. (2004): The Burberry Business Model: Creating an INternational Luxury Fashion Brand, in: International Journal of Retail & Distribution Management, Vol. 32, No. 8, pp. 412–422.

Moore, C.M., Doherty, A.M., & Doyle, S.A. (2010): Flagship Stores As A Market Entry Method: The Perspective of Luxury Fashion Retailing, in: European Journal of Marketing, Vol. 44, No. 1/2, pp. 139–161.

Motorauthority.com (2015): Lamborghini Renews Ad Personam Personalization Program, retrieved February 9, 2015 from http://www.motorauthority.com/news/1090560_lamborghini-renews-ad-personam-personalization-program.

Mülder, W., & Weis, H.C. (1996): Computerintegriertes Marketing [Computer-Integrated Marketing], 1st ed., Ludwigshafen: Kiehl.

Müller-Hagedorn, L. (2002): Handelsmarketing [Retail Marketing], 3rd ed., Stuttgart: Kohlhammer.

Nagasawa, S. (2008): Marketing Principles of Louis Vuitton: The Strongest Brand Strategy, in: Waseda Business & Economic Studies, Vol. 44, pp. 41–54.

Nagle, T.T., Hogan, J.E., & Zale, J. (2011): The Strategy and Tactics of Pricing: A Guide to Growing More Profitably, 5th ed., Upper Saddle River, NJ: Pearson.

Nelson, P. (1970): Information and Consumer Behavior, in: Journal of Political Economy, Vol. 78, No. 2, pp. 311–329.

Nelson, P. (1974): Advertising as Information, in: Journal of Political Economy, Vol. 82, No. 4, pp. 729–754.

Nielsen, J., & Tahir, M. (2001): Homepage Usability: 50 Websites Deconstructed, 1st ed., Upper Saddle River, NJ: New Riders Publishing.

Nieschlag, R., Dichtl, E., & Hörschgen, H. (2002): Marketing [Marketing], 19th ed., Berlin: Duncker & Humblot.

Nueno, J.L., & Quelch, J.A. (1998): The Mass Marketing of Luxury, in: Business Horizons, Vol. 41, No. 6, pp. 61–68.

Nymphenburg.com (2014): Auszubildende, retrieved October 6, 2014 from http://www.nymphenburg.com/de/manufaktur/people/auszubildende.

Nymphenburg.com (2015a): Cumberland, retrieved February 10, 2015 from http://www.nymphenburg.com/de/produkte/service/cumberland.

Nymphenburg.com (2015b): FAQ, retrieved February 10, 2015 from http://www.nymphenburg.com/de/faq.

Nymphenburg.com (2015c): Rhinoceros Clara, retrieved February 6, 2015 from http://www.nymphenburg.com/de/shop/best.of.seasonals/rhinozeros.clara/15562.html.

Odyssee.Cartier.us. (2014): Film, retrieved October 7, 2014 from http://www.odyssee.cartier.us/#/film.

Okonkwo, U. (2007): Luxury Fashion Branding: Trends, Tactics, Techniques, 1st ed., Basingstoke & New York, NY: Palgrave Macmillan.

Okonkwo, U. (2009): Sustaining the Luxury Brand on the Internet, in: Journal of Brand Management, Vol. 16, No. 5/6, pp. 302–310.

Okonkwo, U. (2010): Luxury Online: Styles, Systems, Strategies. 1st ed., Basingstoke & New York, NY: Palgrave Macmillan.

Omas.com (2014): History, retrieved September 22, 2014, from http://www.omas.com/en/manufacture/.

Outnet.com (2015a): Designers, retrieved March 23, 2015 from http://www.theoutnet.com/en-DE/Shop/Designers.

Outnet.com (2015b): Home, retrieved March 23, 2015 from http://www.theoutnet.com/en-DE/.

Overby, J.W., & Lee, E.-J. (2006): The Effects of Utilitarian and Hedonic Online Shopping Value on Consumer Preference and Intentions, in: Journal of Business Research, Vol. 59, No. 10/11, pp. 1160–1166.

OVK, & BVDW (2013): OVK Online Report 2013/02: Zahlen und Trends im Überblick [OVK Online Report 2013/02: An Overview of Figures and Trends], retrieved August 2, 2014, from http://www.bvdw.org/medien/ovk-online-report-2013-02?media=5152.

Oxforddictionaries.com (2014): Rarity, retrieved October 6, 2014 from http://www.oxforddictionaries.com/definition/english/rarity.

Pantzalis, I. (1995): Exclusivity Strategies in Pricing and Brand Extension, doctoral dissertation, The University of Arizona, retrieved August 31, 2014 from http://arizona.openrepository.com/arizona/bitstream/10150/187351/1/azu_td_9620410_sip1_m.pdf.

Parguel, B., Delécolle, T., & Valette-Florence, P. (2014): The Impact of Price Display on Luxury Perceptions, in: Proceedings of the 2014 Monaco Symposium on Luxury, April 10th–11th, 2014, Monaco.

Park, C., & Kim, Y. (2003): Identifying Key Factors Affecting Consumer Purchase Behavior in An Online Shopping Context, in: International Journal of Retail & Distribution Management, Vol. 31, No. 1, pp. 16–29.

Patek.com (2014a): 5078R, retrieved July 2, 2014 from www.patek.com/contents/default/de/5078R_001.html.

Patek.com (2014b): Company: History, retrieved September 22, 2014 from http://www.patek.com/contents/default/en/timeline.html.

Patek.com (2014c): Manufacturing, retrieved October 6, 2014 from http://www.patek.com/en/company/workshops/manufacturing.

Patek.com (2014d): Product Advertising, retrieved October 6, 2014 from http://www.patek.com/contents/default/en/advertisingcampaign.html.

Patek.com (2014e): The Manufacture, retrieved October 6, 2014 from http://www.patek.com/en/company/the-manufacture.

Patek.com (2015a): Calatrava Cross Cuff Links, retrieved February 12, 2015 from http://www.patek.com/en/collection/jewelry.

Patek.com (2015b): The Patek Philippe Salons, retrieved March 31, 2015 from http://www.patek.com/en/retail-network/patek-philippe-salons.

Paton, E. (2012): Flagship Stores: Groups Look East As Clients Head West, in: Financial Times, retrieved July 19, 2015 from http://www.ft.com/cms/s/0/061f100c-a33d-11e1-ab98-00144feabdc0.html#axzz3gLUzZe5L.

Peterson, R.A., Balasubramanian, S., & Bronnenberg, B.J. (1997): Exploring the Implication of the Internet for Consumer Marketing, in: Journal of the Academy of Marketing Science, Vol. 25, No. 4, pp. 329–346.

Peterson, R.A., & Jolibert, A.J.P. (1995): A Meta-Analysis of Country-of-Origin Effects, in: Journal of International Business Studies, Vol. 26, No. 4, pp. 883–900.

Pew Research Center (2013a): Age Distribution of Social Network Users in the United States in June 2012 (in percent), retrieved August 3, 2014 from http://www.statista.com/statistics/243582/age-distribution-of-internet-users-in-the-united-states-since-2008/.

Pew Research Center (2013b): Share of Internet Users Who Use Social Networking in the United States in May 2013 (by Annual Income), retrieved August 3, 2014 from http://www.statista.com/statistics/265068/share-of-us-social-network-users-by-annual-income/.

Phau, I., & Prendergast, G. (2000): Consuming Luxury Brands: The Relevance of the "Rarity Principle", in: Journal of Brand Management, Vol. 8, No. 2, pp. 122–138.

Piaget.com (2014a): History, retrieved September 22, 2014 from http://www.piaget.com/history.

Piaget.com (2014b): Screenshot of Piaget Website, retrieved July 24, 2014 from http://www.piaget.com.

Piaget.com (2015a): Piaget Altiplano Skeleton Watch, retrieved January 19, 2015 from http://www.piaget.com/watches/white-gold-ultra-thin-skeleton-watch-g0a37132.

Piaget.com (2015b): Piaget Altiplano Watch, retrieved January 19, 2015 from http://www.piaget.com/watches/white-gold-ultra-thin-mechanical-watch-g0a29112.

Porsche.com (2014): Thank You – A 1'000'000 Times, retrieved July 21, 2014 from http://www.porsche.com/microsite/facebook/international.aspx.

Probe, A. (2007): Die Handels-WG [Retail Alliances], in: Textilwirtschaft, retrieved May 21, 2015 from http://www.textilwirtschaft.de/suche/show.php?ids%5B%5D=597274.

PRWeb (2005): Did-It, Enquiro, and Eyetools Uncover Google's Golden Triangle, retrieved July 29, 2014 from http://www.prweb.com/releases/2005/3/prweb213516.htm.

Puri, R. (2014): The Top 5 Content Marketing Metrics Your CMO Cares About, retrieved July 30, 2014, from http://blog.newscred.com/article/the-top-5-content-marketing-metrics-your-cmo-cares-about/43298b61109cd2af43a85a7edbd9f27d.

Quelch, J.A. (1987): Marketing the Premium Product, in: Business Horizons, Vol. 30, No. 3, pp. 38–45.

Quintavalle, A. (2012): Retailing in the Luxury Industry, in: Hoffmann, J., & Coste-Manière, I. (Eds.): Luxury Strategy in Action, 1st ed., Basingstoke: Palgrave Macmillan, pp. 74–107.

Rae, J. (1905): The Sociological Theory of Capital, reprint of 1834, Macmillan, retrieved September 10, 2014 from https://ia600300.us.archive.org/25/items/sociologicaltheo00raejuoft/sociologicaltheo00raejuoft.pdf.

Ralphlauren.de (2014): Home, retrieved July 1, 2014 from m.ralphlauren.de/home.

Rao, A.R., & Monroe, K.B. (1989): The Effect of Price, Brand Name, and Store Name on Buyers' Perceptions of Product Quality: An Integrative Review, in: Journal of Marketing Research, Vol. 26, No. 3, pp. 351–357.

Rao, V.R. (1984): Pricing Research in Marketing: The State of the Art, in: The Journal of Business, Vol. 57, No. 1, pp. 39–60.

Rebelle.de (2014): Louis Vuitton, retrieved October 6, 2014 from https://www.rebelle.de/louis-vuitton.

Reddy, M., Terblanche, N., Pitt, L., & Parent, M. (2009): How Far Can Luxury Brands Travel? Avoiding the Pitfalls of Luxury Brand Extension, in: Business Horizons, Vol. 52, No. 2, pp. 187–197.

Reich, C. (2005): Faszinationskraft von Luxusmarken: Eine empirische Untersuchung der Determinanten der Begehrlichkeit im Hinblick auf Luxusmarken und der resultierenden Wirkung auf die Kaufabsicht [Fascination Luxury Brands: An Empirical Investigation on The Determinants of Desirability of Luxury Brands And Its Impact On Purchase Intention], 1st ed., München & Mering: Rainer Hampp.

Reuters.com (2013): Louis Vuitton Slows Down Expansion to Protect Image, retrieved March 9, 2015 from http://www.reuters.com/article/2013/01/31/lvmh-results-idUSL5N0B0GM820130131.

Richemont.com (2006): Richemont Annual Report and Accounts 2006, retrieved January 26, 2015 from https://www.richemont.com/images/investor_relations/reports/annual_report/2006/richemont_annual_report_2006.pdf.

Richemont.com (2014): Our Businesses, retrieved October 2, 2014 from https://www.richemont.com/our-businesses.html.

Riley, F.D., & Lacroix, C. (2003): Luxury Branding on the Internet: Lost Opportunity or Impossibility?, in: Marketing Intelligence & Planning, Vol. 21, No. 2, pp. 96–104.

Robeson, M. (2012): How Luxury Brands Can Reinvent the Customer Experience, retrieved July 16, 2014, from http://loyalty360.org/loyalty-management/2012-q1/how-luxury-brands-can-reinvent-the-customer-experience.

Rohm, A.J., & Swaminathan, V. (2004): A Typology of Online Shoppers Based on Shopping Motivations, in: Journal of Business Research, Vol. 57, No. 7, pp. 748–757.

Roland Berger, & Meisterkreis (2013): High-End Online Deutschland, retrieved September 12, 2013 from http://www.rolandberger.com/media/pdf/Roland_Berger_High_end_Online_D_20130523.pdf.

Rolex.com (2015a): About Rolex: Oyster Case, retrieved March 31, 2015 from http://www.rolex.com/about-rolex/oyster-case.html.

Rolex.com (2015b): About Rolex: Rolex History, retrieved March 31, 2015 from http://www.rolex.com/about-rolex/rolex-history/1905-1919.html.

Rolls-roycemotorcars.com (2012): Phantom Coupé, retrieved February 11, 2015 from https://www.press.rolls-roycemotorcars.com/rolls-royce-motor-cars-pressclub/photoDetail.html?title=rolls-royce-phantom-coupÉ&docNo=P90103188.

Rolls-roycemotorcars.com (2013a): 40/50 HP Silver Dawn, retrieved February 11, 2015 from https://www.press.rolls-roycemotorcars.com/rolls-royce-motor-cars-pressclub/photoDetail.html?title=rolls-royce-40-50-hp-the-silver-dawn-on-the-2013-centenary-alpine-trial&docNo=P90129307.

Rolls-roycemotorcars.com (2013b): 1933 Phantom II, retrieved February 11, 2015 from https://www.press.rolls-roycemotorcars.com/rolls-royce-motor-cars-press-club/photoDetail.html?title=1933-rolls-royce-phantom-ii&docNo=P90140900.

Rolls-roycemotorcars.com (2013c): 1965 Silver Cloud III, retrieved February 11, 2015 from https://www.press.rolls-roycemotorcars.com/rolls-royce-motor-cars-pressclub/photoDetail.html?title=1965-rolls-royce-silver-cloud-iii-james-young-sports-saloon-at-the-2013-goodwood-revival&docNo=P90133666.

Rolls-roycemotorcars.com (2014a): 1904 Rolls-Royce 10HP, retrieved February 11, 2015 from https://www.press.rolls-roycemotorcars.com/rolls-royce-motor-cars-pressclub/photoDetail.html?title=1904-rolls-royce-10hp-two-cylinder-car&docNo=P90157893.

Rolls-roycemotorcars.com (2014b): Silver Ghost, 1916, retrieved February 11, 2015 from https://www.press.rolls-roycemotorcars.com/rolls-royce-motor-cars-press-club/photoDetail.html?title=colonel-t-e-lawrence-and-rolls-royce-silver-ghost-tender-1916&docNo=P90157907.

Rolls-roycemotorcars.com (2014c): Silver Seraph, retrieved February 11, 2015 from https://www.press.rolls-roycemotorcars.com/rolls-royce-motor-cars-pressclub/photoDetail.html?title=rolls-royce-silver-seraph&docNo=P90166835.

Rolls-roycemotorcars.com (2014d): Silver Shadow I, retrieved February 11, 2015 from https://www.press.rolls-roycemotorcars.com/rolls-royce-motor-cars-pressclub/photoDetail.html?title=rolls-royce-silver-shadow-i-london&docNo=P90166855.

Rolls-roycemotorcars.com (2015a): Find a Dealer, retrieved February 25, 2015 from http://www.rolls-roycemotorcars.com// (pop-up window).

Rolls-roycemotorcars.com (2015b): Ghost Rim, retrieved February 12, 2015 from https://www.press.rolls-roycemotorcars.com/rolls-royce-motor-cars-pressclub/photoDetail.html?title=rolls-royce-ghost&docNo=P90134182.

Rolls-roycemotorcars.com (2015c): Service & Aftercare, retrieved February 10, 2015 from http://www.rolls-roycemotorcars.com/ownership/service-and-aftercare/.

Rolls-roycemotorcars.com (2015d): Spirit of Ecstasy, retrieved February 12, 2015 from https://www.press.rolls-roycemotorcars.com/rolls-royce-motor-cars-press club/photoDetail.html?title=rolls-royce-spirit-of-ecstasy&docNo=P90105170.

Roper, S., Caruana, R., Medway, D., & Murphy, P. (2013): Constructing Luxury Brands: Exploring the Role of Consumer Discourse, in: European Journal of Marketing, Vol. 47, No. 3/4, pp. 375–400.

Rosenbaum, M. (2014): Commercial Friendships Between Gay Sales Associates and Straight Female Customers in Luxury Settings, in: Proceedings of the 2014 Monaco Symposium on Luxury, April 10th–11th, 2014, Monaco.

Rosenberg, M. (1979): Conceiving the Self. New York, NY: Basic Books.

Rosow, D. (2013): Luxury Online Stores: An Empirical Examination of Luxury-Specific Web Store Characteristics, unpublished thesis at the WHU – Otto Beisheim School of Management, Vallendar.

Rumpf, K. (2010): Preis und Markendehnung: Eine Empirische Analyse [Price and Brand Extension: An Empirical Analysis], 1st ed., Frankfurt am Main: Peter Lang.

Ryan, D., & Jones, C. (2012): Understanding Digital Marketing: Marketing Strategies for Engaging the Digital Generation, 2nd ed., London et al.: Kogan Page.

Rydercup.com (2008): Rolex extends Partnership with The Ryder Cup, retrieved July 16, 2014 from http://www.rydercup.com/2008/news/2008/europe/09/11/rolex_091108/index.html.

Sabharwal, V. (2015): The Customer Comes First, in: The Luxury Institute News, retrieved May 25, 2015 from http://luxuryinstitute.com/blog/?cat=11&paged=2.

Sanderson, R. (2013): Bottega Veneta Hits Luxury Sweet Spot, in: Financial Times, April 8, 2013, retrieved January 13, 2014 from http://www.ft.com/intl/cms/s/0/9a85b706-97b5-11e2-b7ef-00144feabdc0.html#axzz2qIDxYVrK.

Sarett, M.R. (1960): Effective Marketing of Jewelry, in: Journal of Marketing, Vol. 24, No. 3, pp. 51–54.

Schaal, S. (2014): "Niemand braucht einen Rolls-Royce, um von A nach B zu kommen" ["No One Needs a Rolls-Royce In Order to Get From A To B], in: Wiwo.de, retrieved September 25, 2014, from http://www.wiwo.de/unternehmen/auto/rolls-royce-chef-niemand-braucht-einen-rolls-royce-um-von-a-nach-b-zu-kom men/10749182.html.

Schmitt, B., & Simonson, A. (1998): Marketing-Ästhetik [Marketing Aesthetics], 1st ed. München et al.: Econ.

Schmitt, B., & Simonson, A. (2005): Marketing-Ästhetik für Marken [Aesthetics for Brands], in: Esch, F.-R. (Ed.): Moderne Markenführung [Modern Brand Management], 4th. ed. Wiesbaden: Gabler, pp. 305–327.

Schögel, M. (2012): Distributionsmanagement: Das Management der Absatzkanäle [Distribution Management: Managing Sales Channels], 1st ed., München: Vahlen.

Schweiger, G., & Schrattenecker, G. (2013): Werbung: Eine Einführung [Advertising: An Introduction] (8th ed.), Konstanz & München: UVK.

Sebastian, K.-H., & Maessen, A. (2003): Optionen im strategischen Preismanagement [Aspects of Strategic Pricing], in: Diller, H., & Herrmann, A. (Eds.): Hand buch Preispolitik: Strategien – Planung – Oragnisation – Umsetzung [Pricing Handbook: Strategies – Planning – Organization – Implementation], 1st ed., Wiesbaden: Gabler, pp. 49–68.

Seiders, K., Voss, G.B., Godfrey, A.L., & Grewal, D. (2007): SERVCON: Development and Validation of A Multidimensional Service Convenience Scale, in: Journal of the Academy of Marketing Science, Vol. 35, No. 1, pp. 144–156.

Seringhaus, F.H.R. (2005): Selling Luxury Brands Online, in: Journal of Internet Commerce, Vol. 4, No. 1, pp. 1–25.

Sethuraman, R., Tellis, G.J., & Briesch, R.A. (2011): How Well Does Advertising Work? Generalizations from Meta-Analysis of Brand Advertising Elasticities, in: Journal of Marketing Research, Vol. 48, No. 3, pp. 457–471.

SevenOne Media (2014): Media Activity Guide 2014, retrieved July 19, 2015 from http://viewer.zmags.com/publication/b9c9d2fc#/b9c9d2fc/1.

Simon, H., & Fassnacht, M. (2009): Preismanagement: Strategie – Analyse – Entscheidung – Umsetzung [Price Management: Strategy – Analysis – Decision – Implementation], 3rd ed., Wiesbaden: Gabler.

Sirgy, M.J. (1982): Self-Concept in Consumer Behavior: A Critical Review, in: Journal of Consumer Research, Vol. 9, No. 3, pp. 287–300.

Smith, A. (2005): An Inquiry Into The Nature And Causes Of The Wealth of Nations, repring from 1766, in: Electronic Classics Series, retrieved September 2, 2014 from http://www2.hn.psu.edu/faculty/jmanis/adam-smith/wealth-nations.pdf.

Snyder, C.R. (1992): Product Scarcity by Need for Uniqueness Interaction: A Consumer Catch022 Carousel, in: Basic & Applied Social Psychology, Vol. 13, No. 1, pp. 9–24.

Snyder, C.R., & Fromkin, H.L. (1977): Abnormality as A Positive Characteristic: The Development and Validation of A Scale Measuring Need for Uniqueness, in: Journal of Abnormal Psychology, Vol. 86, No. 5, pp. 518–527.

Snyder, C.R., & Fromkin, H.L. (1980): Uniqueness: The Human Pursuit of Difference. New York, NY: Plenum Press.

Soller, K. (2014): Luxury Brands Are Stupid to Snub the Internet, in: Bloomber Business, retrieved May 25, 2015 from http://www.bloomberg.com/bw/articles/2014-04-03/luxury-brands-should-sell-their-products-online.

Som, A., & Blanckaert, C. (2015): The Road To Luxury: The Evolution, Markets and Strategies of Luxury Brand Management, 1st ed., Hoboken: Wiley.

Sombart, W. (1913): Luxus und Kapitalismus [Luxury and Capitalism], 1st ed., München & Leipzig: Duncker & Humblot.

Specht, G., & Fritz, W. (2005): Distributionsmanagement [Distribution Management], 4th ed., Stuttgart: Kohlhammer.

Spieler, S. (2011): Luxus im Netz [Luxury in the Internet], in: Textilwirtschaft, Vol. 14, pp. 20–22.

Stankeviciute, R. (2012): Internet, Social Media and Luxury Strategy, in: Hoffmann, J. & Coste-Manière, I. (Eds.): Luxury Strategy in Action, 1st ed., Basingstoke: Palgrave Macmillan, pp. 49–68.

Statistisches Bundesamt (2014): Wirtschaftsrechnungen: Laufende Wirtschaftsrechnungen, Einnahmen und Ausgaben privater Haushalte 2012 [Economic Facts & Figures: Income and Expense of Private Households] Vol. 15, No. 1, retrieved March 31, 2015 from https://www.destatis.de/DE/Publikationen/Thematisch/EinkommenKonsum Lebensbedingungen/LfdWirtschaftsrechnungen/EinnahmenAusgabenprivaterHaushalte2150100127004.pdf?__blob=publicationFile.

Statistisches Bundesamt (2015): Monatstatistik im Einzelhandel [Monthly Retail Sales], retrieved from https://www-genesis.destatis.de/genesis/online/data;jsessionid=652A7EFBAC6B6564CDD68EEE02434228.tomcat_GO_1_1?operation=abruftabelleBearbeiten&levelindex=2&levelid=1420722951351&auswahloperation=abruftabelleAuspraegungAuswaehlen&auswahlverzeichnis=ordnungsstruktur&auswahlziel==werteabruf&selectionname=45212-0004&auswahltext=%23SWZ08E6-WZ08-4771%2CWZ08-4777%23Z-01.01.2013%2C01.01.2012%2C01.01.2011%2C01.01.2010%2C01.01.2009%23SQUARTG-QUART2%2CQUART3%2CQUART4%2 CQUART1&nummer=8&variable=4&name=QUARTG&werteabruf=Value+retrieval.

ST-Dupont.com (2014): History, retrieved September 22, 2014 from http://www.st-dupont.com/en/maison-s-t-dupont/history.html.

Steel, E. (2013): Luxury Brands Experiment With Social Media, in: Financial Times November 8, 2013, retrieved Decemer 12, 2013 from http://www.ft.com/intl/cms/s/0/b3658eb0-2f6b-11e3-8b7e-00144feab7de.html#axzz2nHnwc7DJ.

Stolpmann, M. (2000): Online-Marketingmix: Kunden finden – Kunden binden im E-Business [Online Marketing Mix: Customer Acquisition and Retention with e-Business], 1st ed., Bonn: Galileo Press.

Sullivan, M., & Adock, D. (2002): Retail Marketing, 1st ed., London: Thomson.

Swatchgroup.com (2015): Brands and Companies, retrieved March 31, 2015 from http://www.swatchgroup.com/en/brands_and_companies.

Sweeney, J.C., & Soutar, G.N. (2001): Consumer Perceived Value: The Development of A Multiple Item Scale, in: Journal of Retailing, Vol. 77, No. 2, pp. 203–220.

Szymanski, D.M., & Hise, R.T. (2000): E-Satisfaction: An Initial Examination, in: Journal of Retailing, Vol. 76, No. 3, pp. 309–322.

Tellis, G.J. (1986): Beyond the Many Faces of Price: An Integration of Pricing Strategies, in: Journal of Marketing, Vol. 50, No. 4, pp. 146–160.

Thecorner.com (2015): Shop by Corner, retrieved March 20, 2015 from http://www.thecorner.com/gb/women/shop-by-corner.

The Future of Luxury (2013): Luxury Affiliate Marketing: 5 Tips For Success In 2013, retrieved August 2, 2014 from http://www.thefutureofluxury.co.uk/luxury-affiliate-marketing-5-tips-for-success-in-2013/.

Thomas, T. (2007): Luxus: Statusstreben und demonstratives Konsumverhalten [Luxury: Need for Status and Conspicuous Consumption], 1st ed., Marburg: Tectum.

Tian, K.T., Bearden, W.O., & Hunter, G.L. (2001): Consumers' Need for Uniqueness: Scale Development and Validation, in: Journal of Consumer Research, Vol. 28, No. 1, pp. 50–66.

Tiedtke, D. (1998): Bedeutung des Online-Marketing für die Kommunikationspolitik [The Importance of Online Marketing in Communications Management], in: Link, J. (Ed.): Wettbewerbsvorteile durch Online-Marketing [Competitive Advantage Through Online Marketing], 1st ed., Berlin & Heidelberg: Springer.

Tiffany.com (2015): Return to Tiffany, retrieved February 9, 2015 from http://press.tiffany.com/ViewBackgrounder.aspx?backgrounderId=29.

Trusov, M., Bucklin, R.E., & Pauwels, K. (2009): Effects of Word-of-Mouth Versus Traditional Marketing: Findings from an Internet Social Networking Site, in: Journal of Marketing, Vol. 73, No. 5, pp. 90–102.

Twitter.com/Burberry (2014): Burberry Branded Twitter Page, retrieved July 21, 2014 from https://twitter.com/burberry.

UDG Consulting (2012): Cross Channel Excellence im Luxusgütermarketing [Cross-Channel Excellence in Luxury Goods Marketing], presented at the Meisterkreis members' meeting, March 23, 2013, Berlin.

UN Comtrade. (2012): Weltweit führende Exportnationen von Uhren nach Exportwert im Jahr 2012 [Worldwide Leading Watch Export Countries by Export Value in 2012], retrieved March 31, 2015 from http://de.statista.com/statistik/daten/studie/ 276839/umfrage/weltweit-fuehrende-exportnationen-von-uhren/.

Vacheron-constantin.com (2015): Our Heritage, retrieved March 31, 2015 from http://heritage.vacheron-constantin.com/en2/heritage.

Valtin, A. (2005): Der Wert von Luxusmarken [The Luxury Brand Equity], 1st ed., Wiesbaden: Deutscher Universitäts-Verlag.

Vancleefarpels.com (2015a): Alhambra, retrieved March 31, 2015 from http://www.vancleefarpels.com/eu/en/line/6/alhambra.

Vancleefarpels.com (2015b): Stones, retrieved from http://www.vancleefarpels.com/eu/en/the-maison/65/68/van-cleef-arpels-stones#1.

Vancleefarpels.com (2015c): Store Locator, retrieved from http://www.vancleefar pels.com/ww/en/store-locator.

Vancleefarpels.com (2015d): The Mystery Set, retrieved March 31, 2015 from http://www.vancleefarpels.com/ww/en/article/210/mystery-set-

Varian, H.R. (2010): Intermediate Microeconomics: A Modern Approach, 8th ed., New York & London: W.W. Norton & Company.

Veblen, T. (1960): The Theory of the Leisure Class: An Economic Study of Institutions, reprint of 1899, New York, NY: Macmillan Mentor Edition.

Venkatesh, A., Joy, A., Sherry Jr., J.F., & Deschenes, J. (2010): The Aesthetics of Luxury Fashion, Body and Identify Formation, in: Journal of Consumer Psychology, Vol. 20, No. 4, pp. 459–470.

Vente-privee.com (2015): Kostenlos Anmelden [Register For Free], retrieved March 23, 2015 from https://secure.de.vente-privee.com/registration/signup2?partnerid=11834&xtor=SEC-1118-GOO----[%7Bkeyword%7D]&CountryCode=DE.

Verhallen, T.M.M. (1982): Scarcity and Consumer Choice Behavior, in: Journal of Economic Psychology, Vol. 2, No. 4, pp. 299–322.

Verhallen, T.M.M., & Robben, H.S.J. (1995): Unavailability and The Evaluation of Goods, in: Kyklos, Vol. 48, No. 3, pp. 369–387.

Versace.com (2015): Ring Medusa and Greca, retrieved February 12, 2015 from http://de.versace.com/Ring-Medusa-und-Greca/DG54710-DMT1,de_DE,pd.html&q=medusa#!i%3D20%26color%3DD00HS%26start%3D75%26sz%3D25.

Veuve-clicquot.com (2015a): Yellow Label, retrieved February 8, 2015 from http://www.veuve-clicquot.com/sites/default/files/optimized/bouteille-champ_yellow-prod.png.

Veuve-clicquot.com (2015b): Yellow Label Offers, retrieved February 8, 2015 from http://www.veuve-clicquot.com/de/champagne/yellow-label-offers#scroll-to-Traveller.

Vickers, J.S., & Renand, F. (2003): The Marketing of Luxury Goods: An exploratory study--three conceptual dimensions, in: Marketing Review, Vol. 3, No. 4, pp. 459–478.

Vigneron, F., & Johnson, L.W. (1999): A Review and a Conceptual Framework of Prestige-Seeking Consumer Behavior, in: Academy of Marketing Science Review, Vol. 1999, No. 1, pp. 1–15.

Vigneron, F., & Johnson, L.W. (2004): Measuring Perceptions of Brand Luxury, in: Journal of Brand Management, Vol. 11, No. 6, pp. 484–506.

Vitra.com (2015): Eames Plastic Armchair, retrieved January 23, 2015 from http://www.vitra.com/de-de/product/eames-plastic-armchair#t/tab-colors.

Voigt, K.-I. (2003): Presibildung für neue Produkte und Dienstleistungen [Pricing New Products and Services], in: Diller, H. & Herrmann, A. (Eds.): Handbuch Preispolitik: Strategien – Planung – Organisation – Umsetzung [Pricing Handbook: Strategies – Planning – Organization – Implementation], 1st ed., Wiesbaden: Gabler, pp. 651–718.

Völckner, F. (2006): Determinanten der Informationsfunktion des Preises: Eine empirische Analyse [Determinants of the Indicator Role of Price: An Empirical Analysis], in: ZfB – Zeitschrift Für Betriebswirtschaft, Vol. 76, No. 5, pp. 473–497.

VolkswagenAG.com (2013): Annual Report 2013, retrieved February 18, 2015 from http://www.volkswagenag.com/content/vwcorp/info_center/en/publications/2014/03/Y_2013_e.bin.html/binarystorageitem/file/GB+2013_e.pdf.

Vrechopoulos, A.P., O'Keefe, R.M., Doukidis, G.I., & Siomkos, G.J. (2004): Virtual Store Layout: An Experimental Comparison in the Context of Grocery Retail, in: Journal of Retailing, Vol. 80, No. 1, pp. 13–22.

Walster, E., Walster, G.W., & Berscheid, E. (1971): The Efficacy of Playing Hard-to-Get, in: The Journal of Experimental Education, Vol. 39, No. 3, pp. 73–77.

Walster, E., Walster, G.W., Piliavin, J., & Schmidt, L. (1973): "Playing Hard to Get": Understanding an Elusive Phenomenon, in: Journal of Personality and Social Psychology, Vol. 26, No. 1, pp. 113–121.

Walter, V. (1999): Die Zukunft des Online-Marketing: Eine explorative Studie über zukünftige Marktkommunikation im Internet [The Future of Online Marketing: An Explorative Study on the Future Market Communication in the Internet], 1st ed., München & Mering: Rainer Hampp.

Ward, M., & Dahl, D.W. (2014): Should the Devil Sell Prada? Retail Rejection Increases Aspiring Consumers' Desire for the Brand, in: Journal of Consumer Research, Vol. 41, No. 3, pp. 590–609.

Watchuseek.com (2011): Annual Production Numbers/Production Per Year for Watch Brands, retrieved September 22, 2014 from http://forums.watchuseek.com/f2/annual-production-numbers-production-per-year-watch-brands-607424.html.

Weinberg, T. (2011): Social Media Marketing: Strategien für Twitter, Facebook & Co. [Social Media Marketing: Strategies for Twitter, Facebook & Co.], 2nd ed., Köln et al.: O'Reilly.

Wetlaufer, S. (2001): The Perfect Paradox of Star Brands, in: Harvard Business Review, Vol. 79, No. 9, pp. 116–123.

WHITE Communications. (2012): Digital Luxury 2012: Eine Studie über die Zukunft [Digital Luxury 2012: A Study on the Future], retrieved January 23, 2014, from http://de.statista.com.login.bibproxy.whu.edu/statistik/studie/id/16514/dokument/informations-und-kaufverhalten-von-luxuskunden-im-internet-2013/.

Wicklund, R.A., Cooper, J., & Linder, D.E. (1967): Effects of Expected Effort on Attitude Change Prior to Exposure, in: Journal of Experimental Social Psychology, Vol. 3, No. 4, pp. 416–428.

Wiedmann, K., Hennigs, N., Klarmann, C., & Behrens, S. (2013): Creating Multi-Sensory Experiences in Luxury Marketing, in: Marketing Review St. Gallen, Vol. 30, No. 6, pp. 60–69.

Wiedmann, K.-P., Hennigs, N., & Klarmann, C. (2011): Positionierung von Luxusmarken im digitalen Umfeld: Marketingchance oder Erosion der Exklusivität? [Positioning of Luxury Brands in the Digital Space: Marketing Opportunity or Erosion of Exclusiveness?], 1st ed., Saarbrüclen: Südwestdeutscher Verlag für Hochschulschriften.

Wiedmann, K.-P., Hennigs, N., Schmidt, S., & Wuestefeld, T. (2011): Drivers and Outcomes of Brand Heritage: Consumers' Perception of Heritage Brands in the

Automotive Industry, in: Journal of Marketing Theory & Practice, Vol. 19, No. 2, pp. 205–220.

Wiedmann, K.-P., Hennigs, N., & Siebels, A. (2009): Value-Based Segmentation of Luxury Consumption Behavior, in: Psychology & Marketing, Vol. 26, No. 7, pp. 625–651.

Wieseke, J., Alavi, S., Habel, J., & Dörfer, S. (2013): Erfolgsstrategien im persönlichen Verkauf von Luxusmarken [Success Strategies for Personal Selling Luxury Brands], in: Marketing ZFP – Journal of Research and Management, Vol. 35, No. 2, pp. 131–143.

Wieseke, J., Mauer, M., & Alavi, S. (2013): Personal Selling for Luxury Brands, in: Wiedmann, K.-P. & Hennigs, N. (Eds.): Luxury Marketing, 1st ed., Wiesbaden: Gabler, pp. 359–376.

Wiesmann.com (2015): MF 4 Roadster, retrieved February 7, 2015 from http://www.wiesmann.com/en/models/roadster-mf4--mf4-s.

Wikiquote.org. (2015): Coco Chanel, retrieved February 7, 2015 from http://en.wikiquote.org/wiki/Coco_Chanel.

Wiles, M.A., & Danielova, A. (2009): The Worth of Product Placement in Successful Films: An Event Study Analysis, in: Journal of Marketing, Vol. 73, No. 4, pp. 44–63.

Williams, C. (2015): Effective Management, 7th ed., Boston, MA: Cengage Learning.

Wilson, A., Zeithaml, V.A., Bitner, M.J., & Gremler, D.D. (2012): Services Marketing: Integrating Customer Focus Across the Firm, 2nd European ed., Maidenhead: McGraw-Hill.

Wolfinbarger, M., & Gilly, M.C. (2001): Shopping Online for Freedom, Control, and Fun, in: California Management Review, Vol. 43, No. 2, pp. 34–55.

Wolf, V. (2007): E-Marketing [e-Marketing], 1st ed., München: Oldenbourg.

Worchel, S. (1992): Beyond a Commodity Theory Analysis of Censorship: When Abundance and Personalism Enhance Scarcity Effects, in: Basic & Applied Social Psychology, Vol. 13, No. 1, pp. 79–92.

Worchel, S., Lee, J., & Adewole, A. (1975): Effects of Supply and Demand on Ratings of Object Value, in: Journal of Personality & Social Psychology, Vol. 32, No. 5, pp. 906–914.

World Luxury Association (2012): The World's Most Valuable Luxury Brands 2012, retrieved March 31, 2015 from http://careers.blogs.ie.edu/files/2012/01/TOP-100-LUJO.pdf.

Wu, C., & Hsing, S. (2006): Less is More: How Scarcity Influences Consumers' Value Perceptions and Purchase Intents through Mediating Variables, in: Journal of American Academy of Business, Vol. 9, No. 2, pp. 125–132.

Wu, M.-S., Chen, C.-H., & Chaney, I. (2013): Luxury Brands in the Digital Age – the Trust Factor, in: Wiedmann, K.-P., & Hennigs, N. (Eds.), Luxury Marketing, 1st ed., Wiesbaden: Gabler, pp. 207–219.

Yooxgroup.com (2015): What We Do, retrieved March 31, 2015 from http://www.yooxgroup.com/pages/what-we-do/.

Youtube.com/user/Burberry (2014): Burberry Branded YouTube Channel, retrieved July 21, 2014 from http://www.youtube.com/user/Burberry.

Zanger, C. (2007): Leistungskern [Product Core], in: Albers, S., & Herrmann, A. (Eds.): Handbuch Produktmanagement: Strategieentwicklung – Produktplanung – Organisation – Kontrolle [Strategy Formulation – Product Planning – Organization – Control], 3rd ed., Wiesbaden: Gabler, pp. 97–117.

Zarella, D. (2010): Das Social Media Marketing Buch [The Social Media Marketing Book], 1st ed., Köln et al.: O'Reilly.

Zeithaml, V.A. (1981): How Consumer Evaluation Processes Differ Between Goods and Services, in: Donelly, J.H., & George, W.R. (Eds.): Marketing of Services, 1st ed., Chicago: American Marketing Association.

Zentes, J., Morschett, D., & Schramm-Klein, H. (2011): Strategic Retail Management, 2nd ed., Wiesbaden: Gabler.

準建築人手札網站 Forgemind ArchiMedia (2011a): Hermes 愛馬仕- Festival des Metiers 工藝節展覽 poster 01.jpg, retrieved March 31, 2015 (under CC BY 2.0 license) from https://www.flickr.com/photos/eager/6286006355/in/photolist-aztqFV-ajtMfD-ajtQA4-ajvVqE-ajtUzH-ajwuW3-ajvZDJ-ajt5rt-ajwjBE-ajtBYZ-ajthyH-ajtose-azw6Ay-akCvMd-azw6km-azw6p9-deJNnX-azum88-azue4B-azwJxj.

準建築人手札網站 Forgemind ArchiMedia (2011b): IMG_0453.JPG, retrieved March 31, 2015 (under CC BY 2.0 license) from https://www.flickr.com/photos/eager/6286006355/in/photolist-aztqFV-ajtMfD-ajtQA4-ajvVqE-ajtUzH-ajwuW3-ajvZDJ-ajt5rt-ajwjBE-ajtBYZ-ajthyH-ajtose-azw6Ay-akCvMd-azw6km-azw6p9-deJNnX-azum88-azue4B-azwJxj.

準建築人手札網站 Forgemind ArchiMedia (2011c): IMG_0470.JPG, retrieved March 31, 2015 (under CC BY 2.0 license) from https://www.flickr.com/photos/eager/6286654992/in/photolist-azugRV-azwNQm-azwWVE-azwRnu-azwJBQ-azx1Ty-aztqFV-azw6p9-azw6km-azw6Ay-azujJg-azwJxj-aztswK-aztscZ-azw7pU-azw7Ty-azueHZ-azwQu3-azx1of-azwVsd-azufaZ-azwJXw-azu21p-azu6Ka-azuaDe-azwPKC-azwJcw-azubhK-azu9B2-azwMXL-azu2Xz-azuecB-azuizi-azwTK7-azumzM-azu7ni-azwFyQ-azudpc-azucJH-azwKvj-azu7Gc-azwGX7-azwMxd-azu3GR-azwXp9-azu9Pv-azu13R-8MJvmR-8MJv62-8MMyMq.

準建築人手札網站 Forgemind ArchiMedia (2011d): 愛馬仕工藝節展覽 現場照片 05.jpg, retrieved March 31, 2015 (under CC BY 2.0 license) from https://www.flickr.com/photos/eager/6286616566/in/photolist-azwy5N-azx1d9-azwUsN-azu47nazuksZ-azwLsd-azwV7S-azuiYX-azu4vp-azugRV-azwNQm-azwWVE-azwRnu-azwJBQ-azx1Ty-aztqFV-azw6p9-azw6km-azw6Ay-azujJg-azwJxj-aztswK-aztscZ-azw7pU-azw7Ty-azueHZ-azwQu3-azx1of-azwVsd-azufaZ-azwJXw-azu21p-azu 6Ka-azuaDe-azwPKC-azwJcw-azubhK-azu9B2-azwMXL-azu2Xz-azuecB-azuizi-azwTK7-azumzM-azu7ni-azwFyQ-azudpc-azucJH-azwKvj-azu7Gc.

Appendix

Appendix 1 – List of journals by number of luxury-related articles 1948–2013

Journal	# Luxury-related articles	VHB Jourqual 3.0 Rank	Database	Date of access
Journal of Brand Management	27	C	ProQuest	16.01.2014
International Journal of Retail & Distribution Management	20	C	ProQuest	16.01.2014
Journal of Business Research	20	B	ScienceDirect	16.01.2014
European Journal of Marketing	10	C	ProQuest	16.01.2014
Marketing Review St. Gallen	9	D	ProQuest	16.01.2014
Journal of Consumer Research	8	A+	EBSCO	16.01.2014
Journal of Marketing	7	A+	EBSCO	16.01.2014
Psychology & Marketing	7	B	EBSCO	17.01.2014
Journal of Marketing Theory and Practice	6	C	EBSCO	17.01.2014
Marketing ZFP – Journal of Research and Management	6	C	Beck eBibliothek	16.01.2014
Harvard Business Review	5	C	EBSCO	16.01.2014
Journal of Consumer Psychology	5	A	ScienceDirect	16.01.2014
Journal of Marketing Research	5	A+	EBSCO	16.01.2014
Marketing Letters	5	B	EBSCO	16.01.2014
International Marketing Review	4	B	ProQuest	17.01.2014
Business Horizons	4	C	ScienceDirect	17.01.2014
Journal of Advertising	4	B	EBSCO	17.01.2014
Journal of Advertising Research	4	C	EBSCO	17.01.2014
Journal of the Academy of Marketing Science	4	A	EBSCO	16.01.2014
Quarterly Journal of Economics	4	-	EBSCO	17.01.2014
International Journal of Research in Marketing	3	A	ScienceDirect	16.01.2014
Marketing Science	2	A+	EBSCO	16.01.2014
California Management Review	1	B	EBSCO	16.01.2014
Décision Marketing	1	-	JSTOR	17.01.2014
European Business Review	1	-	Google Scholar	17.01.2014
Journal of Internet Commerce	1	-	EBSCO	17.01.2014
Journal of Retailing	1	A	ScienceDirect	16.01.2014
Marketing Intelligence & Planning	1	-	ProQuest	17.01.2014
Sloan Management Review	1	C	EBSCO	16.01.2014
Total: Journals	**176**			
Book chapters	49			
Books	25			
TOTAL	**250**			

Note: based an analysis of journals, book chapters, and books searched for the keywords "luxury", "prestige", "status", "conspicuous", "symbolic", and "scarcity" as of January 2014.
Source: author

Appendix 2 – List of top 40 luxury brands by segment

Apparel	**Cars**	**Watches**	**Jewellery**
Hermès	Rolls-Royce	Patek Phililppe	Cartier
Chanel	Bentley	Vacheron Constantin	Van Cleef & Arpels
Louis Vuitton	Ferrari	Piaget	Boucheron
Dior	Lamborghini	Jaeger Le-Coultre	Harry Winston
Salvatore Ferragamo	Maserati	Audemars Piguet	Chaumet
Versace	Aston Martin	Blancpain	Kloybateri
Prada	Bugatti	Rolex	Bulgari
Fendi	Spyker	Breguet	MONTBLANC
Giorgio Armani	Pagani	IWC	Tiffany & Co.
Zegna	Koenigsegg	Franck Muller	Mikimoto

Source: World Luxury Association (2012)

Appendix 3 – Pre-study: expert interview quotes

Quote #	Expert	Quote in original language
Q1	Expert F	"...ein starker Konflikt aus ähm... eben Hürden aufbauen, Grenzen aufbauen, dadurch die Marke attraktiv zu erhalten und eben möglichst viel Umsatzsteigerung abzuliefern."
Q2	Expert B	"Natürlich ist es die Exklusivität der Distribution. Ein Luxusprodukt darf ich nicht überall haben. Und das ist auch die große Kunst eines Luxusproduktes: diese Gleichung zu finden zwischen Umsatzoptimierung... [und Exklusivität; Annahme des Autors] [...] diese Gradwanderung eigentlich immer der Selbstbeschränkung und der Optimierung innerhalb dieser Selbstbeschränkung."
Q3	Expert G	"Wenn ich es mir unternehmerisch leisten könnte, würde ich auf E-Commerce verzichten [...] Ich würde empfehlen, sich am E-Commerce, am Internet auf jeden Fall zu beteiligen. Die Kunden sind online. Aber ähm... diese Verfügbarkeit würde ich trotzdem da zurückhaltender machen, weil ich glaube, dass ähm.. der Wert der Marke langfristig unter so etwas leidet."
Q4	Expert F	"Eine begrenzte Zugänglichkeit ist ebenfalls eine Kennzeichen von Luxusmarken. Mit anderen Worten, wenn es an jeder Ecke zu bekommen ist – das meine ich auch Online – geht natürlich ein großer Teil des Reizes verloren."
Q5	Expert C	"Natürlich hat man... hat man durch den Online-Vertriebskanal nicht die Interaktion mit dem Kunden, die man benötigt, um sein Geschäft fein zu justieren und halt auch dieses... diese Markenwelt zu transportieren."
Q6	Expert D	"I don't believe we will go through an online selling experience considering the products we have. I think human mediation will be always important in our case."
Q7	Expert C	"...ich glaube in den Preislagen ähm... kaufe ich jetzt nicht ohne es vorher schon mal irgendwo anders gesehen zu haben."
Q8	Expert E	"Ich weiß von einigen Schmuckmarken, die Einzelteile über 100.000 Dollar im letzten Weihnachtsgeschäft online verkauft haben. Also das würde wahrscheinlich bei mir auch eher den Wunsch eines physischen Auseinandersetzens mit dem Teil im Laden bedeuten. Aber da gibt es halt auch unterschiedliche ähm... Präferenzen und unterschiedliche Kaufkraft"
Q9	Expert E	"Also aus meiner Sicht gehört das Internet heute zu einem Kanalmix, dem man sich nicht verwehren kann und auch nicht verwehren sollte."
Q10	Expert B	"Ich glaube, grundsätzlich ist es unsere Aufgabe dorthin zu gehen, wo die Verbraucher sind."
Q11	Expert A	"Wir gehen durch unsere Kommunikation, unsere Werbung in jeden kleinsten Haushalt in irgendeinem Dörfchen, sind dort aber nicht im stationären Handel verfügbar. Und heute mit dem Internet ist das eigentlich die einzige Möglichkeit für sehr, sehr viele Kunden Luxusmarken zu akquirieren."
Q12	Expert A	"Also wir sehen natürlich eine Möglichkeit – ich muss zugeben ein bisschen gezwungen. Die Luxusindustrie war da nicht sehr offen und nicht sehr proaktiv mit dem Internetgeschäft. Wir sind sehr, sehr vorsichtig..."
Q13	Expert F	"Weil was auch zum Beispiel zum Luxus gehört während eines Kaufprozesses ist es zu wissen, woher man etwas bekommt, also den Code zu beherrschen, wo bekomme ich dieses oder jenes Produkt. [...] Wenn ich eben gewisse Grenzen aufgebe, was ich ja tue durch online, [...] dann muss ich sie anderer Stelle umso höher ziehen."
Q14	Expert C	"...haben wir sozusagen ein Produktbereich und wir haben sozusagen den Kaufbereich. Im Kaufbereich werden's 25, 30 Artikel sein, die man online kaufen kann. [...] Die Klassiker."
Q15	Expert G	"Doch diese kleinen Schals macht ja auch Hermès zum Beispiel da ja [im Online Store; Annahme des Autors]. Aber die Kelly Bag zum Beispiel: no way. Niemals."
Q16	Expert B	"E-Commerce muss auch für den Kunden zugänglich, einfach, praktisch sein."
Q17	Expert A	"Man muss halt eine Balance haben zwischen schön und praktisch."
Q18	Expert F	"im Luxusbereich muss da noch geforscht und experimentiert werden, bis da markengerechte Shops entstehen. Die sind da alle ganz am Anfang erst. Und die wissen alle nicht wirklich damit umzugehen. Insofern sind Forschungsarbeiten auch sehr sinnvoll."

Note: quotes are listed in the order of appearance within the text.
Source: authors

Schriften zu Marketing und Handel

Herausgegeben von Martin Fassnacht

Band 1 Ibrahim Köse: Qualität elektronischer Dienstleistungen: Messung und Auswirkungen. 2007.

Band 2 Christina Reith: Convenience im Handel. 2007.

Band 3 Christina Müller: Differenzierung von Handelsunternehmen. 2007.

Band 4 Sonja Klose: Gefährdung existierender Kundenbeziehungen. 2008.

Band 5 Saskia Hardwig: Der Einfluss des Geschäftsstättenimages auf die Produktbewertung von Handelsmarken. 2008.

Band 6 Andreas Ettinger: Auswirkungen von Einkaufsconvenience. 2010.

Band 7 Jochen Mahadevan: Wahrgenommene Preisfairness bei personenbezogener Preisdifferenzierung. 2010.

Band 8 Christian M. Wiegner: Preis-Leistungs-Positionierung. Konzeption und Umsetzung. 2010.

Band 9 Frank Breitschwerdt: Preismanagement von Konsumgüterherstellern. Konzeption, Umsetzung und Erfolgsauswirkungen. 2011.

Band 10 Christian Stallkamp: Betriebsformen im Automobilhandel. Konzeptualisierung und empirische Ergebnisse einer multiattributiven Präferenzstrukturmodellierung. 2011.

Band 11 Katia Rumpf: Preis und Markendehnung. Eine empirische Analyse. 2011.

Band 12 Henning Mohr: Der Preismanagement-Prozess für Luxusmarken. Gestaltung und Erfolgsauswirkungen. 2013.

Band 13 Yorck Nelius: Organisation des Preismanagements von Konsumgüterherstellern. Eine empirische Untersuchung. 2013.

Band 14 Rebecca Winkelmann: Preisdifferenzierung aus Kundensicht. Eine verhaltenswissenschaftliche Untersuchung wahrgenommener Komplexität von Preisdifferenzierung. 2013.

Band 15 Sabine El Husseini: EDLP versus Hi-Lo Pricing Strategies in Retailing. Literature Review and Empirical Examinations in the German Retail Market. 2014.

Band 16 Evelyn Friedel: Price Elasticity. Research on Magnitude and Determinants. 2014.

Band 17 Eva Schuckmann: Shopping Enjoyment. Determinanten, Auswirkungen und moderierende Effekte. 2015.

Band 18 Toni Schmidt: Shopper Behavior at the Point of Purchase. Drivers of In-Store Decision-Making and Determinants of Post-Decision Satisfaction in a High-Involvement Product Choice. 2016.

Band 19 Philipp Nikolaus Kluge: Marketing Luxury Goods Online. 2016.

www.peterlang.com

www.ingramcontent.com/pod-product-compliance
Ingram Content Group UK Ltd.
Pitfield, Milton Keynes, MK11 3LW, UK
UKHW041824031026
15587UKWH00002B/536